AF875227

SOTHIS PRESS

Sothis Press aims to completely reimagine the public domain book with an emphasis on universal access to captivatingly designed print editions. We believe that technology will enable every single book ever published to be perpetually accessible in beautiful print form. Sothis is beauty in ubiquity.

www.sothis.press
1 Waterhouse Square, London, ECIN 2ST

A Digest of the Law Relating to Private Trusts and Trustees

Walter Gray Hart

SOTHIS PRESS

ISBN 978-1-0365-0290-4

A Digest of the Law Relating to Private Trusts and Trustees is in the public domain.

A DIGEST

OF THE LAW

RELATING TO PRIVATE

TRUSTS AND TRUSTEES.

BY

WALTER GRAY HART, LL.D.

LONDON:
THE "LAW NOTES" PUBLISHING OFFICES,
25 & 26, CHANCERY LANE, W.C.

1909

PREFACE.

THIS book contains the materials on which the Trusts Bill, 1908, to codify the law relating to private trusts and trustees, was based.

Were any evidence necessary of the importance to the lay public of this branch of the English law, it would be sufficient to refer to the report of the Select Committee of the House of Commons appointed in 1895 to ascertain whether further legislative enactment might be made for securing the adequate administration of private trusts. The committee estimated that no less than a twentieth part of the whole capitalised value of property, real and personal, comprising the wealth of the United Kingdom, was held on trust. Taking the capitalised value of that property as then estimated by the Treasury to be between nine and ten thousand million pounds—and the figures have certainly not decreased in the interval—this gives a sum of nearly five hundred millions sterling held upon trust. Whether these figures are accurate or not, there is no doubt that thousands of people in this country are at the present moment trustees: still larger numbers are beneficiaries; almost everyone who has any property at all is at some time of his or her life concerned, in the one capacity or the other, with this branch of the law.

The law relating to this system is now for the most part settled, and, having regard to modern amendments, seems in substance satisfactory enough, but in the form of its expression, like so many other branches of the English law, it is of the most chaotic description. Slowly evolved generation by generation, its principles and rules lie embedded in countless reported decisions of the courts from the time of the Year Books to the present, the effect of which has from time to time been modified, amended, and extended by a large number of acts of parliament passed chiefly during the last seventy years.

In such a state of the law it is not to be wondered at that the lay trustee should often err from ignorance of his obligations. Even the lawyer can easily go wrong. A distinguished member of the Chancery Bar, lecturing on the duties and liabilities of trustees some time since, gave an apt illustration of this:—"Towards the end of last sittings," he said, "and almost at the close of a case relating to trustees then being tried in the Chancery Division, it became apparent from an observation made from the bench that all the four counsel engaged in the case, learned and experienced men as they were, had not considered the provisions of the most recent Trustee Act, that of 1894, though such provisions bore directly upon the subject-matter" (*a*). It is not to be wondered at when the law, to use the lecturer's phrase, "lurks in volumes of reports to be counted by hundreds or lies buried, but with a hideous power of inopportune resurrection, in some partially repealed statute."

For this state of things the only remedy is codification, and the law of trusts seems to have arrived at a

(*a*) Birrell, "Duties and Liabilities of Trustees," 3.

stage at which it might with advantage be stated in the form of a code of the type of the Bills of Exchange Act, 1882, the Partnership Act, 1890, the Sale of Goods Act, 1882, and the Marine Insurance Act, 1906.

The manner in which these acts have codified the law with which they deal is to reproduce as exactly as possible in statutory form the principal rules of the existing law without attempting any amendment, save in respect of a few matters of uncontroversial character, in which amendment was feasible without raising opposition, and the success which has attended them seems to have disposed, by the test of practical experience, of the arguments advanced against the system, so far as they are applicable to codification of this kind. A useful aid to the preparation of a code of trusts law of this kind is to be found in the Indian Trusts Act, 1882, which, although framed with a view to the requirements of India, and differing in some respects from English law, is, nevertheless, admittedly based on the latter (*b*).

The belief that a code of trusts law would be of value to laymen led the writer to make the attempt to draft a bill on similar lines to those above mentioned. The bill was introduced in the House of Commons by Mr. Athelstan Rendall in 1907, but no opportunity was obtained of proceeding with it. It was, however, re-introduced in the following session, and was read a second time on March 11th, 1908, and referred to a Select Committee, consisting of Mr. W. Phipson Beale, K.C. (Chairman), Mr. Clancy, Mr. Cave, K.C., Dr. Hazel, Mr. J. W. Hills, Mr. Micklem, K.C., Mr. John

(*b*) See Dr. Whiteley Stokes' "Introduction to the Act in the Anglo-Indian Codes" (Clarendon Press), Vol. I.

O'Connor, Mr. G. H. Radford, Mr. A. Rendall, Mr. Stewart Smith, K.C., and Mr. Clavell Salter, K.C.

The Select Committee held a large number of meetings, and devoted much time and labour to the examination of the clauses of the bill and the authorities on which they were founded, and after suggesting various amendments, requested the Attorney-General to obtain criticisms on the amended draft from legal authorities and experts.

Numerous replies, some of them containing criticisms of great interest and value, were received from judges of the Chancery Division of the High Court, the Law Society, and other authorities. These replies disclosed a curious conflict of opinion with respect to the desirability of codification. Some were wholly favourable to the principle, but others showed that there still exists a considerable body of opinion adverse to it. In consequence the majority of the committee came to the conclusion that it was impossible to proceed with the bill, but recommended "that in the next or a subsequent session a bill should be introduced for consolidating and codifying such parts of the law of trusts as are the subject of statute laws, or are as firmly established by judicial decision as the propositions and rules of trust law and administration, which have already been embodied in statute law."

In the meantime, it has been suggested that it might be useful to publish the notes on which the clauses of the bill were based in the form of a text-book.

CONTENTS.

Part IV.—Obligations of the Trustee.

Part V.—Investment of Trust Funds.

Part VI.—Rights and Powers of the Trustee.

Part VII.—Disabilities of the Trustee.

Part VIII.—Liabilities of the Trustee for a Breach of Trust.

Part IX.—Rights of the Beneficiary.

Part X.—Retirement of Trustee and Appointment of New Trustees.

Part XI.—Judicial Trustees.

Part XII.—Determination of the Trust.

Part XIII.—Miscellaneous and Supplemental.

APPENDIX.

TABLE OF CASES.

C.

D.

E.

F.

G.

L.

M.

T.

V.

W.

Y.

Part I.—TRUSTS IN GENERAL.

SECTION I.—DEFINITION OF A TRUST.

(1) A TRUST is an obligation imposed either expressly or by implication of law whereby the obligor is bound to deal with property over which he has control for the benefit of a certain person or persons of whom he may himself be one, and who, or any one of whom, may enforce the obligation.

Where the obligation is expressly imposed the person who imposes it is called the settlor;
the person on whom the obligation is imposed is called the trustee;
the person for whose benefit it is imposed is called the beneficiary or *cestui que trust;*
the subject-matter of the trust is called the trust property.

(2) When the only obligation upon the trustee is to convey or transfer the trust property to or at the direction of the beneficiary, the trust is called a "bare trust," and the trustee a "bare trustee"; every other trust is called an "active trust," and the trustee an "active trustee."

In law, as in all other human sciences, it has been said, those ideas which seem to be the most simple are really the most difficult to grasp with certainty and express with accuracy (*a*). It is perhaps not surprising, therefore, that the definition of fundamental

(*a*) Pollock, First Book of Jurisprudence, 1.

terms has always proved a matter of difficulty to lawyers; so much so that they have come to look askance at all efforts in this direction—a frame of mind that has found expression in the maxim, "omnis definitio in jure periculosa est." Nevertheless, in order to attain clear ideas definitions are essential, and this is no less so in the law of trusts than in any other branch of our law; before the scope and detail of the subject can be known it must be determined what the nature and definition of a trust is.

Many attempts to define a trust have been made, but it cannot be said that any of them is entirely satisfactory. The following are the most important, placed in their chronological order:—

Lord Hardwicke (1734) (*b*).—"A trust is where there is such a confidence between parties that no action at law will lie, but is merely a case for the consideration of this court" (*i.e.*, of course, the High Court of Chancery).

This definition accentuates one of the most striking characteristics of a trust at the time at which it was enunciated, but, though frequently cited by later writers (*c*), is obviously insufficient at a time when the distinction between courts of equity and courts of law has ceased to exist in England. It only regards two of the peculiar features of a trust, neither of which is now essential. It makes no allusion to the fact that a trust is concerned only with property (*d*), nor to the separation between the beneficial and legal ownership of that property, nor to the obligation to which it gives rise. It was, in fact, framed merely to emphasize a point in the case then under discussion.

Mr. Justice Story (1835) (*e*).—"A trust, in the most enlarged sense in which the term is used in English jurisprudence, may be defined to be an equitable right, title, or interest in property real or personal, distinct from the legal ownership thereof."

This definition was adopted by Lord Justice Brett, in the case of *Wilson* v. *Lord Bury* (*f*); but, as pointed out by Mr.

(*b*) *Sturt* v. *Mellish* (1734), 2 Atk. 211; Lord Keeper Henley gave a definition in substantially the same terms in *Burgess* v. *Wheate* (1759), 1 Wm. Blackstone, 123.

(*c*) *E.g.*, Holland, Jurisprudence, 6th ed. 218.

(*d*) *In re Barney*, (1892) 2 Ch. 265.

(*e*) Story, Equity Jurisprudence, 2nd Eng. ed. § 964.

(*f*) (1880), 5 Q. B. D. 530.

Underhill (*g*) and by Mr. H. A. Smith (*h*), it is rather a definition of the interest of the person in whose favour a trust is created than of the trust itself, and omits to take account of active or special trusts in which the object of the trust is the performance of some particular obligation rather than the vesting of the beneficial ownership in some person other than the legal owner.

Mr. Lewin (1837) (*i*).—"A trust in the words applied to the use [*i.e.*, by Coke, Lit. 272 b] may be said to be 'a confidence reposed in some other, not issuing out of the land, but as a thing collateral annexed in privity to the estate of the land and to the person touching the land, for which *cestui que trust* has no remedy but by subpœna in Chancery.'"

This does not profess to be anything more than an adaptation of Coke's definition of a use, and is rightly regarded by Mr. Underhill (*j*) as defective (1) in being confined to trusts of land, (2) in conveying the impression that the trustee must be some other than either the person who creates the trust or the beneficiary under it, and (3) in that the subpœna in Chancery has long since become obsolete.

Mr. Wharton (1848) (*k*).—"A trust is simply a confidence reposed either expressly or impliedly in a person (hence called a trustee) for the benefit of another (hence called the *cestui que trust* or beneficiary), not, however, issuing out of real or personal property, but as a collateral incident accompanying it, annexed in privity to (*i.e.*, commensurate with) the interest in such property and also to the person touching such interest, for the accomplishment of which confidence the *cestui que trust* or beneficiary has his remedy in equity only."

This is evidently based on Mr. Lewin's work, and, though a considerable improvement on his effort, is open to the second and third objections urged against it above. It is, moreover, undesirably long for a definition, and the precise meaning (if, indeed,

(*g*) Law of Trusts and Trustees, 6th ed. 3.

(*h*) Principles of Equity, 2nd ed. 23.

(*i*) Trusts, 11th ed. 11.

(*j*) Trusts and Trustees, 6th ed. 2.

(*k*) Law Lexicon, 9th ed. s. v.

there be one) of the words "not, however, issuing out of real or personal property, but as a collateral incident accompanying it, annexed in privity to (*i.e.*, commensurate with) the interest in such property and also to the person touching such interest," is by no means clear.

Judge J. W. Smith (1849) (*l*) and *Mr. Snell* (1868) (*m*).—"A trust . . . . is a beneficial interest in, or a beneficial ownership of, real or personal property, unattended with the [possessory and] (*n*) legal ownership thereof."

This definition is attributed by Snell, H. A. Smith, and Underhill, erroneously, it would seem, to Mr. Spence (at any rate, it is not to be found at 2 Sp. 875, cited by them). It appears to have been either devised by Judge Smith, or to have been adapted by him from Mr. Justice Story, and is subject to the same criticism as the definition of the latter.

The Draft Civil Code of the State of New York (1865) defines a trust as follows :—§ 1167, "A trust is either (1) voluntary, or (2) involuntary." § 1168, "A voluntary trust is an obligation arising out of a personal confidence reposed in and voluntarily accepted by one for the benefit of another." § 1169, "An involuntary trust is one which is created by operation of law."

This short definition fails to mark the fact that a trust is concerned with property merely, and it seems to imply that the trustee must be somebody other than the creator of the trust, and that the trustee cannot himself be a beneficiary.

Mr. Watson (1873) (*o*).—"A trust may be described generally as an obligation affecting property legally vested in one or more (the trustee or trustees), which obligation he is or they are bound to perform, wholly or partially for the benefit of another or others (the *cestui que trust* or *cestuis que trust*) in whom the equitable estate is vested."

(*l*) Manual of Equity, 13th ed. § 224.

(*m*) Equity, 12th ed. 53.

(*n*) Snell omits the words in brackets.

(*o*) Compendium of Equity, 2nd ed. 959.

Mr. Watson's definition is a distinct advance on the efforts of earlier text-book writers, but is subject to the objection that the trustee is not necessarily the legal owner of the trust property; he may, for example, be trustee of a mere equity, like an equity of redemption or an equitable interest arising under another trust (*p*). It is also silent as to the difference between express and implied or constructive trusts.

Mr. H. A. Smith (1882) (*q*).—" A trust is rather a duty deemed in equity to rest on the conscience of a legal owner. This duty may be either passive, such as to allow the beneficial ownership to be enjoyed by some other person named the *cestui que trust*, in which case the legal owner is styled a bare trustee; or it may be some active duty, such as to sell or to administer for the benefit of some other person or persons; such as the duties of a trustee in bankruptcy."

The objection to this is that it is at once too wide and too narrow. Too wide because it would be almost if not quite as good a definition of any other equitable obligation; and too narrow because, as shown above, a person may be a trustee without being the *legal* owner of property. The introduction of the word " duty " is also open to objection (*r*).

The Indian Trusts Act, 1882, § 3.—" A trust is an obligation annexed to the ownership of property and arising out of a confidence reposed in and accepted by the owner, or declared and accepted by him, for the benefit of another, or of another and the owner."

This statutory definition was framed, of course, with special reference to the law of India, and is not entirely suitable to English law. It scarcely seems, for instance, to recognize the fact that the author of the trust may be himself the trustee, and does not pretend to cover implied or constructive trusts, which indeed are separately dealt with in later sections of the act.

(*p*) See Underhill, Trusts and Trustees, 6th ed. 3.

(*q*) Equity, 2nd ed. 23.

(*r*) See Anson, Contracts, 10th ed. 6.

Mr. Underhill (1888) (*s*).—"A trust is an equitable obligation, either expressly undertaken or constructively imposed by the court, under which the obligor (who is called a trustee) is bound to deal with certain property over which he has control (and which is called the trust property) for the benefit of certain persons (who are called the beneficiaries or *cestuis que trust*), of whom he may or may not himself be one."

Mr. Underhill's is undoubtedly the best definition yet given, but even his is not beyond criticism. It is not satisfactory, for example, in an analytical definition to insist on the fact that the obligation is "equitable." The fact that trusts were enforceable only in courts of equity and not in courts of law is in this country a matter of history merely, and cannot at the present time be said to be one of their distinguishing marks. Further, it is scarcely accurate to distribute all trusts into the classes of those "expressly undertaken" and constructive trusts. The trustee (save when the author of the trust constitutes himself a trustee), even in the case of express trusts, generally does not *express* his assent to undertake it. It would be more correct to distinguish between trusts which are *imposed* expressly and constructive trusts. It should be added that in the 5th and 6th editions of his book, Mr. Underhill has modified his definition so as in part to meet the criticisms here advanced.

Lord Justice Lindley (1897) (*t*).—"A trust is really nothing except a confidence reposed by one person in another and enforceable in a court of equity."

This is substantially the same as Lord Hardwicke's, given above, and is subject to the same objections as his.

Now, in order to construct a definition which shall not be open to the criticisms urged against those set out above, it is necessary to inquire what are the distinguishing marks of a trust, for the definition should include all those and none others.

"A definition, in order to be satisfactory, ought to give with precision the marks whereby the thing to be defined is distinguished from all other things" (*u*).

(*s*) Trusts and Trustees, 4th ed. 1.

(*t*) *In re Williams*, (1897) 2 Ch. 19.

(*u*) Lawrence, International Law, 1.

For this purpose it is advisable to see, in the first place, what relation the law of trusts bears to other branches of our law.

There can be no doubt that a trust possesses some characteristics which are closely analogous to those of a contract (*v*).

This analogy is specially marked in the case of that class of contracts known as bailments. These, indeed, are not infrequently spoken of as trusts (*w*), and it seems impossible to distinguish a depositum bailment from what is sometimes called a simple or bare trust. It is common usage to speak of a depositee as a trustee (*x*), and authority may even be found for extending this to all bailments. Thus it is stated by Mr. Justice Story in his work on Bailments (*y*) that "a bailment is strictly a trust in the common judicial sense of the word"; and he quotes a passage from Comyns' Digest (*z*), in which it is even said that "if a man give goods upon trust to deliver them to a stranger, Chancery will oblige him to do it," which apparently amounts to saying that equity would enforce the duties of a bailee as though he were a trustee of the goods carried by him. Conversely we find another eminent writer, Sir William Markby (*a*), admitting the question why the liability of a trustee should not be considered a contractual liability, to be one to which he does not find any clear answer.

On the other hand, historically speaking, there is, of course, an immense distinction between contract and trust. The one is the creation of common law, the other of equity; and in the old days, when courts of law and equity were distinct tribunals, probably no one would ever have felt any doubt (in spite of the dicta of Story and Comyns cited above) but that except perhaps in the case of a depositum bailment a bill in equity against a bailee would be bad for want of equity. Even at the present time, when the differences between the old jurisdictions have become obscured, one cannot but feel that it is going to an extreme to speak of some kinds of

(*v*) See Pollock, Contracts, 6th ed. 195; Anson, Contracts, 10th ed. 9; Encyc. Brit. Art. "Trust"; Encyc. Eng. Law, Intro. vol. i. 11; Underhill, Trusts and Trustees, 6th ed. 3.

(*w*) See, *e.g.*, Blackstone, Comm. iii. 432.

(*x*) See, *e.g.*, *Lord Hollis's Case* (1686), 2 Vent. 345; the judgment of Holt, C. J., in *Coggs* v. *Bernard* (1702), Sm. L. C. 10th ed. vol. i. 167; and both argument and judgment in *In re Tidd*, (1893) 3 Ch. 154.

(*y*) 8th ed., note at the foot of p. 8.

(*z*) Chancery, 4 W. 5.

(*a*) Elements of Law, § 617.

bailees—say, *e.g.*, common carriers—as trustees of the goods bailed to them (*b*).

It seems desirable, therefore, that the definition of a trust should, if possible, be so narrowed as to prevent its confusion with a bailment in particular and all other classes of contract in general. But it is not satisfactory to make what is purely a matter of history a basis of the distinction. An endeavour should be made to find a logical rather than a historical difference, if possible.

Dr. Whitely Stokes (*c*) purports to have effected this in the Indian Trusts Act by making his definition emphasize the fact that the obligation of the trust is annexed to the *ownership* of the property, and arises out of a *confidence* reposed in and accepted by the owner, or declared and accepted by him. But this is not satisfactory, for the double reason that the trustee is not necessarily the legal owner of the trust property, and, secondly, that the reposal of a confidence, although a characteristic which many, perhaps most, trusts possess, is not an invariable characteristic; for it is quite clear that the author of the trust may himself be, and often is, the trustee (*d*), and it is meaningless to speak of a person reposing a confidence in himself.

Mr. Underhill (*e*), however, notes two distinctions of the kind sought. These are:—

(1) That a trust, no matter how created, can be enforced against the trustee apart altogether from any consideration being given him, while a contract, except when under seal, cannot, as a rule, be enforced against the promisor unless such consideration be shown.

(2) That a contract cannot be enforced by anyone who is not a party to it (*f*), while it is one of the most conspicuous characteristics of a trust that it can always be enforced by the person for whose benefit it was declared or created, although he is generally no party to its creation.

The first, however, is not in itself sufficient for the purpose, for it is just that group of contracts which most resemble trusts, viz., bailments, which forms the exceptional class of simple contracts that can be enforced without proof of consideration. But in (2)

(*b*) See, further, Pollock, Contracts, 6th ed. 196; Anson, Contracts, 10th ed. 240.

(*c*) Anglo-Indian Codes, vol. i. 823.

(*d*) See Lewin, Trusts, 11th ed. 12.

(*e*) Trusts and Trustees, 4th ed. 5.

(*f*) *Price* v. *Easton* (1833), 4 B. & Ad. 433; *Tweddle* v. *Atkinson* (1861), 1 B. & S. 393.

bailments fall into line with all other contracts and differ from trusts, so that this seems to be a true point of distinction between every trust and every contract. If, then, the definition is so framed as to cover it, it would seem to sufficiently differentiate trust from contract.

Having settled the dividing line between trusts and contracts, the other characteristics exhibited by the former may be summarized thus:—

First, the word trust in common speech no doubt imports confidence, and at first sight it might be thought that the legal description of a trust should necessarily have reference to this fact; but it has already been shown that, however it may have been formerly, the notion of confidence is not now essential to what lawyers mean by a trust (*g*). For trust also connotes obligation, and an obligation which, though at one time merely moral, has long since become legal. When the obligation was merely moral, it was natural that the notion of confidence involved in a trust should be uppermost in men's minds, and it is not surprising to find that the old writers generally made it the pivot of their ideas (*h*), but now that all trusts have for so long been enforced by the courts the notion of confidence has fallen into the background, and that of obligation has come into prominence in its stead (*i*).

Secondly, the obligation is one which may be expressly imposed by act of the party, as in the case of express or declared trusts, or which may be imposed by operation of law as in implied or constructive trusts.

Thirdly, the obligations to which trusts give rise can only exist in connection with property (*j*). "An obligation to do or forbear some act not relating to property is not a trust, whatever else it may be." Property is here used as meaning the subject of a right of ownership, for, as has already been said, it is not essential that the trustee should have the legal estate or ownership so long as he has the control of the trust property.

(*g*) Lewin, Trusts, 11th ed. 7, 12.

(*h*) Compare the older definitions set out above.

(*i*) Compare the later definitions set out above. See also per Lindley, L. J., in *In re Williams*, (1897) 2 Ch. 12.

(*j*) Underhill, Trusts and Trustees, 6th ed. 4; Godefroi, Trusts and Trustees, 2nd ed. 7; *In re Barney*, (1892) 2 Ch. 265; and see *The Buckhurst Peerage* (1876), 2 App. Cas. 1; and *In re Brooke and Fremlin's Contract*, (1898) 1 Ch. at p. 651.

Fourthly, the obligation involves a separation between the complete control of the property to which it is annexed and the complete beneficial interest therein, although the obligor may himself be the party imposing the obligation and is not necessarily excluded from being beneficially interested under it.

Lastly, the obligation is of equitable origin, *i.e.*, in former times was not universally enforceable in courts of justice, but only in those known as courts of equity. This feature, however, has become merely historical in England since the fusion of courts of law and equity effected by the Judicature Acts.

Since, then, the first and last of these cannot at the present time be said to be distinguishing marks of a trust, they should be disregarded. We thus reduce the fundamental facts which the definition ought to express to the following :—

(1) An obligation which may be imposed expressly or by implication of law ;

(2) The restriction of the obligation to the dealing with property over which the obligor has control ;

(3) The separation between the control of the property and the entirety of the beneficial interest in it, subject to the possibility of the obligor being one of the persons entitled ;

(4) The capacity of any one of the persons beneficially interested to enforce the obligation.

These may be combined to form a definition, as follows :—

"A trust is an obligation imposed either expressly or by implication of law whereby the obligor is bound to deal with property over which he has control for the benefit of certain persons of whom he may himself be one, and any one of whom may enforce the obligation."

It is not straining language to speak of a person imposing an obligation on himself, while it is submitted that the use of the words "any one of whom may enforce the obligation" sufficiently marks the distinction between trust and contract ; even if the definition is still wide enough to include a depositum bailment, such as that in *In re Tidd* (*k*), it is submitted that that particular kind of bailment is really a trust and that it is therefore unobjec-

(*k*) (1893) 3 Ch. 154.

tionable to call it one. On the other hand, it may perhaps be objected that it is not wide enough to cover trusts in which there is no *cestui que trust*, like a trust for the erection of a monument, such as that in *Mitford* v. *Reynolds* (*l*), or for the care of animals, as in *In re Dean* (*m*); it is true that these have been decided to be valid trusts, although they are not enforceable by anybody. In conflict with this decision, however, it has been said to be elementary law that for the creation of a trust there are three requisites—a trustee, a *cestui que trust*, and property which one man holds on trust for another (*n*). Such trusts are therefore not trusts in the ordinary sense in which the term is used by lawyers. The trust so called is only valid in this sense—that the person who would take if it were not carried out cannot complain if the trustee does what the settlor has requested (*o*). They may perhaps be called trusts of imperfect obligation.

There remains one other distinction. A trust may be either an active trust or a bare trust. The terms special trust and simple trust are synonymous and are sometimes used, but the former are preferable, as they have been adopted by the legislature. The distinction is of "general practical importance," to adopt the words of Vice-Chancellor Hall, in *Christie* v. *Ovington* (*p*), since the rights and duties of a bare trustee differ in several important respects from those of an active trustee. The expression bare trustee occurs in several Acts of Parliament, *e.g.*:—

The Fines and Recoveries Act, 1833, ss. 27, 31;
The Vèndor and Purchaser Act, 1874, ss. 5, 6;
The Land Transfer Act, 1875, s. 48; and
The Trustee Act, 1893, s. 16.

The decisions as to what the term "bare trustee" means, however, are conflicting. In *Christie* v. *Ovington* Vice-Chancellor Hall defined the expression as used in the Vendor and Purchaser Act and the Land Transfer Act to mean "a trustee whose trust is to convey, and the time has arrived for a conveyance by him." In *Morgan* v. *Swansea Urban Sanitary Authority* (*q*) Sir George Jessel said: "I should have thought that a 'bare trustee,' or a 'naked

(*l*) (1848), 16 Sim. 105.
(*m*) (1889), 41 Ch. D. 552.
(*n*) *In re Brooke and Fremlin's Contract*, (1898) 1 Ch. at p. 651.
(*o*) See Ashburner, Equity, 124.
(*p*) (1875), 1 Ch. D. 279.
(*q*) (1878), 9 Ch. D. 582.

trustee,' meant a trustee without any beneficial interest." In *In re Cunningham and Frayling* (*r*), Mr. Justice Stirling preferred the opinion of Vice-Chancellor Hall, as being more in accordance with the general view of the profession.

The decision of Vice-Chancellor Bacon, in *In re Docwra* (*s*), supports the view of Vice-Chancellor Hall and Mr. Justice Stirling, but the remarks of Mr. Justice Kekewich, in *In re Brooke and Fremlin's Contract* (*t*), seem to accord rather with the view of Sir George Jessel.

The text book writers appear to be on the side of Vice-Chancellor Hall, and it seems, therefore, that in the opinion of the majority of lawyers a bare trustee is one the only obligation upon whom is to convey the trust property to or at the direction of the beneficiary.

(*r*) (1891) 2 Ch. 567. (*s*) (1885), 29 Ch. D. 693.
(*t*) (1898) 1 Ch. at p. 651.

SECTION II.—CLASSIFICATION OF TRUSTS.

EVERY trust is either—

(1) Express, or

(2) Implied.

An express trust is one which is created by words indicating an intention to create a trust.

An implied trust is one which is not created by words indicating an intention to create a trust, but by implication of law.

"All trusts," said Lord Nottingham in the case of *Cook* v. *Fountain* (*a*), "are either first express trusts which are raised and created by act of the parties, or implied trusts which are raised or created by act or construction of law."

This classification certainly marks a fundamental distinction between the kinds of trusts. It corresponds with the distinction drawn by the Statute of Frauds, enacted only a few years later, between "declarations" of trusts of land and conveyances of land "by which a trust or confidence shall or may arise or result by the implication or construction of law," and it has been substantially adopted by most writers on the subject since, though there is a good deal of variation in the language used to denote the distinction.

Mr. Justice Story, for example, classifies trusts as express trusts and implied trusts, the latter comprehending all those trusts which are called constructive and resulting trusts (*b*). And the same classification is given in the notes to the case of *Keech* v. *Sandford* in White & Tudor's Leading Cases in Equity (*c*).

Mr. Lewin (*d*), it is true, begins by dividing them into simple and special—the former being those in which property is vested in

(*a*) (1676), 3 Swanst. at p. 591.

(*b*) Equity Juris. 2nd Eng. ed. § 980.

(*c*) 7th ed. vol. ii. 694.

(*d*) Trusts, 11th ed. 16.

one person in trust for another, but the nature of the trust not being prescribed by the settlor is left to the construction of law; the latter those in which the machinery of a trustee is introduced for the execution of some purpose particularly pointed out, and the trustee is not, as before, a mere passive depositary of the estate, but is called upon to exert himself actively in the execution of the settlor's intention. But this distinction he treats as of no importance for the purpose of the exposition of his subject, and later on he divides them into (1) those created by act of the party, and (2) those created by operation of law, sub-dividing the latter into resulting and constructive, which classification is adopted by Mr. H. A. Smith in his treatise on Equity (*e*).

In substance Mr. Underhill's treatment of the subject (*f*) is the same, though the terms he uses are different. He says, "In relation to their inception, trusts are divisible into two classes: (1) an express trust means a trust created by words importing an intention to create a trust . . . . (2) a constructive trust means a trust which is not created by any words importing an intention to create a trust, but is implied by courts of equity in order to prevent the inequitable acquisition of another's property." And Mr. Watson's language in his Compendium of Equity (*g*) is somewhat similar. Lastly, the Trustee Act, 1888, s. 1 (3) distinguishes between express trusts and trusts arising by construction or implication of law.

On the other hand, trusts are sometimes divided into three kinds: express, implied (*i.e.*, resulting), and constructive, a classification adopted by Judge Josiah W. Smith, in his Manual of Equity (*h*), and by Mr. Snell (*i*). The former writer admits, however, that the two last are frequently confounded, or at least classed together, and they are obviously both species of trusts arising by operation or implication of law.

Mr. Ashburner (*j*) distinguishes between cases in which there is an intention to create a trust and a trust is created in fulfilment of that intention, and cases in which, though there is no intention to create a trust, a court of equity holds that a trust has arisen. But he, following Lord Nottingham apparently, would put some

(*e*) 2nd ed. 33.
(*f*) Trusts and Trustees, 6th ed. 8.
(*g*) 2nd ed. 962.
(*h*) 14th ed. 147, 148.
(*i*) Equity, 12th ed. 53.
(*j*) Equity, 124.

kinds of resulting trusts, like those illustrated by the case of *Dyer* v. *Dyer* (*k*), under the first head.

On the whole, the weight of opinion and reason seems to be in favour of distinguishing trusts created by act of the party from those arising by operation of law, and it seems best to mark the distinction as Mr. Justice Story does, by the accustomed antithesis "express" and "implied," treating resulting and constructive trusts as sub-divisions of the latter.

It may be added that the term implied trusts is sometimes used to designate what are more commonly called "precatory trusts." Mr. Lewin uses the term in this sense (*l*), and he treats such trusts as a species of those created by act of the party. Mr. W. W. Watson also regards precatory trusts as implied, and treats them as a sub-class of trusts which, though not express, are such as equity will enforce. But as Mr. Underhill (*m*) points out, trusts arising from precatory words are essentially express trusts—that is to say, they are *expressed*, although in ambiguous and uncertain language. Moreover, the whole of the law as to express trusts is applicable to trusts created by precatory expressions; and there is, therefore, no justification for treating them as a separate and distinct class.

(*k*) (1788), 2 Cox, 92.

(*l*) See 10th ed. 117; 11th ed. 120.

(*m*) 6th ed. 9.

SECTION III.—CAPACITY OF PARTIES.

(1) CAPACITY to create a trust is regulated by the general law concerning capacity to dispose of property.

(2) Capacity to be a trustee or beneficiary is regulated by the general law concerning capacity to acquire and hold property.

(3) A married woman is able, without her husband, to dispose of, or to join in disposing of, real or personal property held by her solely or jointly with any other person as trustee or personal representative in like manner as if she were a *feme sole* (*a*).

(4) This section operates to render valid and confirm all such dispositions made after the 31st day of December, 1882, whether before or after the commencement of this act; but where any title or right has been acquired through or with the concurrence of the husband before the 1st day of January, 1908, that title or right shall prevail over any title or right which would otherwise be rendered valid by this section (*a*).

(5) Property vested in any person on any trust or by way of mortgage shall not, in case of that person becoming a convict within the meaning of the Forfeiture Act, 1870, vest in any such administrator as may be appointed under that act, but shall remain in the trustee or mortgagee, or survive to his co-trustee or descend to his representative as if he had not become a convict; provided that this enactment shall not affect the title to

(*a*) Married Women's Property Act, 1907, s. 1.

the property so far as relates to any beneficial interest therein of any such trustee or mortgagee (*b*).

Generally speaking, a person who can legally dispose of property can create a trust of it. A person who cannot legally dispose of property can make no trust of it. Similarly a person who can legally acquire and hold property can be a trustee or beneficiary and *vice versâ* (*c*). The persons subject to incapacity with regard to the acquisition or disposition of property are :—

1. Infants.
2. Lunatics.
3. Married women.
4. Convicts.
5. Corporations.

Since the Naturalization Act, 1870, aliens have been as capable of taking, acquiring, holding, and disposing of all property real and personal of every description as British subjects (*d*), with the exception that no alien can be the owner of a British ship (*e*).

But in the law of trusts some of these possess special capacities, or are subject to special incapacities, which require consideration.

I.—Capacity to Create a Trust.

Dealing with the various classes of persons subject to incapacity in the order above mentioned, the law may be shortly stated as follows :—

Infants.—An infant is incapable, subject to exceptions stated below, of making an irrevocable disposition of his property, and therefore cannot create an irrevocable trust of it. A disposition *inter vivos*, however, whether by way of trust or otherwise, made by an infant is not void, but voidable; *i.e.*, it can be repudiated, but until repudiated is binding. Moreover, if the infant elects to repudiate it he must do so within a reasonable time after he comes of age; otherwise he will be bound (*f*).

(*b*) Trustee Act, 1893, s. 48.

(*c*) Lewin, Trusts, 11th ed. 19 *et seq.*

(*d*) s. 2.

(*e*) s. 13.

(*f*) *Edwards* v. *Carter*, (1893) A. C. 360.

There are two exceptions :—

1. By the custom of Kent an infant, whether male or female, not being below the age of fifteen years, seised in fee simple in possession of land subject to the custom of gavelkind, may indefeasibly alienate it by feoffment made for valuable consideration (*g*). It is said that the custom extends only to sales (*h*), and if this is correct it does not enable an infant to create a trust.

2. Under the Infant Settlements Act, 1855, an infant can, with the sanction of the Chancery Division of the High Court, make a settlement, subject to certain qualifications, which will be as binding as if the settlor were of full age (*i*).

The sanction of the court is (notwithstanding s. 3 of the act, which required it to be by petition) obtained by summons in chambers under R. S. C. Ord. 55, r. 2 (10). The infant if a male must be of the age of twenty, and if a female of the age of seventeen (*j*).

In the case of a girl infant who married, a very curious situation was sometimes developed, the practical effect of which was that, although she had theoretically the right of repudiating her settlement, the right could not be effectively exercised. The result was reached in this way. At common law all personal property of a woman (except her paraphernalia) in her possession in her own right at the date of her marriage, or vesting in her in possession in her own right during it, became by the fact of the marriage the absolute property of her husband. This rule was abrogated by ss. 2 and 5 of the Married Women's Property Act, 1882; but s. 19 of that Act provides that nothing in the Act contained "shall interfere with or affect any settlement or agreement for a settlement, made or to be made, whether before or after marriage, respecting the property of any married woman." It was accordingly decided that if a man of full age were about to marry a girl under age and a settlement of her property were made without the leave of the court being obtained under the act of 1855, although when she attained twenty-one she could repudiate the settlement, her personal property still remained bound by it. For nothing in the Married Women's Property Act was to "interfere with" the settlement; since therefore she could only claim the property—unless it were settled for

(*g*) Challis, Real Property, 3rd ed. 368.

(*h*) Davidson, Prec. vol. ii. pt. 1, 245.

(*i*) s. 1.

(*j*) s. 4.

her separate use—by virtue of either s. 2 or s. 5 of that act, and neither section could be set up against the settlement, she could not, notwithstanding the repudiation, get her property. It belonged to the husband, who was bound by the settlement, and it had accordingly to be handed to the trustees of the settlement. *Hancock* v. *Hancock* (*k*), *Stevens* v. *Trevor-Garrick* (*l*), and *Buckland* v. *Buckland* (*m*) were the authorities for the construction of the act. It made no difference whether the trust instrument expressed that settlement of the wife's property was made or agreed to be made by husband alone, or by both husband and wife, or by wife alone. In *Hancock* v. *Hancock* (*k*), where the parties were married before 1883, there was an agreement by the husband alone; in *Stevens* v. *Trevor-Garrick* (*l*) there was an assignment by both; in *Buckland* v. *Buckland* (*m*) there was a recital that it had been agreed that the wife's property should be settled, followed by a declaration by the wife alone that the trustees should stand possessed of the property on the trusts specified; in each case the result was the same —the husband was bound by the settlement.

Of course, if the property in respect of which this question arose were given to the wife for her separate use, the decisions did not apply. The wife did not claim under the Married Women's Property Act then, and if she repudiated the settlement her husband did not become entitled to the property settled. The trustees of the repudiated settlement could not, therefore, claim on the ground that the property belonged to the husband, and that he was bound by the settlement.

And in the case of a settlement made after the 1st of January, 1908, the decisions are abrogated by the Married Women's Property Act, 1907, s. 2 of which provides that:—"(1) Notwithstanding section 19 of the Married Women's Property Act, 1882, a settlement or agreement for a settlement made after the commencement of this act by the husband or intended husband, whether before or after marriage, respecting the property of any woman he may marry or have married, shall not be valid unless it is executed by her if she is of full age, or confirmed by her after she attains full age.

"But if she dies an infant any covenant or disposition by her husband contained in the settlement or agreement shall bind or pass any interest in any property of hers to which he may become

(*k*) (1888), 38 Ch. D. 78. (*l*) (1893) 2 Ch. 307.
(*m*) (1900) 2 Ch. 534.

entitled on her death, and which he could have bound or disposed of if this act had not been passed.

"(3) Nothing in this section shall render invalid any settlement or agreement for a settlement made or to be made under the provisions of the Infant Settlements Act, 1855."

By s. 7 of the Wills Act, 1837, no will made by any person under the age of twenty-one years is valid, so that an infant is absolutely incapable of creating a trust by will.

Lunatics.—A disposition of property, whether by instrument *inter vivos* or by will, by a person usually of unsound mind is valid if made during a lucid interval (*n*). A disposition for valuable consideration made by a person while of unsound mind is valid, unless it can be shown that the person in whose favour it was made was aware of the insanity, in which case it is voidable. This applies to sales (*o*), to mortgages (*p*), to contracts (*q*), and presumably also to dispositions by way of trust.

But if a disposition of property by a person of unsound mind is gratuitous, it is not merely voidable but void (*r*). It would follow from this that a voluntary trust, whether created by deed or will, by a person of unsound mind at the time, is wholly void whether the beneficiaries or trustees were cognizant of the insanity or not.

What amount of insanity is sufficient and required to invalidate the disposition is a difficult question. It was discussed in the case of *Banks* v. *Goodfellow* (*s*) with reference to a will, and it was held that the mere existence of delusions in the testator's mind is not sufficient if they have not affected the dispositions made by the will. There seems to be no reason why there should be any different rule for an instrument *inter vivos*.

Where such a disposition is impeached on the ground of insanity, if the lunatic has since been found by inquisition to have been insane at the date when the disposition was made, the burden of proof that it was made during a lucid interval is thrown on the party claiming under it. If he is not bound by the inquisition because not a

(*n*) *Hall* v. *Warren* (1805), 9 Ves. 605.

(*o*) *Molton* v. *Camroux* (1848), 2 Exch. 487; 4 Exch. 17; *Elliot* v. *Ince* (1857), 7 De G. M. & G. 475.

(*p*) *Campbell* v. *Hooper* (1855), 3 Sm. & G. 153.

(*q*) *Imperial Loan Co.* v. *Stone*, (1892) 1 Q. B. 599.

(*r*) *Elliot* v. *Ince*, *supra*; *Manning* v. *Gill* (1872), L. R. 13 Eq. 485.

(*s*) (1870), L. R. 5 Q. B. 549.

party to it, and can satisfy another jury that the disposition he is supporting was made during a lucid interval, he will be entitled; otherwise he will not (*t*). It has recently been decided, however, that if a lunatic has been so found any disposition of property by deed made after the inquisition is absolutely void, even though made during a lucid interval, since it conflicts with the rights of the crown (*u*).

Married Women.—By the Married Women's Property Act, 1882, s. 1 (1), "A married woman shall, in accordance with the provisions of this act, be capable of acquiring, holding, and disposing, by will or otherwise, of any real or personal property as her separate property, in the same manner as if she were a *feme sole*, without the intervention of any trustee."

s. 2. "Every woman who marries after the commencement of this act shall be entitled to have and to hold as her separate property, and to dispose of in manner aforesaid, all real and personal property which shall belong to her at the time of marriage, or shall be acquired by or devolve upon her after marriage." . . . .

s. 5. "Every married woman married before the commencement of this act shall be entitled to have and to hold and to dispose of in manner aforesaid as her separate property all real and personal property her title to which, whether vested or contingent, and whether in possession, reversion, or remainder, shall accrue after the commencement of this act." . . . .

The enactment of s. 1 appeared to give a married woman as full capacity to dispose of property either *inter vivos* or by will as a *feme sole*, but it was construed by the courts to give her power to dispose by will only of property of which she was possessed while under coverture, and unless she re-executed her will after she had become discovert, it would not be effectual to dispose of property acquired by her after the coverture had come to an end (*v*). It was accordingly provided by s. 3 of the Married Women's Property Act, 1893, that s. 24 of the Wills Act, 1837, shall apply to the will of a married woman made during coverture whether she is or is not possessed of or entitled to any separate property at the time of making it, and such will shall not require

(*t*) *Hall* v. *Warren*, *supra*; *Snook* v. *Watts* (1848), 11 Beav. 105.

(*u*) *In re Walker*, (1905) 1 Ch. 160.

(*v*) *In re Price*, *Stafford* v. *Stafford* (1885), 28 Ch. D. 709.

to be re-executed or re-published after the death of her husband. S. 24 of the Wills Act provides that every will shall be construed with reference to the real and personal estate comprised in it to speak and take effect as if it had been executed immediately before the death of the testator, unless a contrary intention appears by the will.

These provisions place a married woman in the same position with reference to the creation of a trust of property as a man or an unmarried woman, subject to the provision of s. 19 that nothing in the act contained shall interfere with or affect a settlement and the construction which the courts have put upon it above referred to.

Convicts.—By the Forfeiture Act, 1870, s. 8, every convict, during the time while he is subject to the operation of the act (as to which see s. 7), is incapable of alienating or charging any property, or of making any contract save as therein provided. This would prevent the creation of a trust by an instrument operating *inter vivos.* But the incapacity imposed by the act ceases at death, and there appears to be nothing to prevent a convict disposing of his property by will.

Corporations.—A *common law corporation* has generally the same capacity of alienation as an individual. By the Municipal Corporations Act, 1882, s. 108, however, the council of a municipal corporation may not, unless authorized by act of parliament, sell, mortgage, or alienate any corporate land without the approval of the Local Government Board (*w*), or in the case of a site for a place of worship, under the Places of Worship Sites Acts, 1873 and 1882, of the Treasury. Restrictions have also been imposed on ecclesiastical corporations by a great number of statutes; and also on the principal universities, and some colleges and other institutions, and on the alienation of crown land (*x*).

A *statutory corporation* is restricted as regards the alienation of its property by the purposes of its incorporation as defined by its memorandum of association or special act (*y*).

(*w*) See Local Government Act, 1888, s. 72.

(*x*) See Dart, Vendors and Purchasers, 6th ed. vol. i. 20.

(*y*) See Williams, Vendor and Purchaser, vol. ii. 856.

II.—Capacity to be a Trustee.

Infants.—An infant is not incapable of being a trustee (*z*), but since he cannot make a binding disposition of property (exceptions excepted), he cannot effectively act as such. In *King* v. *Bellord* (*a*), for example, a testator devised land to A., B., and C., in trust, at their discretion to sell it. C. was an infant, and it was held that, as a consequence, the trustees could not sell. Moreover, apparently, he cannot be made liable for a breach of trust (*b*); though Lord Justice Fry said, in the case of *In re Garnes* (*c*), that he could conceive circumstances under which an infant trustee might be made liable for moneys received by him. When this was said, the trustee before the court had attained full age. When an infant is appointed a trustee, the court will appoint a new trustee in his place (*d*).

Lunatics.—Lunacy does not prevent a person from acquiring or holding property, but since it renders him incapable of disposing of it to some extent, it renders him incapable of administering it. By the Lunacy Act, 1890, therefore (s. 116), powers of management and administration are conferred on the judge in lunacy; and by s. 128 it is provided that in the case of a trustee becoming lunatic his powers as trustee may be exercised by his committee, and by s. 129 the latter may appoint new trustees under a power vested in the lunatic.

Lunacy also gives the court power to appoint a new trustee in the place of the lunatic (*e*).

Married Women.—A married woman may be a trustee. It is provided by s. 1 (2) of the Married Women's Property Act, 1882, that a married woman shall be capable of entering into and rendering herself liable in respect of and to the extent of her separate property on any contract, ... and by s. 24 the word

(*z*) Per Jeffreys, L. C., *Jevons* v. *Bush* (1685), 1 Vern. 342.

(*a*) (1863), 1 H. & M. 343.

(*b*) *Whitmore* v. *Weld* (1685), 1 Vern. 326; *Hindmarsh* v. *Southgate* (1827), 3 Russ. 324.

(*c*) (1885), 31 Ch. D. at p. 151. He can be sued after attaining full age for a breach of trust committed after attaining full age. *Jevons* v. *Bush* (1685), 1 Vern. 342.

(*d*) *In re Shelmerdine* (1864), 33 L. J. Ch. 474.

(*e*) See Rudall & Greig, Trustee Acts, 3rd ed. 112.

contract includes the acceptance of any trust. But it is in most cases hardly advisable to appoint a married woman. At one time the court would not have a married woman trustee, and in *Lake* v. *De Lambert* (*f*) it removed a female trustee who had married subsequently to the commencement of the trust, merely on the ground of her coverture. It is scarcely likely that the court would take this drastic step now, since most of the disabilities to which married women were formerly subject have been removed.

With regard to pure personal property it is provided by s. 18 of the Married Women's Property Act, 1882, that a married woman who is a trustee alone or jointly may transfer or join in transferring *annuities, stocks, and securities*, without her husband, as if she were a *feme sole*.

And by s. 16 of the Trustee Act, 1893, when any freehold or copyhold hereditament is vested in a married woman *as a bare trustee*, she may convey or surrender it as if she were a *feme sole*.

It was, however, decided that a married woman trustee (other than a bare trustee) could not convey the legal estate in freehold land except by means of a deed acknowledged as required by the Fines and Recoveries Act, 1833, ss. 77 *et seq.* (*g*). And it seemed to follow that copyhold and leasehold land vested in her as trustee could only be disposed of according to the ancient forms.

This disability of a married woman trustee, which caused much inconvenience, was removed by the Married Women's Property Act, 1907, s. 1 of which provides that—"(1) A married woman is able, without her husband, to dispose of or to join in disposing of real or personal property held by her solely or jointly with any other person as trustee or personal representative in like manner as if she were a *feme sole*.

"(2) This section operates to render valid and confirm all such dispositions made after the 31st day of December, 1882, whether before or after the commencement of this act, but where any title or right has been acquired through or with the concurrence of the husband before the commencement of this act that title or right shall prevail over any title or right which would otherwise be rendered valid by this section."

Convicts.—Conviction for treason or felony does not incapacitate the convict from acquiring or holding property, but by the For-

(*f*) (1799), 4 Ves. 492.

(*g*) *In re Harkness and Allsopp's Contract*, (1896) 2 Ch. 358.

feiture Act, 1870, an administrator of his property may be appointed (*h*), and on such appointment all the property of the convict vests in him (*i*). By s. 48 of the Trustee Act, 1893, property vested in the convict as trustee or mortgagee does not vest in the administrator so appointed. By s. 25 (1) of the Trustee Act, 1893, however, the court may make an order for the appointment of a new trustee in substitution for a trustee who is convicted of felony.

Corporations.—In the early days of the Court of Chancery it was laid down that a corporation could not be seised of a use, for it had no soul, and how, then, it was asked, could any confidence be reposed in it? But the technical rules upon which this doctrine proceeded have long ceased to operate in respect of trusts; and at the present day every corporation is compellable in equity to execute a trust (*j*). Indeed, there are several incorporated societies now in existence which have been established for the purpose of undertaking trusteeships amongst other things. A corporation cannot, it is true, acquire or hold land, and therefore cannot be made a trustee of it, without a license from the crown, under the Mortmain and Charitable Uses Act, 1888, s. 1; but there are a very great number of exceptions.

A practical difficulty also arises in regard to the appointment of a corporation as one of several trustees of a will, inasmuch as a grant of probate cannot be made to a corporation and an individual, even though both are appointed executors. The court will make a grant of probate to the individual trustee or trustees, or, if these decline to take it, will make a grant of letters of administration with the will annexed to the corporation, but it will not do both (*k*).

Another difficulty which arose out of the rule of the common law that a corporation could not hold property in joint tenancy has been recently removed by the Bodies Corporate (Joint Tenancy) Act, 1899; and it has accordingly been decided that there is nothing to prevent a company registered under the Companies Acts being appointed a trustee jointly with a natural person, even though the trust property include real estate, since s. 18 of the Companies Act,

(*h*) s. 9.

(*i*) s. 10.

(*j*) Lewin, Trusts, 11th ed. 30.

(*k*) *In the goods of Martin* (1904), 90 L. T. 264.

1862, enables such a company to hold land without the license of the crown (*l*).

III.—Capacity to be a Beneficiary.

Neither an infant, nor a lunatic, nor a married woman, nor an alien, nor a convict is now under any incapacity to acquire property legal or equitable, so that any of them may be made a beneficiary under a trust (*m*).

The only incapacity to take under a trust is in the case of a corporation, which (exceptions excepted) cannot acquire land as beneficiary under a trust without the license of the crown to hold it in mortmain, and in the case of a charity in whose favour a trust of land must be made to comply with the provisions of the Mortmain and Charitable Uses Acts, 1888, 1891, and 1892, although this last is not strictly a case of incapacity.

(*l*) *In re Thompson's Settlement*, (1905) 1 Ch. 229.

(*m*) Lewin, Trusts, 11th ed. 43 *et seq.*

Section IV.—The Trust Property.

All property, whether real or personal and whether legal or equitable, of which a valid assignment may be made, may be made the subject of a trust, unless in the case of land the tenure under which it is held is inconsistent with the trust sought to be created.

"As a general rule," Mr. Lewin says, "all property, whether real or personal and whether legal or equitable, may be made the subject of a trust, provided the policy of the law or any statutory enactment does not prevent the settlor from parting with the beneficial interest in favour of the intended *cestui que trust*" (*a*).

The cases of *Kekewich* v. *Manning* (*b*) and *Shafto* v. *Adams* (*c*) show that a future interest in property such as a reversionary interest, may be made the subject of a trust.

The cases of *Knight* v. *Bowyer* (*d*) and *Gilbert* v. *Overton* (*e*) may be cited as authority that a mere equity is capable of being the subject of a trust.

Similarly, a right which arises under a contract or "chose in action" may be the subject of a trust (*f*). For a chose in action was always assignable in equity, and by s. 25 (6) of the Judicature Act, 1873, an assignment of "any debt or other legal chose in action," answering to the conditions there stated, is made effectual in law to pass and transfer the legal right thereto; and though the section requires that the assignment shall be absolute—not purporting to be by way of charge only—it was held in *Burlinson* v. *Hall* (*g*) that an assignment upon trust for the assignee to pay himself a debt due to him from the assignor and pay the surplus

(*a*) Lewin, Trusts, 11th ed. 47.
(*b*) (1851), 1 De G. M. & G. 176.
(*c*) (1864), 4 Giff. 492.
(*d*) (1857), 23 Beav. at p. 635.
(*e*) (1864), 2 H. & M. 110.
(*f*) For an instance of such a trust being enforced, see *Roberts* v. *Lloyd* (1840), 2 Beav. 376.
(*g*) (1884), 12 Q. B. D. 347.

to the assignor was absolute within the meaning of the section; and in *Comfort* v. *Betts* (*h*) that a similar assignment upon trust for the assignors alone was equally valid.

If, however, the property is incapable of assignment, either from its nature or on the ground of public policy, or by express statutory enactment, it cannot be made the subject of a trust. So it was held in the *Buckhurst Peerage* (*i*) that a title of honour such as a peerage cannot be made the subject of a trust, because it is a personal possession and cannot be held by one person in trust for another. And in *Davis* v. *Duke of Marlborough* (*j*) that the pension granted by the stat. 5 Anne, c. 4, to the great Duke of Marlborough and his posterity as a reward for his public services could not be validly assigned upon trust. The principle on which property is held incapable of being assigned in cases like the last is explained by Lord Langdale in *Grenfell* v. *The Dean and Canons of Windsor* (*k*). "There are various cases," he says, "in which public duties are concerned, in which it may be against public policy, that the income arising for the performance of those duties should be assigned; and for this simple reason, because the public is interested, not only in the performance from time to time of the duties, but also in the fit state of preparation of the party having to perform them. Such is the reason in the cases of half pay, where there is a sort of retainer and where the payments which are made to officers from time to time are the means by which they, being liable to be called into public service, are enabled to keep themselves in a state of preparation for performing their duties. If, therefore, they were permitted to deprive themselves of their half pay, they might be rendered unable promptly to enter upon their duties when called upon, and the public service would be thereby greatly injured. So also where pension or remuneration is given for a purpose which tends less directly to the public benefit, as, for instance, was the case in *Davis* v. *The Duke of Marlborough*. . . . In that case the pension was held inalienable, because it was considered that one of the objects of giving the pension, namely, for having a perpetual memorial of national gratitude for public services, would be entirely lost; and so in the course of the case Lord Eldon said, in the way of illustration and in allusion to the pension of a great public officer, that it could

(*h*) (1891) 1 Q. B. 737.
(*i*) (1876), 2 App. Cas. 1.
(*j*) (1818), 1 Swanst. 74.
(*k*) (1840), 2 Beav. at p. 549.

not be aliened because that public officer must not be allowed to fall into such a situation as to make it difficult for him in consequence of any pecuniary embarrassment to maintain the dignity of his office."

Further, the subject of the trust must be *property*. A mere expectancy or *spes successionis* is not a title to property by English law, and although an assignment of an expectancy made for valuable consideration would be enforced as a contract, a voluntary assignment of it would not, and therefore a voluntary trust of an expectancy is not enforceable against the settlor if he refuses to hand over the trust property to the trustee when the expectancy is realized (*l*).

However, it is provided by s. 6 of the Real Property Act, 1845, that a contingent, an executory and a future interest, and a possibility *coupled with an interest* in real estate may be disposed of by deed.

In the case of trusts of land regard must be had to the tenure by which it is held. For instance, according to Sir George Jessel, an equitable estate tail of copyhold land cannot be created in a manor in which there is no custom to entail (*m*), and the same, no doubt, applies to leaseholds. Again, in the case of land situate in a country in which "trust substitution" is forbidden—as in Italy—a trust of the land is invalid here (*n*). It may, indeed, be that trusts of land in a foreign country can never be enforced in England. Mr. Lewin says that "the few authorities upon the subject tend to confirm this view, but there is little light to be obtained from them, and the law must be regarded as still somewhat unsettled" (*o*). Yet in *Rochefoucauld* v. *Boustead* (*p*), the Court of Appeal enforced a trust of land situate in Ceylon, to the extent of decreeing an account of the trustee's dealings and transactions with the land.

(*l*) *In re Ellenborough*, (1903) 1 Ch. 697.

(*m*) *Allen* v. *Bewsey* (1877), 7 Ch. D. at p. 466.

(*n*) *In re Piercey*, (1895) 1 Ch. 83.

(*o*) Trusts, 11th ed. 50.

(*p*) (1897) 1 Ch. 196.

Part II.—EXPRESS TRUSTS.

SECTION V.—CREATION OF EXPRESS TRUSTS OF LAND.

(1) ALL declarations or creations of trusts or confidences of any lands, tenements, or hereditaments shall be manifested and proved by some writing signed by the party who is by law enabled to declare such trust, or by his last will in writing, or else they shall be utterly void and of none effect (*a*).

(2) Provided always that where any conveyance shall be made of any lands or tenements by which a trust or confidence shall or may arise or result by the implication or construction of law, or be transferred or extinguished by an act or operation of law, then and in every such case such trust or confidence shall be of the like force and effect as the same would have been if this statute had not been made, anything herein contained to the contrary notwithstanding (*b*).

(3) The provisions of this act do not apply where they would operate to effectuate a fraud.

"Trusts," says Mr. Lewin (*c*), "like uses, are of their own nature *averrable*," which means that they may be proved by word of mouth without any writing.

And this was the law for all trusts until the year 1677, when the Statute of Frauds was passed, which made it necessary for

(*a*) Statute of Frauds, s. 7. (*b*) *Ibid.* s. 8.
(*c*) Trusts, 11th ed. 51.

trusts of lands, tenements, or hereditaments to be manifested and proved by writing.

The seventh and eighth sections of the statute, which are those in point, as printed in the last edition of Chitty's Statutes, are as follows :—

Sect. 7 :—

"All declarations or creations of trusts or confidences of any lands, tenements, or hereditaments shall be manifested and proved by some writing signed by the party who is by law enabled to declare such trust, or by his last will in writing, or else they shall be utterly void and of none effect."

Sect. 8 :—

"Provided always that where any conveyance shall be made of any lands or tenements by which a trust or confidence shall or may arise or result by the implication or construction of law, or be transferred or extinguished by an act or operation of law, then and in every such case such trust or confidence shall be of the like force and effect as the same would have been if this statute had not been made, anything herein contained to the contrary notwithstanding."

It is also provided by sect. 9 of the statute that :—

"All grants and assignments of any trust or confidence shall likewise be in writing, signed by the party granting or assigning the same, or by such last will or devise, or else shall likewise be utterly void and of none effect."

It may be observed that the statute only requires the trust to be "manifested and proved" by writing; it does not require it to be made in writing. So Lord Alvanley said in the case of *Forster* v. *Hale* (*d*) : "It is not required by the statute that a trust should be created by a writing . . . but that it shall be manifested and proved by writing; plainly meaning that there should be evidence in writing proving that there was such a trust."

The "party who is by law enabled to declare the trust" within the meaning of the act is the party in whom the absolute beneficial interest in the property is vested when the trust is created.

Consequently, if A. purchases land and takes a conveyance in the name of B., and A. subsequently delivers to B. a paper writing signed by him (A.) which declares trusts of the land after A.'s

(*d*) (1798), 3 Ves. at p. 707.

death, this is a valid declaration of trust within the statute, although the writing be not signed by B., for, since there is a resulting trust of the property in favour of A., he is the beneficial owner of it and the person enabled to declare the trust (*e*).

The statute, however, does not apply where it would operate to effectuate a fraud. In *Rochefoucauld* v. *Boustead* (*f*), Lord Justice Lindley, delivering the judgment of the Court of Appeal (Lord Halsbury, L. C., and Lindley and A. L. Smith, L. JJ.), said : "It is . . . established by a series of cases, the propriety of which cannot now be questioned, that the Statute of Frauds does not prevent proof of a fraud ; and it is a fraud on the part of a person to whom land is conveyed as a trustee, and who knows it was so conveyed, to deny the trust and claim the land himself. Consequently, notwithstanding the statute, it is competent for a person claiming land conveyed to another to prove by parol evidence that it was so conveyed upon trust for the claimant, and that the grantee, knowing the facts, is denying the trust and relying upon the form of conveyance and the statute in order to keep the land himself. This doctrine was not established until some time after the statute was passed. In *Bartlett* v. *Pickersgill* (*g*), the trust was proved, and the defendant, who denied it, was tried for perjury and convicted, and yet it was held that the statute prevented the court from affording relief to the plaintiff. But this case cannot be regarded as law at the present day. The case . . . . is inconsistent with all modern decisions on the subject."

In America the law is different. The trustee may repudiate the trust and keep the land upon payment of its fair market value (*h*).

"Land" in s. 7 of the Statute of Frauds is said by Lewin to include copyhold land (*i*), and he cites *Withers* v. *Withers* (*j*). The report of this case states that Lord Hardwicke was of opinion "that resulting trusts of copyholds as well as of freeholds are within the Statute of Frauds and Perjuries." But, as Mr. Hargrave in a note to this passage points out, there must be some misprint, or reporter's mistake, here, for resulting trusts are

(*e*) *Tierney* v. *Wood* (1854), 19 Beav. 330; *Kronheim* v. *Johnson* (1877), 7 Ch. D. 60.

(*f*) (1897) 1 Ch. 196.

(*g*) (1759), 1 Eden, 515.

(*h*) See Harvard Law Review, vol. xviii. No. 8, 614.

(*i*) Trusts, 11th ed. 53.

(*j*) (1752), Amb. 152.

excepted from the statute by the eighth section. However, all the text-book writers treat the case as deciding that copyhold land is within the act. It seems to be clear that leasehold land is within it from the cases of *Skett* v. *Whitmore* (*k*) and *Forster* v. *Hale* (*l*), and, if leaseholds are, it is difficult to see why copyholds should not be, although Mr. Hargrave in the passage cited says distinctly that they are not.

(*k*) (1705), 2 Freem. 280.

(*l*) (1798), 3 Ves. 696.

SECTION VI.—CREATION OF OTHER EXPRESS TRUSTS.

SUBJECT to the provisions of the Statute of Frauds and of any other statute in that behalf, an express trust may be created by writing (either with or without seal) or by word of mouth, or partly in writing and partly by word of mouth, and in any form of words, provided only that the settlor indicates with reasonable certainty—

(a) An intention on his part to thereby create a trust;
(b) The trust property; and
(c) The beneficiary.

Besides the Statute of Frauds, there are a number of statutes which may be required to be complied with in order to create a valid trust. Among them may be mentioned the Wills Act, 1837, by s. 9 of which every will must be in writing executed in manner therein prescribed; the Mortmain and Charitable Uses Act, 1888, s. 4; the Gifts for Churches Act, 1803, s. 1; and the Judicature Act, 1873, s. 25 (6).

Where any such statute applies it must be complied with or the trust will be invalid.

Illustration.

A. executes a will by which he gives all his property to B., his solicitor, informing B. that he is to take the property as trustee to deal with it according to further written directions to be given him. No directions are given by A. during his life, but after his death a letter is found addressed by A. to B., in which A. expresses a wish that X. should have his property. This is not a valid declaration of trust for X, the letter not being executed as a will. *In re Boyes, Boyes* v. *Carritt* (1884), 26 Ch. D. 531.

However, as in the case of the Statute of Frauds, the provisions of the Wills Act do not prevent the proof of a fraud, and where a gift is made by will verbal evidence is admissible to affix a trust upon the donee. "Where a person," as Lord Cairns said (*a*), "knowing that a testator, in making a disposition in his favour, intends it to be applied for purposes other than his own benefit, either expressly promises or by silence implies that he will carry the testator's intention into effect, and the property is left to him upon the faith of that promise or undertaking, it is in effect a case of a trust, and in such cases the court will not allow the devisee to set up the Statute of Frauds, or rather the Statute of Wills by which the Statute of Frauds is now in this respect superseded, and for this reason:—The devisee by his conduct has induced the testator to leave him the property, and as the Lord Justice Turner says in *Russell* v. *Jackson*, no one can doubt that if the devisee had stated that he would not carry into effect the intentions of the testator the disposition in his favour would not have been found in the will" (*b*).

Illustration.

A. by his will gives the residue of his property to B. and C. On his death-bed A. communicates this to B. and C. and exacts from them a promise to pay an annuity of 300*l*. a year to X. This may be proved by verbal evidence, and when proved constitutes a trust enforceable by X. *Norris* v. *Frazer* (1873), L. R. 15 Eq. 318.

Subject to statutory enactment, a trust need not be in writing, verbal declarations being sufficient. This follows from the statement quoted from Lewin in the previous section, that "trusts are of their own nature averrable." Where no statute has modified it that rule still holds good (*c*).

(*a*) *Jones* v. *Badley* (1868), L. R. 3 Ch. App. 362.

(*b*) To the same effect are the cases of *Russell* v. *Jackson* (1852), 10 Hare, 204; *Tee* v. *Ferris* (1856), 2 K. & J. 357; *McCormick* v. *Grogan* (1869), L. R. 4 H. L. 82; and *Norris* v. *Frazer* (1873), L. R. 15 Eq. 318.

(*c*) *Fordyce* v. *Millis* (1791), 3 Br. Ch. Ca. 577; *Bayley* v. *Boulcott* (1829), 4 Russ. 347; *Benbow* v. *Townsend* (1833), 1 M. & K. 506; *Kilpin* v. *Kilpin* (1833), *ibid.* 520; *Jones* v. *Lock* (1865), L. R. 1 Ch. App. 25.

The following are examples of trusts created by word of mouth :—

Illustrations.

1. A. lends money to B. on mortgage, giving B. verbal directions to make out the security in the name of C., "as he intended the mortgage to be for his benefit, and that it would be his." This creates a trust in favour of C. *Benbow* v. *Townsend* (1833), 1 M. & K. 506.

2. A. transfers stock into the names of B., C., D., and E., stating verbally that the transfer is for the benefit of D., E., F., and G. This creates a trust in favour of the latter. *Kilpin* v. *Kilpin* (1834), 1 M. & K. 520; see especially at p. 538.

3. A., being owed a sum of money by B., verbally intimates to B. his desire that B. shall hold the sum in trust for C. B. consents, and pays over a part. C. is entitled to an injunction restraining B. from paying the remainder otherwise than to himself. *M'Fadden* v. *Jenkyns* (1842), 1 Hare, 458.

It seems that the trust may even be partly in writing and partly by word of mouth. In *Kilpin* v. *Kilpin*, *supra*, the court received evidence from the testator's solicitor of verbal declarations made to him, and also entries in a memorandum book proved to be in the handwriting of the deceased, in order to make out the trust.

Nor is any special form of words needed to create a trust. "It is not necessary that the precise words 'trust' or 'confidence' should be used in order to create a trust . . . . any expressions will suffice from which it is clear that the party using them considers himself a trustee and adopts that character" (*d*). "Trusts can be imposed by any language which is clear enough to show an intention to impose them," said Lord Justice Lindley in 1897 (*e*).

Illustration.

A. and B. enter into partnership under articles which contain a provision that if A. dies during the partnership leaving a widow surviving, the widow may, if she thinks fit, continue to carry on

(*d*) See *Dipple* v. *Corles* (1853), 11 Hare, at p. 184.

(*e*) *In re Williams*, (1897) 2 Ch. at p. 18; see also *Page* v. *Cox* (1852), 10 Hare, at p. 169; and *Kekewich* v. *Manning* (1851), 1 De G. Mac. & G. 176.

the partnership business with the surviving partner, and shall be entitled to A.'s share in the profits and excess of capital. This creates a trust in favour of A.'s widow. *Page* v. *Cox* (1852), 10 Hare, 163.

But there must be an intention to create a trust by the words used. A transaction will not be deemed to create a trust, whatever its form may be, unless it appears that a trust was intended (*f*). The mere use of the word "trust" will not necessarily create a trust. There is no magic in the word "trust," said Lord Hagan (*g*); "in various circumstances it may represent many things." "An instrument does not become a trust enforceable and cognizable in a court of law because that word is used," said Lord Justice James (*h*).

The following cases illustrate this :—

Illustrations.

1. A. directs his agent to purchase stock in the names of himself and his wife "in trust" for his infant son. The agent makes the investment, but no trust is expressed, because the bank object to trust accounts appearing on their books. A. allows the stock to remain without any trust being declared, and receives the dividends down to the date of his death. This is not a trust. *Smith* v. *Warde* (1845), 15 Sim. 56.

2. A., after depositing in a savings bank to the full extent allowed by the act 9 Geo. IV. c. 92, opens another account in the name of "A., in trust for B.," over which he has full control under the act. His object being to evade the act and not to create a trust in favour of B., the latter is not entitled to the amount standing to the credit of the account at the date of A.'s death. *Field* v. *Lonsdale* (1850), 13 Beav. 78.

3. By a royal warrant booty of war is granted to the Secretary of State for India "in trust" for the officers and men of certain

(*f*) *Gaskell* v. *Gaskell* (1828), 2 You. & J. 502; *Hughes* v. *Stubbs* (1842), 1 Hare, 476; *Smith* v. *Warde* (1845), 15 Sim. 56; *In re Weekes' Settlement*, (1897) 1 Ch. 289; and see per Fry, L. J., in *In re Diggles* (1888), 39 Ch. D. at p. 258; and per Rigby, L. J., in *In re Williams*, (1897) 2 Ch. at p. 28.

(*g*) *Kinlock* v. *Sec. State, &c.* (1882), 7 App. Cas. at p. 630.

(*h*) 15 Ch. D. at p. 8.

forces, to be distributed by the Secretary of State or by any other person he may appoint, according to certain scales and proportions; any doubt arising to be determined finally by the Secretary of State, or by such persons to whom he may refer them, unless the Queen otherwise orders. This does not create a trust, the Secretary of State being merely the agent of the crown. *Kinlock* v. *Sec. State, &c.* (1882), 7 App. Cas. 619.

Even though an intention to confer a benefit be shown, that intention must be a clear intention to create a *trust*. It is of no avail to show an intention to confer a benefit in some other way. If the intention appears to have been not to create a trust but to make a *gift*, however clearly it may appear, the court will not, in order to prevent the gift failing, aid the intended donee by construing the imperfect gift as a declaration of trust. "For a man to make himself a trustee there must be an expression of intention to become a trustee, whereas words of present gift show an intention to give over property to another, and not to retain it in the donor's own hands for any purpose, fiduciary or otherwise" (*i*). The following cases illustrate this:—

Illustrations.

1. A., being entitled to ten shares in the X. company, writes upon a receipt for calls due thereon and signs the following indorsement:—"I do hereby assign to my daughter B. all my right, title, and interest of and in the enclosed call, and all other calls of my subscription in the X. company." This is not a declaration of trust, but an invalid gift. *Antrobus* v. *Smith* (1805), 12 Ves. 39.

2. A father puts a cheque into the hands of his son of nine months old, saying, "I give this to baby for himself," and then takes back the cheque and puts it away. He has previously expressed his intention of investing the money represented by it for the benefit of his son. This is not a declaration of trust in favour of the baby. *Jones* v. *Lock* (1865), L. R. 1 Ch. App. 25.

(*i*) See *Richards* v. *Delbridge* (1874), L. R. 18 Eq. 11; *Dillon* v. *Coppin* (1839), 4 M. & Cr. 647; and *In re Lucan* (1890), 45 Ch. D. 470.

3. A., being possessed of leasehold business premises and stock-in-trade, shortly before his death indorses on the lease and signs the following memorandum :—"This deed and all thereto belonging I give to B. from this time forth, with all the stock-in-trade." This does not create a trust in favour of B. *Richards* v. *Delbridge* (1874), L. R. 18 Eq. 11.

4. A., two years before his death, hands to his wife certificates for some railway stock standing in his own name, saying, "These are yours." This is not a declaration of trust by A., but an imperfect gift. *Moore* v. *Moore* (1874), L. R. 18 Eq. 474.

5. A. signs a memorandum as follows :—"I wish to communicate to my executors that I have to-day given to B. my 1,000*l.* debenture bond of the M. S. & L. Ry. Co. ; but as I shall require the annual dividends to meet my necessary expenses, I retain the document in my own possession for my lifetime, requesting you on my decease to hand it over to B. and communicate to the secretary of the said railway company at the Manchester office relative to the transfer of the said bond being entered in their books." This is not a declaration of trust, but an invalid gift, the reference being to 1,000*l.* debenture *stock*, transferable only in the books of the company. *Pethybridge* v. *Burrow* (1885), 53 L. T. 5.

Not only must there be a clear indication of the settlor's intention to create a trust, but he must also indicate with reasonable certainty the trust property and the beneficiary (*j*).

Nearly all the cases in which the question of the certainty of the trust property or of the beneficiaries has been raised are cases in which it has been sought to found the trust on precatory words. Under the modern view of such words, no trust would have been created in any of them, even if the trust property and beneficiary had been certain, so that they are not very satisfactory authorities. However, it is plain that in some such cases, at any rate, even if the precatory words had been the plainest words of trust, the trust

(*j*) *Knight* v. *Knight* (1840), 3 Beav. 172 ; *Briggs* v. *Penney* (1851), 3 Mac. & G. 554.

would have failed for want of certainty of subject-matter or of object (*k*). Of these the following are examples :—

Illustrations.

1. A. devises real estate to B. and her heirs for ever, in fullest confidence that after her decease she will devise "the property" to A.'s "family." This does not create a trust, because neither the subject nor the object is sufficiently certain. *Wright* v. *Atkyns* (1823), T. & R. 143.

2. A., after explaining in her will why she has left the largest share of her property to her two eldest daughters, adds, "if they die single, of course they will leave 'what they have' amongst their brothers and sisters or their children." This does not create a trust, because of the uncertainty of the property. *Lechmere* v. *Lavie* (1832), 2 My. & K. 197.

It may be added that the rule requiring certainty of beneficiary does not apply to a trust in favour of a charity (*l*).

(*k*) *Mussoorie Bank* v. *Raynor* (1882), 7 App. Cas. at p. 331.

(*l*) Tudor, Charitable Trusts, 3rd ed. 29 *et seq.*

SECTION VII.—RULES FOR DETERMINING INTENTION TO CREATE A TRUST.

IN determining whether or not a trust has been created, regard must be had to the following rules:—

Rule I.—A gift of property, coupled with words expressive of the wish, hope, recommendation, entreaty or prayer of the donor that the property shall be dealt with in a specified manner, or with other words of similar import, does not create a trust of that property, unless (regard being had to the whole of the instrument, if any, in which such words appear, and to the circumstances of the case) it appears that an obligation to so deal with it is thereby imposed.

Rule II.—A power to appoint property to a specified person, or among a class of persons, without any gift over in default of such appointment, creates a trust (subject to the donee's right of selection) in favour of such person or persons, if it appears that the donor intended the property to be appointed to him or some one or more of them.

Rule III.—A conveyance or assignment of property to a trustee in trust to pay debts or other sums of money does not of itself create a trust in favour of the creditors or persons to whom such sums are payable, but a trust is created in the following cases, namely:—

(a) When any of such creditors or persons is a party to and executes the deed of conveyance or assignment, a trust in favour of the party so executing it; or

(b) When it is communicated to any of them who expressly or impliedly assents thereto, a trust in favour of the party so assenting; or

(c) When the trust is in favour of creditors existing at the settlor's death, and the settlor dies without having revoked the trust; or

(d) When an intention to create a trust otherwise appears.

The rules stated above are really only an elaboration of that stated in the last preceding section, that in order to the validity of a trust an intention to create a trust is essential, although given the intention the form of the transaction is immaterial. In order to determine whether such an intention has been indicated, certain presumptions are made in the case of gifts accompanied by precatory words, gifts of powers of appointment, and assignments for the benefit of creditors.

Precatory Trusts.

It is pointed out by Mr. Underhill (*a*) that when the peculiar origin and history of uses and trusts is kept in mind, it is not unnatural that words expressive of the settlor's wish, hope, recommendation, entreaty, or prayer—precatory words, as they are called—should have been regarded in former times as just as binding on the donee of the property in respect of which they were used as more precisely imperative forms of expression. The old rule on the subject was stated by Sir Pepper Arden in the case of *Malim* v. *Keighley* (*b*), as follows :—" Wherever any person gives property and points out the object, the property, and the way it shall go, that does create a trust, unless he shows clearly that his desire expressed is to be controlled by the party, and that he shall have an option to defeat it."

There can be no doubt that words of request may still amount to a command (*c*) ; but the leaning of the courts is now strongly

(*a*) Trusts and Trustees, 5th ed. 16 ; 6th ed. 23.

(*b*) (1794), 2 Ves. Jun. at p. 335.

(*c*) See per Lindley, L. J., in *In re Williams*, (1897) 2 Ch. at p. 18.

against construing precatory words as creating trusts. The modern view of the subject dates from the case of *Lambe* v. *Eames* in 1871 (*d*), in which Lord Justice James, in deciding that no trust had been created, said: "In hearing case after case cited, I could not help feeling that the officious kindness of the Court of Chancery in interposing trusts where in many cases the father of the family never meant to create trusts must have been a very cruel kindness indeed. I am satisfied that the testator in this case would have been shocked to think that any person calling himself a next friend could file a bill in this court, and, under pretence of benefiting the children, have taken the administration from the wife. I am satisfied that no such trust was intended, and that it would be a violation of the clearest and plainest wishes of the testator if we decide otherwise."

This view of the meaning of precatory words having been followed in several other cases, the conflict between the older and modern authorities was at length settled by the Court of Appeal in favour of the latter, in 1884, in *In re Adams and the Kensington Vestry* (*e*), in which Lord Justice Cotton said: "I have no hesitation in saying myself that I think some of the older authorities went a great deal too far in holding that some particular words appearing in a will were sufficient to create a trust. . . . . Having regard to the later decisions, we must not extend the old cases in any way or rely upon the mere use of any particular words, but, considering all the words which are used, we have to see what is their true effect, and what was the intention of the testator as expressed in his will."

These opinions have frequently been approved, and the decisions have been uniformly followed by the Court of Appeal (*f*), save that in *In re Williams*, Lord Justice Rigby, who dissented from the opinion of the majority, said: "In theory I do not think there ever has been, at any rate for a century, any doubt as to the principles on which a trust or condition should be deduced, if at all. . . . . On these fundamental points there never has been any real difference, though the application of them to particular cases

(*d*) (1871), L. R. 6 Ch. App. 597.

(*e*) (1884), 27 Ch. D. 394.

(*f*) See, *e.g.*, *In re Diggles*, *Gregory* v. *Edmondson* (1888), 39 Ch. D. 258; *In re Hamilton*, *Trench* v. *Hamilton*, (1895) 2 Ch. 370; *Hill* v. *Hill*, (1897) 2 Ch. 18; *In re Hanbury*, *Hanbury* v. *Fisher*, (1904) 1 Ch. 415, reversed by H. L. on another ground sub nom. *Comiskey* v. *Bowring-Hanbury*, (1905) A. C. 84; and *In re Oldfield*, *Oldfield* v. *Oldfield*, (1904) 1 Ch. 549.

has not always been satisfactory. Of course the Court of Appeal cannot in recent cases have intended in any way to alter the settled law on the subject, or to have assumed a jurisdiction to deal with the question as if it were independent of authority" But, notwithstanding the Lord Justice's "of course," one cannot help feeling, when the older cases are compared with the newer, that the law has been altered, or, to adopt a commonly used phrase, "the current of authority has been changed."

Precatory trusts are usually found in wills, but the doctrine is not confined to wills; it extends to instruments *inter vivos* (*g*)—although some doubt as to this was expressed by Lord Justice Chitty (*h*)—and there seems to be no reason why the doctrine should not apply to verbal trusts as well (*i*). The old cases on the subject will be found collected in the notes to *Harding* v. *Glyn*, White & Tudor, L. C. Eq. (7th ed.) vol. ii. 335; in Encyc. Eng. Law, cited below; and Lewin on Trusts, 11th ed. 144 *et seq.;* but, except such of them as decide against the existence of a trust, they cannot now be relied on.

Illustrations.

1. A. by his will gives his estate to his widow (B.), "to be at her disposal in any way she may think best for the benefit of herself and family." This does not constitute a trust in favour of A.'s children; and a gift under B.'s will to the illegitimate child of one of A.'s sons is valid. *Lambe* v. *Eames* (1871), L. R. 6 Ch. App. 597.

2. A. by his will gives all the rest, residue, and remainder of his estate both real and personal to B., her heirs and assigns for ever "to and for her own proper use and benefit for ever" separately from her husband, "and the proceeds to be applied by her in the bringing up and maintenance of" all B.'s children. This does not constitute a trust in favour of B.'s children. *Mackett* v. *Mackett* (1872), L. R. 14 Eq. 49.

3. A. bequeaths all his property to B. and for her "to do justice to those relations on my side such as she think worthy of

(*g*) *Lidiard* v. *Lidiard* (1860), 28 Beav. 266.

(*h*) In *Hill* v. *Hill*, (1897) 1 Q. B. at p. 493.

(*i*) See Encyc. Eng. Law, sub tit. Precatory Trust, vol. x. 292.

remuneration, but under no restriction to any stated property, but quite at liberty to give and distribute what and to who" B. "may please." This does not create a trust. *In re Bond, Cole* v. *Hawes* (1876), 4 Ch. D. 238.

4. A. gives her property in trust for such of her nieces X. and Y. as should be living at her death, adding, "my desire being that they shall distribute such residue as they think will be most agreeable to my wishes." X. and Y. take for their own benefit and not as trustees. *Stead* v. *Mellor* (1877), 5 Ch. D. 225.

5. A. gives all his property to his wife, X., "absolutely, with full power for her to dispose of the same as she may think fit for the benefit of my family with full confidence that she will do so." This does not create a trust in favour of A.'s children, and X. takes absolutely. *In re Hutchinson and Tenant* (1878), 8 Ch. D. 540.

6. A. gives to B. "the whole of my real and personal property for her sole use and benefit. It is my wish that whatever property my wife might possess at her death be equally divided between my children." This is not a trust. *Parnall* v. *Parnall* (1878), 9 Ch. D. 96.

7. A. gives to B. the whole of his property both real and personal, "feeling confident that she will act justly to our children in dividing the same when no longer required by her." This does not create a trust and B. takes an absolute interest. *The Mussoorie Bank* v. *Raynor* (1882), 7 App. Cas. 321.

8. A. gives all his real and personal estate unto and to the absolute use of his wife, her heirs, executors, administrators and assigns, "in full confidence that she will do what is right as to the disposal thereof between my children either in her lifetime or by will after her decease." This does not constitute a trust in favour of the children. *In re Adams and the Kensington Vestry* (1884), 27 Ch. D. 394.

9. A. bequeaths 4,000*l.* to his brother B. in trust for his sisters C., D. and E., adding, "they are hereby enjoined to take care of my nephew X. as may seem best in the future." This does not constitute a trust in X.'s favour. *In re Moore, Moore* v. *Roche* (1886), 34 W. R. 343.

10. A. gives all her real and personal property to her daughter B., "her heirs and assigns," adding, "and it is my desire that she allows to C. an annuity of 25*l.* during her life, and that the said C. shall, if she desire it, have the use of such portions of my household furniture, linen, &c., as may not be required by my daughter" B. This does not create a trust in favour of C. *In re Diggles, Gregory* v. *Edmondson* (1888), 39 Ch. D. 253 (*j*).

11. A. gives diamonds to B., saying, "I give these diamonds to you for your life with the request that at your death they may be left as heirlooms." This is an absolute gift to B., and no trust is created. *Hill* v. *Hill*, (1897) 1 Q. B. 483.

12. A. by his will gives his residuary estate to his wife B., her heirs, executors, administrators and assigns absolutely, "in fullest confidence that she will carry out my wishes in the following particulars," viz., to pay the premiums due during her life on a policy of insurance on her own life (which is B.'s own property), and that B. by her will should leave the moneys payable under the policy, and also the moneys payable at A.'s death in respect of a policy on his life (which is A.'s property) to his daughter X. This does not constitute a trust in favour of X. *In re Williams, Williams* v. *Williams*, (1897) 2 Ch. 12 (*k*).

Trust Powers.

It is well established that the execution of a mere power of appointment will not be compelled. But if a person gives to another a power to appoint property among a class or in favour of an individual, and makes no provision for the destination of the property in the event of the power not being exercised, it is presumed that the class or individual were intended to have the property, in some shares. The donee of the power has the right to say in what shares they shall take it, but if he does not exercise this right, they are entitled equally.

"Where there appears a general intention in favour of a class,

(*j*) *In re Oldfield, Oldfield* v. *Oldfield*, (1904) 1 Ch. 549, is to the same effect.

(*k*) *In re Hanbury, Hanbury* v. *Fisher*, (1904) 1 Ch. 415, is to the same effect. This case was reversed by H. L., sub nom. *Comiskey* v. *Bowring-Hanbury*, (1905) A. C. 84, on the ground that there was an executory gift over.

and a particular intention in favour of individuals of a class to be selected by another person, and the particular intention fails from that selection not being made, the court will carry into effect the general intention in favour of the class" (*l*).

But there must be a clear indication by the donor that he intended the power to be regarded as a trust (*m*).

The rule applies to a power of appointment in favour of an individual (*n*). But it does not apply if there is a gift over in default of appointment (*o*), even though the gift over in default is void (*p*).

The following cases illustrate the application of this principle:—

Illustrations.

1. A. by will gives property to his wife, desiring her at or before her death to give the same "unto and amongst such of his own relations as she should think most deserving and approve of." This creates a trust in favour of A.'s next of kin. *Harding* v. *Glyn* (1799), 1 Atk. 469 (*q*).

2. A. by will directs that certain property, in case his two children shall both die without leaving lawful issue, shall be disposed of as after mentioned, that is to say, the survivor of his two children shall have power to dispose by will of the property "amongst my nephews and nieces, or their children, either all to one of them or to as many of them" as his surviving child "shall think proper." This creates a trust in favour of the class, subject to a power of selection and distribution in A.'s surviving child. *Burrough* v. *Philcox* (1840), 5 My. & Cr. 73.

3. A. by his will, after giving a fund to his wife for life, directs that after her death it shall be paid to such and so many of the "relations or friends" of the wife as she shall by will appoint.

(*l*) *Burrough* v. *Philcox* (1840), 5 My. & C. 72; *Gude* v. *Worthington* (1849), 3 De G. & Sm. 389; *Salusbury* v. *Denton* (1857), 3 K. & J. 529; *Reid* v. *Reid* (1858), 25 Beav. 469; *In re Caplin's Will* (1865), 2 Dr. & Sm. 527; *Wilson* v. *Duguid* (1883), 24 Ch. D. 244.

(*m*) *In re Weekes' Settlement*, (1897) 1 Ch. 289.

(*n*) *Tweedale* v. *Tweedale* (1878), 7 Ch. D. 633.

(*o*) *Richardson* v. *Richardson* (1885), 16 Q. B. D. 85.

(*p*) *Miley* v. *Cape* (1880), W. N. 151.

(*q*) Having regard to the modern view of precatory trusts, probably this case would now be decided differently.

This creates a trust in favour of the wife's next of kin. *In re Caplin's Will* (1865), 2 Dr. & Sm. 527.

4. A. gives his trustees power, if his daughter marries with their consent, to appoint part of her fortune on her death to her husband. This creates a trust in favour of the husband. *Tweedale* v. *Tweedale* (1878), 7 Ch. D. 633.

5. X. by deed assigns property upon trust for A. for life, and after her decease for B. for life, and after the decease of the survivor amongst such of the children of A. and B. then living, in such manner, shares, times, and proportions as A. and B. jointly, or the survivor of them separately, shall appoint, and in case there should be no such child or children, then upon trust for C. for life, and, after his decease, amongst such of his children in such manner, shares, times, and proportions as he shall appoint. This is a trust in favour of C.'s children, and upon the death of A. and B. without issue, and failure of C. to exercise his power of appointment, all his children are entitled as tenants in common. *Wilson* v. *Duguid* (1883), 24 Ch. D. 244.

6. A. bequeaths to her husband a life interest in certain real property, and gives him "power to dispose of all such property by will amongst our children." This is a mere power, and not a trust. *In re Weekes' Settlement*, (1897) 1 Ch. 289.

Illusory Trusts.

An assignment of property to trustees in trust to pay debts, although at first sight it appears to create a trust, is generally not enforceable by the creditors unless they are parties to it. The rule was first laid down in *Walwyn* v. *Coutts*, in 1815 (*r*), where it was held that the creditors could not prevent the revocation of the deed. This was expressly followed in *Garrard* v. *Lauderdale*, in 1831 (*s*), and again in *Acton* v. *Woodgate*, two years later (*t*). The rule was stated in *Bill* v. *Cureton* (*u*) to have been adopted "to promote the views and intentions of parties"; and though doubts

(*r*) (1815), 3 Sim. 14.

(*s*) (1831), 3 Sim. 1; 2 Russ. & My. 451.

(*t*) (1833), 2 My. & K. 492.

(*u*) (1835), 2 My. & K. 503.

as to the propriety of the decision were sometimes expressed in former days (*v*), the rule is now established beyond question. "It appears to me to be too late now to question the principle of *Garrard* v. *Lauderdale*," said Lord Justice James, in *Johns* v. *James* (*w*). That case "seems to me to have proceeded upon the plainest notions of common sense. It is quite obvious that a man in pecuniary difficulties, having a great number of debts which he could not meet, might put his property in the hands of certain persons to realize and pay the creditors in the best way they could. . . . . If it were supposed that such a deed as that created an irrevocable trust in favour of every one of the persons who happened at the time to be a creditor, the result might have been very often monstrous. It would give him no opportunity of paying a creditor who was pressing; no opportunity of settling an action; no opportunity of getting any food for himself or his family the next day, or redeeming property pledged. . . . . Such a deed as this is to be construed as a mandate, the same sort of mandate that a man gives when he gives his servant money, with directions to pay it in a particular way; it does not create any equitable or legal right in favour of a particular creditor." The principle has been applied in, amongst other cases, *Wilding* v. *Richards* (*x*), *Cornthwaite* v. *Frith* (*y*), *Johns* v. *James* (*z*), *Kinlock* v. *Secretary of State for India* (*a*), *Henderson* v. *Rothschild* (*b*), and *In re Ashby* (*c*).

The rule applies not only to trusts for the payment of debts, but of other sums of money. In *Walwyn* v. *Coutts*, for instance, the trust was for payment of annuities. It applies whether the debts or sums of money are owing by the assignor or another—in *Walwyn* v. *Coutts* they were owing by the assignor's son—and it is immaterial whether the creditors or persons to whom the sums are owing are specified or not; in *Walwyn* v. *Coutts* and *Garrard* v. *Lauderdale* they were specified; in *Acton* v. *Woodgate* they were not.

(*v*) *E.g.*, by Knight Bruce, V.-C., in *Wilding* v. *Richards* (1845), 1 Coll. Ch. R. 659, and by Sugden, L. C., in the Irish case, *Simmonds* v. *Palles* (1845), 2 Jo. & Lat. 504.

(*w*) (1878), 8 Ch. D. 744.

(*x*) (1845), 1 Coll. Ch. R. 655.

(*y*) (1851), 4 De G. & Sm. 552.

(*z*) (1878), 8 Ch. D. 744.

(*a*) (1882), 7 App. Cas. 619.

(*b*) (1886), 33 Ch. D. 459.

(*c*) (1892) 1 Q. B. 872.

Although the trust is revocable, the property in these cases vests in the trustee until the trust is revoked, and he can maintain a suit therefor without joining the creditors (*d*).

The following cases are illustrations of the application of the rule :—

Illustrations.

1. A. conveys property to X. and Y. for the purpose of paying off annuities granted by B. (A.'s son). The annuities are mentioned in a schedule, but the annuitants are not parties to the deed. A. can revoke the deed and the annuitants are not entitled to restrain X. and Y. from reconveying the property. *Walwyn* v. *Coutts* (1815), 3 Sim. 14.

2. A. conveys property to B. and C. upon trust to pay the debts owing by A. to the creditors specified in the schedule to the conveyance. The creditors are made parties to the deed, but they neither execute it nor conform to its terms. They cannot enforce the trust. *Garrard* v. *Lauderdale* (1831), 3 Sim. 1; 2 Russ. & My. 451.

3. A. conveys property to B. and C. upon trust to pay the debts due to them and all other debts then due from A. No creditor other than B. and C. is a party to the conveyance, nor is it communicated to any other creditor. No other creditor can enforce it, and A., B. and C. are entitled to execute a subsequent deed by which the first is partially revoked. *Acton* v. *Woodgate* (1833), 2 My. & K. 492.

4. A., being obligor of several bonds of which B. is surety, conveys property to B. upon trust to pay the bond creditors. The creditors neither execute nor have they notice of the deed. They cannot enforce it, but B. can retain the property until released from his liability as surety. *Wilding* v. *Richards* (1845), 1 Coll. Ch. R. 655.

5. A. conveys all his property to B. upon trust to pay thereout a sum of 5,000*l.* (to be raised by B. on A.'s behalf) and also all

(*d*) *Glegg* v. *Rees* (1871), L. R. 7 Ch. App. 71.

other debts due from him, including a debt due to C. The deed is not communicated to any of the creditors of A. C. cannot require an account from B. *Johns* v. *James* (1878), 8 Ch. D. 744.

The general rule is subject to several qualifications, however. These are :—

(a) *When any of such creditors or persons is party to and executes the deed of assignment.*—It was laid down in *Mackinnon* v. *Stewart* (*e*) that a trust deed for creditors which was executed by the majority of them was irrevocable, and therefore a dissenting creditor could not in the absence of fraud have it set aside. So in *Synnot* v. *Simpson* (*f*), while the general rule was admitted, it was said that " the case is obviously different where the creditor is a party to the arrangement." And in *Siggers* v. *Evans* (*g*) an assignment to a trustee who was himself a creditor was held irrevocable as against him even before he executed it, and the effect is the same even though the creditor executes the deed not *quâ* creditor but in some other capacity (*h*).

It seems, however, from *Acton* v. *Woodgate* that, although the trust is binding as regards the creditors executing the deed, it remains revocable as to creditors who do not execute it.

Illustrations.

1. A. conveys all his property to X., Y. and Z., three of his creditors, in trust to pay the debts due from him to themselves and his other creditors who shall execute the deed. X., Y. and Z. and some of the other creditors execute the deed. B., a dissenting creditor, cannot get the deed set aside as being a mere voluntary deed of agency. *Mackinnon* v. *Stewart* (1850), 1 Sim. N. S. 76.

2. A. conveys all his property to B., a creditor, in trust for B. and his other creditors. On the same day that A. communicates this to B., X., another creditor, seizes A.'s goods in execution. This is an irrevocable trust, and X. is not entitled as against B. *Siggers* v. *Evans* (1855), 5 Ell. & Bl. 367.

(*e*) (1850), 1 Sim. N. S. 76.

(*f*) (1854), 5 H. L. C. 121.

(*g*) (1885), 5 Ell. & Bl. 367.

(*h*) *Montefiore* v. *Browne* (1858), 7 H. L. C. 241; *Cosser* v. *Radford* (1863), 1 De G. J. & S. 585; and *Hobson* v. *Thellusson* (1867), L. R. 2 Q. B. 642, are to the same effect.

3. A. and B., father and son, convey estates to trustees with a power to sell on consent in writing of A. and B., or the survivor, and to apply the produce in payment of the debts of A. therein specified. A. is indebted (*inter alios*) to D., as trustee for an infirmary, this debt being specified in the deed, and D., having some legal interest in the properties, is a party to the deed in respect of that interest and executes it. This creates a trust in favour of the infirmary. *Montefiore* v. *Browne* (1858), 7 H. L. C. 241.

4. A. conveys property to B. upon trust (*inter alia*) to pay to specified creditors the sums due to them, giving B. power to prefer one creditor to another. C., a creditor, executes the deed and receives under it a payment on account. C. is entitled to a decree for the execution of the trust. *Cosser* v. *Radford* (1863), 1 De G. J. & S. 585.

(b) *When it is communicated to any of them who expressly or impliedly assents thereto.*—In *Garrard* v. *Lauderdale*, it seems to have been held that even the communication to the creditors of the fact that the trust has been made would not defeat the power of revocation, but this was dissented from in *Acton* v. *Woodgate*, where the Master of the Rolls, Sir John Leach, says: "It appears to me, however, that this doctrine is questionable; because the creditors being aware of such a trust might be thereby induced to a forbearance in respect of their claims which they would not otherwise have exercised"; a view with which Lord Chancellor Sugden agreed in the Irish case of *Field* v. *Donoughmore* (*i*), where he said: "It is not absolutely necessary that the creditor should execute the deed; if he had assented to it, if he had acquiesced in it, or acted under its provisions and complied with its terms, and the other side expressed no dissatisfaction, the settled law of the Court is that he is entitled to its benefits." The same judge subsequently (*j*) expressly assented to the above statement of the law by Sir John Leach, though he goes on to say: "I do not mean to bind myself to hold that in every case a representation to a creditor will give him the benefit of the trust. It must depend on the character of the representation and the manner it is acted on. On the other hand, I should be sorry to have it

(*i*) (1841), 1 Dru. & War. 228.

(*j*) In *Browne* v. *Cavendish* (1844), 1 Jo. & Lat. 635.

understood that a man may create a trust for the benefit of his creditors, communicate it to them, and obtain from them the benefit of their lying by until perhaps the legal right to sue was lost, and then insist that the trust was wholly within his power." The point was again discussed in *Kirwan* v. *Daniel* (*k*), and the statement in *Garrard* v. *Lauderdale* dissented from, although the actual decision went upon another ground; while in *Griffith* v. *Ricketts* (*l*), it was said plainly, although again only by way of dictum, that such a deed would not be revocable against creditors between whom and the trustees such communications had taken place "as would give them an interest under the deed." The decision in *Garrard* v. *Lauderdale*, therefore, must, on this point, be regarded as overruled by the later cases. In *Harland* v. *Binks* (*m*), for example, it was expressly decided that the trust became binding when the assignment was communicated to the creditors, and they expressed themselves "satisfied" and took no steps to enforce their claims. Again, in *Synnot* v. *Simpson* (*n*), Lord Cranworth said: "If the debtor has notice given him [*sic*—qy., has given him, *i.e.*, the creditor, notice] of the existence of the deed, and has expressly or impliedly told him that he may look to the trust property for payment of his demand, the creditor may thereby become a *cestui que trust*." In *Cosser* v. *Radford* (*o*), it was said by Lord Justice Turner that "if the creditors act upon the deed it becomes binding"; but there the creditor had, as a matter of fact, executed the deed; and in *Johns* v. *James* (*p*), Lord Justice James said: "If the creditor has executed the deed himself, and been a party to it and assented to it—if he has entered into obligations on the faith of the deed, of course that gives him a right." But it appears from *Cornthwaite* v. *Frith* (*q*), that it must be clearly proved that the trust has been communicated; mere communications by the trustee with the creditors about their claims was held insufficient to entitle them to a decree for the execution of the trust.

Exactly what must be the nature of the communication with creditors in order to prevent the deed being revocable seems, then, not to be quite clear.

(*k*) (1847), 5 Ha. 493.
(*l*) (1849), 7 Ha. 307.
(*m*) (1850), 15 Q. B. 713.
(*n*) (1854), 5 H. L. C. at p. 138.
(*o*) (1863), 1 De G. J. & S. 585.
(*p*) (1878), 8 Ch. D. 744.
(*q*) (1851), 4 De G. & Sm. 552.

It does not seem to matter whether the communication is made by the settlor or the trustee. In *Synnot* v. *Simpson* (*t*), Lord Cranworth spoke of communication *by the debtor* being sufficient; while in *Harland* v. *Binks* (*q*), it was held that communication *by the trustee* was sufficient (*r*).

Again, it does not seem necessary that the assent of the creditors should be an express one. If the creditor incurs obligations on the faith of the deed it becomes binding, according to Lord Justice James, in *Johns* v. *James*.

Whether a sufficient communication of the deed to some only of the creditors renders it irrevocable as to all cannot be gathered from the cases, but, having regard to the cases as to the effect of execution by some only of the creditors (*s*), it is submitted that it would not.

Illustrations.

1. A. assigns all his property to B. in trust for such of A.'s creditors as shall execute the deed. B. communicates the existence of the assignment to X., Y. and Z., creditors of A., who express themselves "satisfied," but do not execute the deed. This constitutes B. a trustee for X., Y. and Z., and in the absence of fraud, C., a creditor, cannot have the assignment set aside. *Harland* v. *Binks* (1850), 15 Q. B. 713.

2. A. on going abroad conveys property to B. upon trust to pay A.'s debts, and the surplus, if any, to A. A. does not give his creditors notice of the deed, but B. communicates with them about their claims. This alone does not give the creditors the right to have the trusts executed. *Cornthwaite* v. *Frith* (1851), 4 De G. & Sm. 552.

(c) *When the settlor dies without having revoked the trust.*—In *Synnot* v. *Simpson* (*t*), Lord Cranworth said: "I began by saying that I did not at all question *Garrard* v. *Lauderdale* and the other cases, neither have I the least doubt of the propriety of those

(*q*) (1850), 15 Q. B. 713.

(*r*) See also *Griffith* v. *Ricketts* (1849), 7 Ha. 307.

(*s*) See above, 51.

(*t*) (1854), 5 H. L. C. 121.

decisions. . . . . The trust for the payment of the debts of F. S. [the settlor in the case then under discussion] was during his life a trust which he might revoke or vary at his pleasure . . . . *such revocation became by his death impossible*" (*u*). Again, in *In re Fitzgerald's Settlement* (*v*), the head-note is that "the doctrine of *Garrard* v. *Lauderdale* does not apply to provisions for creditors which do not come into operation till after the death of the settlor." Perhaps this is rather too broad a statement, however. Lord Justice Cotton says (*w*), "Probably *the settlor* might have disregarded the trusts"; and it would seem to be more correct to say that where the trust is not to come into operation till after the death of the settlor, although *Garrard* v. *Lauderdale* applies so as to render the trust revocable *by him*, yet if he dies without revoking it, it then becomes irrevocable. The same point came for decision before Mr. Justice Kekewich, in *Priestley* v. *Ellis* (*x*), who held, following *Synnot* v. *Simpson*, that where the trust is for the creditors existing at the time of the settlor's death, a trust is created which cannot be revoked, at any rate *after* the settlor's death; but whether the settlor himself could have revoked the trust before his death was expressly left open (*y*).

There is a decision of Vice-Chancellor Malins in *In re Sander's Trusts* (*z*) which conflicts with these, but it seems to be the only case in conflict with what has been said, and must, having regard to the weight of authority against it, be considered of doubtful authority.

Illustration.

By deed of "family arrangement" made by A. and B. (father and son) in 1867, an estate is limited to A. for life, with remainder to trustees upon trust with consent of A. and B. during their joint lives, or of the survivor, and after the death of the survivor at the discretion of the trustees to sell and apply the proceeds in payment as therein mentioned of all debts owing by A.; and subject thereto to hold any unsold hereditaments to the uses of a deed of even date under which A. and B. are successive tenants for life with remainder to an infant son of B. in tail. A.'s creditors are neither parties to nor named in the deed, nor is it ever communicated to them.

(*u*) Compare the remarks of the same judge in *Montefiore* v. *Browne* (1858), 7 H. L. C. 241.

(*v*) (1887), 37 Ch. D. 18.

(*w*) P. 22 of the report.

(*x*) (1897) 1 Ch. 480.

(*y*) See p. 503 of the report.

(*z*) (1878), 47 L. J. Ch. 667.

After A.'s death the trustees sell part of the estate with B.'s consent, and out of the proceeds pay all A.'s debts except one due to X. (A.'s sister), of which they are unaware. In 1889 the trustees, with the concurrence of B. (who is A.'s executor), convey the unsold property to the uses of the second deed of 1867. B. cannot revoke the trust, and the infant tenant in tail takes the property subject to the liability for the debt due to X. *Priestley* v. *Ellis*, (1897) 1 Ch. 489.

(d) *When an intention to create a trust otherwise appears.*—In *Wilding* v. *Richards* (a), Vice-Chancellor Knight Bruce, while admitting that if an instrument in favour of creditors, though in form a trust, is intended to be a mere instrument of agency, the intention must have effect given to it, went on to say that it is not every deed in favour of creditors to which no creditor is a party that is of that description; the Court in each case must be guided by the particular circumstances. Again, in *Smith* v. *Hurst* (b), Vice-Chancellor Turner said in cases of deeds purporting to be executed for the benefit of creditors, and to which no creditor is a party, the motive of the party executing the deed may have been either to benefit his creditors or to promote his own convenience; and the Court there has to examine into the circumstances for the purpose of ascertaining what was the true purpose of the deed. And this was followed by the Court of Appeal in *New Prance and Garrard's Trustee* v. *Hunting* (c).

Illustrations.

1. A. borrows money from B. and C. for which he gives them bonds, at the same time conveying property to X., a creditor, upon trust to secure repayment of a number of specified debts, including those due to B., C. and X. The deed is not executed by the creditors, but they are informed of its existence. The deed is binding on A. *Wilding* v. *Richards*, 2nd dec. (1845), 1 Coll. Ch. R. 655.

2. A. conveys to B. and C. all his real estate upon trust to sell and pay off his mortgage and other debts, and after satisfying the

(a) (1845), 1 Coll. Ch. R. 655.

(b) (1852), 10 Hare, 30.

(c) (1897) 2 Q. B. 19. See also *Godfrey* v. *Poole* (1888), 13 App. Cas. 497.

same in trust to pay the surplus to trustees in trust for A.'s wife for life, and after her death for their children in equal shares as tenants in common. This trust is irrevocable by A. *Godfrey* v. *Poole* (1868), 13 App. Cas. 497.

3. A., a trustee, by deed conveys an estate to B. upon trust to raise thereout by sale or mortgage 4,200*l.*, and with this sum to make good certain breaches of trust which A. has committed in respect of the trust estates specified in a schedule to the deed. The existence of the deed is not communicated to any of the beneficiaries or to A.'s creditors. The deed is not revocable by A. or by the trustee in A.'s bankruptcy. *New Prance and Garrard's Trustee* v. *Hunting*, (1897) 2 Q. B. 19.

SECTION VIII.—ENFORCEABILITY OF EXPRESS TRUSTS.

A VOLUNTARY trust is not enforceable, unless:—

(a) The settlor has transferred or done all in his power to transfer the trust property to the trustee; or

(b) has declared himself, or directed the person in whose control it is, to be a trustee thereof.

In order to determine whether or not a trust will be enforced by the courts—setting aside any question of fraud, mistake, illegality, or other invalidating cause—it is necessary to distinguish between (1) trusts created, or intended to be created, for valuable consideration, and (2) voluntary trusts; and in the case of the latter, between (a) perfect voluntary trusts and (b) imperfect voluntary trusts.

I.—TRUSTS FOR VALUE.

Where there is valuable consideration, and a trust is intended to be created, formalities are of minor importance, since, if the transaction cannot take effect as a perfectly created trust, it may be enforced by a court of equity as a contract (*a*). The matter then becomes one of contract law, and since (exceptions excepted) no one can sue on a contract unless he is a party to the consideration, no one can enforce the contract to create the trust unless he is a party to the consideration. However, in the ordinary case of a marriage settlement, the children of the contemplated marriage itself are said to be "within the consideration of the marriage," and may enforce any covenant for their benefit contained in the

(*a*) Lewin, Trusts, 11th ed. 68; Underhill, Trusts and Trustees, 6th ed. 35. See *Lee* v. *Lee* (1876), 4 Ch. D. 175.

settlement (*b*) ; and the trustees may sue on behalf of the intended beneficiaries instead of the latter suing for themselves.

II.—Voluntary Trusts.

Where no valuable consideration has been given for the creation of the trust, whether it will be enforced by the courts or not depends on whether it has been perfected or not.

The rule is stated by Lord Eldon (*c*) as follows :—" I take the distinction to be that if you want the assistance of the court to constitute you *cestui que trust*, and the instrument is voluntary, you shall not have that assistance for the purpose of constituting you *cestui que trust :* as upon a covenant to transfer stock, &c., if it rests in covenant and is purely voluntary, this court will not execute that voluntary covenant. But if the party has completely transferred stock, &c., though it is voluntary, yet the legal conveyance being effectually made the equitable interest will be enforced by this court " (*d*).

" The question, I conceive, must be simply this, whether the relation of trustee and *cestui que trust* has actually been established or not," as Vice-Chancellor Wigram put it (*e*).

(a) *Perfect Voluntary Trusts.*—The manner in which the relationship may be constituted, or in other words a perfect trust created, is pointed out by Lord Justice Turner, in *Milroy* v. *Lord* (*f*), where he says : " I take the law of this court to be well settled that, in order to render a voluntary settlement valid and effectual, the settlor must have done everything which, according to the nature of the property comprised in the settlement, was necessary to be done in order to transfer the property and render the settlement binding upon him. He may, of course, do this by actually transferring the property to persons for whom he intends to provide, and the provision will then be effectual, and it will be equally effectual if he transfers the property to a trustee for the

(*b*) Pollock, Contracts, 7th ed. 210.

(*c*) In *Ellison* v. *Ellison* (1802), 6 Ves. 656.

(*d*) See also *Pulvertoft* v. *Pulvertoft* (1811), 18 Ves. Jun. at p. 99; *Petre* v. *Espinasse* (1834), 2 My. & K. 496; *Bill* v. *Cureton* (1835), *ibid.* 503; *Henry* v. *Armstrong* (1881), 18 Ch. D. 668; *Paul* v. *Paul* (1882), 20 Ch. D. 742; *Harding* v. *Harding* (1886), 17 Q. B. D. 442.

(*e*) In *Meek* v. *Kettlewell* (1842), 1 Hare, at p. 470.

(*f*) (1862), 4 De G. F. & J. at p. 274.

purposes of the settlement or declares that he himself holds it in trust for these purposes."

It appears, moreover, from the case of *Tierney* v. *Wood* (*g*), that there is another method not mentioned by the Lord Justice, viz.: that where the legal estate in the trust property is outstanding, it is sufficient if the settlor directs the trustee to hold the property for the benefit of the *cestui que trust*.

These three methods of perfecting a voluntary trust are illustrated as follows:—

Illustrations.

Where the Settlor has Transferred the Trust Property to the Trustee.

1. A. by voluntary deed conveys property in trust for himself (A.) for life, and after his death to pay thereout various annuities and, subject thereto, in trust for sale and division of the proceeds among his children, with power of revocation *by deed attested by two or more credible witnesses.* This creates a binding trust, and it is not revoked by a reconveyance of the property by B. to A. by deed *not attested by two witnesses*, nor by A.'s will. *Ellison* v. *Ellison* (1802), 6 Ves. 656.

2. A., being of improvident habits and being in prison for debt, executes a voluntary settlement by which he assigns to B. all his interest in the property of his late brother upon certain trusts for the benefit of A. during his life and after his death for his children, with trusts over. A. marries and has a child. He cannot get the deed set aside on the ground that it is voluntary. *Petre* v. *Espinasse* (1834), 2 My. & K. 496.

3. A., a single woman not immediately contemplating marriage, transfers a sum of stock to which she is absolutely entitled to trustees upon trust to pay the dividends to her until marriage, and after marriage upon the usual trusts of a marriage settlement. This is an irrevocable trust, and A. cannot have the deed set aside on the ground that it is voluntary. *Bill* v. *Cureton* (1835), 2 My. & K. 503.

4. A. by ante-nuptial marriage settlement assigns a reversionary interest in certain trust funds standing in the names of X.,

(*g*) (1854), 19 Beav. 330.

the life tenant, and A., to B. and C. upon the usual trusts of a marriage settlement and, subject thereto, for D. (A.'s niece). The legal interest in the trust funds is never transferred to B. and C., and subsequently A. purports to settle the property on other trusts. The first settlement is enforceable by B. and C. and D., and A. will be restrained from carrying out the second. *Kekewich* v. *Manning* (1851), 1 De G. M. & G. 176 (*h*).

5. A., being about to go into business on the Stock Exchange, executes a voluntary deed conveying all his property except 1,000*l.* to trustees upon trust for the separate use of his wife for life, with remainder to his children. A. cannot have the deed set aside merely on the ground that it does not contain a power of revocation. *Henry* v. *Armstrong* (1881), 18 Ch. D. 668.

6. A., having previously told B. that if she would continue in her service until her death she would leave in the care of C. a present for her beyond what she might leave her in her will, hands to C., her solicitor and one of her executors, a promissory note signed by herself and payable on demand to B., telling C. not to mention the note to anyone but B., but to retain it till the death of A., and then to give it to B. if she should remain in A.'s service until her death. This is a trust in B.'s favour, who is entitled to prove for the amount in the administration of A.'s estate. *In re Richards* (1887), 36 Ch. D. 541.

Where the Settlor has done all in his power to transfer the Trust Property to the Trustee.

1. A. by voluntary deed assigns a policy of assurance on his life to B. and C. upon trust for the benefit of D. and her children. A. delivers the deed to C., but retains the policy of assurance. No notice of assignment is ever given to the assurance office, and A. subsequently surrenders the policy to them. This is a perfect trust, since no act remains to be done by A., and the trust is enforceable against him. *Fortescue* v. *Barnett* (1834), 3 My. & K. 36 (*i*).

(*h*) This decision was explained in *In re Ellenborough*, (1903) 1 Ch. 697, below, p. 64.

(*i*) This decision is at first sight a little curious, since by s. 3 of the Policies of Assurance Act, 1867, it is provided that

2. A. by a voluntary deed assigns a plot of land which he holds under an agreement for a lease, with the agreement and all his interest therein, to trustees upon certain trusts. Subsequently a lease of the premises is granted to A., but the legal term thereby vested in him is never assigned to the trustees. This creates a perfect trust, the settlor having completely assigned the equity vested in him at the date of the settlement, and the subsequent grant of the lease being immaterial. *Gilbert* v. *Overton* (1864), 2 H. & M. 110.

3. A. writes to B., one of the trustees of his marriage settlement, a letter stating that he is desirous of making a settlement upon his four children of six policies of assurance on his own life, the particulars of which he gives. Three of the policies are handed to B., but the other three are deposited with the office as collateral security, but A. undertakes to pay off the loan. The letter describes the trusts upon which the policies are to be held, and until the settlement is executed "A. is to be bound by this agreement in the same manner as if the settlement were actually executed." No notice of the letter is given to the office, no formal settlement is ever executed, and no notice is ever given to the other trustees. B. dies, and the letter and policies are returned to A. This is a complete assignment of the policies to B., and the trust is enforceable. *In re King, Sewell* v. *King* (1879), 14 Ch. D. 179.

4. On the marriage of A. with B., A.'s property is settled upon B. and A. successively for life, remainder to the children of the marriage, remainder in default of children to A. absolutely if she survives B., but if she dies in his lifetime, as she may by will appoint, remainder in default of appointment to her next of kin, excluding her husband. A. and B. cannot revoke the settlement

no assignment of a policy of life assurance is to confer on the assignee any right to sue for the amount of the policy until a written note of the date and purport of such assignment has been given to the assurance company. But it seems that it is no part of the duty of the assignor to give the notice; this is for the assignee to do; so far as the assignor is concerned, the assignment is complete as soon as he has executed the assignment. "The trustees ought to have given notice of the assignment, but their omission to give notice cannot affect the *cestui que trust*," Sir John Leach, M. R., says at p. 43 of the report. This case was followed in *Pearson* v. *The Amicable Assurance Office* (1859), 27 Beav. 229.

as against the next of kin, even though there be no issue of the marriage and no possibility of issue. *Paul* v. *Paul* (1882), 20 Ch. D. 742.

Where the Settlor has declared Himself, or the Person in whose control the Property is to be, a Trustee.

1. The legal estate in fee in lands is vested in A. in trust for B. B. signs a document addressed to A., directing that the lands and other property shall after his death be held for the benefit of certain persons. This is an enforceable trust. *Tierney* v. *Wood* (1854), 19 Beav. 330.

2. A. by voluntary settlement covenants to surrender copyholds to B., C. and D. on certain trusts, and that until the surrender is made she will stand possessed thereof in trust for B., C. and D. This constitutes A. a trustee upon the trusts of the settlement. *Steele* v. *Waller* (1860), 28 Beav. 466.

(b) *Imperfect Voluntary Trusts.*—" In order to render the [voluntary] settlement binding," says Lord Justice Turner in *Milroy* v. *Lord* (*j*), " one or other of the modes [above mentioned] must, as I understand the law of this court, be resorted to, for there is no equity in this court to perfect an imperfect gift. The cases, I think, go further to this extent, that if the settlement is intended to be effectuated by one of the modes to which I have referred, the court will not give effect to it by applying another of those modes. If it is intended to take effect by transfer, the court will not hold the intended transfer to operate as a declaration of trust, for then every imperfect instrument would be made effectual by being converted into a perfect trust " (*k*).

The rule that a voluntary trust is not enforceable if it is imperfect is illustrated by the following cases:—

Illustrations.

1. A. by voluntary deed covenants with B. and C. to surrender

(*j*) (1862 , 4 De G. F. & J. at p. 274.

(*k*) See also *Colman* v. *Sarrel* (1789), 1 Ves. 50; *Jefferys* v. *Jefferys* (1841), Cr. & Ph. 141; *Marler* v. *Tommas* (1873), L. R. 17 Eq. 8; *In re D'Angibau* (1879), 15 Ch. D. 228; *In re Anstis* (1886), 31 Ch. D. 596; *Green* v. *Paterson* (1886), 32 Ch. D. 95.

copyholds to them upon trusts for the benefit of his three daughters. A. dies without surrendering the copyholds, and by his will devises part of them to his wife, who is admitted. A.'s daughters cannot enforce the covenant to surrender the copyholds against the wife. *Jefferys* v. *Jefferys* (1841), Cr. & Ph. 138.

2. A., being contingently entitled to a reversionary interest in a trust fund (*i.e.*, having a mere expectancy or *spes successionis*), executes a voluntary assignment thereof to B., upon trust as to part for A. and as to the remainder for B. himself. No notice is given to the trustees of the fund. This does not establish the relation of trustee and *cestui que trust*, and B. cannot enforce the assignment. *Meek* v. *Kettlewell* (1842), 1 Hare, 464; (1843) 1 Ph. 342 (*l*).

3. A. by voluntary settlement purports to assign copyholds to trustees upon trust for himself for life with remainder to B., and the settlement contains a covenant for further assurance. A. dies without surrendering the copyholds. B. cannot enforce his interest in the copyholds. *Dening* v. *Ware* (1856), 22 Beav. 184.

4. A. executes a voluntary deed purporting to assign bank shares to B. upon trust for C. B. at the same time has a general power of attorney from A. authorizing him to transfer the shares and a further power authorizing him to receive the dividends, but no transfer is in fact made. This is not a valid trust of the shares, since it was not A.'s intention to constitute himself a trustee, but to vest the trust in B., and this has not been done, the bank shares being transferable only in the books of the bank and no transfer having been made to B. *Milroy* v. *Lord* (1862), 4 De G. F. & J. 264.

5. A. executes a voluntary settlement containing a recital that a sum of 2,000*l.* has been paid to B., and declaring that B. shall stand possessed thereof upon trust for A. for life, with an ultimate

(*l*) This decision is not overruled by *Kekewich* v. *Manning* (*supra*, p. 61, see *In re Ellenborough*, *Towry Law* v. *Burne*, (1903) 1 Ch. 697). In *Kekewich* v. *Manning* there was a voluntary assignment of a future interest in property, which is valid under 8 & 9 Vict. c. 106, s. 6. In *Meek* v. *Kettlewell* and *In re Ellenborough*, there was a purported voluntary assignment of a mere *spes successionis*, which is not enforceable.

trust in favour of A.'s next of kin. The recital is untrue, and A. dies without paying B. A.'s next of kin cannot enforce the trust. *Marler* v. *Tommas* (1873), L. R. 17 Eq. 8.

6. A. voluntarily covenants with trustees to assign a fund to them upon certain trusts with ultimate remainder to A.'s next of kin. A. dies without having executed an assignment of the fund. The fund belongs to A.'s personal representatives, and the next of kin have no claim upon it. *In re D'Angibau* (1879), 15 Ch. D. 228.

Imperfect Voluntary Trusts in Wills.—It is sometimes stated that the court will enforce a voluntary trust in a will, as if this were an exception to the general rule that an imperfect voluntary trust will not be enforced (*m*); but it is difficult to imagine a trust created by will in which the testator does not either transfer, or do all in his power to transfer, the trust property to the trustee, or make himself or the person in whose control it is a trustee thereof. The case, therefore, seems to be covered by the rule stated above.

Imperfect Voluntary Trusts for Charities.—Statements are also to be found which appear to suggest that if the trust is charitable it will be sustained even though voluntary and imperfect (*n*). The case cited in support of this is *Sayer* v. *Sayer* (*o*). In this case A. had power to appoint stock by her will "signed, sealed and published in the presence of and attested by two or more witnesses." A. made an unattested will prior to the Wills Act, 1837, by which she purported to give the stock to or to the treasurers of certain charitable societies, and this was held a good exercise of the power of appointment.

On the other hand, it is said that the mere existence of an intention to devote property to charity, when that intention has not been carried into effect, is not sufficient to create a charitable

(*m*) See, *e.g.*, Underhill, Trusts and Trustees, 6th ed. 34.

(*n*) Snell, Equity, 12th ed. 118.

(*o*) (1849), 7 Hare, 377; affirmed on appeal as *Innes* v. *Sayer* (1851), 3 Mac. & G. 606.

trust. Thus, money deposited by a testatrix in a bank in her own name, "as trustee for charitable purposes," was held to form part of her estate in *Sinnett* v. *Herbert* (*p*). And the case above cited seems to be really only an example of the rule that a defective execution of a power will be aided in favour of certain classes of persons, among whom are charities.

(*p*) (1871), L. R. 12 Eq. 201. See Tudor, Charitable Trusts, 3rd ed. 40.

SECTION IX.—DISCLAIMER OF EXPRESS TRUST.

(1) EVERY person appointed a trustee may disclaim the trust either by writing with or without seal or by word of mouth or by conduct showing an intention to disclaim.

(2) A disclaimer must be of the whole trust, and must be made within a reasonable period, and before the trustee has done any act showing an intention to accept the trust.

(3) A disclaimer by one of two or more persons appointed co-trustees vests the trust property in the other or others, and makes him or them sole trustee or trustees from the date of the creation of the trust.

(4) A disclaimer by a person appointed sole trustee revests the trust property in the settlor or his representatives, and renders him or them subject to the obligation of the trust.

In the reports of Lord Nottingham's time are two cases (*a*) in which it was sought to compel trustees to accept trusts: in *Clifton* v. *Sacheverell* the trustee was ordered to accept on having a full indemnity from the *cestui que trust*, and in *Hussey* v. *Markham* a similar decree was made on the following conditions, suggested by the trustee, that the master be directed to take accounts every year, and to allow costs and charges, and that the trustee be not chargeable with any money but what he or others by his orders should actually receive, and be not obliged to pay for any loss unless it were occasioned by his wilful negligence or default (*b*).

It is plain, however, that nowadays a trustee is not compellable to accept a trust unless he has contracted to do so, and even if he

(*a*) Cas. temp. Finch, 32, 258.

(*b*) Kerly, History of Equity, 199.

has he is only liable in damages if he changes his mind and breaks his contract.

Mr. Lewin says: "It may be laid down as a clear and undisputed rule that no one is compellable to undertake a trust" (*c*). It follows that any person appointed a trustee has a right to disclaim the office.

A disclaimer should be made by deed, for a deed is clear evidence and admits of no ambiguity; but a deed is not necessary, and a verbal disclaimer has been held sufficient (*d*), as has also a disclaimer by mere conduct (*e*). And since the trustee cannot disclaim the office without also disclaiming the legal estate in the trust property, if his conduct shows that he has disclaimed the trusteeship, it also shows that the legal estate is not in him (*f*).

The disclaimer must be of the whole trust; a disclaimer of part only is invalid. It is not competent for any trustee to say: "I will attend to some of the trusts, and I will not attend to others." So that even though part of the trust property be in England and part in a foreign country, and the trustee be resident in the foreign country, if he accepts the trusts as to the foreign property he accepts them wholly, or, putting it conversely, if he executes a disclaimer of the trusteeship so far as it relates to the English property only, it does not operate as a disclaimer at all (*g*).

A disclaimer ought to be made without delay. If the trustee allows more than a reasonable length of time to elapse a presumption arises that he has accepted. It is then a question of fact whether his acquiescence amounts to an acceptance of the office (*h*). And the disclaimer must be made before the trustee has entered on the duties of the office, for a trustee who has once accepted the trust cannot afterwards renounce it (*i*).

Sect. 7 of the Real Property Act, 1845, provides that an estate or interest in any tenements or hereditaments in England of any tenure may be disclaimed by a married woman by deed; and that every such disclaimer shall be made conformably to the provisions

(*c*) Trusts, 11th ed. 214.

(*d*) *Foster* v. *Dawber* (1860), 8 W. R. 646.

(*e*) *Stacey* v. *Elph* (1833), 1 My. & K. 195; *In re Gordon* (1877), L. R. 6 Ch. App. 531; *In re Birchall* (1889), 40 Ch. D. 436.

(*f*) *In re Birchall*, *supra*.

(*g*) *In re Lord and Fullerton's Contract*, (1896) 1 Ch. 228.

(*h*) Lewin, Trusts, 11th ed. 215, 219.

(*i*) Snell, Equity, 12th ed. 151; Underhill, Trusts and Trustees, 6th ed. 148.

of the Fines and Recoveries Act, 1833. Having regard to the decision in *In re Harkness and Allsopp's Contract* (*j*), the Married Women's Property Act, 1882, did not apparently affect this provision where the married woman was a trustee, so that a trustee who was a married woman had apparently to disclaim a trusteeship of land by deed acknowledged. But the effect of sect. 1 of the Married Women's Property Act, 1907, which enables her to "dispose of" property held by her either solely or jointly with any other person as trustee or personal representative "as if she were a *femme sole*," seems to render this obsolete.

The effect of disclaimer by a trustee where there is a co-trustee is to vest the whole legal estate in the co-trustee: and as regards the exercise of the office, even if the trust be accompanied with a power, the continuing trustee may administer the trust without the concurrence of the trustee who has chosen to disclaim, and without the appointment of a new trustee. . . . . And when the disclaimer has been executed it operates retrospectively, and makes the other trustee the sole trustee *ab initio* (*k*).

When the trustee is a sole trustee the effect of the disclaimer is to revest the trust property in the settlor or those deriving title under him, and to render him or them subject to the obligations of the trust (*l*).

(*j*) (1896) 2 Ch. 358.

(*k*) Lewin, Trusts, 11th ed. 218.

(*l*) *Mallott* v. *Wilson*, (1903) 2 Ch. 494, following *Jones* v. *Jones* (1874), W. N. 190.

Section X.—Construction of Express Trusts.

(1) When the limitations of the trust property are completely expressed in the instrument creating it, the trust is called an executed trust. An executed trust must be construed in accordance with the technical meaning of the words used by the settlor.

(2) When the limitations of the trust property are not completely expressed in the instrument creating the trust, but are only indicated in general terms with a view to a complete declaration in a subsequent instrument, the trust is called an executory trust. An executory trust must be construed in such manner as will best give effect to the intention of the settlor, and the words used by him may be subordinated to such intention.

(3)—(a) In the case of an executory trust in an antenuptial settlement or agreement for a settlement there is a presumption that the intention of the settlor is to provide for the issue of the marriage.

(b) There is no presumption of intention in the case of an executory trust in any other instrument.

For the purposes of interpretation, trusts are divided into executed trusts and executory trusts.

The distinction between executed and executory trusts was taken as long ago as 1705 in *Leonard* v. *Earl of Sussex* (*a*), and was recognized in several subsequent cases (*b*). It is generally regarded,

(*a*) (1705), 2 Vern. 526.

(*b*) *E.g.*, *Sweetapple* v. *Bindon* (1705), 2 Vern. 536; *Bale* v. *Colman* (1708), 1 P. Wms. 145; *Stamford* v. *Hobart* however, as having been finally established by the leading case of *Glenorchy* v. *Bosville* (c) in 1733.

Although, however, it is now completely settled that the distinction exists for the purposes of interpretation (d), the precise method of determining to which class a trust belongs is not so clearly stated in the cases (e). "The words 'executory trust,'" said Lord Northington in *Austen* v. *Taylor* (f), "seem to me to have no fixed signification." Lord King, in the case of *Papillon* v. *Voice* (g), describes an executory trust to be where the party must come to this court to have the benefit of the will. But that is the case of every trust. Later on in the same case he says: "The true criterion is this: wherever the assistance of trustees, which is ultimately the assistance of this court, is necessary *to complete a limitation*, that is sufficient evidence of the testator's intention that the court should model the limitations. But *where the trusts and limitations are already expressly declared*, the court has no authority to interfere, and make them different from what they would be at law."

"All trusts are in a sense executory," said Lord St. Leonards in *Egerton* v. *Earl Brownlow* (h), "because a trust cannot be executed except by a conveyance, and therefore there is always something to be done. But this is not the sense which a court of equity puts upon the term 'executory trust.' A court of equity considers an executory trust as distinguished from a trust executing itself, and distinguishes the two in this manner: Has the testator been what is called, and very properly called, his own conveyancer? Has he left it to the court to make out from general expressions what his intention is, or has he so defined that intention that you have nothing to do but to take the limitations he has given to you and to convert them into legal estates?"

"It is of the essence of an executory trust that it should not be fully expressed or declared in the instrument creating it, but

(1710), 3 Bro. P. C. Toml. 31; *Trevor* v. *Trevor* (1720), 1 P. Wms. 622; and *Papillon* v. *Voice* (1728), 2 P. Wms. 471.

(c) (1733), Cas. t. Talbot, 3; Wh. & Tud. L. C. Eq. 7th ed. vol. ii. 763. See Lord Hardwicke's remark at 2 Atk. 582.

(d) See *Sackville-West* v. *Viscount Holmesdale* (1870), L. R. 4 H. L. 543.

(e) See Wh. & Tud. L. C. Eq. 7th ed. vol. ii. 771.

(f) (1759), 1 Eden, 366.

(g) (1728), 2 P. Wms. 471.

(h) (1853), 4 H. L. C. at p. 211.

that it should require some further deed or instrument for its complete legal expression," said Lord Westbury in *Sackville-West* v. *Viscount Holmesdale* (*i*).

"An executory trust," according to Lord Cairns in the same case (*j*), is "a trust which is to be executed by the preparation of a complete and formal settlement, carrying into effect, through the operation of an apt and detailed legal phraseology, the general intention compendiously indicated."

Sir George Jessel (*k*) thought a true executory trust was perhaps a little more narrow, "as where a conveyance has been directed to be executed by a testator, but it is called an executory trust, and perhaps not incorrectly, where instead of expressing exactly what he means, that is, filling up the terms of the trust, he tells the trustees to do their best to carry out his intention."

From these dicta it seems that a trust is executory if (1) the limitations of the trust property are not completely expressed in the instrument creating it, but are only indicated in general terms, and (2) a further instrument is required in order to completely declare them. Any other trust is executed.

Executed Trusts.

In the case of *Bale* v. *Colman* (*l*), Lord Harcourt laid it down that the same words of limitation ought to receive the same construction in a court of equity as they have at law. And Lord Talbot, in the leading case of *Glenorchy* v. *Bosville* (*m*), said: "I think in cases of trusts executed or immediate devises, the construction of courts of law and equity ought to be the same; for there the testator does not suppose any other conveyance will be made."

Lord Hardwicke appears to have thrown some doubt on this in *Bagshaw* v. *Spencer* (*n*), but he subsequently altered his opinion (*o*).

(*i*) (1870), L. R. 4 H. L. at p. 566.

(*j*) At p. 571.

(*k*) In *Miles* v. *Harford* (1879), 12 Ch. D. at p. 699.

(*l*) (1711), see 2 P. Wms. 473.

(*m*) (1733), Cas. t. Talbot, 3.

(*n*) (1748), 2 Atk. at p. 582.

(*o*) *Exel* v. *Wallace* (1751), 2 Ves. at p. 323. And see note at 2 Cox, 8, and 3 Ves. 396.

Illustrations.

1. A. devises land to B., C., D. and E. for payment of debts, and afterwards to the use of them and their heirs, save that B. is to have his share for life with power to make leases, remainder to the heirs male of his body, remainders over. This is a trust [executed], and B. takes an estate tail male. *Bale* v. *Colman* (1711), 1 P. Wms. 141; 2 P. Wms. 474.

2. A. devises lands on certain trusts, and subject thereto to the use of B. for life, remainder to trustees to support contingent remainders, remainder to the use of the heirs male of the body of B. and their heirs. This is a trust [executed], and B. takes an estate tail [male]. *Wright* v. *Pearson* (1758), 1 Eden, 119.

3. A. devises land to trustees in trust to pay certain annuities, and subject thereto in trust for B. and his assigns for life, without impeachment of waste, remainder to the trustees to preserve contingent remainders, remainder to the use of the heirs of the body of B., remainder to testator's own right heirs. He then gives the residue of his personal estate to be laid out in land, which shall thereafter remain, continue, and be to the like uses. B. takes an estate tail in the land to be purchased. *Austen* v. *Taylor* (1759), 1 Eden, 361.

It should be mentioned here that although technical words of limitation have the same construction in executed trusts as in legal limitations, where no technical words of limitation are used at all, trusts, executed as well as executory, are sometimes construed more liberally. The authorities are somewhat confusing, and there appears to be some conflict between the older text-book writers and the more modern. The subject is dealt with in Cruise's Digest, vol. i. 343 (which seems to give the rule too favourably to trusts); Hayes, Conveyancing, 5th ed. vol. i. 91; Preston, Estates, vol. ii. 64; Williams, Real Property, 19th ed. 181; Lewin, Trusts, 11th ed. 120, 121; and Elphinstone, Interpretation of Deeds, rule 104—which seems to give the rule too narrowly.

Perhaps the rule may be stated to be that a limitation of a trust of real estate without words of inheritance will give the beneficiary a life estate only unless an intention on the part of the settlor or grantor to pass a fee simple or fee tail appears in the instrument containing the limitation (*o*).

Executory Trusts.

"In matters executory or in cases of articles or a will directing a conveyance, where the words of the articles or will are improper or informal the court will not direct a conveyance according to such improper or informal expressions, but will order the conveyance or settlement to be made in a proper or legal manner, so as may best answer the intent of the parties" (*p*).

"In construing an executory trust a court of equity exercises a large authority in subordinating the language to the intent," said Lord Westbury in *Sackville-West* v. *Viscount Holmesdale* (*q*).

The origin of the rule, according to Lord Hatherley (*r*), may be traced to the desire to obviate the consequence of the extremely technical doctrine in *Shelley's Case*.

Lord Eldon seems at one time to have felt some hesitation in accepting the doctrine (*s*), but he afterwards fully assented to it (*t*).

Executory trusts are most frequently to be found in, although they are not confined to, marriage articles and wills, and these require separate consideration.

Executory Trusts in Marriage Articles.—In the case of marriage articles there is a presumption arising from the nature of the document that the intention of the settlor was to make a provision for

(*o*) The cases of *Holliday* v. *Overton* (1852, 15 Beav. 480); *Lucas* v. *Brandreth* (1860, 28 Beav. 274); *Tatham* v. *Vernon* (1861, 29 Beav. 604); *Meyler* v. *Meyler* (1883, 11 L. R. Ir. 532); *In re Whiston's Settlement* (1894, 1 Ch. 661); *Dearberg* v. *Letchford* (1895, 72 L. T. 892); and *In re Irwin* (1904, 2 Ch. 753), are instances of the absence of any indication of such intention. The cases of *Pugh* v. *Drew* (1869, 17 W. R. 988); *In re Tringham's Trusts* (1904, 2 Ch. 487); and *In re Oliver's Settlement* (1905, 1 Ch. 191), are instances in which sufficient indication of an intention to pass the fee simple was found.

(*p*) *Stamford* v. *Hobart* (1710), 3 Bro. P. C. 31. And see *Glenorchy* v. *Bosville* (1733), Cas. t. Talbot, 3; *Austen* v. *Taylor* (1759), 1 Eden, 361; *White* v. *Carter* (1766), 2 Eden, 367; *Jervoise* v. *Duke of Northumberland* (1820), 1 J. & W. 570.

(*q*) (1870), L. R. 5 H. L. at p. 565. See also other cases cited below.

(*r*) L. R. 4 H. L. at p. 553.

(*s*) See his judgment in *Newcastle* v. *Lincoln* (1806), 12 Ves. 236.

(*t*) *Jervoise* v. *Duke of Northumberland* (1820), 1 J. & W. at p. 571. And see L. R. 6 Eq. at p. 548.

the children of the marriage, and the construction of the instrument is controlled by this presumption (*u*).

"When the object," as Sir W. Grant said (*v*), "is to make a provision by the settlement of an estate for the issue of a marriage, it is not to be presumed that the parties meant to put it in the power of the father to defeat that purpose and to appropriate the estate to himself. If, therefore, the agreement is to limit an estate for life with remainder to the heirs of the body, the court decrees a strict settlement in conformity with the presumable intention."

The case of *Newcastle* v. *Lincoln* (*infra*) shows that the same method of construction must be applied to an executory trust in an ante-nuptial settlement.

Illustrations.

1. A. by marriage articles *covenants to settle* land upon trustees to the use of him, A., for life without waste, remainder to the use of B., his intended wife, for her life, remainder to the use of the heirs male of him on her body begotten, remainders over. The settlement must limit the property to A. for life, remainder to his first son in tail. *Trevor* v. *Trevor* (1720), 1 P. Wms. 622.

2. A. in an ante-nuptial marriage settlement *covenants to settle* leasehold estates in trust for such persons and such or the like estates as far as the law will allow, as declared concerning real estates limited to the first and other sons of the marriage in tail male with several remainders. The settlement in pursuance of this covenant must be so framed that no person shall be entitled to the absolute property in the leaseholds until he attains twenty-one. *Newcastle* v. *Lincoln* (1797), 3 Vesey, 387 ; 12 Vesey, 217.

Executory Trusts in Wills.—"In a will there is no presumption that the testator means one quantity of interest rather than another, an estate for life rather than an estate in fee." . . . Even in a will, however, "if it is clearly to be ascertained from anything in the will that the testator did not mean to use the expressions which he has employed in their strict proper technical sense, the court in

(*u*) *Rochford* v. *Fitzmaurice* (1842), 2 Dr. & War. at p. 18.

(*v*) In *Blackburn* v. *Stables* (1814), 2 V. & B. 369.

decreeing such settlement as he has directed will depart from his words in order to execute his intention" (*w*).

"The only difference," said Lord Hatherley, "in the case of a will, or deed of gift, not being marriage articles, is this, that the intent must appear in some manner on the face of the instrument in order to justify the court in directing a settlement which does not follow the exact words employed in the instrument containing the executory trust, but by varying them effects the presumed intention of the parties" (*x*).

Illustrations.

1. A. devises property to B. for payment of debts and legacies and afterwards *to settle* the remainder; and what remains unsold a moiety to C. and the heirs of his body by a second wife; *taking special care in such settlement that it never be in the power of C. to dock the entail during his life.* C. is only entitled to a life estate. *Leonard* v. *Earl of Sussex* (1705), 2 Vern. 526.

2. A. devises [*sic*] 300*l. to be laid out by her executrix in lands and settled* to the only use of her daughter B. and her children; and if she die without issue the lands to be equally divided between her brothers and sisters then living. There being no evidence of a contrary intent, B. takes an estate tail. *Sweetapple* v. *Bindon* (1705), 2 Vern. 536.

3. A. devises real estate to X., Y. and Z. upon trust (*by advice of counsel*) *to convey* the same to the first son of B. for ninety-nine years if he should so long live, remainder to the heirs male of the body of such first son, with remainders over. The intention being to make as strict a settlement as possible, the conveyance in pursuance of this will must, after the limitation to the first son of B., contain a limitation to trustees during his life to preserve contingent remainders. *Stamford* v. *Hobart* (1710), 3 Brown P. C. 31 (*y*).

(*w*) *Blackburn* v. *Stables*, *supra*. And see the judgment of Lord Eldon in *Jervoise* v. *Duke of Northumberland* (1820), 1 J. & W. at p. 574; and *Sackville-West* v. *Viscount Holmesdale* (1870), L. R. 4 H. L. at p. 555.

(*x*) *Sackville-West* v. *Viscount Holmesdale* (1870), L. R. 4 H. L. at p. 554.

(*y*) If the limitation to trustees to preserve contingent remainders were not inserted, the contingent remainder to the heirs male of the first son of B. would fail for want of a particular estate of freehold.

4. A. by will gives personal estate to be laid out in the purchase of lands for B. and the heirs male of his body to be begotten for ever; and for want of such issue, to C. and the heirs male of his body to be begotten for ever; with remainders over, and appoints C. his executor. B. takes an estate tail. *Seal* v. *Seal* (1715), Precedents in Chancery, 421 (*z*).

5. A. devises [*sic*] 1,000*l*. to trustees to be laid out in the purchase of lands, *and to be settled* on B. for life without impeachment of waste, and from and after the determination of that estate to trustees to preserve contingent remainders, remainder to the heirs of the body of B., remainders over *with power to B. to make a jointure*. This is an executory trust, and B. is entitled to an estate for life merely. *Papillon* v. *Voice* (1728), 2 P. Wms. 470.

6. A. devises land to trustees in trust to sell, and thereout to purchase other lands or stock and to permit B. to receive the interest and profits for life, and after A.'s decease to permit C. to receive the interest and profits during his natural life, and after his decease then in trust for the use of the issue of the body of B. lawfully begotten. From the terms of the will it appears that B. is intended to take a life estate only. B. is entitled to a life estate only and not to an estate tail. *Meure* v. *Meure* (1737), 2 Atk. 265.

7. A. devises land to trustees upon trust on the marriage of B., *to convey it* with all convenient speed to the use of B. for life *sans waste*, voluntary waste in houses excepted, remainder to her husband for life, remainder to the issue of her body with remainders over. This is an executory trust (p. 9), and the conveyance must be to B. for life with remainders in strict settlement. *Glenorchy* v. *Bosville* (1733), Cas. t. Talbot, 3.

8. A. by his will directs his trustees *to convey* freeholds in trust for the separate use of his daughter B. for and during the term of her natural life, and so as she alone or such person as she shall

(*z*) This case is also reported in 1 P. Wms. 290, and 2 Eq. Abr. 346, which state that there was a direction *to settle* the lands on B. and his heirs male, which would make it an executory trust, but this is omitted in the Prec. in Ch. report, and in its absence the trust would seem to be an executed one. See Brett, L. C. Eq. 3rd ed. 38.

appoint shall take and receive the rents and profits thereof, *and so as her husband is not to intermeddle therewith;* and from and after her decease in trust for the heirs of the body of B. This is an executory trust, and B. takes an estate for life only. *Roberts* v. *Dixwell* (1738), 1 Atk. 606.

9. A. bequeaths personal estate to trustees upon trust to lay out the same in the purchase of land, *to be settled and assured as counsel shall advise* for the use of B. and his issue in tail male *to take in succession and priority of birth;* remainders over. This is an executory trust, and B. takes an estate for life merely. *White* v. *Carter* (1766), 2 Eden, 365.

10. A. devises land to trustees upon trust on B.'s attaining the age of twenty-one years or being married that they shall, *as counsel shall advise, convey, settle and assure* the same to B. for life, and after her death then on the heirs of her body lawfully issuing. This is an executory trust, and B. is entitled to an estate for life only, with remainder to her first and other sons in tail general. *Bastard* v. *Proby* (1788), 2 Cox, 6.

11. A. by will gives the residue of his property to his executors in trust for B., adding, "my will is that he shall not be put into possession of any of my effects till he attains the age of twenty-four years, *nor shall my executors give up their trust till a proper entail be made to the heir male by him.*" This is an executory trust, but, there being nothing to show that the words are not used in their technical sense, B. takes an estate tail. *Blackburn* v. *Stables* (1813), 2 V. & B. 367.

12. A. devises to B. all his real and personal estate upon trust that the same *shall be settled by able counsel* to go to and amongst his grandchildren of the male kind and their issue in tail male, remainder over. This is an executory trust, but, there being no evidence of a contrary intention, the grandchildren take estates tail. *Marshall* v. *Bousfield* (1817), 2 Maddock, 166.

13. A. bequeaths jewels to B. "to go and be held as heir-looms by him, and by his eldest son on his decease, and to go and descend to the eldest son of such eldest son, and so on, to the eldest son of his descendants, as far as the rules of law or equity

will permit. *And I request B. to do all in his power by will or otherwise to give effect to this my wish.*" This is an executory trust (p. 545), and B. takes only a life interest, and the jewels must be settled on B. for life, remainder to his eldest son for life, remainder to the eldest son of such eldest son, to be vested at twenty-one. *Shelley* v. *Shelley* (1868), L. R. 6 Eq. 540 (*a*).

14. A. devises land on trust to *convey, assign and assure* it to B. and the heirs of his body lawfully issuing, but in such manner and form nevertheless and subject to such limitations and restrictions as that, if B. shall die without leaving issue, it may descend unencumbered and belong to C., her heirs, executors, administrators and assigns, according to the respective nature and tenure thereof. This is an executory trust (p. 209), and B. takes a life interest only. *Thompson* v. *Fisher* (1870), L. R. 10 Eq. 207.

15. A. by will gives property to trustees upon trust "*to convey, settle and assure*" it "in a course of entail to correspond, as nearly as may be, with the limitations of a barony, in such manner and form" as the trustees "shall consider proper, or as their counsel shall advise." The limitations of the barony are to A. for life, and after the death of A. to B. (the second son of A.) and the heirs male of his body; and in default of issue, in the same manner to the third, fourth, and fifth sons of B. successively, and the heirs male of their bodies; with a shifting clause, by which in certain events the barony is to go over. A.'s intention being to attach the property to the barony as far as possible, the settlement must be to B. and the other sons of A. for their respective lives, with remainder to their sons successively in tail. *Sackville-West* v. *Viscount Holmesdale* (1870), L. R. 4 H. L. 543.

16. A. devises freeholds in Worcestershire to his third son and his issue male, with remainder to his fourth son and his issue male, in strict settlement; and devises freeholds in Cardiganshire to his fourth son and his issue male, with remainder to his fifth son and his issue male in strict settlement. By a shifting clause, it is provided that if his fourth son, or any issue male of his fourth son,

(*a*) Having regard to the decisions as to precatory trusts above, pp. 42—46, and especially to the case of *Hill* v. *Hill*, (1897) 1 Q. B. 483, this might now be regarded as not a trust at all.

become actually entitled to the Worcestershire estates, and if his fifth son, or any of his issue male, are then living, the limitations of the Cardiganshire estates in favour of his fourth son or his issue male are to absolutely cease. A. also bequeaths leaseholds in Cardiganshire to trustees *upon such trusts as, regard being had to the difference in tenure of the premises respectively, will best or most nearly correspond with the uses declared of the Cardiganshire freeholds.* This is an executory trust (p. 699), and on the third son dying a bachelor in the lifetime of the fourth, the Cardiganshire leaseholds go over to the fifth son, the shifting clause, assuming it to be bad for remoteness if applied verbatim to leaseholds, being modified so as to make it good. *Miles* v. *Harford* (1879), 12 Ch. D. 691.

17. A. bequeaths the contents of her house to trustees upon trust to select the best paintings, statuary, and china for the Earl of E., *to be held and settled as heirlooms, and to go with the title.* This is an executory trust (p. 548), and a settlement will be directed, giving a life interest to the earl, with remainder to the next heir of the earldom for his life. *Cockerell* v. *Earl of Essex* (1884), 26 Ch. D. 538.

Executory Trusts in Deeds.—It is sometimes stated that executory trusts are to be found only in marriage articles and wills (*b*). But this is not correct, as appears from such cases as *Rochford* v. *Fitzmaurice* and *Mayn* v. *Mayn* below.

Executory trusts in settlements not upon marriage, whether voluntary or for value, must be construed in the same manner as executory trusts in wills—*i.e.*, the intention must appear on the face of the instrument (*c*).

Illustrations.

1. By a post-nuptial settlement for value, A. covenants *to settle lands as counsel shall advise or direct* to the use of B. for life, and after his decease to the use of the heirs male of the body of B., remainders over. This is an executory trust (p. 173), and the intention being to provide for B.'s issue and others, B. takes an

(*b*) See Snell, Equity, 12th ed. 56.

(*c*) *Rochford* v. *Fitzmaurice* (1842), 1 Conn. & Laws. at p. 172; 2 Dr. & War. at p. 20; *Sackville-West* v. *Viscount Holmesdale* (1870), L. R. 4 H. L. at p. 554.

estate for life merely. *Rochford* v. *Fitzmaurice* (1842), 1 Conn. & Laws. 158; 2 Dr. & War. 1.

2. A., B., C. and D. execute a voluntary deed by which it is declared that D. shall raise out of certain hereditaments 800*l.*, and invest the same upon trusts *to be declared* for the benefit of X. for life with remainder to her children, and as to X. for her separate use, and *with all powers for charging the security and for maintenance, and other powers and trusts which are usually inserted in a money settlement of the like nature.* This is an executory trust (p. 153), and the settlement must limit the money to the children as tenants in common and not as joint tenants. *Mayn* v. *Mayn* (1867), L. R. 5 Eq. 150.

SECTION XI.—INVALIDATING CAUSES.

A TRUST is invalid if its creation has been induced by fraud, duress, undue influence or mistake, or if it is created for a fraudulent purpose or any purpose forbidden by law.

A trust, like a sale, gift, mortgage or contract, is liable to be invalidated by fraud, duress, undue influence, mistake or illegality.

The detailed consideration of these matters does not, strictly speaking, form part of the law of trusts, but they qualify what has been said in the preceding sections, and there are certain instances in which they have a special importance in that branch of law.

FRAUD.

"Fraud vitiates everything," and if a party has been induced to enter into a transaction by the fraud of another the transaction is void. There seem to be but few reported decisions in which a trust has been set aside on this ground as distinct from the particular species of fraud known as undue influence, but in the case of *Evans* v. *Carrington* (*a*), where a wife had fraudulently induced her husband to execute a separation deed which constituted a trust in her favour, the deed was set aside on the husband's application. Where, however, the trust has been created for valuable consideration, in order to obtain relief there must be *restitutio in integrum*. If, therefore, the trust is contained in an ante-nuptial settlement, being founded on a valuable consideration which cannot be restored, it cannot be set aside even though it was induced by fraudulent misrepresentation. In *Johnston* v. *Johnston* (*b*), the action was brought by a husband to set aside an

(*a*) (1860), 2 D. F. & J. 481.

(*b*) (1884), 53 L. J. Ch. 1014.

ante-nuptial settlement which he had made on his wife, who had falsely asserted that she had obtained a divorce from her first husband by reason of his adultery and cruelty, and that she had not cohabited with her second husband before her marriage with him. As a matter of fact, however, the wife had been divorced by her first husband by reason of her adultery with her second husband. Mr. Justice Pearson refused to set the settlement aside, on the ground that the marriage was valid; the consideration was given, and could not be undone. And this decision was affirmed by the Court of Appeal (c).

Fraud as a cause of invalidity of a trust is more important where it affects the purpose for which the trust is created. This will be dealt with later.

Undue Influence.

Closely connected with fraud is undue influence. "As no court has ever attempted to define fraud, so no court has ever attempted to define undue influence, which includes one of its many varieties," Lord Justice Lindley said in *Allcard* v. *Skinner* (d).

Undue influence may be actual or presumed. Where a gift (which term is here used to include a benefit under a trust) is proved to have been obtained as a result of the exercise of undue influence, the donor can always recall it.

Further, there are cases in which the relation between donor and donee, at or shortly before the making of the gift, is such as to raise a presumption of undue influence, and the court then sets aside the gift unless the donee can prove that it was the result of a free exercise of the donor's will. It is immaterial in such a case that the donor makes the gift without pressure or solicitation by the donee, or that the donor perfectly understands the nature of what he is doing. In these cases the court interferes, not on the ground that any wrongful act has in fact been committed by the donee, but on the ground of public policy and to prevent an abuse of the relation which existed between the parties and of the influence which arises from it. The principle on which the law is based is that it is right and expedient to save people from being victimised by others. "To protect people from being forced,

(c) *Johnston* v. *Johnston* (1885), 52 L T. 76.

(d) (1887), 36 Ch. D. at p. 183.

tricked, or misled in any way by others into parting with their property, is one of the most legitimate objects of all laws," as Lord Justice Lindley said (*e*).

The principal relations which give rise to a presumption of undue influence are those of:—

Parent and child and similar relations (*f*);
Guardian and ward (*g*);
Minister of religion and disciple and the like (*h*);
Lawyer and client (*i*);
Medical adviser and patient (*j*).

But it is not confined to these. It applies "to all the variety of relations in which dominion may be exercised by one person over another," to quote from the argument of Sir S. Romilly in *Huguenin* v. *Baseley* (*h*).

Gifts liable to be set aside by the court on the ground of undue influence have always been treated as voidable and not void. *Wright* v. *Vanderplank* (*f*) and *Mitchell* v. *Homfray* (*j*) are authorities for this. Moreover, such gifts are voidable on equitable grounds only. The right to set them aside may therefore be lost by laches and acquiescence, as the case of *Allcard* v. *Skinner* (*h*) itself shows.

Mistake.

If a settlement is made under a mistake, or a misapprehension of the effect of it, it is likewise not binding on the settlor, and can be set aside by the court. The case of *Forshaw* v. *Welsby* (*k*) is an instance of this. The settlement in that case was made when the settlor was very ill and, as the court found (*l*), when he thought

(*e*) See Ashburner, Equity, 412, and the judgment of Lindley, L. J., in *Allcard* v. *Skinner*, above.

(*f*) *Wright* v. *Vanderplank* (1856), 8 D. M. & G. 136; *Powell* v. *Powell*, (1900) 1 Ch. 243.

(*g*) *Hatch* v. *Hatch* (1804), 9 Ves. 292; *Maitland* v. *Irving* (1846), 15 Sim. 437.

(*h*) *Huguenin* v. *Baseley* (1807), 14 Ves. 273; *Allcard* v. *Skinner* (1887), 36 Ch. D. 145; *Morley* v. *Loughnan*, (1893) 1 Ch. 736.

(*i*) *Carter* v. *Palmer* (1841), 8 Cl. & F. 659; *Brown* v. *Kennedy* (1863), 33 Beav. 133 (barrister); *Liles* v. *Terry and Wife*, (1895) 2 Q. B. 679; *Willis* v. *Barron*, (1902) A. C. 271; *Wright* v. *Carter*, (1903) 1 Ch. 27 (solicitor).

(*j*) *Mitchell* v. *Homfray* (1881), 8 Q. B. D. 587.

(*k*) (1860), 30 Beav. 243.

(*l*) See p. 247 of the report.

he was going to die, and he did not intend it to be operative if he survived. He, however, recovered from his illness, having in the meantime lost all recollection of having executed the settlement. Although there was no undue influence or pressure exercised on the settlor, the court set the settlement aside on his application.

Everett v. *Everett* (*m*) was a somewhat similar case, the settlement there being set aside apparently on the ground that the settlor—a young lady who had only just attained twenty-one—had not understood the effect of it; but the court was also influenced by the fact that she had not had independent advice, and that it was a rather imprudent disposition of her property.

In such cases there is really no intention on the part of the settlor to create the particular trust in fact created; the mistake is fundamental; but apparently the trust is not void, it is only voidable; so that if the title of a *bonâ fide* purchaser for value without notice has intervened, as against him, the trust cannot be revoked (*n*).

This is, of course, a different matter from mistake in the expression of intention. That also gives a right to relief, but it seems to belong to the sphere of contract law rather than the law of trusts. It is fully dealt with in Pollock on Contracts, 7th ed. pp. 498 *et seq.*; and in White & Tudor's Leading Cases in Equity, 7th ed. vol. ii. 798 *et seq.*

Fraudulent Purpose.

A trust may likewise be void if the purpose for which it is created be fraudulent. There are two classes of cases in which this has acquired a special importance: (1) where the purpose is to defraud the creditors of the settlor, and (2) where it is to defraud purchasers from him.

Trusts in Fraud of Creditors.—A trust may be void as against the creditors of the settlor, either under the statute 13 Eliz. c. 5, or under the Bankruptcy Act, 1883, s. 47.

13 Eliz. c. 5—omitting unnecessary verbiage—is an act for "avoiding gifts, grants and conveyances, as well of lands and tenements as of goods and chattels devised to the intent to delay,

(*m*) (1870), L. R. 10 Eq. 405.

(*n*) See Pollock, Contracts, 7th ed. 596 and 605.

hinder, or defraud creditors and others," and s. 1 declares that every gift, grant and conveyance of lands, tenements, hereditaments, goods and chattels, or any of them, by writing or otherwise, to or for any intent or purpose before declared, shall be deemed (only against that person hindered, delayed or defrauded) to be void.

By s. 5 the act is not to extend to any estate or interest in lands, tenements or hereditaments, goods or chattels upon good consideration and *bonâ fide* conveyed or assured to any person not having at the time any notice of such fraud.

The statute speaks of fraudulent, not voluntary conveyances. Consequently, a conveyance cannot be set aside under it merely because it is voluntary; it must also be shown to be fraudulent. Conversely, the exception only being in favour of conveyances upon good (which here means valuable) consideration *and bonâ fide*, a conveyance may be set aside under it, even though for value, if shown to be fraudulent.

A. *Conveyances for Value.*—Trusts created for valuable consideration are found in ante-nuptial settlements. These may be void under the statute if made with intent to delay creditors, unless they are made *bonâ fide* and the beneficiary has no notice of the fraud.

Illustrations.

1. A. by ante-nuptial settlement assigns property to trustees upon trust for himself until bankruptcy, and then over to B. The settlement is void, and A.'s trustee in bankruptcy is entitled to the property. *Higginbotham* v. *Holme* (1811), 19 Vesey, 88.

2. A. has cohabited with a woman for seven years. Being in insolvent circumstances and intending to secure his property from his creditors, he marries the woman, and by an ante-nuptial settlement assigns the whole of his property to trustees upon trust for his wife, with a joint power to them to appoint amongst their children. The woman is aware of the facts. The settlement is void. *Columbine* v. *Penhall* (1853), 1 Sm. & Giff. 228; *Bulmer* v. *Hunter* (1869), L. R. 8 Eq. 46.

3. A. executes an ante-nuptial settlement of all his property on B., whom he subsequently marries. The only object of both A.

and B. is to endeavour, under cover of the marriage, to put A.'s property out of the reach of his creditors. The settlement is void. *In re Pennington, Ex parte Cooper* (1888), 59 L. T. 774.

B. *Voluntary Conveyances.*—It was formerly thought that, if the effect of the settlement were to deprive the settlor of the means of paying his then existing debts, an intent to defraud must be presumed in the case of a voluntary settlement (*o*). It is certain, however, that the court is not bound to presume an intent to defeat or delay creditors merely because they are defeated or delayed as a necessary consequence of the settlement. A settlement which has this effect will be good if it appears from the evidence that the settlor had no such intent (*p*).

The effect of the decision of the Court of Appeal in the case last cited seems to be that there must be sufficient evidence to warrant a judge or jury in finding that the settlement was intended to delay, hinder, or defraud creditors. *In the absence of any evidence at all, such an intent may be inferred from the fact that the necessary result of the settlement was to defeat or delay the creditors.* This inference is, however, one of fact only and not of law, and may be rebutted if the evidence as a whole shows that no such intention existed (*q*).

Illustrations.

1. A., who is solvent at the time, but has contracted a considerable debt, which will fall due in the course of a few weeks, makes a voluntary settlement, by which he withdraws a large portion of his property from payment of his debts. He then collects the rest of his assets and spends them recklessly, and as a consequence the expectant creditor remains unpaid. The settlement is void. *Spirett* v. *Willows* (1864), 3 De G. J. & S. 293.

2. A. has a life income of about 1,000*l.* a year, his only other property being a policy on his life for 1,000*l.*, a copyhold cottage worth 50*l.*, and some furniture. His creditors are pressing him, and in order to pay the most urgent he borrows from B. 350*l.*, in consideration of which he conveys to B. the copyhold cottage and

(*o*) *Freeman* v. *Pope* (1870), L. R. 5 Ch. App. 540.

(*p*) *Ex parte Mercer, In re Wise* (1886), 17 Q. B. D. 290.

(*q*) See Hunt, Fraudulent Conveyances, 2nd ed. 54, 55.

gives her a bill of sale on his furniture. The arrangement does not, however, enable him to discharge the whole of his indebtedness, and being still indebted, he executes a voluntary settlement of his life policy in favour of C., the result of which is to leave him insolvent. He then contracts a debt to D. The settlement is void as against D. *Freeman* v. *Pope* (1870), L. R. 5 Ch. App. 538.

3. A. is married on May 31, 1881. In August, 1881, an action for breach of promise is commenced against him, and the writ is served on October 8, 1881. About the same time A. learns that he has become entitled to a legacy under his stepfather's will, and on the 17th October, 1881, he executes a voluntary settlement of the legacy on his wife for life, with remainders over. A. is not influenced in doing this by the action, which he then thinks will come to nothing. On July 20, 1882, judgment is given against him in the action for 500*l.*, and he becomes bankrupt. The settlement is not void. *Ex parte Mercer, In re Wise* (1886), 17 Q. B. D. 290.

Trusts void under the Bankruptcy Acts.—By s. 47 of the Bankruptcy Act, 1883, it is provided that:—

"(1) Any settlement of property, not being a settlement made before and in consideration of marriage, or made in favour of a purchaser or incumbrancer in good faith and for valuable consideration, or a settlement made on or for the wife or children of the settlor of property which has accrued to the settlor after marriage in right of his wife, shall, if the settlor becomes bankrupt within two years after the date of the settlement, be void against the trustee in the bankruptcy, and shall, if the settlor becomes bankrupt at any subsequent time within ten years after the date of the settlement, be void against the trustee in the bankruptcy, unless the parties claiming under the settlement can prove that the settlor was, at the time of making the settlement, able to pay all his debts without the aid of the property comprised in the settlement, and that the interest of the settlor in such property has passed to the trustee on the execution thereof.

"(2) Any covenant or contract made in consideration of marriage for the future settlement on or for the settlor's wife or children of any money or property wherein he had not, at the date of his marriage, any estate or interest, whether vested or contingent in possession or remainder, and not being money or property of or in right of his wife, shall, on his becoming bankrupt before the property or money has been actually transferred or paid pursuant to the contract or covenant, be void against the trustee in bankruptcy.

"(3) 'Settlement' shall, for the purposes of this section, include any conveyance or transfer of property."

It has been held that the word "void" in the section should be read as "voidable," so that a purchaser of the property comprised in the settlement before the trustee's title has accrued cannot be disturbed (*r*).

Trusts in Fraud of Purchasers.—Trusts of *land* may be void against subsequent purchasers of the land under 27 Eliz. c. 4.

s. 2 of this statute provides that "every conveyance, grant, charge, lease, estate, incumbrance, and limitation of use or uses of, in or out of any lands, tenements, or other hereditaments whatsoever . . . . for the intent and of purpose to defraud and deceive such person or persons, bodies politic or corporate as have purchased or shall afterwards purchase in fee simple, fee tail, for life, lives, or years, the same . . . . or any part thereof, or . . . . any rent, profit, or commodity in or out of the same, or any part thereof, shall be deemed and taken only as against that person and persons, bodies politic and corporate, his and their heirs, successors, executors, administrators, and assigns, and . . . . every other person and persons lawfully claiming by, from or under them, . . . to be utterly void, frustrate, and of none effect."

s. 4 excepts any conveyance, &c., made upon good consideration and *bonâ fide*.

Upon this statute it was formerly held that, if the owner of land made a voluntary conveyance or settlement of it and then subsequently sold the same land to a purchaser for value, the mere fact of the subsequent sale was evidence of the fraudulent character of the previous conveyance or settlement, which was void in consequence (*s*). This has now been altered by the Voluntary Conveyances Act, 1893, which is as follows:—

s. 2. Subject as hereinafter mentioned, no voluntary conveyance of any lands, tenements, or hereditaments, whether made

(*r*) *In re Vansittart*, (1893) 2 Q. B. 377; *In re Carter and Kenderdine's Contract*, (1897) 1 Ch. 776; *In re Tankard, Ex parte The Official Receiver*, (1899) 2 Q. B. 57.

(*s*) *Doe* v. *Manning* (1807), 2 East, 59.

before or after the passing of this act, if in fact made *bonâ fide* and without any fraudulent intent, shall hereafter be deemed fraudulent or covinous within the meaning of the act 27 Eliz. c. 4, by reason of any subsequent purchase for value, or be defeated under any of the provisions of the said act by a conveyance made upon any such purchase, any rule of law notwithstanding.

s. 3. This act does not apply in any case in which the author of a voluntary conveyance of any lands, tenements, or hereditaments has subsequently, but before the passing of this act, disposed of or dealt with the same lands, tenements, or hereditaments, to or in favour of a purchaser for value.

s. 4. The expression "conveyance" includes every mode of disposition mentioned or referred to in the said act of Elizabeth.

The act came into force on the 29th June, 1893.

Unlawful Purpose Generally.

Trusts involving a Perpetuity.—Any trust the purpose of which is prohibited by law is void, and since the law prohibits any disposition of property which renders it inalienable in perpetuity, a trust which offends the rule against perpetuities is void.

The rule as established in the case of *Cadell* v. *Palmer* (*t*) may be stated as follows:—

"Every limitation of either real or personal property is void, if the vesting in the case of real property of an estate in fee simple or fee tail, or in the case of personal property of an absolute interest in the same, is or may possibly be thereby postponed for longer than a period comprising the duration of the lives of any number of ascertainable persons in existence at the date when the limitation comes into operation, and a further period of twenty-one years from the death of the last survivor of such persons, without reference to the infancy of any person; provided that the property may be limited to vest in a person *en ventre sa mère* at the expiration of such period."

The following are recent cases illustrating the application of the rule to trusts:—

Illustrations.

1. Testator gives his real and personal estate to trustees in

(*t*) (1833), 7 Bligh, N. S. 202.

trust for A. for life, and after A.'s death in trust for all her sons and daughters who shall attain the age of twenty-two. At the testator's death A. has no child who has attained the age of twenty-two. The trust for A.'s children is void for remoteness. *Thomas* v. *Wilberforce* (1862), 31 Beav. 299.

2. Real estate is limited to the use of trustees for 500 years and, subject thereto, to the use of A. for life, remainder to his first and other sons in tail, remainder to B. for life, remainder to his first and other sons in tail, remainders over; and a power is given to the trustees during the minority of any person from time to time to take possession of and manage the estate. The power is void for remoteness. *Floyer* v. *Banks* (1869), L. R. 8 Eq. 115.

3. Testator gives 3,000*l.* to A. for life, and after A.'s death in trust for all the children of A. who shall attain the age of twenty-one, and the issue of such of them as shall die under that age, which issue shall attain the age of twenty-one or die under that age leaving issue, *per stirpes.* A. is unmarried at testator's death. The trust for A.'s children and their issue is void for remoteness. *Pearks* v. *Moseley* (1880), 5 App. Cas. 729 (*u*).

4. Testator gives real estate to trustees and their heirs in trust for A. for life, and after her death to retain the rents for their own use during the life of B., and after his death to convey the real estate to such son of C. as shall first attain the age of twenty-five in fee. At testator's death C. has no son who has attained the age of twenty-five. The limitation to the son of C. is void for remoteness. *Abiss* v. *Burney* (1881), 17 Ch. D. 211.

(*u*) This is a trust for A.'s children and their issue as a class, and the total number of the members of the class is not necessarily ascertainable within the limits of the rule. For example, so far as can be known at the testator's death, the whole class may consist of A.'s grandchildren who may not attain twenty-one within twenty-one years from A.'s death. Again, suppose A. has three children (as in the case cited he had), each must take at least 1,000*l.*; but if one or more dies without leaving issue who attains twenty-one (which need not necessarily happen within twenty-one years from A.'s death) the share of the survivor or survivors would be increased proportionately. The grounds of the decision are clearly explained in the judgment of Sir G. Jessel in *Hale* v. *Hale* (1876, 3 Ch. D. 643), which case the House of Lords approved in *Pearks* v. *Moseley*.

5. Testator gives real estate unto and to the use of trustees in trust for A. for life, remainder to the first son of A. who attains the age of twenty-five. At testator's death A. has no son who has attained the age of twenty-five. The remainder is void for remoteness. *Ibid.*

6. Testator devises a freehold house to trustees in trust, after the expiration of a lease which has forty-nine years to run, to sell and distribute the proceeds among specified persons ascertainable within the limits of the rule. The trust is void for remoteness, but the legatees of the proceeds are entitled to the property as real estate. *In re Daveron*, (1893) 3 Ch. 421; approved and followed by the Court of Appeal in *In re Appleby*, (1903) 1 Ch. 565.

7. Testator directs his trustees to carry on his business of a gravel contractor until his freehold gravel pits are worked out, and then to sell them, with power for his sons to bid at the sale; and directs the proceeds of sale to be held in trust for such of his children as are then living. Both the trust for sale and the trust of the proceeds are void for remoteness. *In re Wood, Tullett* v. *Colville*, (1894) 3 Ch. 381.

8. Testator gives his residuary estate in trust after the death of A. and her husband for all the daughters of A. who attain twenty-one or marry; with a proviso that the share of any daughter shall be held in trust for her for her life, and after her death in trust for her children. The proviso is void for remoteness so far as it relates to daughters born after the death of the testator. *In re Russell*, (1895) 2 Ch. 698.

It should be added that charitable trusts are valid although they offend the rule against perpetuities, provided that if the occurrence of an event is a condition precedent of the gift the event must necessarily occur within the period prescribed by the rule (*v*).

Trusts for Accumulation of Income.—Before the year 1800 any trust for the accumulation of the income of property which did not offend the rule against perpetuities was valid. But an alteration in the law was made as a consequence of the will of Mr. Peter Thellusson, a wealthy London merchant, who died in 1797, and

(*v*) Tudor, Charitable Trusts, 3rd ed. 56.

who directed the income of the bulk of his property, amounting to over 600,000*l.*, to be accumulated during the lives of his three sons and their descendants living at the date of his death for the benefit of some future descendants to be living at the decease of the survivor. It was calculated that if the survivor of the persons during whose lives the trust was to continue lived to be seventy, the property would then amount to over 19,000,000*l.* (*w*), and that it might conceivably amount to 140,000,000*l.* (*x*). The testator's intention evidently was to found three families who should be wealthier than any other in the land, and it was urged that to permit the attainment of such an object would constitute a source of danger to the commonwealth; but the will was held valid by the Courts (*y*). It appears from the report of the case of *Thellusson* v. *Rendlesham* (*z*), that the trust actually lasted fifty-nine years, the survivor of the lives dying in 1856; and then, owing to the vast amount of litigation to which the will gave rise, the fortune to which the beneficiaries succeeded was of only moderate dimensions, so that the danger in that particular case did not arise. But in the meantime, even before the will was ultimately pronounced valid by the House of Lords, the Accumulations Act, 1800, was passed in order to prohibit the creation of such a trust for the future.

The Accumulations Act, 1800, s. 1, provides that no person . . . . shall . . . . settle or dispose of any real or personal property, so . . . . that the rents, issues, profits or produce thereof shall be wholly or partially accumulated for any longer term than—

(a) The life of any such grantor or settlor; or

(b) The term of twenty-one years from the death of such grantor, settlor, or testator; or

(c) During the minority or respective minorities of any person or persons who shall be living or *en ventre sa mère* at the time of the death of such grantor, settlor, or testator; or

(d) During the minority or respective minorities only of any person or persons who under the . . . . trusts . . . . directing such accumulations would for the time being, if of full age, be

(*w*) 4 Ves. 237.

(*x*) Dict. Nat. Biog. lvi. 110.

(*y*) *Thellusson* v. *Woodford* (1798), 4 Ves. 227; 11 Ves. 112.

(*z*) (1859), 7 H. L. C. 429.

entitled to the rents . . . . or annual produce so directed to be accumulated (*a*).

And where any accumulation is directed otherwise, the direction shall be null and void. . . . .

By s. 2, however, an exception is made in favour of provisions—

(1) for payment of debts,
(2) for raising portions, or
(3) touching the produce of timber,

all of which may be made as if the act had not been passed.

The act has been amended by the Accumulations Act, 1892, which prohibits accumulations for the purchase of land only for any longer period than during the minority or respective minorities of any person or persons who under the trusts directing such accumulation would for the time being, if of full age, be entitled to receive the income so directed to be accumulated.

If a trust offends the rule against perpetuities it is void altogether; if it exceeds the limits of the Accumulation Acts it is good *pro tanto* (*b*).

Immoral Trusts.—A trust against public morality is likewise unenforceable. It is for this reason that a trust for illegitimate children *thereafter to be born* has been said to be void; though a trust for illegitimate children *in esse* or *en ventre sa mère* at the date of the instrument creating the trust is valid, and it may be that the trust is valid in favour of all illegitimate children born before the instrument comes into operation. This was the decision of the majority of the Court of Appeal in *Occleston* v. *Fullalove* (*c*), though Lord Selborne dissented. In discussing the rule that future illegitimate children cannot take under a trust, Lord Justice James in that case (p. 160) says: "If the expression 'future children' be limited to what I conceive to be its more accurate meaning—children to come into existence after the will itself has really come into existence as the last will of the testator, viz., after his death—then I would at once, for reasons subse-

(*a*) This period is not confined to minority of persons born in the testator's lifetime, so that a trust to accumulate during the minority of a specified person not born till after the testator's death is good. *In re Cattell*, (1907) 1 Ch. 567.

(*b*) *Griffiths* v. *Vere* (1803), 9 Ves. 127.

(*c*) (1874), L. R. 9 Ch. App. 147. See also *In re Hastie's Trusts* (1887), 35 Ch. D. 728; *In re Loveland*, (1906) 1 Ch. 542.

quently given, concede that there is or may be such a rule of law as that referred to. But if it be extended to apply to children coming into existence between the date or execution of the will and the death of the testator, then, in my humble judgment, the proposition is not one to be assumed as it appears to have been." . . . . Lord Justice Mellish, in the same case, draws a distinction between a trust for future illegitimate children in a deed and one in a will on the ground that the former operates from the date of its execution, the latter from the death of the testator. He granted that in the former case the gift is void as tending to immorality (p. 171), but held that in the latter it is good as regards children born or *en ventre sa mère* before the testator's death, although after the date of the will. It seems clear that a trust cannot be effectively made in favour of illegitimate children to be born after the date when the will comes into operation, namely, the death of the testator.

Trusts against Public Policy.—Finally, any trust the purpose of which is contrary to public policy is void. The leading case on this subject is *Egerton* v. *Earl Brownlow* (*d*). The case arose upon the will of the seventh Earl of Bridgewater, who devised very large real estates to trustees to make a settlement according to the limitations stated in the will. One of these was to Lord Alford for the term of ninety-nine years, if he should so long live; remainder to trustees to preserve contingent remainders; remainder to the use of the heirs male of his body, with remainder in default of such issue to the use of Charles Henry Cust for the term of ninety-nine years, if he should so long live; remainder to trustees to preserve contingent remainders; remainder to the use of the heirs male of his body, subject as to all these estates to the provisoes thereinafter contained. One of these was, "that if Lord Alford shall die without having acquired the title of Duke or Marquis of Bridgewater to him and the heirs male of his body, then and in such case the use and estate hereinbefore directed to be limited to the heirs male of his body shall cease and be absolutely void." The judges were called in to advise the House of Lords, and the latter held by a majority of four to one, in accordance with the opinion of two judges against eight, that the limitations

(*d*) (1853), 4 H. L. C. 1.

were void, as being against public policy; the *ratio decidendi* being that the limitations "amounted in effect to a gift of pecuniary means to be used in obtaining a peerage, and offered a direct temptation to the improper use of such means, and the improper admission of private motives of interest in political conduct: in short, because in the opinion of the court they had a manifest tendency to the prejudice of good government and the administration of public affairs" (*e*).

(*e*) Pollock, Contracts, 7th ed. 317.

Part III.—IMPLIED TRUSTS.

SECTION XII.—RESULTING TRUST WHERE NO TRUST DECLARED, &c.

(1) WHERE the owner of property transfers it, but appears not to intend to give the transferee the whole beneficial interest therein, if

(a) No trust is expressed by the owner, or

(b) The trust expressed by the owner is incapable of being executed, or

(c) The trust or other purpose for which the transfer is made by the owner is completely executed without exhausting the property,

the transferee holds the property or so much thereof as is unexhausted in trust for the owner or those deriving title through him.

(2) Where a voluntary transfer of personal property is made otherwise than by will, there is a presumption that the transferee is intended to hold it in trust for the transferor unless a contrary intention appears;

Provided that if the transferor is the parent or husband of, or stands *in loco parentis* to, the transferee, there is a presumption that he intends the transferee to take the property beneficially and not in trust, unless a contrary intention appears.

(3) Where the transferee is expressed to take as trustee, evidence is not admissible to prove that the transfer is intended to include the beneficial interest;

otherwise it is admissible to prove the intention with which the transfer is made.

The rules relating to implied trusts or trusts arising by operation of law are an artificial extension of the law of trusts, for the sake of justice and convenience, to various cases in which a legal interest in, or a control over, property has been gained in circumstances which make it inequitable for the person having that interest or control to deal with the property as beneficial owner. These trusts answer to the class of "implied contracts," or "quasi-contracts" in the field of contract law (*a*). In the words of Lord Justice Kay (*b*), the person whom it is sought to affect with the trust is not a trustee at all, although he may be liable as if he were. In the Indian Trusts Act, 1882, they are perhaps more properly termed "obligations in the nature of trusts." As has been shown in Section II., they are by English lawyers sometimes called "implied trusts," sometimes "constructive trusts"; and one species is known as "resulting trusts," and sometimes the term "implied trusts" is used to denote the latter. On the whole, it seems best to term them generically "implied trusts," and to subdivide them into A., resulting trusts, and B., constructive trusts—the difference between resulting and constructive trusts being that the former are based upon the presumed intention of the parties; the latter are independent of any such intention, being raised by construction of law merely.

Resulting trusts arise in four classes of cases:—

1. When no trust is expressed or the trust expressed is incapable of taking effect, or is executed without exhausting the trust property.

2. When property is purchased by one person, but the conveyance or transfer is made to another.

3. When property is conveyed to two or more persons as joint tenants, but such persons are in equity tenants in common.

4. When the purpose of a trust or transfer is illegal.

With regard to the first class, the rule may be stated to be that where the owner of property transfers it, but appears not to intend

(*a*) See Encyc. Eng. Law, vol. i. 11. (*b*) (1893) 2 Q. B. at p. 400.

to give the transferee the whole beneficial interest, there is a resulting trust if

(a) No trust is expressed by the owner, or
(b) The trust expressed by him is incapable of taking effect, or
(c) The trust or other purpose for which the transfer is made is completely executed without exhausting the property.

The following cases afford illustrations of trusts of this kind :—

Illustrations.

(a) *No Trust declared.*

1. A. devises real estate to "my trustees," but declares no trusts of the property. The trustees hold it in trust for the testator's heir. See per Lord Eldon in *Dawson* v. *Clark* (1811), 18 Ves. 247 (*c*).

2. Testator gives to the trustees of Mount Zion Chapel 3,500*l.*, and appoints as trustees to the same A. and G., "the money to be appropriated according to statement appended." There is no statement appended. The 3,500*l.* falls into the residue. *Aston* v. *Wood* (1868), L. R. 6 Eq. 419.

3. Testator devises and bequeaths all his estate and effects to trustees, their *heirs*, executors, and administrators, upon trusts only applicable to personalty. There is a resulting trust of testator's real estate to his heir. *Longley* v. *Longley* (1871), L. R. 13 Eq. 133.

4. A. transfers to his son B. shares in the X. Company. His reason for doing so, though not stated by him, appears to be to qualify B. to be appointed director of the company. B. always hands the dividends to A., and A. keeps the share certificates. B. is a trustee for A. *In re Gooch, Gooch* v. *Gooch* (1890), 62 L. T. 384.

(b) *Trust incapable of being Executed.*

5. Testator gives his real and personal estate to trustees upon trust to sell and convert it into money, and divide the proceeds between A., B., C. and D. A. and B. predecease the testator. The trustees must hand their shares, so far as they represent the

(*c*) See also *Morice* v. *Bishop of Durham* (1805), 10 Ves. at p. 526.

proceeds of sale of real estate, to the testator's heir-at-law, and so far as they represent the proceeds of the personalty, to his next of kin. *Ackroyd* v. *Smithson* (1780), 1 Bro. Ch. 503.

6. Testator directs his executors to lay out 30,000*l.* in land, and to pay the income to A. for life, with remainder to a charity. The executors do not actually lay out the money before A.'s death. The gift to the charity failing under the Charitable Uses Act (*d*), testator's next of kin are entitled to the 30,000*l.* *Cogan* v. *Stephens* (1835), 1 Beav. 482, n.; 5 L. J. Ch. 17.

7. Testatrix gives B. a promissory note "for the purpose of enabling B. to present to either branch of my family, and principal and interest therein, as A. may consider most prudent." This being a trust which cannot be enforced, B. holds the note in trust for testatrix's estate. *Stubbs* v. *Sargon* (1838), 3 My. & Cr. 507.

(c) *Trust Executed without Exhausting Property.*

8. A wife mortgages her estate to secure her husband's debt, and the equity of redemption is reserved to the heirs of the husband. The husband holds the property in trust for the wife and her heirs. *Brend* v. *Brend* (1683), 1 Vern. 213 (*e*).

9. A. devises real estate to a trustee on trust to pay his debts. If after paying all A.'s debts there is any surplus, the trustee holds it in trust for the heir. *King* v. *Denison* (1813), 1 V. & B. 279 (*f*).

10. A., being in want of money, induces his wife to assign to him a leasehold house to enable him to raise money by mortgaging it. A., after effecting the mortgage, holds the equity of redemption in trust for his wife. *In re Duke of Marlborough*, (1894) 2 Ch. 133.

(*d*) Money directed to be laid out in the purchase of land could only be given to a charity by deed before the Mortmain and Charitable Uses Act, 1891, came into force.

(*e*) Conf. *Huntingdon* v. *Huntingdon* (1702), 2 Br. P. C. Toml. 1; and *Jackson* v. *Innes* (1819), 1 Bligh, 104.

(*f*) *In re West*, (1900) 1 Ch. 84, is to the like effect.

11. A fund is raised by subscription for the maintenance of two distressed ladies, a portion of which remains unapplied at the death of the survivor. There is a resulting trust of the balance of the fund for the subscribers to it. *In re the Trusts of the Abbott Fund*, (1900) 2 Ch. 326.

Where, however, the owner appears to intend to dispose of the whole beneficial interest by the transfer there will be no resulting trust, although the transfer is made for a particular object which is satisfied without exhausting the property (*g*).

It seems that on a voluntary transfer *inter vivos* of personal property there is a presumption of a resulting trust in favour of the transferor. Lord Thurlow evidently thought so (*h*). Sir G. Jessel so decided in *Fowkes* v. *Pascoe* (*i*), and in the same case Lord Justice James "assumed" it, though apparently he felt some doubt (*j*), while Lord Justice Mellish treated it as the law (*k*). Lastly, Lord Justice Cotton, in *Standing* v. *Bowring* (*l*), asserted that "the rule is well settled that where there is a transfer by a person into his own name jointly with that of a person who is not his child or adopted child, there is *primâ facie* a resulting trust for the transferor." These authorities seem to outweigh the one or two opposite dicta. But the presumption is only a "*presumptio hominis*" or *primâ facie* rule, and as the above cases show is not applied if the circumstances evidence an intention that the transferor is to take the whole beneficial interest.

On the other hand, it has been said that on a voluntary conveyance of land from A. "unto and to the use of" B. there is no such presumption of a resulting trust. According to Lord Hardwicke, "if a trust by implication was to arise . . . . it would be to contradict the Statute of Frauds; for it might be said in every case where a voluntary conveyance is made that a trust shall arise by implication; *but that is by no means the rule of the court;* trusts by implication or operation of law arise in such cases where one

(*g*) See *Cook* v. *Hutchinson* (1836), 1 Keen, 42. Recent illustrations are *Sayre* v. *Hughes* (1868), L. R. 5 Eq. 376; *Fowkes* v. *Pascoe* (1875), L. R. 10 Ch. App. 343; *Batstone* v. *Salter* (1875), *ibid.* 431; *Standing* v. *Bowring* (1885), 31 Ch. D. 282; *Cooke* v. *Smith*, (1891) A. C. 297; and *Cumack* v. *Edwards*, (1896) 2 Ch. 679.

(*h*) See *Scultthorp* v. *Burgess* (1790), 1 Ves. Jun. 91.

(*i*) *Supra*, at p. 345, n.

(*j*) p. 348.

(*k*) p. 352.

(*l*) *Supra*, at p. 287.

person pays the purchase-money and the conveyance is taken in the name of another, or in some other cases of that kind; but the rule is by no means so large as to extend to every voluntary conveyance" (m). Lord Justice James likewise said in *Fowkes* v. *Pascoe*, that there would certainly not be a trust in such a case. Yet Lord Justice Turner was strongly of opinion that a trust could be made out notwithstanding the Statute of Frauds (n), and the decisions of the Court of Appeal (James and Mellish, L. JJ.) in *Haigh* v. *Kaye* (o), and of Vice-Chancellor Bacon in *Rudkin* v. *Dolman* (p), seem hardly consistent with Lord Hardwicke's statement of the law, though the former case can no doubt be explained on the ground of fraud. Apart from authority it is difficult to see why there should be any difference between personal property and land. Before the Statute of Uses, as Chief Baron Eyre pointed out in *Dyer* v. *Dyer*, if a feoffment were made without consideration, the use resulted to the feoffor. One would have thought, therefore, that after the statute there would have been a resulting trust on a voluntary conveyance "unto and to the use of" the grantee, and that this resulting trust would have been saved by sect. 8 of the Statute of Frauds.

Whatever may be the true view as to this, it is clear that where a transfer of property is made to a wife or child, or one to whom the transferor stands *in loco parentis*, there is a presumption of the same kind that the transferor intended it as an advancement, just as in the case of a purchase in the name of such persons (q). In the case of *In re Orme* (r), Mr. Justice Kay says, "Now I think it is quite clear by authority that if advances are made to a person to whom the individual who makes the advances is *in loco parentis*, that those advances are *primâ facie* gifts," and decided that the money advanced in that case by a mother to her son for business purposes was a gift to the son.

Illustrations.

1. A widow transfers certain East India Stock which stands in her own name into the names of herself and her unmarried

(m) In *Young* v. *Peachey* (1741), 2 Atk. at p. 256.

(n) *Childers* v. *Childers* (1857), 1 De G. & J. at p. 495.

(o) (1869), L. R. 7 Ch. App. 469.

(p) (1876), 35 L. T. 791.

(q) Lewin, Trusts, 11th ed. 159. See *Devoy* v. *Devoy* (1857), 3 Sm. & G. 403; and see *Sayre* v. *Hughes*; *Fowkes* v. *Pascoe*; *Batstone* v. *Salter*; and *Standing* v. *Bowring*, *supra*.

(r) (1884), 50 L. T. 51.

daughter. There is a presumption of intention to benefit the daughter, and in the absence of evidence the daughter is entitled on the death of her mother. *Sayre* v. *Hughes* (1868), L. R. 5 Eq. 376.

2. A., widow, makes small advances from time to time to her son B., to whom she is *in loco parentis*, to enable him to carry on business or for his maintenance. A. never attempts to recover these moneys, nor does she take any acknowledgment of them. After A.'s death B. cannot be charged with them in the administration of A.'s estate. *In re Orme, Evans* v. *Maxwell* (1884), 50 L. T. 51.

But here also the presumption may be rebutted by evidence, even though it be only the evidence of the father that he did not intend an advancement (*s*).

Where the transferee is expressed to take as trustee verbal evidence is not admissible to prove that the transfer is intended to include the beneficial interest (*t*). It was admitted in the old case of *Docksey* v. *Docksey* (*u*), but only to prove that the transferee was intended to take in trust for a person other than the plaintiff. In the case of *Gladding* v. *Yapp* (*t*), where the testator had nominated his sister to be his executrix, and directed her to keep a proper account, verbal evidence was admitted, and was held sufficient, to show that she was intended to take beneficially, the Vice-Chancellor (Sir John Leach) saying that "parol evidence is not admissible to contradict a will; and if a will contain express declarations that the executor is to be a trustee, evidence cannot be received against the effect of that declaration; but if there be no express declaration of trust in the will, and only circumstances which afford inference or presumption of trust in the executor, there parol evidence is admissible to answer that inference or presumption" (*v*). On the other hand, in the case of *Cook* v. *Hutchinson* (*w*), which was a case of a transfer by deed *inter vivos*,

(*s*) *Devoy* v. *Devoy* (1857), 3 Sm. & G. 403.

(*t*) *Langham* v. *Sandford* (1811), 17 Ves. 442; 19 Ves. 643; *Gladding* v. *Yapp* (1820), 5 Madd. 56; *Barrs* v. *Fewkes* (1865), 13 W. R. 987; *Irvine* v. *Sullivan* (1869), L. R. 8 Eq. 673; *Croome* v. *Croome* (1888), 59 L. T. at p. 584; W. N. 37.

(*u*) (1708), 2 Eq. Ca. Ab. 506.

(*v*) Cited and approved in *Croome* v. *Croome* (1888), 59 L. T. at p. 584.

(*w*) (1836), 1 Keen, at p. 50.

where the transferee was expressed to take upon trust, the Master of the Rolls (Lord Langdale) says distinctly that the resulting trust may be rebutted by parol evidence, and held it to be rebutted. But the circumstances of the case alone showed that it was not intended that there should be a resulting trust.

It is sometimes stated that there is no resulting trust of unexhausted residue when the *cestui que trust* is a charity; this is, however, scarcely accurate; the question is purely one of construction. "We must look at the instruments," said Lord Campbell in *Att.-Gen.* v. *Dean of Windsor* (*x*), "and see whether taking them altogether we discover an intention on the part of the donors that the rents should be divided in certain proportions and given to the different objects of the bounty of the donors in those proportions, or whether the intention manifested is that specified sums should be permanently paid to particular objects of the bounty of the donors, and that they should be entitled to nothing more than the payment of those specified sums, without abatement and without augmentation" (*y*).

(*x*) (1860), 8 H. L. C. at pp. 393 and 394.

(*y*) See Tudor, Charitable Trusts, 3rd ed. 46 *et seq.*

SECTION XIII.—RESULTING TRUST ON PURCHASE IN NAME OF ANOTHER.

(1) WHERE property is transferred to a person or persons other than the person paying or providing the consideration therefor, whether for the whole interest purchased or for an interest jointly with or in succession to him, the transferee or transferees hold the property in trust for the person paying or providing the consideration, unless a contrary intention appears.

Provided that if the person paying or providing the consideration is the parent or husband of, or stands *in loco parentis* to, the transferee, there is a presumption that he intends the transferee to take the property beneficially and not in trust, unless a contrary intention appears.

(2) Evidence is admissible to prove by whom the consideration is paid or provided, and the intention with which the transfer is made.

(3) The provisions of sub-sect. (1) of this section do not apply where the result would be to defeat the policy of an act of parliament, nor where an advance of purchase-money is made by way of loan.

"The clear result of all the cases," said Chief Baron Eyre in the case of *Dyer* v. *Dyer* (*a*), "without a single exception, is that the trust of a legal estate, whether freehold, copyhold, or leasehold; whether taken in the names of the purchaser and others jointly, or in the names of others without that of the purchaser; whether in

(*a*) (1788), 2 Cox, 92; 2 R. R. 14.

one name or several; whether jointly or *successive*, results to the man who advances the purchase-money."

This judgment goes only to real estate and leaseholds, but the principle of a resulting trust in favour of the purchaser applies to pure personal estate as well (*b*).

Mr. Justice Story (*c*) says of this doctrine that "in truth it has its origin in the natural presumption, in the absence of all rebutting circumstances, that he who supplies the money means the purchase to be for his own benefit rather than for that of another, and that the conveyance in the name of the latter is a matter of convenience and arrangement between the parties for other collateral purposes."

This, however, sounds like an afterthought, and Chief Baron Eyre seems to have considered that it was founded simply on analogy to the common law rule that where a feoffment was made without consideration the use resulted to the feoffor.

It has been suggested, that the origin of the presumption of resulting use on a feoffment of land was the practice of making feoffments of land to the use of the feoffor's will, and of taking a purchase of land in the name of another in order to bar the dower of the purchaser's wife. That is to say, because it was common to find that when a feoffment was made without consideration being given by the feoffee but by someone else, the feoffee was only intended to hold the property on the latter's behalf, in order to prevent fraud it was natural to presume such an intention in all cases (*d*).

The following cases are illustrations of this class of resulting trusts:—

Illustrations.

1. A. pays the purchase-money for land conveyed to B. B. holds it in trust for A. *Anon.* (1684), 2 Vent. 361.

(*b*) See judgment of Joyce, J., in *In re a Policy*, (1902) 1 Ch. at p. 285; and *Soar* v. *Foster; James* v. *Holmes;* and *The Venture*, below.

(*c*) Eq. Jur. 13th ed. § 1200.

(*d*) Strahan and Kenrick, Digest of Equity, 177. Prof. Ames, of Harvard, seems to hold a similar view. See Harvard Law Review, vol. xx. 555. The doctrine has been abolished by statute in several States of the American Union: *ibid.*

2. A pays the purchase-money for land which is conveyed to A., B. and C. for their lives. B. and C. are trustees for A. *Howe* v. *Howe* (1686), 1 Vern. 415.

3. A. and B. join in providing the purchase-money for the Blackacre estate, which is conveyed to A. alone. A. is trustee for B. for his proportion of the purchase-money. *Wray* v. *Steele* (1814), 2 V. & B. 388.

4. A. purchases stock in the name of himself and B., his deceased wife's sister, with whom he has gone through the form of marriage. B. is a trustee for A. *Soar* v. *Foster* (1858), 4 K. & J. 152.

5. A. hands money to B. (with whom she is cohabiting), without any specific directions as to its application, and B. invests it in the purchase of leaseholds and other property. B. is a trustee for A. *James* v. *Holmes* (1862), 4 De G. F. & J. 470.

6. A. takes out a policy of insurance on his own life "for behoof of B.," his wife's sister, and the policy provides that B., her executors, administrators and assigns shall be entitled to receive the policy moneys on A.'s death. A. survives B., retains the policy, and pays the premiums till his death. B.'s representative is a trustee of the policy moneys for A.'s executor. *In re a Policy*, (1902) 1 Ch. 282.

7. A yacht is bought for 1,050*l*., and is registered in the name of X.; 550*l*., part of the purchase-money, is, in fact, provided by X.'s brother Y. Y. is entitled to fifty-five 105ths of the yacht or her proceeds of sale after she is sold. *The Venture*, (1908) P. 218.

But the foundation of the doctrine is the desire of courts of equity to give effect to the intention of the parties, and there is therefore no resulting trust if it appears to have been the intention of the purchaser that the transferee should take beneficially. "It is the established doctrine of a court of equity that this resulting trust may be rebutted by circumstances in evidence," Chief Baron Eyre said in *Dyer* v. *Dyer*. And this doctrine was extended by the case of *Fowkes* v. *Pascoe* (*e*), where it was held

(*e*) (1875), L. R. 10 Ch. App. 343.

that in determining whether a trust or a gift was intended, regard must be had as well to the circumstances of the case as to the evidence adduced by the party who alleges that he was intended to take beneficially. In *Fowkes* v. *Pascoe* the facts were that Sarah Baker, a widow, had an only child, a son, who had married and had died, leaving a widow but no children. The widow married again and had a son, T. J. Pascoe, and other children. The evidence showed that Sarah Baker looked upon her daughter-in-law, her children and grandchildren as if they had been her own descendants, and T. J. Pascoe lived with her for several years before his marriage in the year 1844. In 1843 she bought certain stock in the names of herself and T. J. Pascoe. In 1845 she bought more, and at various times afterwards she bought and transferred more, so that at her death in 1850 there was standing in the names of herself and him some 7,000*l.* worth. She gave him part of her property by her will, and appointed him one of the trustees. The Court of Appeal held that in the circumstances the sums of stock were a gift to T. J. Pascoe.

Further, the fact that the purchase is made by a father in the name of a child, by a husband in the name of a wife, or by any person in the name of another to whom he is *in loco parentis*, is *primâ facie* evidence of intention to make a gift. Here, according to Sir George Jessel, "the presumption of gift arises from the moral obligation to give" (*e*). This presumption of advancement, as it is called, has been applied in the following cases :—

Illustrations.

1. A. takes bonds in the names of his infant grandchildren, whose father is dead. This is a provision for them, and there is no presumption of a resulting trust. *Ebrand* v. *Dancer* (1680), 2 Ch. Ca. 26.

2. A. purchases property and takes the conveyance to himself and his wife and X. during their lives and the life of the survivor. After A.'s death his wife is not a trustee for A.'s estate. *Kingdon* v. *Bridges* (1688), 2 Vern. 67.

3. A. purchases property in the name of his illegitimate son, to

(*e*) *Bennet* v. *Bennet* (1879), 10 Ch. D. at p. 477.

whom he is *in loco parentis*. This is presumed to be a gift. *Beckford* v. *Beckford* (1774), Lofft, 490.

4. Copyhold land is granted to A. and B., his wife, and C., their son, to take in succession for their lives and the life of the survivor. A. pays the whole of the purchase-money. C. is not a trustee for A. *Dyer* v. *Dyer* (1788), 2 Cox, 92.

5. A. enters into an agreement in the name of himself and his wife to purchase land, and dies before the whole of the purchase-money is paid. The land belongs to the wife, and the remainder of the purchase-money must be paid out of A.'s estate. *Drew* v. *Martin* (1864), 2 H. & M. 130.

6. A. buys debentures in a railway company in the name of himself, his wife, and X., one of the trustees of his marriage settlement. This is an advancement, and on A.'s death X. holds merely as trustee for the wife. *In re Eykin's Trusts* (1877), 6 Ch. D. 115.

But again the circumstances of the case must be taken into consideration, and if these go to show that the purchaser did not intend a gift, the mere fact that the purchase is made in the name of a wife or child is not sufficient to rebut the presumption of a resulting trust (*f*).

It is doubtful whether this presumption of advancement applies in the case of a purchase by a mother in the name of a child, although the better opinion seems to be that it does. It seems to have been assumed that it did in *Garrett* v. *Wilkinson* (*g*), and so decided in *Sayre* v. *Hughes* (*h*), and that it did not in *In re De Visme* (*i*) and in *Bennet* v. *Bennet* (*j*), where Sir George Jessel says: "In the case of a father you have only to prove the fact that he is the father, and when you have done that the obligation at once arises; but in the case of a person *in loco parentis* you must prove that he took upon himself the obligation. But in our law there is no moral obligation—I do not know how to express it more shortly—no obligation according to the rules of equity—on a mother to provide for her child: there is no such obligation as a court of

(*f*) *Marshal* v. *Crutwell* (1875), L. R. 20 Eq. 328.

(*g*) (1848), 2 De G. & Sm. at p. 246.

(*h*) (1868), L. R. 5 Eq. 376.

(*i*) (1863), 2 D. J. & S. 17.

(*j*) (1879), 10 Ch. D. 474.

equity recognizes as such." Since this was said s. 21 of the Married Women's Property Act, 1882, has made a married woman having separate property subject to the same liability for the maintenance of her children as the husband is. This is perhaps not material, since the presumption in the case of the father is not put on the legal liability to maintain, but on the *moral* obligation. But, as Mr. Underhill says (*k*), "Surely there is as much moral presumption of an intention by a mother to benefit her offspring as there is in the case of the father . . . . in reason and in custom there is assuredly as much obligation on the part of a mother, *who has the command of money*, to benefit her children with it as in the case of a father." In such cases, however, Sir George Jessel admits that, even if the mother is not *in loco parentis*, very little evidence beyond the relationship is wanted, there being very little motive required to induce a mother to make a gift to her child, so that the point is not of great importance (*l*).

The trust or advancement in these cases being founded on the presumed intention of the parties, verbal evidence is admissible—

First, to prove by whom the purchase-money is paid (*m*).

Secondly, to prove the intention with which the transfer is made in order to rebut the presumption of a resulting trust (*n*).

Thirdly, to rebut the presumption of advancement (*o*).

Fourthly, to support the presumption of advancement (*p*).

A resulting trust will not, however, arise under the rule stated in *Dyer* v. *Dyer* if the policy of an act of parliament would be thereby defeated (*q*). For instance, there will be no resulting trust in favour of a purchaser who buys land in order to qualify the transferee to act as a justice of the peace (*r*), for this would be to

(*k*) Trusts and Trustees, 6th ed. 126.

(*l*) See also *In re Orme* (1884), 50 L. T. 51.

(*m*) *Gascoigne* v. *Thwing* (1685), 1 Vern. 366; *Knight* v. *Pechey* (1759), 1 Dick. 327; see also *Ryall* v. *Ryall* (1739), 1 Atk. 59; *Willis* v. *Willis* (1740), 2 Atk. 71; and *Groves* v. *Groves* (1829), 3 Y. & J. 163.

(*n*) *Dyer* v. *Dyer* (1788), 2 Cox, 92; *Rider* v. *Kidder* (1805), 10 Ves. 364; and *Fowkes* v. *Pascoe* (1875), L. R. 10 Ch. App. 343.

(*o*) *Williams* v. *Williams* (1863), 32 Beav. 370.

(*p*) *Lamplugh* v. *Lamplugh* (1709), 1 P. Wms. 113.

(*q*) *Ex parte Yallop* (1808), 15 Ves. at p. 71.

(*r*) *Crichton* v. *Crichton* (1894), 13 R. 770.

defeat the statute 18 Geo. II. c. 20, which requires that the ownership shall be a beneficial one. And it may be that this principle goes further, and that there will be no resulting trust where the property has been bought for any illegal purpose. The decision in *Groves* v. *Groves* (*s*) appears to have been partly based on this ground.

Lastly, if A. discharges the purchase-money by way of loan to B., in whose name the conveyance is taken, no trust will result in favour of A., who is merely a creditor of B. (*t*).

It has been said by a learned editor of the 14th ed. of Stephen's Commentaries (*u*) that rules better calculated to promote litigation and perjury than those discussed in this section it has rarely been the evil fortune even of Chancery lawyers to invent.

(*s*) *Groves* v. *Groves* (1829), 3 Y. & J. 163.

(*t*) *Crop* v. *Norton* (1740), 9 Mod. 235; *Bartlett* v. *Pickersgill* (1760), 1 Eden, 516.

(*u*) Vol. iii. 505.

SECTION XIV.—RESULTING TRUST ON JOINT PURCHASE OR MORTGAGE.

(1) WHERE property is conveyed to two or more persons as joint tenants, who, being purchasers, contribute the purchase-money in unequal shares, or, being mortgagees, contribute the mortgage money in either equal or unequal shares, on the death of any of the joint tenants the survivor or survivors hold so much of the property in trust for the representatives of the deceased joint tenant as is proportionate to the amount of the purchase-money or mortgage money, as the case may be, contributed by him, unless a contrary intention appears.

(2) Evidence is admissible to prove the intention with which the purchase or mortgage is made.

The third class of resulting trusts was definitely established by the case of *Lake* v. *Gibson* (*a*), where Sir Joseph Jekyll decreed that five persons to whom land had been conveyed jointly were tenants in common in equity, "and that the survivor should not go away with the whole; for then it might happen that some might have paid or laid out their share of the money, and others who had laid out nothing go away with the whole estate."

"When two or more purchase lands and advance the money in *equal* proportions, and take a conveyance to them and their heirs, this is a joint tenancy; that is, a purchase by them jointly of the chance of survivorship, which may happen to the one of them as well as to the other; but where the proportions of the money are *not equal*, and this appears in the deed itself, this makes them in the nature of partners; and however the legal estate may survive,

(*a*) (1729), 1 Eq. Ca. Abr. 294, pl. 3.

yet the survivor shall be considered but as a trustee for the others in proportion to the sums advanced by each of them."

This was affirmed by Lord Chancellor King under the name *Lake* v. *Craddock* in 1732 (*b*).

It does not seem necessary that the deed itself should show that the purchase-money is advanced in unequal proportions, as Sir Joseph Jekyll states. Lord Hardwicke gave the rule without that qualification in *Rigden* v. *Vallier* (*c*), and the fact that the purchase-money was so advanced may be proved by parol evidence (*d*).

Even though the purchase-money is advanced in equal shares the purchasers are sometimes tenants in common in equity, as *Lake* v. *Gibson* itself shows. In that case five persons had bought a piece of land from the Commissioners of Sewers, by whom it had been conveyed to them jointly. They were held to be tenants in common in equity, and the survivors trustees for one of the purchasers who had died, provided that his representatives paid one-fifth of all moneys expended, on the ground that the purchase of the land was a partnership undertaking, and that in partnership the *jus accrescendi* is never allowed. The Partnership Act, 1890, s. 20, has now made this a statutory rule.

Again, where money is advanced by persons either in equal or unequal shares, who take a mortgage to themselves jointly, although the debt and security will at law belong to the survivor, in equity there will be a tenancy in common, the survivor being a trustee for the personal representatives of the deceased mortgagees. For, as Lord Alvanley said in *Morley* v. *Bird* (*e*), "equity says it could not be the intention that the interest should survive. Though they take a joint security, each means to lend his own and to take back his own." The ground for this distinction between purchases and mortgages is not particularly clear, but it is settled (*f*)

(*b*) (1732), 3 P. Wms. 158.

(*c*) (1751), 2 Ves. at p. 258.

(*d*) See *Harris* v. *Fergusson* (1848), 16 Sim. 308, where it would seem that the fact must have been proved by parol evidence. And see per Page-Wood, V.-C., in *Harrison* v. *Barton* (1860), 1 J. & H. at p. 293, and p. 295.

(*e*) (1798), 3 Ves. 631.

(*f*) *Aveling* v. *Knipe* (1815), 19 Ves. 440; *Robinson* v. *Preston* (1858), 4 K. & J. 505; *Harrison* v. *Barton* (1860), 1 J. & H. 287; *In re Rowe* (1889), 61 L. T. 581.

Illustrations.

1. A. mortgages land to B. and C. and their heirs in consideration of an advance of 2,000*l.*, of which B. contributes 1,450*l.* and C. 550*l.* B. dies. On payment off of the mortgage C. is a trustee for his representatives of 1,450*l.* and interest. *Petty* v. *Styward* (1632), 1 Rep. in Ch. 31.

2. Land is conveyed to five persons and their heirs in consideration of 5,145*l.* One of the purchasers contributes 1,025*l.* towards this sum, and then dies. The survivors are trustees of one-fifth of the land for his representatives, on payment of a sum sufficient to make the contribution of the deceased equal to that of the others. *Lake* v. *Gibson* (1729), 1 Eq. Ca. Abr. 294, pl. 3; *Lake* v. *Craddock* (1732), 3 P. W. 158 (*g*).

3. A., B. and C., being beneficially entitled to money as tenants in common, invest it on mortgage of land. By the mortgage deed the land is conveyed to them as joint tenants, the deed containing a clause that the mortgage money belongs to them on a joint account in equity as well as at law. The evidence showing that they consider themselves entitled to the mortgage in equal shares, they are tenants in common, and the survivor, C., is a trustee for the representatives of A. and B. of their shares. *In re Jackson* (1887), 34 Ch. D. 732.

But in this class of cases, also, the resulting trust is based upon a presumed intention of the parties (*h*), and there will be no resulting trust if the circumstances show that a joint tenancy was intended (*i*). And parol evidence of the circumstances in which the transaction took place is admissible to show what the intention was, notwithstanding the Statute of Frauds (*j*), though it is doubtful whether parol evidence as to their statements of their intention is admissible (*k*).

(*g*) The purchase-money paid by the deceased, as will be seen, was not quite one-fifth of the whole, but the decision really went on the ground that the purchasers were partners.

(*h*) See per Page-Wood, V.-C., in *Robinson* v. *Preston* (1858), 4 K. & J. at p. 515.

(*i*) See for an example *Harris* v. *Fergusson* (1848), 16 Sim. 308.

(*j*) *Harrison* v. *Barton* (1860), 1 J. & H. 287; and see *In re Jackson* (1887), 34 Ch. D. 732.

(*k*) *Harrison* v. *Barton*, *supra*; see at p. 293.

SECTION XV.—RESULTING TRUST WHERE PURPOSE OF TRANSFER ILLEGAL.

WHERE a person transfers property to another for an illegal purpose, but such purpose is not carried into execution, or the effect of permitting the transferee to retain the property might be to defeat the provisions of any act of parliament or rule of law, the transferee holds the property for the benefit of the transferor.

As a rule, where the object of a transfer is illegal, the court will not help the transferor to get his property back. *In pari delicto melior est conditio possidentis* (*a*).

But before the illegal purpose is carried out the transferor is entitled to repudiate the transaction and to recover the property from the transferee. Lord Romilly, M. R., in the case of *Symes* v. *Hughes* (*b*), states the rule as follows:—"Where the purpose for which the assignment was given is not carried into execution, and nothing is done under it, the mere intention to effect an illegal object when the assignment was executed does not deprive the assignor of his right to recover the property from the assignee, who has given no consideration for it." In the case of *In re Great Berlin Steamboat Co.* (*infra*), the transferor was held not entitled to recover money which he had handed to the company for a fraudulent purpose, because he did not repudiate until after the company had been ordered to be wound up, though Lord Justices Baggallay and Lindley admitted his right to recover it if he had repudiated before that. The case therefore appears to turn on the effect of an order for winding up a company on the rights of creditors.

Further, in *Ayerst* v. *Jenkins* (*infra*), although he refused relief to the representatives of the settlor on the ground of the illegality of the purpose of the settlement, Lord Selborne said (p. 283):

(*a*) *Groves* v. *Groves* (1829), 3 Y. & J. 163; *Ayerst* v. *Jenkins* (1873), L. R. 16 Eq. 283; *In re Great Berlin Steamboat Co.* (1884), 26 Ch. D. 616. Conf. *Haigh* v. *Kaye* (1872), L. R. 7 Ch. App. 469.

(*b*) (1870), L. R. 9 Eq. at p. 479.

"When the immediate and direct effect of an estoppel in equity against relief to a particular plaintiff might be to effectuate an unlawful object, or to defeat a legal prohibition, or to protect a fraud, such an estoppel may well be regarded as against public policy."

In each of these cases, therefore, there is a resulting trust in favour of the transferor of the property.

The following cases are illustrations of resulting trusts of this kind:—

Illustrations.

1. A. conveys his real estates to B., with a view to being thereby enabled to swear that he has not sufficient qualification to be made sheriff of London. He does not, however, take the oath, but pays the fine for not serving instead. B. holds as trustee for A. *Birch* v. *Blagrave* (1755), Amb. 264.

2. A. conveys real property upon trusts which are void for remoteness. There is a resulting trust in favour of A., or after his death his heir. *Tregonwill* v. *Sydenham* (1815), 3 Dow, 194.

3. A., fearing that he has committed bigamy and that he may be prosecuted, conveys real estate to B. upon trust to reconvey it when the difficulty he is in has blown over. Subsequently learning that he has a complete defence to any indictment, he calls on B. to reconvey. B. must reconvey accordingly. *Davies* v. *Otty* (1865), 35 Beav. 208.

4. A. assigns leasehold land to a trustee with a view of defeating his creditors. The trustee assigns to X. X. is trustee for A., and A. can have the property reconveyed to him. *Symes* v. *Hughes* (1870), L. R. 9 Eq. 475.

5. A., being (in 1857) in prison on a charge of felony, in order to avoid a forfeiture of his personal property in the event of conviction assigns it to B. absolutely. A. is tried and found not guilty on the ground of insanity. B. is a trustee for A. *Manning* v. *Gill* (1872), L. R. 13 Eq. 485.

Section XVI.—Constructive Trust where Trustee Gains Advantage from his Position as such.

(1) Where a person, being in a fiduciary relation to another, gains for himself any proprietary or pecuniary advantage by virtue of such relation, he holds the advantage so gained in trust for the person or persons to whom he is in the fiduciary relation.

(2) There is no fiduciary relation within the meaning of this section between joint tenants or tenants in common of property by virtue merely of the joint tenancy or tenancy in common.

(3) The trustee is entitled to repayment by the persons in sub-sect. (1) of this section mentioned of any costs and expenses properly incurred by him in obtaining such advantage, together with the value of any permanent improvements made to it by him, and to an indemnity against any liabilities properly contracted in respect thereof, and to a charge therefor on the trust property.

"A constructive trust," said Lord Justice Bowen in the case of *Soar* v. *Ashwell* (*a*), "is one which arises when a stranger to a trust already constituted is held by the court to be bound in good faith and in conscience by the trust in consequence of his conduct and behaviour. Such conduct and behaviour the court considers as involving him in the duties and responsibilities of a trustee, although but for such conduct or behaviour he would be a stranger

(*a*) (1893) 2 Q. B. at p. 396.

to the trust. A constructive trust is therefore, as has been said, 'a trust to be made out by circumstances.'"

The term "constructive trust," however, is used in a wider sense than is covered by this statement. There need be no trust "already constituted" at all. For instance, a vendor of land after contract but before conveyance is said to be a constructive trustee for the purchaser, as in the case of *Shaw* v. *Foster* (*b*) and other cases. Again, if one of several partners entitled to a lease surrenders the lease and takes a new one to himself, he is a constructive trustee for the others, as the case of *Featherstonhaugh* v. *Fenwick* (*c*) shows. Again, if a vendor executes a conveyance before he has received the purchase-money, the purchaser is a constructive trustee for him, as the leading case of *Mackreth* v. *Symmons* (*d*) shows, and so on.

A constructive trust is really a species of trust created by implication or operation of law, being distinguished from the other sub-class of such trusts, namely, resulting trusts, by the characteristic of being independent of any intention to create a trust on the part of the parties concerned, and the cases in which such a trust arises may be conveniently grouped under three heads:—

1. When a trustee or part owner of property gains an advantage from his position as such.

2. Persons receiving trust property from the trustees become constructive trustees in certain cases (*e*); and

3. Where in any other case the legal and beneficial interests in property are not combined in the same person (*f*).

The first of these is a class of trusts long known to the law—the cases go back nearly 250 years—but the leading case illustrating it, which has indeed given its name to the class, is the well-known one of *Keech* v. *Sandford*, decided in 1726 (*g*), and commonly referred to as the Rumford Market case. In this case Lord Chancellor King decided that a trustee of a lease who had renewed the lease in his

(*b*) (1872), L. R. 5 H. L. 338.

(*c*) (1810), 17 Ves. 298; 11 R. R. 77.

(*d*) (1808), 15 Ves. 329; 10 R. R. 85.

(*e*) See for example *Pannell* v. *Hurley* (1845), 2 Coll. C. C. 241; *Bridgman* v. *Gill* (1857), 24 Beav. 302; *Lee* v. *Sankey* (1872), L. R. 15 Eq. 204.

(*f*) See *Hardoon* v. *Belilios*, (1901) A. C. at p. 123; Underhill, Trusts and Trustees, 6th ed. 138.

(*g*) Select Ca. in Ch. 61.

own name and for his own benefit, was a constructive trustee for his *cestui que trust* of the renewed lease, although there was no proof of fraud and the lessor had declined to renew for the benefit of the *cestui que trust*. The Chancellor said that the trustee should rather have let it run out than have had the lease to himself.

"This may seem hard, that the trustee is the only person of all mankind who might not have the lease; but it is very proper that rule should be strictly pursued and not in the least relaxed; for it is very obvious what would be the consequences of letting trustees have the lease on refusal to renew to the *cestui que use*."

The ground on which the rule is based is in fact that of public policy. "The trustee's situation in respect of the estate gives him access to the landlord, and it would be dangerous to permit him to make use of that access for his own benefit" (*h*). There is a goodwill accompanying the possession of the property, as Lord Eldon put it (*i*).

It is now well established that this rule is not confined to the renewal of leases nor to trustees (*j*). It is stated in the notes to *Keech* v. *Sandford* in White & Tudor's Leading Cases in Equity (*k*) in the following terms:—

"Whenever a person clothed with a fiduciary or quasi fiduciary character or position gains some personal advantage by availing himself of such character or position, a constructive trust is raised by courts of equity, such person becomes a constructive trustee, and the advantage gained must be held by him for the benefit of his *cestui que trust*."

The following are cases in which constructive trusts of this kind have been held to be created:—

Illustrations.

1. A. by his will gives 1,000*l.* to his daughters and makes B. and others his executors. A.'s estate comprises a lease which is renewed by the executors. The daughters are entitled to the renewed lease so far as may be necessary to secure their 1,000*l.* *Holt* v. *Holt* (1671), 1 Ch. Ca. 190.

(*h*) See *Blewett* v. *Millett* (1774), 7 Bro. P. C. (Toml.) at p. 373; *Griffin* v. *Griffin* (1804), 1 Sch. & Lef. at p. 354; *In re Biss*, (1903) 2 Ch. at pp. 57, 60. See also *Pickering* v. *Vowles* (1783), 1 Bro. Ch. at p. 198.

(*i*) *James* v. *Dean* (1805), 11 Ves. at p. 395.

(*j*) See examples 2, 4, 6, 9, 10, &c., p. 120, below.

(*k*) 7th ed. vol. ii. 695.

2. A. mortgages a lease to B. B. renews the lease. A. is entitled to the renewed lease on paying B. his charges. *Rushworth's case* (1676), 2 Free. 13 (*l*).

3. A. bequeaths a lease of a market to B. in trust for an infant. B., before the expiration of the term, applies to the lessor for a renewal for the benefit of the infant. The lessor declines to grant a renewal, whereupon B. gets a lease made to himself. B. is a trustee for the infant. *Keech* v. *Sandford* (1726), Sel. Ch. Ca. 61.

4. A. and B. agree to buy property which is subject to incumbrances. Some of the incumbrancers make abatements of interest and give other advantages to A. for his own benefit. He must account for these to B. *Carter* v. *Horne* (1728), 1 Eq. Ca. Abr. 7.

5. Leasehold property is settled upon trust for A. for life and after A.'s death for B. absolutely. A. obtains an extension of the lease. She is a trustee of the extended lease for B. and cannot devise it by her will. *Taster* v. *Marriott* (1768), Amb. 668 (*m*).

6. Leasehold property is settled on A. for life with remainders over. A. applies for a renewal. X. pays her 3,000*l*. to withdraw her application. A. is a trustee of this sum for the remainderman. *Owen* v. *Williams* (1773), Amb. 734.

7. Leasehold property devolves on A. as administratrix and her infant son B. jointly. A. marries X., who thereby acquires the leasehold in right of A. X. obtains a renewal in his own name. He is a trustee for B. *Ex parte Grace* (1799), 1 Bos. & Pull. 376 (*n*).

8. A. by will gives leasehold property to his two infant children. B. by threats persuades the executors to assign the lease to him

(*l*) See also *Rakestraw* v. *Brewer* (1728), 2 P. Wms. 511; *contra*, *Nesbitt* v. *Tredennick* (1808), 1 Ball & B. 29; 12 R. R. 1; but *quære* whether this case is consistent with the authorities. See White & Tud. L. C. Eq. 7th ed. vol. ii. 702.

(*m*) To the same effect are *Rawe* v. *Chichester* (1773), Amb. 715; *Pickering* v. *Fowles* (1783), 1 Bro. Ch. 197; *James* v. *Dean* (1808), 15 Ves. 236; 8 R. R. 178; *Eyre* v. *Dolphin* (1813), 2 Ball & B. 290; 12 R. R. 24; *Rowley* v. *Ginnever*, (1897) 2 Ch. 503.

(*n*) This case was explained in *In re Biss*, (1903) 2 Ch. 40, where it was pointed out that it was as if A. herself had renewed.

and then obtains a renewal. B. is a trustee for the infants. *Mulvany* v. *Dillon* (1810), 1 Ball & B. 409; 12 R. R. 43.

9. A., B. and C. are partners. B. and C., without notice to A., obtain a renewal to themselves of the lease of the partnership premises and then dissolve the partnership. B. and C. are trustees of the renewed lease for A. in proportion to his share. *Featherstonhaugh* v. *Fenwick* (1810), 17 Ves. 298; 11 R. R. 77 (*o*)

10. A., acting on behalf of himself and his partners B. and C., negotiates with X. for a lease to be granted to the firm. X., without the knowledge of B. and C., pays A. a sum of 12,000*l.* in consideration of his procuring the firm to take the lease. A. is a trustee of this sum for the firm. *Fawcett* v. *Whitehouse* (1829), 1 Russ. & My. 132; 32 R. R. 163 (*p*).

11. A. mortgages a lease to B. and afterwards obtains from the reversioner a lease for lives renewable for ever of the reversion. B. is entitled to the benefit of the renewed lease. *Smith* v. *Chichester* (1842), 1 C. & L. 486.

12. A lease for lives renewable by custom is settled on trust to renew and subject thereto on trust for A. for life with remainders over. A. assigns to X. The assignees of the reversion having refused to renew, X. buys the reversion in fee. X. is a trustee for the remainderman. *In re Lord Ranelagh's will* (1884), 26 Ch. D. 590.

13. Testatrix bequeaths property held under a lease renewable by custom to A. for life and after his death for his children in equal shares. A. renews the lease several times and finally purchases the reversion in fee. A. is a trustee of the fee. *Phillips* v. *Phillips* (1884), 29 Ch. D. 673.

14. A. mortgages a lease renewable by custom to B. The lessor assigns the reversion in fee and the assignees refuse to renew.

(*o*) To the same effect is *Clegg* v. *Fishwick* (1849), 1 Mac. & G. 294. Compare *Clegg* v. *Edmondson* (1857), 8 De G. M. & G. 787, where the action was successfully defended on the ground of laches.

(*p*) *Hichens* v. *Congreve* (1828), 1 Russ. & My. 150; 32 R. R. 173, is to the same effect; see also *Bentley* v. *Craven* (1853), 18 Beav. 75.

A. buys the reversion in fee from them. He holds it subject to B.'s mortgage. *Leigh* v. *Burnett* (1884), 29 Ch. D. 231.

15. A. by will gives a house (*q*) which is subject to a mortgage to his daughter B. for life with remainder to her children. B.'s husband C. is entitled in her right, and in order to give effect to the will buys the house from the mortgagee who sells it under his power of sale. C. is a trustee of the house for the children. *Griffith* v. *Owen*, (1907) 1 Ch. 195.

Two questions with reference to the extent of the rule applied in these cases have lately been the subject of decision. The first is—What constitutes a fiduciary relation within the rule? Apart from the cases in which the relation between the parties is that of trustee and *cestui que trust*, executor or administrator and beneficiary, or agent and principal in which the fiduciary character of the relation is obvious (*r*), it is plain that there is a fiduciary relation between tenant for life and remainderman. The cases of *Taster* v. *Marriott* and others (example 5) and *Phillips* v. *Phillips* (example 13), above, show this. It is equally plain that there is a fiduciary relation between mortgagee and mortgagor—*Rushworth's case* (example 2), above, shows this—and between mortgagor and mortgagee—*Smith* v. *Chichester* and *Leigh* v. *Burnett* (examples 11 and 14) show this.

There is likewise a fiduciary relation between partners, as appears from the cases of *Featherstonhaugh* v. *Fenwick* and *Clegg* v. *Fishwick* (example 9), above.

This, however, seems to exhaust the list. It has been asserted sometimes that if a person interested jointly with others in a lease renews, he holds the renewed lease in trust for the others—an assertion based apparently on a passage in the judgment of Lord Bathurst in the case of *Rawe* v. *Chichester* (*s*), and the case of *Palmer* v. *Young* (*t*). But the decision of the Court of Appeal in the case of *In re Biss* (*u*) shows this to be erroneous. In that case a lessor granted a lease for seven years of a house in which the

(*q*) The report does not say whether the house was leasehold or freehold, but apparently it was freehold as no probate of the will was obtained. The testator died in 1879.

(*r*) See judgment of Romer, L. J., in *In re Biss*, (1903) 2 Ch. at p. 61.

(*s*) (1773), Amb. 715.

(*t*) (1684), 1 Vern. 276.

(*u*) (1903) 2 Ch. 40.

lessee carried on a profitable business. On the expiration of the term the lessor refused to renew, but allowed the lessee to remain as tenant from year to year at an increased rent. During that tenancy the lessee died intestate leaving a widow and three children, one being an infant. The widow took out administration to her husband's estate, and she and the two adult children, one of whom was a son, continued to carry on the yearly tenancy. The widow and son each applied to the lessor for a new lease for the benefit of the estate which he refused to grant, but having determined the yearly tenancy by notice, he granted to the son "personally" a new lease for three years at a still further increased rent. The administratrix thereupon applied to have the new lease treated as having been taken by the son for the benefit of the estate, and Mr. Justice Buckley, thinking himself bound by *Ex parte Grace* (example 7), held that he was a trustee of it accordingly. The Court of Appeal, however, pointing out that in that case the renewal was made by a person in a fiduciary position, whereas in the case before the court the parties were tenants in common who do not stand in a fiduciary relation to one another (*v*), held that the son was entitled to the renewed lease for his own benefit.

From the judgment of Lord Justice Collins (*w*) it would seem that in the case of trustees, executors, administrators and agents, and also tenants for life there is a conclusive presumption of personal incapacity to retain the benefit in such cases. But that in the case of mortgagees (and mortgagors ?) and partners there is only a rebuttable presumption of fact. The Lord Justice put joint tenants also in this category, citing *Palmer* v. *Young*, above, but Lord Justice Romer showed that from the records and registrar's notebook it appeared that that case was one of fraud, and was no authority for the proposition for which it is often cited. "On inquiry into the cases," he said, "it appears to me, as a result, that a person renewing is only held to be a constructive trustee of the renewed lease if in respect of the old lease he occupied some special position and owed by virtue of that position a duty towards the other persons interested." Such a duty is owed by tenant for life towards remainderman, by partners towards each other, and by mortgagee to mortgagor and *vice versâ*, but no such duty exists between joint tenants or tenants in common, as such (*x*).

(*v*) See *Kennedy* v. *De Trafford*, (1897) A. C. 180.

(*w*) p. 56 of the report.

(*x*) It should be noted that *Carter* v. *Horne* (example 4, p. 120, above) was not cited.

The second and more recently discussed of the two questions is—When does the purchase by a trustee of a lease of the reversion in fee simple fall within the rule? Plainly it does so sometimes, as the cases of *In re Lord Ranelagh's will*, *Phillips* v. *Phillips*, and *Leigh* v. *Burnett*, above cited, show. Does it do so always? This is the question that the court had to answer in the case of *Bevan* v. *Webb* before Mr. Justice Warrington in 1905 (*y*). The learned judge held that it only applied where the lease is renewable by contract or by custom, and he based his decision on two earlier cases, namely, *Randall* v. *Russell* (*z*) and *Longton* v. *Wilsby* (*a*). In the former a testator, being possessed of property under a lease held from a college, gave the property to his wife during her widowhood with remainders over. After his death the widow renewed the lease and subsequently purchased the reversion from a person to whom the college had assigned it. Sir William Grant held that the renewed lease belonged to the testator's estate, but that the reversion did not.

"No case," he said, "was mentioned in which this sort of equity had been carried to such a length. The ground commonly stated, on which the renewed lease becomes subject to the trusts of a will disposing of the original lease, is that one is merely an extension or continuation of the other. But the fee is a totally different subject, which the testator had it not in his contemplation to acquire or dispose of. Yet if Mrs. Russell (the tenant for life) had purchased from the college, it might be said that she thereby intercepted and cut off the chance of future renewals and consequently made use of her situation to prejudice the interests of those who stood behind her; and there might be some sort of equity in their claim to have the reversion considered as a substitution for those interests; although, as I have already said, I am not aware of any decision to that effect (*b*). But here the situation of the parties was altered by the act of the landlord without any intervention of the tenant for life. The college had aliened the property to an individual. The benefit attending the tenant right of renewal with a public body was gone. A lease at a rack rent was all that was to be expected from the private proprietor. Mrs. Russell's purchase from the first vendee wrought no change whatever in the

(*y*) (1905) 1 Ch. 620.

(*z*) (1817), 3 Mer. 190; 17 R. R. 56.

(*a*) (1897), 76 L. T. 770.

(*b*) This is the point since decided by the Court of Appeal against the trustee in *Phillips* v. *Phillips*, p. 121, above.

situation of those who had had interests in the lease as a college lease. Before she bought, it had become a lease that must expire at the end of fourteen years. Whether Mr. Hull (the purchaser of the reversion) sold or kept the reversion was a matter of indifference to them."

In *Longton* v. *Wilsby* Mr. Justice Stirling simply followed Sir William Grant, quoting the passage above set out. The matter, therefore, wholly rests on Sir William Grant's reasoning. Now it will be seen that the latter says "the ground commonly stated, on which the renewed lease becomes subject to the trusts of a will disposing of the original lease, is that the one is merely an extension or continuation of the other"; and no doubt this has been said from time to time from *Rushworth's case* downwards. But it will be observed that this is not the ground on which the rule was based in the leading case of *Keech* v. *Sandford*, or in *Blewett* v. *Millett*, *Griffin* v. *Griffin* and *In re Biss*. In all these cases it was put on the ground of public policy—the danger to the beneficiary. "The trustee's situation in respect of the estate gives him access to the landlord, and it would be dangerous to permit him to make use of that access for his own benefit," to repeat the passage quoted above. It is submitted that this reason accounts much better than the other for cases like *Owen* v. *Williams* and *Fawcett* v. *Whitehouse* above, and if it be correct it is not easy to see why it should not be applied to the purchase of the reversion as much as to the renewal of a lease. The application of the rule to the latter is not confined to cases in which the lease is renewable by contract or custom (*c*). Why should the former? Is not the danger to the beneficiary likely to be as great in the one case as in the other (*d*)?

The point urged by Sir William Grant that although if the purchase had been from the original lessors, the college, a trust would have been raised, yet, since the college had aliened the property to an individual, "the benefit attending the tenant right of renewal with a public body was gone," seems immaterial if *In re Lord Ranelagh's will* (example 12) and *Leigh* v. *Burnett* (example 14) are correct decisions.

(*c*) See per Romer, L. J., in *In re Biss*, (1903) 2 Ch. at p. 60; and per Warrington, J., in *Bevan* v. *Webb*, (1905) 1 Ch. at p. 630, correcting in this point the report of *Longton* v. *Wilsby*, above.

(*d*) Sir William Grant himself pointed out the danger in *Hardman* v. *Johnson* (1815), 3 Mer. 347; 17 R. R. 95, although next day he decided against the *cestui que trust* without giving any reasons for his decision.

Perhaps, however, this distinction between leases renewable by contract or custom and those to which no such "tenant right" is attached is not destined to prevail. At any rate, Mr. Justice Parker in a judgment discussing the principle involved has said, "If it were proved affirmatively that the purchase of a reversion had only been obtained by virtue of the purchaser being interested in the leaseholds—for example, because the landlord was giving all his leaseholders an opportunity to enfranchise their holdings—I see no reason why, if there existed on the part of the purchaser the necessary fiduciary relationship or duty, the principle of *Keech* v. *Sandford* should not be applied whether the lease were renewable of right or not renewable at all" (*e*).

When a trust of this sort is raised the trustee is entitled, on accounting for the advantage gained by him, to repayment of any costs and expenses properly incurred by him in obtaining such advantage, together with interest thereon and the value of any permanent improvements made to it by him, and to an indemnity against any liabilities properly contracted in respect thereof.

"He who seeks equity must do equity." "If," as Mr. Justice Kekewich has put it (*f*), "you insist upon a man performing his duties as trustee and making over property as trustee, you must treat him as a trustee throughout, and you cannot expect him to perform his duties without at the same time exonerating him from expenditure incurred which benefits the property of which he is trustee" (*g*).

The trustee is also entitled to a lien or charge for such expenses, &c. on the trust property (*h*).

(*e*) *Griffith* v. *Owen*, (1907) 1 Ch. at p. 205.

(*f*) *Rowley* v. *Ginnever*, (1897) 2 Ch. at p. 507.

(*g*) See *Holt* v. *Holt* (1671), 1 Ch. Ca. 190; *Keech* v. *Sandford* (1726), Sel. Ca. Ch. 61; *Rawe* v. *Chichester* (1773), Amb. 715; *Eyre* v. *Dolphin* (1813), 2 Ball & B. 290; *Ex parte Grace* (1799), 1 Bos. & Pull. 376; *Giddings* v. *Giddings* (1826), 3 Russ. 241; *In re Lord Ranelagh's will* (1884), 26 Ch. D. 590; *Rowley* v. *Ginnever*, (1897) 2 Ch. 503.

(*h*) *Rowley* v. *Ginnever*, *supra*.

SECTION XVII.—CONSTRUCTIVE TRUST FROM RECEIPT OF TRUST PROPERTY.

WHERE a person receives trust property from the trustee, and knowingly deals with it in a manner inconsistent with the trust, or knowingly assists a trustee to commit a fraudulent breach of trust, he is liable to make good to the beneficiaries any loss sustained by them as a consequence of the breach of trust as if he had been a trustee.

"It is . . . clearly established," said Vice-Chancellor Bacon, in *Lee* v. *Sankey* (*a*), "that a person who receives into his hands trust moneys, and who deals with them in a manner inconsistent with the performance of trusts of which he is cognizant, is personally liable for the consequences which may ensue upon his so dealing."

More recently Lord Justice Kay has stated the rule thus: "A stranger to the trust, who receives the trust money with notice of the trust, or knowingly assists the actual trustee in a fraudulent and dishonest disposition of the trust property, is a constructive trustee" (*b*).

"On the other hand," Lord Selborne said, in *Barnes* v. *Addy* (*c*), with the entire concurrence of the other members of the Court of Appeal, "strangers are not to be made constructive trustees merely because they act as agents of trustees in transactions within their legal powers,—transactions, perhaps, of which a court of equity may disapprove,—unless those agents receive and become chargeable with some part of the trust property, or unless they assist with knowledge in a dishonest and fraudulent design on the part of the trustees." And this statement of the law was adopted by Lord Justice A. L. Smith, in *Mara* v. *Browne* (*d*).

(*a*) (1872), L. R. 15 Eq. at p. 211.

(*b*) *Soar* v. *Ashwell*, (1893) 2 Q. B. at p. 405.

(*c*) (1874), L. R. 9 Ch. App. at p. 251.

(*d*) (1896) 1 Ch. 209.

"What is the general doctrine with reference to constructive trustees of that kind?" said Stirling, J., in *In re Blundell* (*e*). "It is that a stranger to the trust receiving money from the trustee which he knows to be part of the trust estate is not liable as a constructive trustee, unless there are facts brought home to him which show that to his knowledge the money is being applied in a manner which is inconsistent with the trust; or (in other words) unless it be made out that he is party either to a fraud, or to a breach of trust on the part of the trustee."

Again, the substance of Mr. Justice Kekewich's judgment in *In re Barney* (*f*) is that before a person can be declared a constructive trustee, it must be shown that he has actually participated in fraudulent conduct on the part of the trustee, or that trust property is [in breach of the trust, as he knows (*g*)] either actually vested in him, or so far under his control, that he is in a position to require it to be vested in him.

It seems, moreover, from the case of *Coleman* v. *Bucks and Oxon Union Bank* (*h*), that an agent receiving trust money from a trustee is not liable as a constructive trustee merely because he knows the money he is receiving is trust money. He must know that it is a breach of trust for the trustee to pay it to him (*i*).

The following cases illustrate the application of these principles:—

Illustrations.

A.—*Cases in which Stranger held liable as Trustee.*

1. A., a trustee, keeps a trust account and a private account with B. and C., bankers. A., being indebted to B. and C. on his private account, draws a cheque on the trust account and pays it to the credit of his private account. B. and C. know that the moneys represented by the cheque are trust moneys. They are liable as constructive trustees to refund the amount to the beneficiaries. *Pannell* v. *Hurley* (1845), 2 Coll. C. C. 241 (*k*).

(*e*) (1888), 40 Ch. D. at p. 381.

(*f*) (1892) 2 Ch. 265.

(*g*) These words must be inserted, having regard to cases like *Keane* v. *Robarts* (1819), 4 Madd. 332; and *Coleman* v. *Bucks and Oxon Union Bank*, above, and the statements of law quoted above.

(*h*) (1897) 2 Ch. 243.

(*i*) See pp. 254 and 255 of the report.

(*k*) *Foxton* v. *Manchester, &c. Banking Co.* (1881), 44 L. T. 406, is similar. Both cases are distinguished in *Coleman* v. *Bucks and Oxon Union Bank*, (1897) 2 Ch. 243.

2. A. and B., trustees holding a fund in trust for C. for life, remainder for D. for life, with remainder over, open a trust account with X. and Y., their bankers, and pay to the credit of the account a sum of 770*l.* D. owes X. and Y. 750*l.* on a bill of exchange, and being unable to pay it, at the suggestion of X. and Y., and without the authority of A. or B., D. draws a cheque on the trust account for the amount. X. and Y. apply the cheque in discharge of the bill. They know that the 770*l.* is trust money. X. and Y. must repay the 750*l.* to the trust account. *Bridgman* v. *Gill* (1857), 24 Beav. 302.

3. A. and B., trustees, employ X., a solicitor, to receive the proceeds of part of the trust estate from a purchaser. X. pays the money to A. alone, without B.'s authority or receipt. A. misappropriates it and dies insolvent. X. is a constructive trustee, and must make good the loss to the trust estate. *Lee* v. *Sankey* (1872), L. R. 15 Eq. 204.

B.—*Cases in which Stranger held not liable as Trustee.*

1. A. and B., trustees, employ X. and Y., bankers, to collect assets forming part of the trust fund. X. and Y. receive the assets and apply them in payment of bills drawn on them by A. and B. In drawing the bills A. and B. in fact commit a breach of trust, but X. and Y. are unaware of this. X. and Y. are not liable as constructive trustees. *Keane* v. *Robarts* (1819), 4 Madd. 332.

2. A., a sole surviving trustee, desires to retire and appoint B. in his place. He instructs X., a solicitor, to prepare the necessary documents. X. advises A. against appointing B. as sole trustee, but A. insists, and X. prepares a deed of appointment of B. as sole trustee and a deed of indemnity. Y., another solicitor, approves the deeds on behalf of C., the *cestui que trust*, after having pointed out to C. the risk of loss of the trust fund, and obtained C.'s express instructions to carry out the arrangement. B. misappropriates the trust fund. Neither X. nor Y. ever has control of the trust fund, nor have they any apprehension of any fraudulent design on the part of A. or B. Neither X. nor Y. is liable as a constructive trustee. *Barnes* v. *Addy* (1874), L. R. 9 Ch. 244.

3. A. is a sole trustee. It is arranged that A. shall not be entitled to draw on the trust account at the bank without the con-

currence of B. and C., who are to initial her cheques. A. draws and B. and C. initial cheques on the account, for purposes which, as B. and C. are aware, are a breach of the trust. B. and C. do not thereby become constructive trustees. *In re Barney*, (1892) 2 Ch. 265.

4. A. and B. are trustees, B. being the active trustee. It is suspected that B. has invested part of the trust funds on worthless securities, and it is consequently arranged that A. shall retire and X. shall be appointed trustee in his place. A solicitor prepares a deed for the purpose, which, however, is not executed. The solicitor also induces B. to take over the worthless securities himself, and eventually B. pays the whole of the trust funds in cash into a bank in the joint names of himself and X. X. and the beneficiaries ask the solicitor to find other investments for the trust moneys, and at the solicitor's suggestion they are invested on mortgages, X. and B. drawing cheques on the account at the bank, which are handed to the solicitor, who pays the proceeds to the various mortgagors. The mortgages are an improper investment, and the trust moneys are lost. The solicitor is not liable as a constructive trustee. *Mara* v. *Browne*, (1896) 1 Ch. 199.

Constructive trustees, who are such under the rule stated in this chapter, are not entitled to plead the statute of limitations against the beneficiaries, except under s. 8 of the Trustee Act, 1888 (*l*).

(*l*) See *Soar* v. *Ashwell*, (1893) 2 Q. B. 390, especially the judgment of Kay, L. J., at p. 405.

SECTION XVIII.—CONSTRUCTIVE TRUST WHERE LEGAL AND BENEFICIAL INTEREST NOT IN SAME PERSON.

IN any case not within any of the preceding sections, when there is no express trust, but the person having possession or control of property has not the whole beneficial interest therein, he holds the property in trust for the person or persons having such interest or the residue thereof, as the case may be, to the extent necessary to satisfy their lawful demands.

All that is necessary to establish the relation of trustee and *cestui que trust* is to prove that the legal title is in one person and the equitable title is in another (*a*).

Consequently, wherever this state of affairs exists without having been brought about in any of the ways discussed in the previous sections, a constructive trust arises.

Dr. Whiteley Stokes in s. 94 of the Indian Trusts Act, 1882, states the law thus:—

"In any case not coming within the scope of any of the preceding sections, where there is no trust, but the person having possession of property has not the whole beneficial interest therein, he must hold the property for the benefit of the persons having such interest, or the residue thereof (as the case may be), to the extent necessary to satisfy their just demands."

Mr. Underhill (*b*) says of this proposition that it doubtless includes all those relating to constructive trusts which have preceded it; but as it would be an endless task to enumerate every kind of constructive trust (for they are, as has been truly said, conterminous with equity jurisprudence), it seems better to call special attention

(*a*) *Hardoon* v. *Belilios*, (1901) A. C. at p. 123.
(*b*) Trusts and Trustees, 6th ed. 138.

to those classes which are most important and to bring all others within one sweeping general clause.

The following are among the principal cases of constructive trusts within it :—

(i) The case of a vendor of property who has contracted to sell it, but has not executed the conveyance. See *Shaw* v. *Foster* (1872), L. R. 5 H. L. C. 338; *Phillips* v. *Silvester* (1872), L. R. 8 Ch. App. at p. 176; *Lysaght* v. *Edwards* (1876), 2 Ch. D. at p. 506; *Clarke* v. *Ramuz*, (1891) 2 Q. B. at p. 462.

(ii) The case of a purchaser who has obtained a conveyance of the property before he has paid the whole of the purchase-money for it. See *Mackreth* v. *Symmons* (1808), 15 Ves. 329.

(iii) The case of a vendor who has received from a purchaser a deposit in part payment of purchase-money where the contract is not completed. See *Whitbread* v. *Watt*, (1901) 1 Ch. 911, affirmed by C. A., (1902) 1 Ch. 135.

(iv) The case of an owner of property who has created an equitable mortgage of it. See *Russel* v. *Russel* (1783), 1 Bro. Ch. Ca. 269.

(v) The case of a trustee for sale who purchases the trust property himself. See *Fox* v. *Mackreth* (1788), 2 Bro. Ch. Ca. 400.

(vi) The case of a debtor who becomes the legal personal representative of his creditor. See *Ingle* v. *Richards* (1860), 28 Beav. 366.

(vii) The case of a husband who forcibly takes possession of his wife's separate estate. *Wassell* v. *Leggatt*, (1896) 1 Ch. 554.

(viii) The case of an executor in respect of residue not specifically disposed of. Executors Act, 1830, s. 1.

(ix) The case of a mortgagee who has sold under his power of sale as regards the surplus proceeds. Conv. Act, 1881, s. 21 (3).

(x) The case of a tenant for life exercising the powers conferred on him by the Settled Land Acts. S. L. Act, 1882, s. 53.

(xi) The case of a partner having the legal estate or interest in property forming part of the partnership stock. Partnership Act, 1890, s. 20.

(xii) The case of a personal representative taking real estate under Part I. of the Land Transfer Act, 1897. s. 2 of that act.

Part IV.—OBLIGATIONS OF THE TRUSTEE.

Section XIX.—Duty to Perform Trust.

(1) A trustee must deal with the trust property in accordance with the terms of the trust, provided that:—

(a) Where all the beneficiaries have legal capacity to dispose of property, they may demand or assent to any modification of the terms of the trust,

(b) In cases of emergency where circumstances arise which are unprovided for by the terms of the trust, the court may authorize a departure from the terms of the trust to meet the emergency.

(2) Every person in whom the trust property becomes vested during the continuance of the trust, otherwise than by purchase of the legal estate or interest for valuable consideration without notice of the trust, is subject to the same obligation as the trustee.

(3) Where no other obligation is imposed upon the trustee by the terms of the trust he must convey or transfer the trust property to or at the direction of the beneficiary.

In the case of every active trust there are some things which the law or the directions of the settlor in the trust instrument require the trustee to do. There are other things which either the law or the trust instrument leaves to his discretion.

As to either class of things, the terms of the trust instrument override the law (*a*).

Whatever, therefore, the terms of the trust require him to do with the trust property the trustee must do. He has no option in the matter, but must perform his trust (*b*). This is the fundamental rule—the foundation stone on which the law of trusts has been built. "It overshadows," as Mr. Underhill says, "and modifies all other rules, which must be read as if they contained an expressed declaration that they are subject to any provision to the contrary contained in the settlement itself" (*c*).

This rule, however, like most other rules of law, is subject to qualifications.

The first is that *if the sole beneficiary, or all the beneficiaries if more than one, is or are* sui juris, *he or they may put an end to the trust at any time.* "For whatever modifications of the estate the settlor may have contemplated, through whatever channel he may have originally intended his bounty to flow, the *cestuis que trust*, as the persons to be eventually benefited, are in equity from the creation of the trust, and before the trustees have acted in the execution of it, the absolute beneficial proprietors" (*d*).

The second is that *in cases of emergency, or in circumstances not foreseen or anticipated by the settlor and unprovided for by the trust instrument, the court may sanction a departure from the terms of the trust.*

This jurisdiction was only definitely established in 1901 by the decision of the Court of Appeal in *In re New* (*e*), in which the court authorized three different sets of trustees to concur in a shareholders' scheme for the reconstruction of a company the shares in which constituted in each case the trust property, but directed such of the trustees as had no power to invest in shares or debentures of such a company as was intended to be formed to apply for leave to retain them beyond a year. Lord Justice Romer, who delivered the judgment of the court, said:—"As a

(*a*) Story, Eq. Jur., 2nd Eng. ed. § 1276.

(*b*) See, for example, *Deeth* v. *Hale* (1809), 2 Molloy, 317.

(*c*) Underhill, Trusts and Trustees, 6th ed. 157. Compare the Indian Trusts Act, 1882, s. 11.

(*d*) Lewin, Trusts, 11th ed. 864; *In re Cotton's Trustees and the School Board for London* (1882), 19 Ch. D. 624; see for examples, *Saunders* v. *Vautier* (1841), 4 Beav. 115; and *Magrath* v. *Morehead* (1871), L. R. 12 Eq. 491. These cases are not followed in America. See *Claflin* v. *Claflin* (1889), 149 Mass. R. 19.

(*e*) (1901) 2 Ch. 534.

rule the court has no jurisdiction to give, and will not give its sanction to the performance by trustees of acts with reference to the trust estate which are not on the face of the instrument creating the trust authorized by its terms. The cases of *In re Crawshay* (*f*), decided by North, J., and *In re Morrison* (*g*), decided by Buckley, J., are instances where the court was asked to sanction steps to be taken by trustees which it thought unjustifiable, and which it decided it had no jurisdiction to authorize. But in the management of a trust estate, and especially where that estate consists of a business or shares in a mercantile company, it not infrequently happens that some peculiar state of circumstances arises for which provision is not expressly made by the trust instrument, and which renders it most desirable, and it may be even essential, for the benefit of the estate and in the interest of all the *cestuis que trust* that certain acts should be done by the trustees which in ordinary circumstances they would have no power to do. In a case of this kind which may reasonably be supposed to be one not foreseen or anticipated by the author of the trust, where the trustees are embarrassed by the emergency that has arisen and the duty cast upon them to do what is best for the estate, and the consent of all the beneficiaries cannot be obtained by reason of some of them not being *sui juris* or in existence, then it may be right for the court, and the court in a proper case would have jurisdiction to sanction on behalf of all concerned such acts on behalf of the trustees as we have above referred to. By way of illustration we may take the case where a testator has declared that some property of his shall be sold at a particular time after his death, and then, owing to unforeseen change of circumstances since the testator's death, when the time for sale arrives it is found that to sell at that precise time would be ruinous to the estate, and that it is necessary or right to postpone the sale for a short time in order to effect a proper sale; in such a case the court would have jurisdiction to authorize, and would authorize, the trustees to postpone the sale for a reasonable time.

"It is a matter of common knowledge that the jurisdiction we have been referring to, which is only part of the general administrative jurisdiction of the court, has been constantly exercised, chiefly at chambers. Of course, the jurisdiction is one to be exercised with great caution and the court will take care not to

(*f*) (1888), 60 L. T. 357.

(*g*) (1901) 1 Ch. 701.

strain its powers. It is impossible, and no attempt ought to be made, to state or define all the circumstances under which, or the extent to which, the court will exercise the jurisdiction; but it need scarcely be said that the court will not be justified in sanctioning every act desired by trustees and beneficiaries merely because it may appear beneficial to the estate; and certainly the court will not be disposed to sanction transactions of a speculative or risky character. But each case brought before the court must be considered and dealt with according to its special circumstances. As a rule, these circumstances are better investigated and dealt with in chambers. Very often they involve matters of a delicate and private nature, the publication of which is not requisite on any good ground and might cause great injury to the trust estate."

In the later case of *In re Tollemache* (*h*), Mr. Justice Kekewich mentioned as common instances of the exercise of this jurisdiction the authorization of a trustee:—

(i) to make advances for the benefit of an infant out of capital not sanctioned by the trust instrument;
(ii) to carry on a business belonging to a testator which can only be realized at break-up prices;
(iii) to sell a business forming part of the trust property to a joint stock company in consideration of shares or stock where no power for that purpose is contained in the trust instrument;
(iv) to concur in the reconstruction of a company (*i*);
(v) to foreclose a mortgage.

But the court will only exercise the jurisdiction in cases of emergency. It is not sufficient to show that the departure from the terms of the trust proposed will be to the advantage of the beneficiaries (*j*), as indeed Lord Justice Romer said in the passage from the judgment in *In re New* quoted above. Therefore the court will not authorize trustees to take—merely on the ground that it is beneficial—an investment which the settlor has not authorized (*j*).

It is not the trustee alone who is bound by the obligations of the trust, but everyone in whom the trust property becomes vested

(*h*) (1903) 1 Ch. 457, affirmed by C. A., (1903) 1 Ch. 955.

(*i*) *In re New*, *supra*, was a case of this kind.

(*j*) *In re Tollemache*, (1903) 1 Ch. 955.

during the continuance of the trust, except a purchaser for value without notice who has the legal estate or interest.

For example, the representatives of a deceased trustee in whom the legal estate or interest in the trust property is vested from time to time are capable of performing, and bound to perform, the obligations of the trust (*k*) unless they disclaim (*l*).

Something like this has been the rule from very early times. There is, for example, a case reported in the Year Book of 14 Hen. VIII. (1522), folio 4, pl. 5 (*m*), in which Fitzherbert says: "If I enfeoff B. to hold to him his heirs and assigns, my trust and confidence are in him his heirs and assigns: and this is easily shown, for his heirs will be bound to perform the feoffor's will as much as the father, and the second feoffee as much as the first if there is no consideration." And Pollard adds: "But if [the feoffee enfeoff one] upon consideration without notice the use is changed, and if with notice though upon consideration, the first use remains; and this is the diversity."

It is plainly the law now (*n*). "No equitable doctrine is better established than this, that if the person who purchases an estate, although for valuable consideration, after notice of a prior equitable estate or right, will not be enabled, by means of the legal estate or otherwise, to defeat such prior equitable interest" (*o*).

Similarly, if the transferee of trust property, though without notice of the trust, gives no consideration, he stands in no better position than the transferor (*p*).

Further, if the transferee of the trust property, though he gives value and is without notice, does not obtain the legal estate or interest from the trustee, he takes subject to the right of the *cestui que trust;* for where the equities are otherwise equal, the first in time prevails (*q*).

On the other hand, as Lord Justice Mellish said in 1872, "when a trustee in breach of trust conveys away a legal estate which he possesses, and that legal estate comes into the possession

(*k*) *In re Waidanis, Rivers* v. *Waidanis*, (1907) 1 Ch. 123.

(*l*) *Legg* v. *Mackrell* (1860), 2 D. F. & J. 551; *In re Ridley*, (1904) 2 Ch. 774; *In re Bennett*, (1906) 2 Ch. 216.

(*m*) Ames, Cases on Trusts, 2nd ed. 283.

(*n*) Lewin, Trusts, 11th ed. 270.

(*o*) Snell, Equity, 12th ed. 29; *Le Neve* v. *Le Neve* (1747), Amb. 436; 3 Atk. 646; Wh. & Tud. L. C. Eq. 7th ed. vol. ii. 175.

(*p*) See per Cotton and Bowen, L. JJ., in *Taylor* v. *Blakelock* (1886), 32 Ch. D. 560.

(*q*) See *Shropshire Union Railway and Canal Co.* v. *The Queen* (1875), L. R. 7 H. L. 496.

of a purchaser for valuable consideration without notice, that purchaser can hold the property against the *cestuis que trust* who were defrauded by the conveyance of the trustee" (*r*).

Yet even then the purchaser must be able to show that he obtained a transfer of the legal estate or interest at the time he paid his consideration; for he cannot protect himself against the *cestui que trust* by getting in the legal estate from the trustee after he has notice of the trusts on which it is held, although he had no notice of them when he paid his consideration (*s*).

It may be that there are two exceptions to the above rule, (1) a lord taking land by escheat, and (2) a disseisor, since neither of these takes through or under the trustee, but claims by title paramount (*t*).

In the case of the lord taking by escheat, however, there is the high opinion of Lord Mansfield that he would be bound by the trust (*u*), and the tendency of modern decisions seems to be in this direction (*v*). The point is of no practical importance, however, as escheat is not likely to occur since the 30th section of the Conveyancing Act, 1881, came into operation.

The case of the disseisor of land or the converter of a chattel is more important. Formerly it is clear that he would not have been bound by a trust. It was resolved by all the judges in a case referred to them by Queen Elizabeth, that "the disseisor was subject to no trust nor any subpœna was maintainable against him, not only because he was in the post, but because the right of inheritance or freehold was determinable at the common law and not in the chancery, neither had *cestui que use* (while he had his being) any remedy in that case" (*w*). And Lord St. Leonards was clearly of the same opinion, for he says: "At this day everyone is bound by a trust who obtains the estate without a valuable consideration, or even for a valuable consideration if with notice, unless perhaps the lord by escheat. But persons claiming the legal estate by an actual disseisin without collusion with the

(*r*) *Pilcher* v. *Rawlins* (1872), L. R. 7 Ch. App. 259. See also *Dodds* v. *Hills* (1865), 2 H. & M. 424; and *Taylor* v. *Blakelock*, *supra*.

(*s*) *Saunders* v. *Dehew* (1692), 2 Vern. 271; *Allen* v. *Knight* (1846), 5 Ha. 272; *Mumford* v. *Stohwasser* (1874), L. R. 18 Eq. 556.

(*t*) Lewin, Trusts, 11th ed. 271, 274.

(*u*) *Burgess* v. *Wheate* (1759), 1 W. Blackstone, at p. 162 *et seq.*; 1 Eden, at p. 227 *et seq.*

(*v*) Lewin, *supra*, 272.

(*w*) *Earl of Worcester* v. *Sir Moyle Finch* (1600), 4 Inst. 85.

trustee will not be bound by the trust. Therefore, if I oust A., who is a trustee for B., and a claim is not made in due time, A. will be barred and his *cestui que trust* with him, although I had notice of the trust" (*x*).

This also seems to be the accepted view in the United States, where it has been held that if A., having a judgment against X., levies on and sells chattels belonging to B. as trustee for C., C. has no right of action against A. (*y*).

But the reasons given for the rule, namely, that the *cestui que use* had no remedy at common law, and that the legal title could not be determined in Chancery (*z*), does not seem to be a very forcible one in England since the Judicature Acts, and it certainly appears strange that a wrongdoer should be in a better position than a person claiming by a rightful title, and the tendency of English courts seems to be to hold a disseisor bound by equities, whether he had notice of them or not (*a*).

If no other obligation is imposed on a trustee, he must convey or transfer the trust property to the trustee, or as he may direct. "The simple trust," says Mr. Lewin, "is where property is vested in one person upon trust for another, and the nature of the trust not being prescribed by the settlor is left to the construction of law. In this case the *cestui que trust* has *jus habendi*, or the right to be put into actual possession of the property, and *jus disponendi*, or the right to call upon the trustee to execute conveyances of the legal estate as the *cestui que trust* directs" (*b*).

(*x*) Sugd., Gilbert on Uses, 429, note (61).

(*y*) Ames, Cases on Trusts, 2nd ed. 372.

(*z*) See *Sir Moyle Finch's case, supra; Ames, supra; Chuddleigh's case* (1595), 1 Rep. 120 a, at 139 b.

(*a*) See *In re Nisbet and Pott's Contract*, (1906) 1 Ch. 386. See the whole subject discussed in the *Solicitors' Journal*, vol. 51, 141 *et seq.*, 155 *et seq.*

(*b*) Lewin, Trusts, 11th ed. 16.

SECTION XX.—DUTY TO ASCERTAIN THE STATE OF THE TRUST PROPERTY AND PLACE IT IN SECURITY.

A TRUSTEE must acquaint himself, as soon as reasonably may be after having accepted the trust, with the nature and circumstances of the trust property, and (subject to the provisions of this Digest and of the terms of the trust) must, unless there is good reason to the contrary, obtain payment or transfer of the trust property to himself, and get in trust money not invested on authorized securities.

"The first duty of trustees," says Mr. Lewin, "is to place the trust property in a state of security" (*a*). To enable them to do this effectively they must, of course, first find out what that property is. Accordingly Mr. Justice Kekewich has said: "I think that when persons are asked to become new trustees they are bound to inquire of what the property consists that is to be handed over to them, and what are the trusts. They ought also to look into the trust documents and papers to ascertain what notices appear among them of incumbrances and other matters affecting the trust" (*b*).

Having ascertained what the trust property is, it immediately becomes the duty of the trustees to obtain payment or transfer of it to them, and if the trust fund is not paid or the trust property handed over to them within a reasonable time to enforce payment or transfer by legal proceedings. If they do not, they are guilty of a breach of trust. The only excuse for not taking action to enforce payment is a well-founded belief on the part of the trustees that

(*a*) Lewin, Trusts, 11th ed. 316. Compare the Indian Trusts Act, 1882, s. 12.

(*b*) *Hallows* v. *Lloyd* (1888), 39 Ch. D. at p. 691. See also Lewin, 220.

such action would be fruitless, and the burden of proving the grounds of such belief is on the trustees (*c*).

The duty of the trustee in the above respects is stated in s. 12 of the Indian Trusts Act, 1882, as follows :—

> "A trustee is bound to acquaint himself as soon as possible with the nature and circumstances of the trust property; to obtain where necessary a transfer of the trust property to himself; and (subject to the provisions of the instrument of trust) to get in trust moneys invested on insufficient or hazardous security";

and the rule is given in almost identical language in Underhill's Trusts and Trustees, Art. 33 (*d*).

The Trustee Act, 1893, s. 21 (which is a re-enactment of s. 37 of the Conveyancing Act, 1881), now provides that an executor or administrator, or two or more trustees acting together, or a sole acting trustee where by the instrument, if any, creating the trust a sole trustee is authorized to execute the trusts and powers thereof may, if and as he or they may think fit, accept any composition or any security, real or personal, for any debt or for any property, real or personal, claimed, and may allow any time for payment for any debt, and may compromise, compound, abandon, submit to arbitration or otherwise settle any debt, account, claim, or thing whatever relating to the testator's or intestate's estate or to the trust, and for any of those purposes may enter into, give, execute and do such agreements, instruments of composition or agreement, releases, and other things as to him or them seem expedient, without being responsible for any loss occasioned by any act or thing so done by him or them in good faith. It has been suggested by no less an authority than Sir George Jessel that this enactment has modified the rule above stated, and that the only question is whether the trustees have acted in good faith instead of on a well-founded belief (*e*). The section was not cited or considered in the case of *In re Brogden* referred to above, and its effect remains obscure.

(*c*) *In re Brogden* (1886), 38 Ch. D. 546, C. A.; adopted by Chitty, J., in *Re Hurst* (1890), 63 L. T. at p. 668; following Sir J. Romilly, M. R., in *Clack* v. *Holland* (1854), 19 Beav. 262. For instances of a successful defence by the trustee on this ground, see *Hobday* v. *Peters* (No. 3) (1860), 28 Beav. 603; *Re Owens* (1882), 47 L. T. 61; and *Re Roberts* (1897), 76 L. T. 479.

(*d*) 6th ed. 165, 166.

(*e*) *Re Owens, Jones* v. *Owens* (1882), 47 L. T. 61. See Underhill, Trusts and Trustees, 6th ed. 210, 212.

It is a consequence of their duty to place the trust property in a state of security, that the trustees must have the muniments of title to the trust property, as well as the securities which represent it, under their own control. They are entrusted with the custody of them, and they are bound within reasonable limits to see that the deeds are kept in a safe place and that no one can take them away (*f*).

But there is no right for one of several trustees to have the documents kept in a box which shall not remain in the physical possession of either trustee, but be placed at a bank in their joint names. Any such rule would make the administration of the trust exceedingly cumbersome. In the absence of special circumstances, therefore, the court will not order one of several trustees who has the title deeds of the trust property in his possession to concur with the other or others in placing the deeds or documents of title and securities relating to the trust in a box accessible only to the trustees jointly and deposited at a bank (*g*). And the rule is subject to the right of the trustees to employ agents in a proper case (*h*).

The following cases are illustrations of the above rule:—

Illustrations.

1. Testator gives the residue of his estate on trust. The residue includes a bond debt due from B. and C. which the executors do not call in. B. becomes a bankrupt and C. absconds, and none of the money can be recovered. The executors are liable. *Powell* v. *Evans* (1800), 5 Vesey, 839 (*i*).

2. A. assigns a leasehold public-house, with the stock-in-trade and household goods therein, to trustees upon trust to realize the sum of 800*l.* and apply it on specified trusts, subject to a proviso that so long as B. pays them 100*l.* a year until the whole 800*l.* be discharged he shall be entitled to occupy the premises. B. pays 250*l.* by instalments and then remains in occupation for four years without paying anything, when he becomes bankrupt. On a sale

(*f*) Per Kekewich, J., in *Field* v. *Field*, (1894) 1 Ch. at p. 429.

(*g*) *In re Sissons' Settlement*, (1903) 1 Ch. 262.

(*h*) See *Field* v. *Field*, (1894) 1 Ch. 425; *In re De Pothonier*, (1900) 2 Ch. 529, below.

(*i*) *Platel* v. *Craddock* (1838), 1 C. P. Cooper's Cases, 481, is similar.

of the house the trustees realize 405*l.*, and this is all they can recover. They are liable for the balance of the 800*l.* *Caffrey* v. *Darbey* (1801), 6 Vesey, 488.

3. By a marriage settlement it is agreed that 5,000*l.* consols belonging to the wife shall be transferred to the trustees on specified trusts. The trustees take no steps to enforce a transfer, and the consols are sold and the proceeds are misapplied by the husband. The trustees are liable. *Fenwick* v. *Greenwell* (1847), 10 Beav. 412 (*j*).

4. A. devises real estate to a trustee for a term upon trust to raise 1,000*l.*, to be invested in trust for B. for life, with remainder to her children. The trustee sells the term for 1,000*l.*, which is paid to him. Subsequently he becomes bankrupt and obtains his discharge. It is the duty of the trustee to prove in his own bankruptcy for the 1,000*l.*, and if he does not do so he will remain liable for 1,000*l.* notwithstanding his discharge. *Orrett* v. *Corser* (1855), 21 Beav. 52.

5. A. assigns all his property to a trustee for his creditors. The trustee allows wine and spirits to the value of 130*l.* to remain in A.'s possession, and these are eventually lost to the trust. The trustee is liable. *Ex parte Ogle, In re Pilling* (1873), L. R. 8 Ch. App. 711.

Just as a trustee is under an obligation to get in outstanding trust property, so where he is not the original trustee he is under an obligation to obtain satisfaction for breaches of trust committed by former trustees of which he is cognizant. But his obligation is limited in the same way as his obligation to get in outstanding trust property. He need not take proceedings if there is no probability of their being successful (*k*). And it would appear that, so long as he sees to it that the trust fund is intact, he has done all that is required of him. "In the case of trustees newly appointed, their liability extends to seeing that they get the trust funds into their hands; but did anybody ever imagine that their liability extended beyond that, or that they are bound to inquire into all

(*j*) *In re Brogden* (1888), 38 Ch. D. 546, is similar.

(*k*) Ashburner, Equity, 166.

the dealings with the trust fund from the origin of the trust, and to pursue every past trustee who might by any means whatever have become liable to pay more than the actual trust funds? The case I would put in illustration is this: Suppose a trust of 10,000*l.* consols, and one of the trustees, with the connivance of the other, sells out the stock and engages with it in trade; ten years afterwards he replaces it; five years after that the trustees retire, and new trustees are appointed in their place, who find the fund intact. One of the trustees is then told, 'It is all right now, but the money has only been paid in five years before,' and is told that one of the former trustees had used it in his trade. It is intolerable to suppose that the new trustee should be made liable for not filing a bill, as it was formerly, under the old procedure, or bringing an action, as it is now, against the former trustee, or his representative supposing he is dead, with the view of getting from him either the extra interest over and above the interest of the consols, or the profits he might have made from the use of the money in his business" (*l*).

(*l*) Per Sir G. Jessel, M. R., *In re Forest of Dean Coal Mining Co.* (1878), 10 Ch. D. at p. 453.

SECTION XXI.—DUTY TO EXERCISE ORDINARY CARE.

(1) SUBJECT to the terms of the trust a trustee must exhibit the same care in the execution of the trust as a person of ordinary prudence would exhibit in the management of his own affairs, having regard to the preservation of the trust property for the benefit of all the beneficiaries.

(2) Subject to the provisions of this Digest, and of the terms of the trust, a trustee who has exhibited such care as aforesaid is not liable for the loss, destruction or deterioration of the trust property.

(3) The provisions of this section apply, whether the trustee is or is not remunerated for his services.

A trustee must perform the duties which the trust instrument or the law imposes on him, but subject to this he need only exhibit the same care in administering the trust as a person of ordinary prudence would take about his own affairs (*a*).

In the case of *Speight* v. *Gaunt* (*b*), Lord Blackburn said: "The authorities cited . . . . I think show that, as a general rule, a trustee sufficiently discharges his duty if he takes in managing trust affairs all those precautions which an ordinary prudent man of business would take in managing similar affairs of his own."

In *Whiteley* v. *Learoyd* (*c*), the Court of Appeal were apparently inclined to put the duty rather higher. "As I understand it," said Lord Justice Cotton, "the rule is this: They (*i.e.*, the trustees) must take such care in conducting the business of the trust as a

(*a*) Lewin, Trusts, 11th ed. 324, 368; Wh. & Tud. L. C. Eq. notes to *Brice* v. *Stokes*, 7th ed. vol. ii. 660 *et seq.*; Underhill, Trusts and Trustees, 6th ed. 208 *et seq.* Compare the Indian Trusts Act, 1882, s. 15.

(*b*) (1883), 9 App. Cas. at p. 19.

(*c*) (1886), 33 Ch. D. 347.

reasonably cautious man would use, having regard not only to the interests of those who are entitled to the income, but to the interests of those who will take in future." In the same case Lord Justice Lindley said, "Care must be taken not to lose sight of the fact that the business of the trustee, and the business which the ordinary prudent man is supposed to be conducting for himself, is the business of investing money for the benefit of persons who are to enjoy it at some future time, not for the sole benefit of the person entitled to the present income. The duty of a trustee is not to take such care only as a prudent man would take if he had only himself to consider; the duty rather is to take such care as an ordinary prudent man would take if he were minded to make an investment for the benefit of other people for whom he felt morally bound to provide" (*d*). These observations, however, met with some criticism when the case reached the House of Lords. Lord Halsbury expressed himself "unable to adopt some observations of the Court of Appeal, which seem to point to a different degree of care in regard to the conduct of the business of a trust according to whether there are persons to take in the future or whether the trust fund is to be created for one beneficiary absolutely. The question must be the due care of the capital sum. Whether that capital sum is one in which there is a life estate only, or absolutely for the use of the beneficiary, seems to me to bear no relation to the question of the due caution which a trustee is bound to exercise in respect of the investment of the fund" (*e*). Lord Fitzgerald also said: "I am satisfied to accept, in substance, the exposition of Cotton, L. J., at p. 350 of 33 Ch. D., though it may be open to some verbal criticism."

Again, in *Rae* v. *Meek* (*f*) Lord Herschell said: "The law bearing upon the liability of trustees has been recently considered by your Lordships in the cases of *Whiteley* v. *Learoyd* (*e*) and *Knox* v. *Mackinnon* (*g*), the one coming from the English, the other from the Scotch courts. I think these cases establish that the law in both countries requires of a trustee the same degree of diligence that a man of ordinary prudence would exercise in the management of his own affairs."

(*d*) *Ibid.* p. 355.

(*e*) *Learoyd* v. *Whiteley* (1887), 12 App. Cas. at p. 732.

(*f*) (1889), 14 App. Cas. at p. 569.

(*g*) (1888), 13 App. Cas. 753.

But of course what is said here presupposes that the trustee has a right to exercise a discretion in the matter in question. In some things the law or the trust instrument leave the trustee no choice whether he will or will not do an act. They impose on him an absolute obligation. In such cases as these, if he does not perform his obligation he commits a breach of trust, and it will not help him to say that a person of ordinary prudence would have acted as he has done. For instance, a trustee must not choose investments other than those which the terms of his trust permit, though they may be such as an ordinary prudent man of business would select for his own money (*h*). Similarly, "no one would contend that a trustee might safely ignore the terms of the instrument of trust, so long as his disposition of the trust property was such as would have been a prudent disposition of his own" (*i*).

The fact that the trustee is remunerated for his services, however, makes no difference in the degree of care he is required to exhibit. In *Speight* v. *Gaunt*, it is true, Lord Blackburn said: "I think where a person is to be remunerated for what he does he ought not to accept the employment unless he has competent knowledge and skill in the business he is to transact, and may properly be held liable if he proves deficient in either"; but in a later case Mr. Justice Romer decided that the fact that the trustee was remunerated made no difference. "I see no reason," he says, "for confining the principle laid down in *Speight* v. *Gaunt* to cases where the trustee is unpaid, though no doubt some of the judges who decided *Speight* v. *Gaunt* did in their judgments refer to the fact that the trustee was not paid for his services. I think the principle ought to be applied in a proper case even where the trustee is remunerated" (*j*).

Illustrations.

1. A servant of a trustee robs his master, taking, among other property, the trust fund. The trustee is not liable. *Morley* v. *Morley* (1678), 2 Cases in Chancery, 2 (*k*).

(*h*) Per Lord Blackburn, at 9 H. L. C. p. 19. See also per Fry, L. J., at 38 Ch. D. p. 571; *Holmes* v. *Dring* (1788), 2 Cox, 1.

(*i*) Per North, J., in *In re Brogden* (1888), 38 Ch. D. at p. 554.

(*j*) *Jobson* v. *Palmer*, (1893) 1 Ch. 71. Compare, however, judgment of the P. C. in *National Trustees Co. of Australasia* v. *General Finance Co. of Australasia*, (1905) A. C. at p. 381.

(*k*) See also *Jobson* v. *Palmer*, (1893) 1 Ch. 71, *infra*, under sect. XXVII.

2. A trustee properly delivers goods forming part of the trust property to her solicitor to be delivered to the beneficiary in due course. They are stolen from the solicitor. The trustee is not liable. *Jones* v. *Lewis* (1750), 2 Vesey, 240.

3. A bankrupt's estate includes a large quantity of tobacco. The trustee employs a broker to sell it by auction. The purchase money is paid to the broker who, about ten days afterwards, dies insolvent. The trustee is not liable for the loss. *Ex parte Belchier* (1754), Amb. 218.

4. A trustee employs a stockbroker whose honesty and solvency he has no reason to suspect to buy securities of certain municipal corporations authorized by the trust. The broker gives him a bought note which purports to be subject to the rules of the London Stock Exchange, and obtains the purchase money from the trustee by telling him that it is payable next day, which is, in fact, the next settling day. The broker never obtains the securities and shortly afterwards becomes insolvent, and the trust money is lost. There being nothing in the transaction to excite the suspicion of an ordinary prudent man of business, the trustee is not liable. *Speight* v. *Gaunt* (1883), 9 App. Cas. 1, affirming C. A., 22 Ch. D. 727 (*l*).

(*l*) See other cases cited *infra*, under sect. XXVII.

SECTION XXII.—DUTY TO BE IMPARTIAL.

SUBJECT to the terms of the trust, where there is more than one beneficiary the trustee must be impartial and must not execute the trust for the advantage of one at the expense of another.

When, as is commonly the case, there is more than one beneficiary, the trustee must consider the interests of all equally. He must not favour one at the expense of another (*a*).

For example, trusts frequently provide for the payment of income to certain persons during their lives, as well as for the ultimate transfer of the *corpus* of the trust property to persons ascertained or to be ascertained, at the termination of the trust; and a trustee must, so far as is reasonably practicable, hold the balance even between the claims of the life tenants and those of the remaindermen (*b*).

Similarly, a trustee must not use influence with third parties to the prejudice of one of several beneficiaries for the purpose of coercing him into abandoning part of his rights in the trust property for the benefit of the others, even though it may seem to the trustee that the settlor has unduly favoured that beneficiary (*c*).

Perhaps the case of most frequent occurrence in which trustees have to bear this principle in mind is that in which they are asked by the tenant for life in possession, in order to improve his income, to make an investment which will probably be disadvantageous to those in remainder, even though it be one which the settlement authorizes. This request they must, of course, refuse, however

(*a*) See Lewin, Trusts, 11th ed. 741, 1065; Underhill, Trusts and Trustees, 6th ed. 175; *Ellis* v. *Barker* (1871), L. R. 7 Ch. App. 104. Compare the Indian Trusts Act, 1882, s. 17.

(*b*) Chief Justice Fuller, in W. A. Dickinson, App. (1890), 152 Mass. R. 184. "I agree as fully as it can be expressed that it is the duty of trustees to hold a perfectly even hand between all their *cestuis que trust*": per Fry, L. J., *In re Lepine*, (1891) 1 Ch. at p. 219.

(*c*) *Ellis* v. *Barker* (1871), L. R. 7 Ch. App. 104.

disagreeable the refusal may be (*d*). It often proves so disagreeable that the trustee yields, with the result that he commits a breach of trust and subsequently finds himself involved in heavy loss.

Any system of trusts which did not require trustees to act with perfect impartiality as between their *cestuis que trust* would, as Lord Macnaghten has said, only be mischievous (*e*).

The following cases illustrate this rule:—

1. Testator gives money on trust to purchase land and settle it to the use of A. for life without impeachment of waste, with remainders over; the trustees must not buy an estate with an exceptionally large quantity of timber on it, for A. may immediately cut and sell the timber for his own benefit. Suggested by Lord Eldon in *Burges* v. *Lamb* (1809), 16 Ves. at p. 187.

2. A. devises real estate to trustees in trust to sell for payment of his debts and, subject thereto, gives it to B. for life, without impeachment of waste, with remainders over. The trustees must not sell the timber on the estate to pay the debts, for this will be benefiting the remaindermen at the expense of B.; and if they do B. is entitled to a charge on the inheritance for the price. *Davies* v. *Wescomb* (1828), 2 Sim. 425.

3. Testator gives the residue of his estate in trust for A. for life, with remainders over. At the request of A. the trustees invest the fund on mortgage of land instead of in consols, in order to obtain for A. a larger income. The security turns out to be insufficient. The trustees must make good the loss. *Raby* v. *Ridehalgh* (1855), 7 De G. M. & G. 104.

4. Testator, after giving various legacies, gives the residue of his estate to trustees for division among his children. The trustees, being requested to realize the estate, sell part of the real estate to the eldest son for 25,000*l.*, because he carries on testator's business there, but leave 12,000*l.* of the purchase-money on loan to him upon various securities, and refuse to call it in, notwithstanding repeated applications to do so by the other beneficiaries. The eldest son fails and the securities turn out to be deficient. The trustees must make good the loss. *Knox* v. *Mackinnon* (1888), 13 App. Cas. 753.

(*d*) Vaizey, Settlements, vol. i. 420.

(*e*) *Knox* v. *Mackinnon* (1888), 13 App. Cas. at p. 768.

SECTION XXIII.—DUTY TO CONVERT WASTING AND REVERSIONARY PROPERTY AND THE LIKE.

(1) WHERE a testator indicates an intention that the residue of his personal estate shall be enjoyed by persons in succession, it is the duty of the trustee, in the absence of evidence of a contrary intention on the part of the testator, to convert so much of the estate as is of a wasting or perishable nature, or consists of securities not authorized for the investment of trust funds by law or the terms of the trust, and so much of the estate as is of a reversionary or expectant nature into authorized investments.

(2) The conversion must be made within a year from the death of the testator, unless it appears to be for the benefit of the estate to postpone it.

The rule above stated is known as the rule in *Howe* v. *Earl of Dartmouth*, decided by Lord Eldon in 1802 (*a*). It is, as Mr. Underhill says, only a corollary from the rule that the trustee must act impartially between all the beneficiaries. It is founded on the presumption that where personal estate is given in terms amounting to a general residuary bequest to be enjoyed by persons in succession, such persons are to enjoy the same thing in succession (*b*). It follows that wasting or perishable property, or what the law considers of too hazardous a character for the investment of trust funds, must be sold for the protection of the remaindermen, and reversionary property must be got in, in fairness to the tenant for life.

(*a*) 7 Vesey, 137; 6 R. R. 96; Wh. & Tud. L. C. Eq. 7th ed. vol. i. 68.

(*b*) Per Thesiger, L. J., in *Macdonald* v. *Irvine* (1878), 8 Ch. D. at p. 121.

Though called the rule in *Howe* v. *Earl of Dartmouth*, it had, according to Lord Cottenham, existed before that case was decided (*c*). Perhaps as good a judicial statement of the rule as can be found is that of Lord Justice Baggallay in *Macdonald* v. *Irvine* (*d*). "The rule," he said, "amounts to this, that where there is a residuary bequest of personal estate to be enjoyed by several persons in succession, a court of equity, in the absence of any evidence of a contrary intention, will assume that it was the intention of the testator that his legatees should enjoy the same thing in succession, and as the only means of giving effect to such intention will direct the conversion into permanent investments of a recognized character of all such parts of the estate as are of a wasting or reversionary character, and also all such other existing investments as are not of the recognized character and are consequently deemed to be more or less hazardous."

The rule seems only to apply to trusts in wills, and not to a settlement of personal property by deed (*e*). It may apply to an absolute gift to one with an executory limitation over to another, but the inference of the testator's intention on which the rule is based is perhaps not so strong in this case, and it is easier to show an intention that the property shall be enjoyed in specie (*f*).

The principle on which all the cases on the subject turn has often been said by judges to be clear enough; it is only in the application of it that difficulty arises.

The rule only applies in the absence of evidence of a contrary intention on the part of the settlor. It is this which has caused difficulty sometimes. But it is now "quite clear that the rule must be applied unless upon the fair construction of the will you find a sufficient indication of intention that it is not to be applied; the burden in every case being upon the person who says the rule ought not to be applied in the particular case" (*g*), and in order to decide whether the testator has expressed a contrary intention the whole will must be looked at (*h*).

The mere absence of a direction to convert is not sufficient

(*c*) *Pickering* v. *Pickering* (1839), 4 My. & Cr. at p. 296. See also per Cozens-Hardy, L. J., in *In re Van Straubenzee, Boustead* v. *Cooper, infra.*

(*d*) (1878), 8 Ch. D. at p. 112.

(*e*) See *In re Van Straubenzee, Boustead* v. *Cooper*, (1901) 2 Ch. 779.

(*f*) *In re Bland, Miller* v. *Bland*, (1899) 2 Ch. 336.

(*g*) Per James, L. J., in *Macdonald* v. *Irvine* (1878), 8 Ch. D. at p. 124.

(*h*) L. R. 18 Eq. 427.

evidence of an intention that the property shall be enjoyed in specie (*i*).

There is no direct authority as to the time at which the trustee ought to convert the property when conversion ought to be made under the rule, but it would appear that it ought to be not later than a year from the testator's death (*j*).

Mr. Justice Kekewich has said that "the conversion must take place as soon as conveniently may be, *that is, as soon as possible after the expiration of one year from the testator's death*" (*k*). But this was said *obiter*, and it is submitted that the weight of authority shows that the conversion ought to be not later than one year from the testator's death.

Illustrations.

A.—Cases in which the Rule applied.

1. Testator gives all his personal estate (subject to specified exceptions) and all his land to A. for life, and afterwards to B. for life, with remainders over. His personal estate comprises long and short terminable Government annuities. These must be sold and re-invested in trustees' securities. *Howe* v. *Earl Dartmouth* (1802), 7 Vesey, 137 (*l*).

2. Testator gives to his wife "the whole interest arising from his property, both real and personal," for her life, and at her death for his children. The estate includes a leasehold house. This must be converted. *Benn* v. *Dixon* (1840), 10 Sim. 636 (*m*).

3. Testator gives certain leaseholds to A., and gives his money in the long (terminable) annuities, and the residue of his property, on trust to pay the dividends and interest thereof, to B. for life, remainder to C. for life, remainders over. A. predeceases the testator. B. and C. are not entitled to the rents of the leaseholds

(*i*) *Morgan* v. *Morgan* (1851), 14 Beav. 72.

(*j*) See *Grayburn* v. *Clarkson* (1868), L. R. 3 Ch. App. 605; *Sculthorpe* v. *Tipper* (1871), L. R. 13 Eq. 232; *Hiddingh* v. *Denyssen* (1887), 12 App. Cas. 624; and *In re Chapman*, (1896) 2 Ch. 763. This seems to follow also from the decision in *Dimes* v. *Scott* (1828), 4 Russ. 195, see below.

(*k*) *In re Bates, Hodgson* v. *Bates*, (1907) 1 Ch. at p. 27.

(*l*) *Lichfield* v. *Baker* (1840), 13 Beav. 447, is to the same effect.

(*m*) *Craig* v. *Wheeler* (1860), 29 L. J. Ch. 374, is similar.

or the annuities in specie. *Sutherland* v. *Cooke* (1845), 1 Coll. Ch. R. 498.

4. Testator gives all his freehold, copyhold *and leasehold* estates, and all other his real and personal estate, upon trust, after payment of debts and legacies, to invest the residue; and as to one-half his freehold, copyhold *and leasehold* estates, and all the trust moneys, stocks, funds and securities, and all other his real and personal estate, on trust for A. and B. for life, with remainder over. The estate includes terminable Government annuities, annuities for years charged on parish rates, furniture and leaseholds. A. and B. are entitled to the leaseholds in specie, but the others must be converted. *Hood* v. *Clapham* (1854), 19 Beav. 90.

5. Testator gives the remainder of the produce of his real and personal estate to be placed out at interest, and the dividends and the produce thereof to be paid to his wife for life. The estate includes a reversionary interest expectant on the life of the wife. The latter is entitled to have this treated as converted [at the end of a year?] from the testator's death. *Johnson* v. *Routh* (1858), 27 L. J. Ch. 305.

6. Testatrix gives the residue of her estate to trustees in trust, as to one-third, to pay the income to A. for life, and after A.'s death to his children, and the other two-thirds to two other persons and their children. The estate comprises an underlease of a house for an unexpired term of fifty-seven years. This must be converted. *In re Shaw's Trusts* (1871), L. R. 12 Eq. 124.

7. Testator gives his residue to trustees on trust to convert and invest on Government or real securities, and to pay the income to his wife for life, with remainders over. He empowers them to continue invested any of his Government stocks or real securities, and directs that his wife shall be entitled to the interest, dividends and annual proceeds of his residuary estate from the day of his decease. The estate includes long (terminable) annuities. These must be converted. *Tickner* v. *Old* (1874), L. R. 18 Eq. 422 (*n*).

8. Testator gives the residue of his estate on trust to pay to his wife the rents, issues and profits for her life, with remainder

(*n*) Compare this case with *Lord* v. *Godfrey*, below.

over, and empowers his trustees to allow his money to remain in the same state of investment in which they shall find it at his decease. The estate includes long (terminable) annuities. These must be converted. *Porter* v. *Baddeley* (1877), 5 Ch. D. 542 (*o*).

9. Testator gives the residue of his estate, which includes at his death Egyptian bonds and household furniture, to his nephew. After the date of the will he marries, and subsequently makes a codicil, giving to his wife for her life "all the income, dividends, and annual proceeds of his entire estate," and postpones the payment of all legacies and the distribution of all estates vested in him, or over which he has a power of appointment, until after her decease, and subject thereto revives and confirms his will. The Egyptian bonds and furniture must be converted. *Macdonald* v. *Irvine* (1878), 8 Ch. D. 101.

10. Testator gives the "*rents* and profits" of his residuary estate to A. for life, remainder to B. for life, subject to certain annuities, remainder to B.'s children, giving the annuitants *a power of distress*. The residuary estate includes both freeholds and leaseholds. The leaseholds must be converted, the reference to "rents" and "distress" being applicable to the freeholds, and therefore not sufficient to take the leaseholds out of the rule. *In re Game, Game* v. *Young*, (1897) 1 Ch. 881 (*p*).

B.—Cases in which the Rule not applied.

1. Testator gives the residue of his stocks *or funds in the books of the Bank of England* to his executors on trust to pay the interest to his wife for life, remainder over; and gives his executors power to alter or vary the investments. The funds include long terminable annuities. The wife is entitled to these and the executors must not convert them. *Lord* v. *Godfrey* (1819), 4 Madd. 455 (*q*).

(*o*) Compare with *Gray* v. *Siggers*, below.

(*p*) The decision was the other way in *Vachell* v. *Roberts* (1863), 32 Beav. 140.

(*q*) Compare *Tickner* v. *Old* and *Porter* v. *Baddeley*, above, where the rule was applied. In these cases there was no specific description of the funds. See 5 Ch. D. at p. 544.

2. Testatrix (after various legacies) bequeaths to A. "the whole of the remainder of her *dividends*" during her life, with remainders over. The only stock possessed by testatrix at the date of her death is 606*l.* long annuities. This is a specific legacy, and the remaindermen are not entitled to have the annuities converted. *Vincent* v. *Newcombe* (1832), Young, Ex. 599.

3. Testator gives the residue of his estate to his executors upon trust to permit his wife B. to receive the "rents, profits, *dividends* and annual proceeds thereof" for her life; and after her death on trust to sell his freehold and leasehold houses; directing X. to be employed as auctioneer "to convert *the whole of his estate* and effects into money." B. is entitled to the income upon long annuities left by the testator. *Alcock* v. *Sloper* (1833), 2 My. & K. 699.

4. Testator gives to his wife "all and every part of his property in every shape *and without any reserve*" for her life, with remainders over. The estate includes leaseholds. The wife is entitled to these in specie. *Collins* v. *Collins* (1833), 2 My. & K. 703 (*r*).

5. Testatrix gives the residue of her property "all I do or may possess *in the funds*, copy or leasehold estates" to A. and B. for their lives, with remainders over. The residuary estate consists of 150*l.* long annuities only. A. and B. are entitled to these in specie. *Bethune* v. *Kennedy* (1835), 1 My. & Cr. 114 (*s*).

6. Testator gives the residue of his estate in trust to permit "the *rents*, issues, profits, interest and annual proceeds" to be received by A. for life, with remainders over. The estate comprises leaseholds, but no other property to which the word "rents" is applicable. A. is entitled to these in specie. *Goodenough* v. *Tremmamondo* (1840), 2 Beav. 512 (*t*).

7. Testator gives the whole of his property to his wife for life, and afterwards to be equally divided between his children. He

(*r*) See note on this case at 1 Ph. 78.

(*s*) It seems doubtful whether this case would be followed now. See per Knight-Bruce, V.-C., 1 Coll. C. C. at p. 501, and per Thesiger, L. J., 8 Ch. D. at p. 122.

(*t*) *Marshall* v. *Bremner* (1854), 2 Sm. & G. 237, is to the same effect. Compare *Pickup* v. *Atkinson* (1846), 4 Hare, 624, where the use of the word "rents" was held insufficient to take the case out of the rule; and *In re Game*, above, where there was freehold property to which it was applicable.

then (*inter alia*) gives "my house 21, North Street, St. Marylebone" (a leasehold), and "20*l*. per annum in the long annuities" to his wife. The wife is entitled to these for her life in specie. *Vaughan* v. *Buck* (1841), 1 Ph. 75 (*u*).

8. Testator gives "all the rest, residue and remainder of my freehold, copyhold and *leasehold* estates and all other my estate and effects" upon trust to pay "the dividends, interest, *rents* and profits and annual produce thereof" to his wife for life, with remainder over. The wife is entitled to the enjoyment of the leaseholds left by the testator in specie. *Blann* v. *Bell* (1852), 5 De G. & Sm. 658.

9. Testator gives all his residuary estate to trustees upon trust to sell so much as they may think necessary, and out of the proceeds and other his residuary estate to pay any mortgages subsisting at his death on his freehold *or leasehold* estates and his just debts, &c., and to invest the surplus; and to stand possessed of such investments and all other his residuary estate upon trust for several persons successively for their respective lives, with remainders over. A.'s estate includes a leasehold, which at his death is subject to a mortgage. The trustees have a discretion to permit the tenants for life to enjoy the leasehold in specie, and after nineteen years the court will not interfere with them. *In re Sewell's Estate* (1870), L. R. 11 Eq. 80.

10. Testator gives his residuary estate to trustees upon trust to sell "when in their discretion it may seem advisable," and until sale (*inter alia*) the rents and profits are to be paid to A. for life, with remainders over. The estate includes a brickfield let to a tenant at a royalty which is being gradually worked out. The trustees believe that by selling the field at a future time as building land a greater price will be obtained. They are not bound to convert it, and the whole profits belong to A. *Miller* v. *Miller* (1872), L. R. 13 Eq. 263.

11. Testator gives all his real estate and also all his "*leasehold estates*" and all his goods, chattels and credits on trust as to a moiety to B. for life with remainders over, and as to a moiety for

(*u*) *Oakes* v. *Strachey* (1843), 13 Sim. 414, is similar.

C. for life, with remainders over, giving C. power to appoint the "rents" and "*profits*" of part of her share. He gives his trustees power to vary the investments of his estate and also "*to conduct, carry on and continue the collieries he is possessed of and to increase or to abridge the business thereof.*" His estate includes some collieries held on lease. B. and C. are entitled to the whole profits of these. *Thursby* v. *Thursby* (1875), L. R. 19 Eq. 395.

12. Testator gives the residue of his personal estate upon trust for his wife for life, with remainders over, and gives his trustees power to retain any portions of his property in the same state in which it should be at his decease, or to sell and convert the same as they shall in their absolute discretion think fit. The estate includes leaseholds. The trustees need not convert them. *Gray* v. *Siggers* (1880), 15 Ch. D. 74.

13. Testator gives property upon trust for X. for life with remainders over, giving his trustees "if and when they shall consider it expedient full power to sell and dispose of all or any" of his estate. The estate includes a reversion expectant on the death of X. The trustees are not bound to convert this for the benefit of X. *In re Pitcairn, Brandreth* v. *Colvin*, (1896) 2 Ch. 199.

14. Testator gives to his wife "all my real and personal estate for her use as long as she remains a widow, and at her death all to be divided" among his children, adding "also my shares and interest in the New H. H. Mining Co. and the New R. V. Brick and Tile Co." The widow is entitled during widowhood to the profits of the shares in specie. *Stanier* v. *Hodgkinson* (1904), 73 L. J. Ch. 179.

15. Testator by his will gives personal estate upon trust for his wife for life and after her death over to others, adding by a codicil "my trustees or trustee may retain any investments belonging to me at the time of my death for such period as to them, him or her may seem proper without being responsible for any loss occasioned thereby." Having regard to these words the trustees need not convert hazardous securities, and the widow is entitled to the income so long as they think fit to retain them. *In re Bates, Hodgson* v. *Bates*, (1907) 1 Ch. 22.

Section XXIV.—Rules for Apportionment of Property which ought to be converted.

(1) Where property ought to be converted, whether under the last preceding section, or by the express direction of the settlor, it must be apportioned between the tenant for life and the remainderman in accordance with the following rules:—

Rule I. The tenant for life is entitled to the whole actual income produced thereby until conversion where the settlor indicates an intention to that effect.

Rule II. Where there is no indication of such intention, but the trustee is empowered by the settlor to postpone the conversion, or the property is not capable of immediate conversion without loss to the estate, then (a) in the case of personal property, a value must be put upon the property as at the death of the settlor, and the tenant for life is entitled until conversion to interest at the rate of three per centum per annum on the amount of such value from the day of the death of the settlor, and the residue, if any, of the income produced thereby must be invested as capital; (b) in the case of real property, the tenant for life is entitled to the whole actual income until conversion.

Rule III. Subject to the preceding rules, where property which ought to be converted is not converted, the tenant for life is entitled as from the death of the settlor to the interest on so much $2\frac{1}{2}$ per cent. new consols as the amount that would have been realized by a conversion at the end of a year after the settlor's death would have purchased.

Rule IV. Where property of a reversionary or expectant nature which ought to be converted is not converted, it must on falling in be apportioned by ascertaining the sum which, lent at interest at the rate of three per cent. per annum on the day of the settlor's death, and accumulating at compound interest at that rate with yearly rests and deducting income tax, would, with the accumulations of income, have produced at the day of receipt the amount actually received; and the sum so ascertained must be treated as capital and the residue as income.

(2) The court may from time to time increase or diminish the rate of interest under the foregoing rules as in its discretion it shall think fit.

It often happens that when property ought to be converted either under the rule in *Howe* v. *Earl of Dartmouth* (*a*), or by the express terms of the trust instrument, it is found impossible to convert it within a year from the settlor's death. Sometimes, especially when conversion is expressly directed, this is foreseen and provided for by the testator, but often it is not. The rights of the parties are then governed by a series of somewhat complicated rules according to the circumstances of the case. The following is believed to be a correct statement of these rules:—

Rule I.

In adjusting accounts between tenant for life and remainderman, the first rule is that *the tenant for life is entitled to the whole*

(*a*) (1802), 7 Vesey, 137; 6 R. R. 96; White & Tudor, Leading Cases in Equity, 7th ed. vol. i. 68.

of the income produced by the property to be converted where the settlor indicates an intention to that effect. In the form of express trust for conversion generally used by conveyancers this intention is clearly expressed. The following cases show that whenever there is a duty to convert, the intention may be inferred from the terms of the will, although not clearly expressed :—

Illustrations.

1. Testator gives his residuary personal estate, consisting partly of ships, to A. for life, with remainder to her children. He directs his executors not to sell any of his ships for seven years from his death, unless the keeping them unsold should cause loss. A. is entitled to the whole income to be derived from the ships while retained. *Green* v. *Britten* (1863), 1 De G. J. & S. 649.

2. Testator gives his estate upon trust for conversion, the proceeds to be invested and held in trust for his wife for life, remainder to his children. The will contains a power to postpone conversion, and a direction that until conversion the rents, profits, and income are to be paid and applied in the same manner as the income of the trust estate. The testator's estate consists principally of a business carried on by him, which the executors carry on with a view to its sale as a going concern. The wife is entitled to the whole of the profits of the business. *In re Chancellor, Chancellor* v. *Brown* (1884), 26 Ch. D. 4.

3. Testator gives his residuary estate amongst beneficiaries for life, with remainders over, and directs that it shall be lawful for his trustees at their discretion to continue all or any part of his personal estate in the state or investment in or upon which the same shall be at his decease, however doubtful or hazardous or limited the description or nature of the property or investment may be. In an action for the administration of his estate the Court directs certain securities not authorized by the investment clause in the will to be retained. The tenants for life are entitled to the whole income produced by them. *In re Sheldon, Nixon* v. *Sheldon* (1888), 39 Ch. D. 50.

4. Testator gives his residuary estate upon trust for conversion and investment of the proceeds on specified securities, with power

to the trustees in their absolute discretion to retain any securities unconverted, and to stand possessed of "the stocks, funds, shares and securities for the time being constituting or representing the residuary personal estate and the income thereof" upon trust to pay the income to certain persons for life, with remainder over. The estate includes redeemable American bonds. The tenants for life are entitled to the whole net income of those which are retained. *In re Thomas, Wood* v. *Thomas*, (1891) 3 Ch. 482 (*b*).

Rule II.

Sometimes, however, although the settlor has foreseen that it will not be possible to convert the property immediately, and has provided for this by giving the trustee power to postpone the conversion, he has furnished no indication of his intention as to the application of the income until conversion. Sometimes the settlor has made no provision at all, but it is impossible to convert the property immediately without loss to the estate. In these cases the rule is that *a value must be put upon the property as at the death of the settlor, and the tenant for life is entitled to 3 per cent. interest on such value from the day of the settlor's death, and the residue of the income must be invested as capital* (*c*). This rule was first formulated by Lord Eldon in the case of *Gibson* v. *Bott* (*c*), and its foundation is that, although there is no breach of trust in delaying to convert in such cases, the delay must not be allowed to prejudice anybody (*d*).

The rate of interest allowed was formerly 4 per cent. But in 1900, in a case in which the conversion of a reversionary interest was in question, the Court of Appeal allowed interest at 3 per cent. only, in view of the rate of interest which can now be obtained on

(*b*) To the same effect are *In re Bates, Hodgson* v. *Bates*, (1907) 1 Ch. 22; *In re Wilson, Moore* v. *Wilson*, (1907) 1 Ch. 397. Compare *In re Chaytor*, (1905) 1 Ch. 233, below, p. 167.

(*c*) *Gibson* v. *Bott* (1802), 7 Ves. at p. 97; 6 R. R. 90; *Meyer* v. *Simonsen* (1852), 5 De G. & Sm. 723; *Re Llewellyn's Trusts* (1861), 29 Beav. 171 (in each of which there was no power to postpone conversion, but it was impossible to convert without loss); *Brown* v. *Gellatly* (1867), L. R. 2 Ch. 751; *Cooper* v. *Laroche* (1869), 38 L. J. Ch. 591; *Furley* v. *Hyder* (1873), 42 L. J. Ch. 626; *In re Chaytor*, (1905) 1 Ch. 233 (in each of which there was a power to postpone).

(*d*) See per Lord Eldon in *Gibson* v. *Bott, supra;* and per Lord Cairns in *Brown* v. *Gellatly, supra.*

securities upon which trustees may invest (*e*), and it has since been held that the same rate must apply in a case within this rule (*f*).

The tenant for life is of course entitled to the income produced by the invested interest (*g*).

In referring to the case of *Gibson* v. *Bott*, Mr. Lewin says that although it does not appear from the report at what time the value was to be taken, according to recent cases it should have been ascertained at the expiration of one year from the testator's death (*h*). The cases he cites are *Caldecott* v. *Caldecott* (*i*), *Sutherland* v. *Cooke* (*j*), *Re Llewellyn's Trusts* (*k*), and *Meyer* v. *Simonsen* (*k*).

In *Caldecott* v. *Caldecott* the order of the court certainly was that the tenant for life was entitled to so much of the dividends and interest of the unauthorized securities as would not exceed 4 per cent. on the sums ascertained to be the value thereof respectively *at the end of one year after the testator's death* (*l*). But in that case the testator had given the residue of his estate to his executors *in trust to be by them from time to time as they should think fit turned into moneys*, and subject thereto to lay out and invest the same on trust for persons in succession, and Vice-Chancellor Knight-Bruce said (p. 322) that he could not read these words as expressing more than the law would direct or imply without them. The case is in fact almost identical with *Brown* v. *Gellatly* (*m*) so far as the third class of securities in that case were concerned. It seems, therefore, to fall rather under Rule III., below, than this one.

Sutherland v. *Cooke* was likewise a case within Rule III., below; there was no power to postpone conversion, and the property which ought to have been converted might easily have been sold, but by an innocent mistake the whole income had been paid to the tenant for life. It was argued that she was entitled only to such interest

(*e*) *Rowlls* v. *Bebb*, (1900) 2 Ch. 107.

(*f*) *In re Woods*, *Gabellini* v. *Woods*, (1904) 2 Ch. 4; *In re Chaytor*, (1905) 1 Ch. 233.

(*g*) *Meyer* v. *Simonsen*, *supra*; *In re Woods*, *Gabellini* v. *Woods*, *supra*.

(*h*) Lewin, Trusts, 11th ed. 336. This is followed by Snell, Equity, 12th ed. 181.

(*i*) (1842), 1 Y. & C. C. C. 312, 737; 57 R. R. 345.

(*j*) (1845), 1 Coll. 503; 66 R. R. 166.

(*k*) (1861), 29 Beav. 171.

(*l*) See the form of order at p. 738 of the report.

(*m*) In *Brown* v. *Gellatly*, *supra*, the testator gave his property to his trustees in trust to realize the same "when and in such manner as they may see fit," and Rule III. was applied by Lord Cairns to the unauthorized securities. See below.

as would have been payable had the property been sold at the end of one year after the testator's death, and the produce invested in Bank 3 per cent. annuities. As will be shown presently this was correct. Vice-Chancellor Knight-Bruce, however, thought there was no positive rule on the subject, and, as he had done in *Caldecott* v. *Caldecott*, allowed 4 per cent. on the value of the property at the end of a year after the testator's death.

In *Re Llewellyn's Trusts* there were two classes of property to be converted—one falling under this rule because it could not be realized immediately, and one under Rule III., below. Sir John Romilly said in the course of his judgment, "the period for ascertaining the value of the property will be twelve months after the death of the testator," but he appears to have been referring to the latter class. There was no question of ascertaining the value of the former class which consisted of unpaid balances of purchase money carrying interest at 5 per cent.

In *Meyer* v. *Simonsen* it is not stated when the value should be taken for a similar reason; the fund in question consisted of a debt of 12,000*l.* payable by eight yearly instalments of 1,500*l.* with interest at 5 per cent.

The cases cited by Mr. Lewin, therefore, do not support his statement, and it is directly contrary to the decision of Lord Cairns in *Brown* v. *Gellatly*, who says in the course of his judgment, "it seems to me that the case falls exactly within the third division pointed out by Sir James Parker in the case of *Meyer* v. *Simonsen*, and that a value must be set upon the ships *as at the death of the testator*, and the tenant for life must have 4 per cent. on such value." And this was the order actually made in the case as appears from the minutes of it given at the foot of the judgment. The statement in Lewin consequently appears to be erroneous. It is the result of a confusion of Rules II. and III.

The above rule was applied by Mr. Justice Kekewich in *Re Eaton* (*n*), but it is submitted that the decision was incorrect. The securities to be converted in that case were unauthorized, and there was no power to postpone conversion, nor was it suggested that they could not be converted without loss. The case therefore fell within the decision in *Dimes* v. *Scott* or Rule III., below.

(*n*) (1894), 70 L. T. 761.

The following cases illustrate the application of this second rule :—

Illustrations.

1. Testator gives his residuary estate upon trust to convert and hold the proceeds in trust to pay the income to A. for life, with remainder over. The residuary estate includes leasehold property which cannot be sold owing to defects in the title. A value must be set upon this, and A. is entitled to interest at [3] per cent. upon that value from the death of the testator. *Gibson* v. *Bott* (1802), 7 Ves. 89.

2. Testator gives the residue of his estate upon trust to pay the income and profits to his widow for life, with a gift over. The will contains no direction as to the conversion of his estate, which includes 12,000*l*. invested in a partnership. Under the provisions of the partnership deed the 12,000*l*. is repayable by instalments of 1,500*l*. with interest at 5 per cent. on the unpaid balances. The tenant for life is entitled to [3] per cent. on the sum from time to time remaining due; the difference between the 3 per cent. and the 5 per cent. must be invested, and the dividends thereon paid to the tenant for life. *Meyer* v. *Simonsen* (1852), 5 De G. & Sm. 723 (*o*).

3. A. by will gives his residuary estate to B. for life, with remainder over. The residuary estate includes ships. A. directs his executors to realize his estate " when and in such manner as they may see fit," and gives them power to sail his ships for the benefit of his estate till they can be satisfactorily sold. B. is entitled as from A.'s death only to [3] per cent. per annum on the value of the ships at the date of A.'s death, and the residue of the profits produced by the ships must be invested. *Brown* v. *Gellatly* (1867), L. R. 2 Ch. App. 751 (*p*).

4. Testator gives his residuary estate upon trust to sell and convert, " with power to postpone such sale and conversion as long as my trustees shall think proper, and to retain any investments subsisting at my death whether of the kind hereinafter authorized

(*o*) *Re Llewellyn's Trusts* (1861), 29 Beav. 171, is similar.

(*p*) *Cooper* v. *Laroche* (1869), 38 L. J. Ch. 591; *Furley* v. *Hyder* (1873), 42 L. J. Ch. 626; *Wentworth* v. *Wentworth*, (1900) A. C. 163, are similar.

or not," and to stand possessed of the residuary trust *moneys* and the investments for the time being representing the same in trust to pay the income to A. for life, with remainders over. The residuary estate includes ordinary shares in a company which are an unauthorized investment. A. is entitled only to 3 per cent. interest on the value of the ordinary shares at the testator's death, and the rest of the dividends must be invested. *In re Chaytor*, (1905) 1 Ch. 233.

If the property to be converted, however, is real estate, apparently this rule does not apply, and the tenant for life is entitled to the whole actual income produced by the property to be converted where the trustees have power to postpone the conversion, or are justified by the circumstances in postponing it. There is, at any rate, a series of decisions to this effect.

Illustrations.

1. Testator devises real estate to trustees upon trust, "as soon as conveniently may be after my death," to sell and to stand possessed of the proceeds on trust for several persons respectively for life, with remainder to their children. The tenants for life are entitled to the rents and profits of the real estate from the death of the testator until sale. *Casamajor* v. *Strode* (1809), 19 Ves. 390, n.

2. By a settlement *inter vivos*, real estate is vested in trustees upon trust to pay the rent to A. for life, and immediately after her death to sell and invest the proceeds, and pay the income of the trust stock to B. for life, with limitations over of the trust stock. There is no power to postpone conversion, but though there is no undue delay, the land is not sold till after B.'s death. B.'s estate is entitled to the rents produced between the deaths of A. and B. *Hope* v. *D'Hédouville*, (1893) 2 Ch. 361.

3. Testator gives his residuary real and personal estate to trustees upon trust to convert, and to pay the income of the proceeds to his wife for life, with remainder to his daughters, with power to postpone conversion as long as they shall think fit during

his wife's life. The wife is entitled to the rents and profits of the real estate until sale. *In re Searle*, (1900) 2 Ch. 829 (*q*).

It is not apparent why there should be a distinction between real and personal estate in this respect, nor is any explanation afforded by the cases, and against them there is a decision of the Privy Council, in which the same rule as in *Meyer* v. *Simonsen* and *Brown* v. *Gellatly* was applied to real estate (*r*).

Rule III.

In any other cases than those falling within the foregoing rules, except that of reversionary interests which need to be dealt with separately, the rule is that *when property which ought to be converted is not converted, the tenant for life is entitled as from the settlor's death to the interest on so much 2½ per cent. consols as the amount that would have been realized by a conversion at the end of a year after the settlor's death would have purchased.*

This rule was laid down by Lord Lyndhurst in the case of *Dimes* v. *Scott* (*s*). It is sometimes confused with the preceding rule. Mr. Lewin, for example, gives this rule, but does not clearly distinguish Rule II., above, from it (*t*). Mr. Underhill (*u*) gives only one rule instead of two. But that there are two distinct rules appears clearly from Lord Cairns' judgment in the case of *Brown* v. *Gellatly* (*v*). The residuary estate in that case comprised three classes of property—(1) certain ships belonging to the deceased which the testator had given his executors full power to sail for the benefit of his estate until they could be satisfactorily sold; (2) investments in securities which the testator had authorized his executors to retain; (3) other investments not within the power of investment contained in the will. Lord Cairns said:—

"I think that with regard to the ships the testator put them simply in the position of property which was to be converted

(*q*) *In re Darnley*, (1907) 1 Ch. 159; and *In re Oliver*, (1908) 2 Ch. 74, are similar, except that there was no power to postpone conversion.

(*r*) *Wentworth* v. *Wentworth*, (1900) A. C. 163.

(*s*) (1828), 4 Russ. 195; 28 R. R. 46.

(*t*) Lewin, Trusts, 11th ed. 334.

(*u*) Trusts and Trustees, 6th ed. 187, Art. 37 (1) b.

(*v*) (1867), L. R. 2 Ch. 751. The distinction between the rules is also drawn by Sir J. Parker in *Meyer* v. *Simonsen*, *supra*, and by Sir J. Romilly in *Re Llewellyn's Trusts*, *supra*. The two rules are also given in White & Tudor, L. C. Eq. 7th ed. vol i. 86, 87; Brett, L. C. Eq. 4th ed. 155, 157; and Gover, Capital and Income, 99, 100.

cautiously, and in proper time, and as to which there was no breach of trust in the executors delaying to convert it, but which when converted was to be invested, and when invested to be enjoyed as the residue of his estate. In that state of things it seems to me that the case falls exactly within the third division pointed out by Sir James Parker in the case of *Meyer* v. *Simonsen*, and that a value must be set upon the ships as at the death of the testator, and the tenant for life must have 4 per cent. on such value, and the residue of the profits must of course be invested and become part of the estate. Then, secondly, as to the authorized securities . . . . the tenant for life is in my opinion entitled to the specific income of the securities just as if they had been 3 per cent. consols. Then comes the third question in the case, the securities not ranging themselves under any of those mentioned in the last clause of the will. . . . I think the proper order to make is that which was made in *Dimes* v. *Scott* followed by Vice-Chancellor Wigram in the case of *Taylor* v. *Clark*, namely, to treat the tenant for life as entitled during the year after the testator's death (*w*) to the dividends upon so much 3 per cent. stock as would have been produced by the conversion and investment of the property at the end of the year."

And there is reason in the distinction between the two rules. When the trustees have a discretion to postpone conversion or the property cannot be converted without loss, the trustees are not guilty of a breach of trust in refraining from converting it. When the property could be sold, and there is no power to postpone the sale, the trustees are guilty—at least, technically—of a breach of trust in not converting it within the year; and though they may not be morally blameworthy, the rights of the beneficiaries must be regulated as if they had performed their duty and sold the property not later than one year after the testator's death. Whether this difference is sufficient to make it worth while to have two rules where one might be made to do may be open to question, but as the authorities stand the two rules clearly exist.

The following cases are illustrations of the application of this rule:—

Illustrations.

1. Testator gives the residue of his personal estate to trustees

(*w*) In the minutes of the order given at p. 760 of the report the words "as from the 6th March, 1862, the day of the testator's death" are substituted for these, and they appear to be more correct.

upon trust to convert and invest it in government or real securities, and to stand possessed thereof in trust for A. for life, with remainders over. The estate includes 2,000*l.* invested in a loan redeemable in ten years with interest meantime at 10 per cent. The trustees must account as if the 2,000*l.* had been converted and invested in consols at the end of a year from the testator's death, and any higher rate of interest than the consols produce paid to A. by them must be refunded. *Dimes* v. *Scott* (1828), 4 Russ. 195; 28 R. R. 46 (*x*).

2. Testator gives the residue of his estate on trusts for persons in succession. He gives his executors full power to realize the same "when and in such manner as they may see fit (*y*), and to invest at their discretion or allow to remain as at present invested all his funds in government and other specified securities. The estate includes stocks, shares and securities not coming under any of these descriptions, and not being proper investments for trust moneys. The tenants for life are entitled as from the day of the testator's death to the interest of so much Bank 3 per cent. annuities (*z*) as the amount that would have been realized by a conversion thereof at the end of the year after the death of the testator would have purchased at the end of the year. *Brown* v. *Gellatly* (1867), L. R. 2 Ch. 751.

Rule IV.

The above rules are not applicable when the property which ought to be converted consists of a reversionary interest or other property which is not got in until more than a year after the testator's death. In the case of such property the rule is that *when the property is received it is apportionable between tenant for life and remainderman by ascertaining the sum which, put out at 3 per cent. per annum on the day of the testator's death and accumulating at compound interest calculated at that rate with yearly rests and deducting income tax would, with the accumulations of interest, have produced at the date*

(*x*) *Taylor* v. *Clark* (1841), 1 Hare, 161; and *Morgan* v. *Morgan* (1851), 14 Beav. 72, are similar.

(*y*) These words do not amount to a power to retain the residue in its existing state of investment. See per Knight-Bruce, V.-C., in *Caldecott* v. *Caldecott* (1842), 1 Y. & C. C. C. at p. 322; 57 R. R. 349.

(*z*) The investment would now be $2\frac{1}{2}$ per cent. consols. See *In re Game, Game* v. *Young*, (1897) 1 Ch. 881, a similar case.

of receipt the amount actually received; and the sum so ascertained ought to be treated as capital and the residue as income (*a*).

Here, also, the rate of interest formerly allowed was 4 per cent., but in view of the rate of interest now obtainable on trustees' securities the court now only allows 3 per cent. (*b*).

The authorities seem to show that it does not matter in this class of cases whether the trustees delay getting in the reversionary or expectant property in the exercise of a power to postpone conversion, or because it was for the benefit of the estate to postpone it, or simply because they did not appreciate that it was their duty to get it in. In each case the tenant for life is entitled to have the income he has lost made good to him. There was a power to postpone in *Beavan* v. *Beavan* (*a*) and in *In re Chesterfield's Trusts* (*a*), but there was apparently no such power in *In re Goodenough* (*a*). There was a power to postpone in *Rowlls* v. *Bebb* (*b*), but the court held it had not been exercised. In each case the rule was applied.

(*a*) *In re Earl of Chesterfield's Trusts* (1883), 24 Ch. D. 643; following *Beavan* v. *Beavan* (1869), *ibid.* 649, n. See also *In re Goodenough*, (1895) 2 Ch. 537.

(*b*) *Rowlls* v. *Bebb*, (1900) 2 Ch. 107.

SECTION XXV.—DUTY TO KEEP ACCOUNTS AND SUPPLY INFORMATION.

(1) SUBJECT to the terms of the trust a trustee must—

(a) keep clear and accurate accounts of the trust property; and

(b) at all reasonable times at the request of the beneficiary furnish him with full and accurate information as to the amount and state of the trust property; and

(c) permit the beneficiary or his duly authorized agent to inspect and take copies of or extracts from the accounts and vouchers, and other documents relating to the trust.

(2) The beneficiary must pay the cost of obtaining any such information or of making copies of or extracts from the accounts, vouchers and other documents relating to the trust required by him, and a trustee is entitled to have such costs guaranteed before complying with any such requisition.

"It is the bounden duty of an executor," said Lord Eldon in 1817, "to keep clear and distinct accounts of the property which he himself is bound to administer" (a). There is the same great lawyer's authority for saying that this is equally applicable to a trustee in the strict sense of the word (b).

It is also the duty of a trustee to afford his *cestui que trust* all reasonable and proper information in reference to the disposition

(a) *Freeman* v. *Fairlie* (1817), 3 Mer. at p. 43.

(b) *Earl of Hardwicke* v. *Vernon* (1808), 14 Ves. at p. 510; see also per Sir T. Plumer, in *Pearce* v. *Green* (1819), 1 Jac. & W. at p. 140.

and investment of the trust property and the administration of the trust generally, and to permit him to inspect vouchers and other trust documents (*c*), and apparently to have extracts or copies of them at his own expense (*d*). And this right to information has been recognized to the extent of requiring the trustee to furnish the beneficiary with an authority to the Bank of England when the trustee stated that the trust fund was invested in consols, to enable him to verify the trustee's statement, and also to enable him to ascertain that the stock was free from any incumbrance or free from any paramount claim in the shape of a charging order or distringas (*e*).

With regard to the right to production and inspection of the trust documents, what a man is entitled to do himself he is generally entitled to do by an agent, and so the beneficiary may inspect the vouchers or other documents himself, or appoint an agent, such as his solicitor, to do it for him (*f*).

There may be circumstances which would justify the trustee in withholding the trust documents from the beneficiary, but the onus of showing them will be on the trustee (*g*). And if a trustee fails in the performance of these duties without being able to satisfy the court that he has a strong reason justifying him in his refusal, he will probably have to pay the costs of the application against him (*h*).

If, however, the trustee performs this duty he does all that the law demands of him in this respect. He is not bound to give any information to strangers. "The duty of a trustee is properly to preserve the trust fund, to pay the income and the corpus to those who are entitled to them respectively, and to give all his *cestuis que*

(*c*) Per Lord Eldon, in *Walker* v. *Symonds* (1818), 3 Swanst. at p. 58; and in *Clarke* v. *Earl of Ormonde* (1821), Jac. at pp. 119, 120; see also per Stuart, V.-C., in *Springett* v. *Dashwood* (1860), 2 Giff. 521; and *Kemp* v. *Burn* (1863), 4 Giff. 348; also per Lindley, L. J., in *Low* v. *Bouverie*, (1891) 3 Ch. at p. 99; see also Lewin, Trusts, 11th ed. 866, 867; Chandler, Guide to Trust Accounts; and compare the Indian Trusts Act, 1882, s. 19.

(*d*) *Ottley* v. *Gilbey* (1845), 8 Beav. 602.

(*e*) *In re Tillott, Lee* v. *Wilson*, (1892) 1 Ch. 86.

(*f*) See *Kemp* v. *Burn*, *supra*; *In re Cowin* (1886), 33 Ch. D. 179; *In re Dartnall*, (1895) 1 Ch. 474.

(*g*) See per North, J., in *In re Cowin* (1886), 33 Ch. D. at p. 186.

(*h*) See *Springett* v. *Dashwood* (1860), 2 Giff. 521; *Kemp* v. *Burn* (1863), 4 Giff. 348; *In re Cowin*, *supra*; *In re Page, Jones* v. *Morgan*, (1892) 1 Ch. 304.

trust on demand information with respect to the mode in which the trust fund has been dealt with, and where it is. But it is no part of the duty of a trustee to tell his *cestui que trust* what incumbrances the latter has created, nor which of his incumbrancers have given notice of their respective charges. It is no part of the duty of a trustee to assist his *cestui que trust* in selling or mortgaging his beneficial interest and in squandering or anticipating his fortune; and it is clear that a person who proposes to buy or lend money on it has no greater rights than the *cestui que trust* himself. There is no trust or other relation between a trustee and a stranger about to deal with a *cestui que trust*, and although probably such a person in making inquiries may be regarded as authorized by the *cestui que trust* to make them, this view of the stranger's position will not give him a right to information which the *cestui que trust* himself is not entitled to demand. The trustee, therefore, is, in my opinion, under no obligation to answer such an inquiry. He can refer the person making it to the *cestui que trust* himself" (*i*).

A trustee is always entitled to have all the expenses of the administration of the trust made good to him. If, therefore, the beneficiary requires any information it must be at his own expense, and the trustee or the solicitor acting for him is entitled to have the cost of obtaining the information paid or guaranteed to him before supplying it (*j*). A very good instance of the right of the trustees to be guaranteed against the cost of supplying information is to be found in the case of *In re Bosworth* (*j*). The plaintiffs, a lady and her husband, believed they were entitled to a beneficial interest under a will of which the defendants, one of whom was a solicitor, were trustees, and applied to them for detailed information with respect to the estate. The trustees replied that there was nothing coming to the plaintiffs, but offered to give the desired information if the plaintiffs would undertake to indemnify them against the cost of the necessary investigation of documents. The plaintiffs thereupon commenced an action for accounts, in the course of which they discovered that there was nothing in fact coming to them, and wished to discontinue without paying costs.

(*i*) Judgment of Lindley, L. J., in *Low* v. *Bouverie*, (1891) 3 Ch. at p. 99.

(*j*) *In re Bosworth, Martin* v. *Lamb* (1889), 58 L. J. Ch. 432; see also *In re Dartnall, Sawyer* v. *Goddard*, (1895) 1 Ch. 474.

In ordering them to pay costs, Mr. Justice Kekewich said, "What are the trustees to do? They must either do one of two things—either say 'Will you pay the costs?' which they did here, or they must either incur expense themselves, and make themselves liable to the solicitor whom they will have to pay out of their own pockets, or they must incur it on behalf of the trust estate. Why they should incur expenses to be paid out of their own pockets I cannot conceive; and it certainly would be wrong of them to incur expenses to be paid out of the trust estate unless the costs were such as ought properly to be thrown on the trust estate. Under those circumstances the reasonable course is to say, 'Guarantee us the costs, and then we shall be happy to do what is right in the matter.' It so happens in this particular case that one of the trustees was a solicitor—that is to say, the gentleman who would have to be consulted and whose costs would have to be paid. Does that make any difference? To my mind none at all. It would be extremely hard to make the independent gentleman pay costs, and I think it is extremely hard to make a solicitor give up a certain amount of his time and a certain amount of the time of his clerk and office staff to produce information for the benefit of somebody else who is not willing to pay for it. To him his time is money, and his means of earning his income, and I think he ought to be paid for information which he has to give."

It is now provided by the Public Trustee Act, 1906, s. 13, that "Subject to rules under the act and unless the court otherwise orders the condition and accounts of any trust shall, on application being made and notice thereof given in the prescribed manner by any trustee or beneficiary, be investigated and audited by such solicitor or public accountant as may be agreed on by the applicant and the trustees or, in default of agreement, by the Public Trustee or some person appointed by him: Provided that (except with the leave of the court) such an investigation or audit shall not be required within twelve months after any such previous investigation or audit, and that a trustee or beneficiary shall not be appointed under this section to make an investigation or audit."

The person making the investigation or audit has a right of access to the books, accounts and vouchers of the trustees, and to any securities and documents of title held by them on account of the trust, and may require from them such information and explanation as may be necessary for the performance of his duties, and upon the completion of the investigation and audit must forward to the applicant and to every trustee a copy of the accounts, together with a report thereon, and a certificate signed by him to the effect that the accounts exhibit a true view of the state of affairs of the trust, and that he has had the securities of the trust fund investments produced to and verified by him, or (as the case may be) that such accounts are deficient in such respects as may be specified in such certificate.

The remuneration of the auditor and other expenses of the investigation and audit must be borne by the estate unless the Public Trustee otherwise directs (*k*).

The application under the section must be made to the Public Trustee in manner prescribed by Rule 37 of the Public Trustee Rules.

Form of Trustee's Account.

The form in which a trustee should keep his accounts is nowhere prescribed. It may be assumed, however, that if the trustee keeps his accounts in the form in which the court requires them to be delivered by an executor, he sufficiently discharges his obligation.

Ord. XXXIII. r. 4, of the Rules of the Supreme Court, 1883, provides that "where any account is directed to be taken the accounting party, unless the court or a judge shall otherwise direct, shall make out his account and verify the same by affidavit. The items on each side of the account shall be numbered consecutively, and the account shall be referred to by the affidavit as an exhibit." . . . .

The form of affidavit prescribed by Ord. LV. r. 75, refers in paragraphs 1 and 2 to a first schedule in which is set forth an account and inventory of the personal estate of which the testator was possessed or entitled to at the time of his death; paragraph 3 gives particulars of the funeral expenses; paragraphs 4 and 5 refer to an account (A) of the personal estate coming to the hands of the executors or any person by their order or for their use, with the times when the names of the persons from whom and on what

(*k*) See also the Public Trustee Rules, 1907, rr. 37—39; Fulton, Law relating to the Public Trustee, 79–85; Champernowne, Johnston & Bridge, Public Trustee Act, 1906, 87 *et seq.*

account received, and a like account of the disbursements, allowances and payments made; paragraphs 6 and 7 refer to a second schedule containing the personal estate of the testator outstanding and undisposed of; paragraphs 8 and 9 refer to a third schedule containing particulars of the real estate which the testator was seised of or entitled to at his death; paragraph 10 refers to a Fourth Schedule containing particulars of the incumbrances affecting the real estate and what part they respectively affect; paragraphs 11 and 12 refer to an account (B) of the rents and profits of the real estate come to the hands of the executors or of any person by their order or for their use, with the times when and the names of the persons from whom, on what account, in respect of what part of such estate the same were received, and the times when they became due, and a like account of disbursements, allowances and payments.

Further, it is the practice of the Paymaster's Office, when the court holds trust funds and securities, to keep an account showing in separate columns on one side every sum of cash and every security received, and on the other side every sum of money paid and every security transferred.

It has therefore been suggested that a trustee's account should show, by entries made as far as practicable in order of date, all property received and investments made, and all property and investments disposed of or parted with, and all moneys received or paid by or on behalf of the trustee in respect of the trust estate, and from or to whom and on what account such moneys are received or paid. The account should also distinguish as far as practicable capital from income, and moneys received or paid in respect of real estate from moneys received or paid in respect of personal estate (*l*).

(*l*) See, generally, Chandler, Guide to Trust Accounts, especially chaps. i. and ii.

Section XXVI.—Duty not to set up Jus Tertii.

A trustee must not, for himself or any other person, set up or aid any title to the trust property adverse to the terms of the trust as between himself and the beneficiary.

It seems to be clearly established that a trustee must not set up a title adverse to that of his *cestui que trust* (*a*).

He must not set up a title for himself, because this places him in a position in which his interest and his duty are in conflict (*b*); and he must not do it for anyone else because, having accepted the trust for one, he is estopped from setting up the claim of another. It is like the case of a tenant who has accepted possession from a landlord and who is estopped from denying the title of him from whom he accepted possession (*c*).

The rule is illustrated by the following cases:—

Illustrations.

1. A. survives his wife, one of several tenants in common. He is advised by counsel that he has no right to an estate by the curtesy, since his wife has never been in possession. He commences a partition suit as next friend of his infant daughter, and under the decree the legal estate in the daughter's share is conveyed to the use of A. during his daughter's infancy in trust for maintenance, and afterwards to her own use in fee. After his

(*a*) Lewin, Trusts, 11th ed. 315; Underhill, Trusts and Trustees, 6th ed. 258; per Knight-Bruce, V.-C., in *Att.-Gen.* v. *Munro* (1848), 2 De G. & Sm. at p. 163; and in *Stone* v. *Godfrey* (1854), 5 De G. M. & G. at p. 86; and per Turner, L. J., *ibid.* at p. 92; per Page Wood, V.-C., in *Frith* v. *Cartland* (1865), 2 H. & M. at p. 420. Compare the Indian Trusts Act, 1882, s. 14.

(*b*) See the judgment of Lord Hatherley in *Tennant* v. *Trenchard* (1869), L. R. 4 Ch. App. 537.

(*c*) *Newsome* v. *Flowers* (1861), 30 Beav. at p. 470; *Neligan* v. *Roche* (1873), 7 Ir. R. Eq. at p. 337.

daughter attains twenty-one A. cannot set up his claim to curtesy. *Stone* v. *Godfrey* (1854), 5 De G. M. & G. 76.

2. A chapel is vested in trustees in trust for the Society of Particular Baptists. A dissension takes place, and part of the congregation secedes and goes to another chapel. Some years after the surviving trustees are induced, not knowing the real object, to appoint new trustees, and vest the property in them, whereupon the new trustees, who are attached to the seceding congregation, take proceedings to recover possession of the chapel. The appointment will be set aside and the action restrained. *Newsome* v. *Flowers* (1861), 30 Beav. 461 (*d*).

But if there is a doubt whether the trust ought to be executed, he may apply to the court for directions. In the case of *Neale* v. *Davies* (*e*), Lord Justice Turner said: "The trustees accepted the trusts of the settlement of 1831, but there is a doubt whether it ought to be held on those trusts. It is said that they knew of this doubt when they accepted the trusts; but I take it to be the law that if a trustee has accepted a fund upon certain trusts, and then receives information, making it doubtful whether he ought to execute those trusts, he has a right to come to the court for its direction whether the trusts ought to be executed. How is the case altered by his knowing of the existence of this doubt at the time when he accepts the trusts? It may be altered in this respect, that he may be liable for the consequences of his having accepted the trusts; but it cannot in my opinion be altered so as to bind him to apply the fund to purposes at variance with the trusts to which the fund is subject, or on which it ought to be held. Suppose a person accepts a fund on certain trusts, and then another claiming the fund under a paramount trust gives notice of his claim to the trustee, and says that he will hold the trustee personally liable if he deals with the fund in a manner contrary to the paramount trust. Could the trustee in face of such a notice transfer the fund to his *cestuis que trust*? In the case which I have put, if all the *cestuis que trust* claiming under the paramount trust were adult, the trustee might protect himself by giving them notice that if they did not within a reasonable specified time take proceedings to enforce their claim, he should proceed to distribute

(*d*) Compare *Neligan* v. *Roche* (1873), 7 Ir. R. Eq. 332, to the same effect.
(*e*) (1854), 5 De G. M. & G. 258.

the fund according to the trusts which he had declared; for then if the paramount *cestuis que trust* did not institute a suit, he would, as I apprehend, be indemnified. But where infants or unborn children are concerned, no such notice could preclude their right to assert their title to the trust fund." Lord Justice Knight-Bruce, however, dissented from this, and expressed the view that the trustees would be bound nevertheless to perform the trusts which they undertook; but the decision was in accordance with Lord Justice Turner's judgment (*f*).

(*f*) V.-C. Chatterton, however, in the Irish case *Neligan* v. *Roche* (1873), 7 Ir. R. Eq. at p. 338, thought the view of Knight-Bruce, L. J., more in accordance with the principle which the authorities appear to have established.

SECTION XXVII.—DUTY NOT TO DELEGATE THE ADMINISTRATION OF THE TRUST.

(1) SUBJECT to the provisions of this Digest, a trustee must perform the trust himself, and must not delegate any of his duties or powers either to a co-trustee or to any other person, unless—

(a) he is authorized to do so by the terms of the trust; or

(b) a person of ordinary prudence would in like circumstances employ an agent in the management of his own affairs.

(2) A trustee is only entitled to employ an agent under paragraph (b) of the preceding sub-section within the ordinary scope of the agent's business.

Trustees are a species of agents, and, like other agents, must perform their duties themselves; they are not entitled to delegate them to someone else. *Delegatus non potest delegare.* Bentham ridiculed this maxim as being founded on nothing more substantial than the harmony of the words composing it (*a*); but the idea it expresses seems reasonable enough when applied to a trustee. It is *he* whom the settlor has trusted, not anyone he in his turn may select. It follows that if a trustee employs another to do work he ought to do himself and any loss is sustained by the beneficiary in consequence, the trustee must make it good (*b*).

Illustrations.

A.—*Cases in which Trustee liable.*

1. A. is a trustee for a woman and her child, and with the woman's consent assigns his trust to B. B. commits a breach of

(*a*) Bentham, Principles of Morals and Legislation, 13.

(*b*) Lewin, Trusts, 11th ed. 276, 277; Underhill, Trusts and Trustees, 6th ed. 240; conf. Indian Trusts Act, 1882, s. 47.

trust. A. must make it good. *Anonymous* (circâ 1700), 3 Swanston, 79, n.

2. A. leaves real estate to B. and C. in trust for payment of his debts and appoints them his executors. B. and C. renounce the executorship and convey the real estate to A.'s heir subject to the trust. The latter not paying A.'s debts, the creditors are entitled to require B. and C. to pay them. *Hardwick* v. *Mynd* (1793), 1 Anst. 109 (*c*).

3. A. and B. are trustees of a marriage settlement. A. allows B. to see to the investment of the trust fund. B. entrusts it to an "outside" stockbroker, who misappropriates a part of it. A. is equally liable to the beneficiaries with B. *Robinson* v. *Harkin*, (1896) 2 Ch. 415.

But there are important qualifications to this rule. First, the trust instrument may authorize the employment of an agent, in which case the trustee is not liable for a loss sustained as a consequence of his employment, at any rate, if he has exercised reasonable care in looking after the agent (*d*). Secondly, as long ago as 1754, Lord Hardwicke laid it down that where trustees act by other hands either from necessity or conformably to the common usage of mankind, they are not answerable for losses (*e*).

"In other words, a trustee is not bound because he is a trustee to conduct business in other than the ordinary and usual way in which similar business is conducted by mankind in transactions of their own," as Sir George Jessel said, in the case of *Speight* v. *Gaunt* (*f*) —now the leading case. Or, as Lord Blackburn put it in the same case (*g*), "where there is a usual course of business the trustee is justified in following it, though it may be such that there is some risk that the property may be lost by the dishonesty or insolvency of an agent employed. The transactions of life could not be carried on without some confidence being bestowed. . . . It would be both unreasonable and inexpedient to make a trustee responsible for not being more prudent than ordinary men of business are."

(*c*) See also *Adams* v. *Clifton* (1826), 1 Russ. 297.

(*d*) See *Kilbee* v. *Sneyd* (1828), 2 Moll. at p. 199.

(*e*) *Ex parte Belchier* (1754), Amb. 218.

(*f*) (1883), 22 Ch. D. 727.

(*g*) (1883), 9 App. Cas. at p. 19.

It is in accordance with this general principle that the Trustee Act, s. 24, exonerates a trustee from liability for the act, neglect, or default "of any banker, broker, or other person with whom any trust moneys or securities may be deposited" (*h*). And s. 17 of the Act expressly authorizes a trustee (1) to appoint a solicitor to be his agent to receive and give a discharge for any money by permitting him to have the custody of and to produce a deed containing any such receipt as is referred to in s. 56 of the Conveyancing Act, 1881, and (2) to appoint a banker or solicitor to be his agent to receive and give a discharge for any money payable to the trustee under or by virtue of a policy of assurance by permitting him to have the custody of and to produce the policy of assurance with a receipt signed by the trustee.

Illustrations.

B.—*Cases in which Trustee not liable.*

1. A bankrupt's estate includes a large quantity of tobacco. The trustee employs a broker to sell it by auction. The purchase-money is paid to the broker, who, about ten days afterwards, dies insolvent. The trustee is not liable for the loss. *Ex parte Belchier* (1754), Amb. 218.

2. A trustee employs a stockbroker, whose honesty and solvency he has no reason to suspect, to buy securities of certain municipal corporations authorized by the trust. The broker gives him a bought note, which purports to be subject to the rules of the London Stock Exchange, and obtains the purchase-money from the trustee by telling him that it is payable next day, which is, in fact, the next settling day. The broker never obtains the securities, and shortly afterwards becomes insolvent, and the trust money is lost. There being nothing in the transaction to excite the suspicion of an ordinary prudent man of business, the trustee is not liable. *Speight* v. *Gaunt* (1883), 9 App. Cas. 1, affirming C. A. 22 Ch. D. 727.

3. The trustee of a deed of assignment for the benefit of creditors having to carry on the debtor's business, which is that of a watchmaker, employs an assistant. The assistant steals a watch.

(*h*) See per Lord Selborne in *Speight* v. *Gaunt*, at p. 4 of the report.

The trustee, having exercised ordinary care in selecting the assistant, is not liable for the loss. *Jobson* v. *Palmer*, (1893) 1 Ch. 71.

4. Trustees invest their trust fund on mortgage of a building estate, and deposit the title deeds of the estate with their solicitors. The development of the estate makes frequent reference to the title deeds necessary. The court will not order the trustees to keep the deeds in their own exclusive control. *Field* v. *Field*, (1894) 1 Ch. 425.

5. Testator authorizes his trustees to retain as part of the trust property bearer bonds with coupons for dividend attached. The trustees are entitled to deposit the bonds with their bankers in their joint names for the bankers to cut off and collect the coupons. *In re De Pothonier*, (1900) 2 Ch. 529 (*i*).

6. One of two co-trustees employs the other, who is a stockbroker of high standing and repute, under a clause in the trust instrument authorizing him to be employed and paid, to sell certain inscribed stock belonging to the trust, and to re-invest the proceeds in certain other inscribed stock. The latter represents that he has bought the stock, and in due course produces a stock receipt in the usual form, and pays the dividends to the beneficiary as they fall due. It subsequently transpires that the stock receipt is a forgery, and that the stockbroker has misappropriated the trust moneys, which are lost in consequence. The co-trustee is not liable, although he has not attended at the bank to accept the transfer, and although he has received a sum from the stockbroker as half commission on the purchase. *Shepherd* v. *Harris*, (1905) 2 Ch. 310.

But the immunity from liability for the intromissions of a factor or agent extends only to the acts of a factor or agent properly appointed and acting within the legitimate scope of his agency (*j*). So a trustee must not employ an agent out of the ordinary course of his business. It is no part of the ordinary business of a solicitor to choose a valuer for trustees intending to invest trust money on

(*i*) The trustees would not be justified in allowing such bonds to remain in the hands of a solicitor: per Kekewich, J., in *Field* v. *Field*, *supra*; approved by Cozens-Hardy, J., in *In re De Pothonier*, *supra*.

(*j*) Per Lord Davey, *Wyman* v. *Paterson*, (1900) A. C. at p. 289.

mortgage, for example, and if the trustees employ a solicitor for this purpose they will be liable for any loss that may result to the trust property (*k*). Nor is it proper to employ a solicitor as if he were a banker, so that if trustees leave trust moneys in their solicitor's hands instead of seeing that they are invested, and the solicitor fails, the trustees will be liable (*l*). And he must not employ an agent whom an ordinary prudent man of business would not employ to manage his own affairs. He is therefore running a great risk if he employs an "outside broker" to invest trust moneys for him (*m*).

In regard to matters of advice, even where a trustee is justified in employing a skilled agent to advise him, it does not follow as a matter of course that he will be protected because he has acted on his advice. He must still exercise the same judgment as a prudent man of business in the like circumstances. As Lord Halsbury once said, "I think it is quite clear that a trustee is entitled to rely upon skilled persons in matters in which he cannot be expected to be experienced. He may perhaps rely upon a lawyer on some matters of law, and in this case I do not deny that he would be entitled to rely upon a valuer upon a pure question of valuation. But unless one examines with reference to what question the skilled person gives advice, it is possible to confuse the reliance which may be properly placed upon the skill of a skilled person with the judgment which the trustee is bound to form on the subject of the performance of the trust" (*n*).

Lord Selborne also has said, "I cannot say that because an action is advised by counsel it is always and necessarily one which trustees may properly bring. The advice of counsel is not an absolute indemnity to trustees in bringing an action, though it may go a long way towards it" (*o*).

And it has been held that trustees are none the less liable for breach of trust if they pay the trust fund to the wrong person because they acted on the advice of their legal advisers (*p*).

(*k*) *Fry* v. *Tapson* (1884), 28 Ch. D. 268.

(*l*) *Wyman* v. *Paterson*, (1900) A. C. 271.

(*m*) See *Robinson* v. *Harkin*, (1896) 2 Ch. 415. If, however, the settlor recommends the employment of a specified agent the recommendation discharges the trustee so far as the matter of selection goes: *Kilbee* v. *Sneyd* (1828), 2 Moll. 199.

(*n*) *Learoyd* v. *Whiteley* (1887), 12 App. Cas. at p. 731.

(*o*) *Stott* v. *Milne* (1884), 25 Ch. D. at p. 714.

(*p*) *National Trustees Co. of Australasia* v. *General Finance Co. of Australasia*, (1905) A. C. 373.

Section XXVIII.—Duty of Co-Trustees to act jointly.

(1) Where there is more than one trustee, all must join in performing the trust unless the terms of the trust otherwise provide, or the court otherwise orders.

(2) This section does not apply to legal personal representatives acting in the administration of a deceased person's estate.

Where there are more trustees than one, they must all join in performing the trust. This follows from the rule that a trustee cannot delegate his duty, for if they do not all perform the trust one or more must be delegating. It is common enough to hear one of several co-trustees spoken of as the "acting trustee," meaning the trustee who really performs the duties of the trust and whose decisions are merely indorsed by the others. But the courts do not recognize any such distinction (*a*).

"The reason why more than one trustee is appointed is that they shall take care that the [trust property or] moneys shall not get into the hands of one of them alone, that they shall take care that the trust [property or] moneys are always under the power or control of every one of them, and they have no right as between themselves and the *cestuis que trust*, unless the circumstances are such as to make it imperatively necessary to do so, to authorize one of them to receive the [property or] moneys" (*b*).

Illustrations.

1. Testator appoints A., B. and C. trustees of his will. A. and B. ask C. to concur with them in making certain investments of

(*a*) Lewin, Trusts, 11th ed. 284; Underhill, Trusts and Trustees, 6th ed. 254; conf. Indian Trusts Act, 1882, s. 48.

(*b*) Kay, J., in *In re Flower and the Metropolitan Board of Works* (1884), 27 Ch. D. at pp. 596, 597.

the trust property. C. refuses to concur. A. and B. are not entitled to make the investments. *Swale* v. *Swale* (1856), 22 Beav. 584.

2. Testator gives real estate to A. and B. on trusts authorizing them to sell all or any part at the request of the beneficiary in possession, or in case he should be under twenty-one, of his guardian. The guardian requests the trustees to sell part of the real estate. A. consents, but B. refuses. No sale can be had, and the court will not interfere. *Marquis Camden* v. *Murray* (1880), 16 Ch. D. 161.

3. Trustees of real estate sell it. They must all attend personally to receive the purchase-money from the purchaser or direct it to be paid to their joint account at a bank. *In re Flower and the Metropolitan Board of Works* (1884), 27 Ch. D. 592 (*c*).

4. Four trustees have power to postpone the conversion or getting in of part of the trust estate. If one of the four does not agree to the retention of any of the securities they must be converted. *In re Roth, Goldberger* v. *Roth* (1896), 74 L. T. 50.

The rule is not applicable to co-executors or co-administrators administering the estate of a deceased person whose authority is joint and several (*d*).

(*c*) They may also now authorize their solicitor to receive the purchase-money under s. 56 of the Conveyancing Act, 1881, as read with s. 17 of the Trustee Act, 1893.

(*d*) Williams, Executors, 10th ed. 715 *et seq.*

Part V.—INVESTMENT OF TRUST FUNDS.

Section XXIX.—Authorized Investments.

A trustee may, unless expressly forbidden by the instrument (if any) creating the trust, invest any trust funds in his hands, whether at the time in a state of investment or not, in manner following: that is to say—

(a) In any of the parliamentary stocks or public funds or government securities of the United Kingdom:

(b) On real or heritable securities in Great Britain or Ireland:

(c) In the stock of the Bank of England or the Bank of Ireland:

(d) In India Three-and-a-half per cent. stock and India Three per cent. stock, or in any other capital stock which may at any time hereafter be issued by the Secretary of State in Council of India under the authority of act of parliament, and charged on the revenues of India:

(dd) In any colonial stock which is registered in the United Kingdom in accordance with the provisions of the Colonial Stock Acts, 1877 and 1892, as amended by the Colonial Stock Act, 1900, and with respect to which there have been observed such conditions (if any) as the Treasury may by order notified in the *London Gazette* prescribe :

(e) In any securities the interest of which is for the time being guaranteed by parliament :

(f) In consolidated stock created by the Metropolitan Board of Works or by the London County Council, or in debenture stock created by the Receiver for the Metropolitan Police District :

(g) In the debenture or rentcharge or guaranteed or preference stock of any railway company in Great Britain or Ireland incorporated by special act of parliament, and having during each of the ten years last past before the date of investment paid a dividend at the rate of not less than three per centum per annum on its ordinary stock :

(h) In the stock of any railway or canal company in Great Britain or Ireland whose undertaking is leased in perpetuity or for a term of not less than two hundred years at a fixed rental to any such railway company as is mentioned in sub-section (g) either alone or jointly with any other railway company :

(i) In the debenture stock of any railway company in India the interest on which is paid or guaranteed by the Secretary of State in Council of India:

(j) In the "B" annuities of the Eastern Bengal, the East Indian, and the Scinde, Punjaub and Delhi Railways, and any like annuities which may at any time hereafter be created on the purchase of any other railway by the Secretary of State in Council of India, and charged on the revenues of India, and which may be authorized by act of parliament to be accepted by trustees in lieu of any stock held by them in the purchased railway; also in deferred annuities comprised in the register of holders of annuity class D, and annuities comprised in the register of annuitants class C, of the East Indian Railway Company:

(k) In the stock of any railway company in India upon which a fixed or minimum dividend in sterling is paid or guaranteed by the Secretary of State in Council of India, or upon the capital of which the interest is so guaranteed:

(l) In the debenture or guaranteed or preference stock of any company in Great Britain or Ireland, established for the supply of water for profit, and incorporated by special act of parliament or by royal charter and having during each of the ten years last past before the date of investment paid a dividend of not less than five pounds per centum on its ordinary stock:

(m) In nominal or inscribed stock issued or to be issued by the corporation of any municipal borough having according to the returns of the last census prior to the date of investment a population exceeding fifty thousand, or by any county council, under the authority of any act of parliament or provisional order:

(n) In nominal or inscribed stock issued or to be issued by any commissioners incorporated by act of parliament for the purpose of supplying water and having a compulsory power of levying rates over an area having, according to the returns of the last census, prior to the date of investment, a population exceeding fifty thousand, provided that during each of the ten years last past before the date of investment the rates levied by such commissioners shall not have exceeded eighty per centum of the amount authorized by law to be levied:

(nn) In Metropolitan Water Stock issued by the Metropolitan Water Board:

(o) In any of the stocks, funds or securities for the time being authorized for the investment of cash under the control or subject to the order of the High Court,

and may also from time to time vary any such investment (*a*).

(*a*) Trustee Act, 1893, s. 1, as extended by the Colonial Stock Act, 1900, s. 2, and the Metropolis Water Act, 1902, s. 17 (4).

Whenever a trustee has money in his hands which he cannot apply to the purposes of the trust within a reasonably short time of its receipt, it is his duty to make the fund productive to the beneficiary by the investment of it (*b*).

In the absence of a special authority conferred by the trust instrument, a trustee was formerly only entitled to invest in government securities. He could not even safely invest on mortgage of real estate, for although some of the chancellors, including Lord Hardwicke (*c*), appear to have thought such a mortgage a proper investment, Lord Thurlow held it to be improper in the year 1785 (*d*), and his view was generally approved (*e*). Nor could he invest in Bank of England stock. "Bank stock," said Lord Eldon, "is as safe, I trust and believe, as any government security, but it is not government security, and therefore this court does not lay out or leave property in Bank stock; and what this court will decree it expects from trustees" (*f*).

However, it became common to confer on trustees a power to invest on mortgage of real estate and other securities by the terms of the instrument creating the trust, and the range of investments has been gradually extended by the legislature until it is now very wide.

First, by s. 32 of the Law of Property Amendment Act, 1859, commonly called Lord St. Leonards' Act, when not expressly forbidden by the trust instrument they were authorized to invest on real securities in any part of the United Kingdom, or on the stock of the Bank of England or Ireland, or on East India Stock.

This was made retrospective by the Law of Property Amendment Act, 1860, s. 12, and by s. 11 of the same act trustees "having power to invest their trust funds upon government securities, or upon parliamentary stocks, funds, or securities or any of them," were authorized to invest them in any of the stocks, funds, or securities in which cash in court might be invested.

In addition to these, by the statute 30 & 31 Vict. c. 132, s. 2, they were authorized to invest in any securities the interest of which was guaranteed by parliament; by the Debenture Stock

(*b*) Lewin, Trusts, 11th ed. 339.

(*c*) See *Knight* v. *Plymouth* (1747), 1 Dick. at p. 126.

(*d*) *Ex parte Cathorpe* (1785), 1 Cox, Eq. Ca. 182.

(*e*) Ames, Cases on Trusts, 2nd ed. 485; Lewin, Trusts, 11th ed. 342.

(*f*) *Howe* v. *Earl of Dartmouth* (1802), 7 Ves. 137; 6 R. R. 96.

Act, 1871, trustees having power to invest in the mortgages or bonds of any railway or other company were authorized to invest in the debenture stock of such company; by the Metropolitan Board of Works (Loans) Act, 1871, they were authorized to invest in the consolidated stock of the Metropolitan Board of Works; and by the Local Loans Act, 1875, s. 27, if authorized to invest in the debentures or debenture stock of any railway or other company, they were authorized to invest in the nominal debentures or nominal debenture stock issued under that act by any local authority.

All of these enactments, except those of the Debenture Stock Act, 1871, and the Local Loans Act, 1875, were repealed and re-enacted by the Trust Investment Act, 1889, which added a number of other investments, but was itself repealed (with immaterial exceptions), together with the sections of the acts of 1871 and 1875, by the Trustee Act, 1893, s. 51, for the purpose of being re-enacted in s. 1 of that act.

Finally, the act of 1893 has been still further extended by the Colonial Stock Act, 1900, s. 2 of which authorizes a trustee to invest in any colonial stock which is registered in the United Kingdom in accordance with the provisions of the Colonial Stock Acts, 1877 and 1892, as amended by the act, and by the Metropolis Water Act, 1902, which adds Metropolitan Water Stock to the list of investments.

The complete list of securities authorized by these statutes is set out in large type above.

It will be observed that a trustee may invest in any of the specified securities, "unless *expressly* forbidden by the instrument (if any) creating the trust." Therefore, even though a settlor directs his trustees to invest the trust fund in a particular way, they are entitled to invest in any of the securities specified in the act, since in such a case they are only impliedly, and not expressly, forbidden (*g*).

The expression—

Parliamentary stocks or public funds or Government securities of the United Kingdom

comprises the

Two and a Half per Cent. Consolidated Stock known as "Consols":

(*g*) *In re Burke*, (1908) 2 Ch. 248.

Two and Three Quarters per Cent. Stock or Two and Three Quarters per Cent. Annuities:

Two and a Half per Cent. Stock or Two and a Half per Cent. Annuities:

Two and Three Quarters per Cent. National War Loan:

Terminable Annuities:

Exchequer Bonds:

Local Loans Stock:

Guaranteed Two and Three Quarters per Cent. Land Stock (Ireland).

Guaranteed Two and Three Quarters per Cent. Stock issued under the Irish Land Act, 1903 (*h*).

Of these terminable annuities are not to be obtained on the open market, and even if they were, could seldom, if ever, be a proper investment for trust money (*i*).

The power to invest on

Real or heritable securities in Great Britain or Ireland

does not authorize a purchase of real estate but only a mortgage of it (*j*). By s. 5 of the Trustee Act, 1893, a power to invest in real securities authorizes an investment on mortgage of leaseholds of the kind specified in the section. The power to invest on a mortgage of real estate is, however, subject to some limitations. For example, in the absence of an express authority, it is a breach of trust for trustees to invest on a contributory mortgage (*k*), and it is probably a breach of trust to invest the trust moneys on a second mortgage. It has indeed been held that a trustee who advances money on a second mortgage is not necessarily liable for a loss arising therefrom; although to escape liability he will have to show that the security was a proper one (*l*), but having regard to the judgments of the Court of Appeal in the case of *Chapman* v. *Browne* (*m*), this is very doubtful, and it would be unsafe for a trustee to rely on it.

There is nothing, however, to prevent a trustee from investing

(*h*) Ellissen, Trust Investments, 2, 3.

(*i*) See Champernowne and Johnston, Trustee Acts, 19.

(*j*) *Ouseley* v. *Anstruther* (1847), 10 Beav. 456.

(*k*) *Webb* v. *Jonas* (1888), 39 Ch. D. 660.

(*l*) *Want* v. *Campain* (1893), 9 Times L. R. 254.

(*m*) (1902) 1 Ch. 785. See at pp. 796, and 800 to 804.

trust funds on a sub-mortgage, *i.e.*, a mortgage of a mortgage, since he gets the legal estate in the property the subject of the mortgages, and (since 1881) all the powers of the original mortgagee, with the additional security of a covenant for repayment from him as well as from the original mortgagor (*n*).

The truth of the matter is that where an investment on real security made by a trustee is impeached by the beneficiary the trustee must show not only that it is an authorized investment but a proper one. In the case of *Learoyd* v. *Whiteley*, in the House of Lords (*o*), Lord Watson said, "as a general rule the law requires of a trustee no higher degree of diligence in the execution of his office than a man of ordinary prudence would exercise in the management of his own private affairs. Yet he is not allowed the same discretion in investing the moneys of the trust as if he were a person dealing with his own estate. It is the duty of the trustee to confine himself to the class of security authorized, and likewise to avoid all investments of that class which are attended with hazard" (*p*). There is hazard in both a contributory and a second mortgage, but none in a sub-mortgage.

Colonial Stock.

As stated above, power for trustees to invest on colonial stocks was added by the Colonial Stock Act, 1900, s. 2. The restrictions mentioned in s. 2, sub-s. (2), of the Trustee Act, 1893, stated below, with respect to the stocks therein referred to apply to colonial stock. The Treasury is to keep a list of any colonial stocks in respect of which the provisions of the act are for the time being complied with, and to publish the list in the *London* and *Edinburgh Gazettes*, and in such other manner as may give the public full information on the subject. Lists have been published in the *Gazette* from time to time.

Debenture, &c. . . Stock of any Railway Company . . . .

By the Rules of the Supreme Court, Ord. XXII. r. 17, funds in court may be invested in debenture, preference, guaranteed or rent-charge stocks of railways in Great Britain or Ireland having

(*n*) *Smethurst* v. *Hastings* (1885), 30 Ch. D. 490; Conv. Act, 1881, ss. 19—24.

(*o*) (1887), 12 App. Cas. at p. 733.

(*p*) See also the remarks of Cotton and Lindley, L. JJ., in the Court of Appeal in the same case (33 Ch. D. 347), quoted above under Sect. XXI.

for ten years next before the date of investment paid a dividend on ordinary stock or shares, and as, under par. (o), these investments are open to trustees they will be safe so long as Ord. XXII. r. 17, remains in force, even though the railway company has paid a less dividend than 3 per cent. on its ordinary stock, provided that some dividend has been paid on it for the ten years before the date of the investment.

Where a trustee invests the trust funds in the stock of a railway company under this section, which subsequently ceases to be an authorized security by failure of the company to pay a dividend on the ordinary stock, he is not liable for continuing to hold the stock (*q*).

Metropolitan Water Stock.

The Metropolitan Water Board was created by the Metropolis Water Act, 1902, s. 1, for the purpose of acquiring and carrying on the undertakings of the metropolitan water companies mentioned in the first schedule to the act, and power was conferred on the Board by s. 17 to create a sufficient amount of stock to be called Metropolitan Water Stock, and in the act referred to as water stock as the Board, with the consent of the Local Government Board, and after consultation with the Governor of the Bank of England, might resolve. And sub-s. (4) of s. 17 provided that—

"Water stock shall be included amongst the securities in which trustees may invest under the powers of the Trustee Act, 1893."

The following are the

. . . . *Securities for the time being authorized for the investment of cash under the control of the High Court,*

by the Rules of the Supreme Court, Ord. XXII. r. 17 :—

Two and a Half per Cent. Consolidated Stock :

Consolidated Three Pounds per Cent. Annuities :

Reduced Three Pounds per Cent. Annuities :

Two Pounds Fifteen Shillings per Cent. Annuities :

Two Pounds Ten Shillings per Cent. Annuities :

Local Loans Stock under the National Debt and Local Loans Act, 1887 :

Exchequer Bills :

Bank Stock :

(*q*) Trustee Act (1893) Amendment Act, 1894, s. 4.

India Three and a Half per Cent. Stock :

India Three per Cent. Stock :

India Two and a Half per Cent. Stock :

Indian guaranteed railway stocks or shares, provided in each case that such stocks or shares shall not be liable to be redeemed within a period of fifteen years from the date of investment:

Stocks of Colonial Governments guaranteed by the Imperial Government; or in respect of which the provisions of the Colonial Stock Act, 1900, and of s. 2 (2) of the Trustee Act, 1893, are for the time being complied with :

Mortgage of freehold and copyhold estates respectively in England and Wales :

Metropolitan Consolidated Stock, Three Pounds Ten Shillings per Cent. :

Three per Cent. Metropolitan Consolidated Stock :

Two and a Half per Cent. Metropolitan Consolidated Stock :

Three per Cent. London County Consolidated Stock :

Inscribed Two and a Half per Cent. Debenture Stock, issued by the Corporation of London, and secured by a trust deed dated the 24th June, 1897 :

Inscribed Three per Cent. Debenture Stock, issued by the Corporation of London, and secured by supplemental trust deed dated June 1st, 1905 :

London County Council Three and a Half per Cent. Stock :

Debenture, preference, guaranteed, or rent-charge stocks of railways in Great Britain or Ireland having for ten years next before the date of investment paid a dividend on ordinary stock or shares :

Debenture, preference, guaranteed, or rent-charge stocks of railways in Great Britain or Ireland guaranteed by railway companies owning railways in Great Britain or Ireland which have for ten years next before the date of investment paid a dividend on ordinary stock or shares :

Nominal debentures or nominal debenture stock under the Local Loans Act, 1875, or under the Isle of Man Loans Act, 1880, provided in each case that such debentures or stock shall not be liable to be redeemed within a period of fifteen years from the date of investment.

SECTION XXX.—PURCHASE AT A PREMIUM OF REDEEMABLE STOCKS.

(1) A TRUSTEE may, under the powers of the Trustee Act, 1893, invest in any of the securities mentioned or referred to in the last preceding (*b*) section, notwithstanding that the same may be redeemable and that the price exceeds the redemption value.

(2) Provided that a trustee may not, under the powers of this act, purchase at a price exceeding its redemption value any stock mentioned or referred to in sub-sections (dd) (*c*), (g), (i), (k), (l) and (m) of that section (*b*), which is liable to be redeemed within fifteen years of the date of purchase at par, or at some other fixed rate, or purchase any such stock as is mentioned or referred to in the sub-sections aforesaid, which is liable to be redeemed at par, or at some other fixed rate, at a price exceeding fifteen per centum above par or such other fixed rate.

(3) A trustee may retain until redemption any redeemable stock, fund, or security which may have been purchased in accordance with the powers of this act (*a*).

Apart from express authority in the trust instrument trustees were formerly not justified in investing in determinable securities (*d*). S. 4 of the Trust Investment Act, 1889, however, authorized the

(*a*) Trustee Act, 1893, s. 2, as read with the Colonial Stock Act, 1900, s. 2.

(*b*) *I.e.*, sect. XXIX., above, which sets out s. 1 of the Trustee Act, 1893.

(*c*) Colonial Stock Act, 1900, s. 2.

(*d*) *Stewart* v. *Sanderson* (1870), L. R. 10 Eq. 26.

investment of trust funds in any of the securities mentioned or referred to in s. 3 of that act, notwithstanding that the same might be redeemable and that the price exceeded the redemption value. But it prohibited the purchase at a price exceeding its redemption value any stock mentioned or referred to in subsections (g), (i), (k), (l) and (m), which was liable to be redeemed within fifteen years of the date of purchase at par, or at some other fixed rate, or to purchase any such stock which was liable to be redeemed at par, or at some other fixed rate, at a price exceeding fifteen per centum above par or such other fixed rate. This was repealed by the Trustee Act, 1893, s. 51, but was re-enacted by s. 2 of that act, which was extended to colonial stock authorized for the investment of trust money by the Colonial Stock Act, 1900, s. 2.

SECTION XXXI.—INVESTMENTS TO BE AT DISCRETION OF TRUSTEES.

EVERY power conferred by the preceding sections shall be exercised according to the discretion of the trustee, but subject to any consent required by the instrument, if any, creating the trust with respect to the investment of the trust funds (*a*).

It has already been pointed out that although as a rule a trustee is only bound to exhibit the same care in the performance of the trust as a person of ordinary prudence would exhibit in the management of his own affairs, yet he has not quite the same discretion with regard to the investment of the trust moneys as if he were a person dealing with his own property (*b*).

It is not sufficient for a trustee to show that an investment made by him is within his powers if it is an improvident investment. This is specially important in connection with the power to invest on real securities. A second mortgage of freehold land and a contributory mortgage of freehold land are both real securities, yet it appears to be a breach of trust for a trustee to take either (*c*). Similarly an investment on mortgage of a freehold brickfield (*d*), a colliery (*e*), or a licensed hotel (*f*), although they may all be real securities, is extremely dangerous, if not absolutely prohibited.

Probably this is what is meant by the third section of the Trustee Act, 1893, which enacts that every power conferred by the preceding sections shall be exercised according to the discretion of the trustee.

(*a*) Trustee Act, 1893, s. 3.

(*b*) See per Lord Watson in *Learoyd* v. *Whiteley* (1887), 12 App. Cas. at p. 733, and *ante*, under Sect. XXIX.

(*c*) *Ante*, under Sect. XXIX.

(*d*) *Learoyd* v. *Whiteley* (1887), 12 App. Cas. 727.

(*e*) See *Sheffield Building Society* v. *Aizlewood* (1889), 44 Ch. D. 412.

(*f*) *Budge* v. *Gummow* (1872), L. R. 7 Ch. App. 719.

Further, it has already been shown that it is the duty of a trustee to be impartial. Therefore, in order properly to exercise his discretion, the trustee must have regard to the rights and interests of all the beneficiaries. This is specially important where there are beneficiaries entitled in succession; for if a trustee has made an investment with a view to favouring one, and this has resulted in a loss to another or others, he has committed a breach of trust and must make good the loss (*g*).

The third section of the Trustee Act, 1893, also provides that the powers of investment conferred by the act are to be subject to any consent required by the instrument, if any, creating the trust. If consent be necessary it must be procured in strict accordance with the requirements of the trust instrument, and it must be contemporaneous with the exercise of the power for which it is required. A prospective consent will not do (*h*), nor will a subsequent consent exonerate the trustees (*i*), but perhaps after a considerable lapse of time a consent might be presumed (*j*).

(*g*) See *Davies* v. *Wescomb* (1828), 2 Sim. 425; *Raby* v. *Ridehalgh* (1855), 7 De G. M. & G. 104.

(*h*) *Child* v. *Child* (1855), 20 Beav. 50.

(*i*) *Bateman* v. *Davis* (1818), 3 Madd. 98.

(*j*) *Re Adrian Birch* (1853), 17 Beav. 358.

SECTION XXXII.—APPLICATION OF PRECEDING SECTIONS.

THE preceding sections shall apply as well to trusts created before as to trusts created after the passing of this act, and the powers thereby conferred shall be in addition to the powers conferred by the instrument, if any, creating the trust (*a*).

When the Trust Investment Act, 1889, extended the range of investments open to trustees, it provided (s. 6) that the act should apply as well to trusts created before as to trusts created after the passing of it, and that the powers thereby conferred should be in addition to the powers conferred by the instrument (if any) creating the trust. This was repealed by s. 51 of the Trustee Act, 1893, but was re-enacted by s. 4 of that act.

The true method of construing the statutory powers, it has been said, is to read them into the deed or will creating the trust (*b*). The words "instrument (if any) creating the trust" seem to leave it doubtful whether the statutory powers of investment are applicable when the trust is not created by an "instrument." The latter word includes act of parliament by s. 50 of the Trustee Act, 1893.

(*a*) Trustee Act, 1893, s. 4.

(*b*) See per Fry, L. J., *In re Dick*, (1891) 1 Ch. at p. 429, and per Lord Field in same case, sub nom. *Hume* v. *Lopes*, (1892) A. C. at p. 117.

Section XXXIII.—Enlargement of Express Powers of Investment (*a*).

(1) A trustee having power to invest in real securities, unless expressly forbidden by the instrument creating the trust, may invest and shall be deemed to have always had power to invest—

(a) on mortgage of property held for an unexpired term of not less than two hundred years, and not subject to a reservation of rent greater than a shilling a year, or to any right of redemption or to any condition for re-entry, except for non-payment of rent; and

(b) on any charge or upon mortgage of any charge, made under the Improvement of Land Act, 1864.

(2) A trustee having power to invest in the mortgages or bonds of any railway company or of any other description of company may, unless the contrary is expressed in the instrument authorizing the investment, invest in the debenture stock of a railway company or such other company as aforesaid.

(3). A trustee having power to invest money in the debentures or debenture stock of any railway or other company may, unless the contrary is expressed in the

(*a*) Trustee Act, 1893, s. 5.

instrument authorizing the investment, invest in any nominal debentures or nominal debenture stock issued under the Local Loans Act, 1875.

(4) A trustee having power to invest money in securities in the Isle of Man or in securities of the government of a colony may, unless the contrary is expressed in the instrument authorizing the investment, invest in any securities of the government of the Isle of Man under the Isle of Man Loans Act, 1880.

(5) A trustee having a general power to invest trust moneys in or upon the security of shares, stock, mortgages, bonds, or debentures of companies incorporated by or acting under the authority of an act of parliament may invest in or upon the security of mortgage debentures duly issued under and in accordance with the provisions of the Mortgage Debenture Act, 1865 (*a*).

Investment on Real Securities.

It was decided in a case tried in 1886 that a power to a trustee to invest in real securities would not authorize him to take a mortgage of leasehold land, however long the term might be (*b*). Previously there had been some doubt, and the decision did not meet with the entire approval of conveyancers, apparently, for it was provided by s. 9 of the Trustee Act, 1888, that a power to invest trust money in real securities should authorize, and should be deemed to have always authorized, an investment upon mortgage of property held for an unexpired term of not less than 200 years, and not subject to any reservation of rent greater than a shilling a year, or to any right of redemption, or to any condition of re-entry except for non-payment of rent. This was repealed by s. 51 of the Trustee Act, 1893, but re-enacted in s. 5 (1) (a) of that act.

The term "real securities" had been extended to a charge made under the Improvement of Land Act, 1864, by s. 60 of that

(*a*) Trustee Act, 1893, s. 5.

(*b*) *Leigh* v. *Leigh* (1886), 35 W. R. 121.

act. This also was repealed by s. 51 of the Trustee Act, 1893, but re-enacted in s. 5 (1) (b), which enacts that—

"A trustee having power to invest in real securities, unless expressly forbidden by the instrument creating the trust, may invest, and shall be deemed to have always had power to invest . . . (b) on any charge or upon mortgage of any charge made under the Improvement of Land Act, 1864."

Debenture Stock.

It was provided by the Debenture Stock Act, 1871, s. 1, in order to remove doubts whether it was lawful for trustees authorized to invest trust funds in the *mortgages* or *bonds* of companies to invest in *debenture stock*, that "where a power has before the passing of this act been, or shall at any time hereafter be, given to trustees to invest trust funds in the mortgages or bonds of a railway company or of any other description of company, such power shall, unless the contrary is expressed in the instrument creating the power, be deemed to include a power to invest such funds in the debenture stock of a railway company or such other company as aforesaid, and an investment of trust funds in debenture stock may be made accordingly."

The Debenture Stock Act, 1871, was repealed by s. 50 of the Trustee Act, 1893, s. 5 (2) of which, however, enacts that—

"A trustee having power to invest in the mortgages or bonds of any railway company or of any other description of company may, unless the contrary is expressed in the instrument authorizing the investment, invest in the debenture stock of a railway company or such other company as aforesaid."

Securities under the Local Loans Act, 1875.

By the Local Loans Act, 1875, provision was made for securing loans raised by local authorities as therein defined under their statutory powers. This might be, amongst other methods, by the issue of debentures, which might be made payable either to the bearer of the debenture or to a person named—a debenture of the last-mentioned kind being termed by the act a "nominal debenture" (*c*)—or by the issue of debenture stock in respect of which a certificate might be issued entitling the bearer to the stock therein

(*c*) s. 5.

described, any stock in respect of which no such certificate should be issued being in the act referred to as "nominal debenture stock" (*d*). By s. 27 of the act, it was provided that "any trustees for the time being authorized or directed to invest any moneys in the debentures or debenture stock of any railway or other company shall, unless the contrary is provided by the instrument authorizing or directing such investment, have the same power of investing such moneys in any nominal debentures or nominal debenture stock issued under this act." This was repealed by s. 50 of the Trustee Act, 1898, s. 5 (3) of which, however, provides that—

"A trustee having power to invest money in the debentures or debenture stock of any railway or other company may, unless the contrary is expressed in the instrument authorizing the investment, invest in any nominal debentures or nominal debenture stock issued under the Local Loans Act, 1875."

Now that act itself provides in s. 1 "a trustee may, unless expressly forbidden by the instrument (if any) creating the trust, invest" . . . . "(g) in the debenture or rent-charge or guaranteed or preference stock of any railway company in Great Britain or Ireland incorporated by special act of parliament. . . . ." And by s. 50 of the act "the expression 'instrument' includes act of parliament." Is this of itself sufficient to enable trustees to invest nominal debentures or nominal debenture stock issued under the act of 1875? The answer is "no." S. 5 (3) is only an enlargement of the express powers of investment contained in the instrument creating the trust, and if that does not expressly authorize an investment on the debentures or debenture stock of any railway or other company the trustee may not invest in nominal debentures or nominal debenture stock issued under the Local Loans Act, 1875 (*e*).

Isle of Man Securities.

In 1880 with a view to making provision for improvements in the harbours and other public works in the Isle of Man, it was provided by the Isle of Man Loans Act that the government of the island might, with the approval of the Treasury and the

(*d*) s. 6.

(*e*) *In re Tattersall* (1906), 54 W. R. 603; (1906) 2 Ch. 399.

Tynwald Court, borrow money for the purposes in the act mentioned by debentures, debenture stock and annuity certificates to which the provisions of the Local Loans Act, 1875, were made applicable, and s. 7 of the act enacted that trustees *in the Isle of Man* authorized to invest moneys in securities in the Isle of Man, and trustees authorized to invest in the securities of the government of a colony should, unless the contrary were provided by the instrument authorizing or directing such investment, have power of investing in any securities under the act.

This was repealed by s. 51 of the Trustee Act, 1893, and instead, s. 5 (4) of the act provides that:—" A trustee having power to invest money in securities in the Isle of Man or in securities of the government of a colony may, *unless the contrary is expressed in the instrument authorizing the investment*, invest in any securities of the government of the Isle of Man under the Isle of Man Loans Act, 1880."

It seems obvious that this also only applies where the trustee has power to invest in the securities mentioned by the express terms of the trust instrument (*f*).

Mortgage Debentures.

By the Mortgage Debenture Act, 1865, it was provided that companies incorporated under the Companies Act, 1862, or under any act of parliament and entitled to advance money on the security of land might (*g*), under the conditions laid down in the act, borrow money upon mortgage debentures to be issued under the act. The security on which the debentures were founded was required to be of the kind specified in the act (*h*), and provision was made for registration of such securities at the Land Registry (*i*) and also for the registration of the debentures founded upon them (*j*).

S. 40 of the act provided that in cases in which, by the instrument creating the trust, trustees have power to invest in shares, stock, mortgages, bonds or debentures of companies, they might invest on the security of mortgage debentures issued under

(*f*) *In re Tattersall*, (1906) 2 Ch. at p. 405.

(*g*) See s. 3.

(*h*) See s. 5.

(*i*) See ss. 6—10.

(*j*) s. 32.

the act. This section also was repealed by s. 51 of the Trustee Act, 1893, s. 5 (5) of which provides that:—"A trustee having a general power to invest trust moneys in or upon the security of shares, stock, mortgages, bonds or debentures of companies incorporated by or acting under the authority of an act of parliament may invest in or upon the security of mortgage debentures duly issued under and in accordance with the provisions of the Mortgage Debenture Act, 1865."

This also appears only to apply where the trustee has power to invest in the securities mentioned by the express terms of the instrument of trust.

SECTION XXXIV.—POWER TO INVEST NOTWITHSTANDING DRAINAGE CHARGES.

A TRUSTEE having power to invest in the purchase of land or on mortgage of land may invest in the purchase or on mortgage of any land notwithstanding the same is charged with a rent under the powers of the Public Money Drainage Acts, 1846 to 1856, or the Landed Property Improvement (Ireland) Act, 1847, or by an absolute order made under the Improvement of Land Act, 1864, unless the terms of the trust expressly provide that the land to be purchased or taken in mortgage shall not be subject to any such prior charge (*a*).

In 1846, with a view to the improvement of agricultural land by the execution of drainage works, it was enacted by the Public Money Drainage Act that the Treasury might make advances to landowners out of the consolidated fund not exceeding 2,000,000*l.* for Great Britain and 1,000,000*l.* for Ireland (*b*). Such advance was to be secured by a rent-charge upon the land in favour of the Crown (*c*), and it was provided that a rent-charge under the act should not be deemed such an incumbrance as to preclude a trustee of money held in trust to be invested in the purchase of land or invested on mortgage from investing the same in the purchase of or upon mortgage of land so charged unless the terms of the trust otherwise provided (*d*).

Analogous provisions were contained in the Landed Property Improvement (Ireland) Act, 1847 (*e*), by which the provisions of the act of 1846 were repealed, so far as they related to Ireland,

(*a*) Trustee Act, 1893, s. 6.

(*b*) 9 & 10 Vict. c. 101, s. 1. The amounts were extended by the Public Money Drainage Act, 1850.

(*c*) s. 34.

(*d*) s. 37.

(*e*) 10 Vict. c. 32, s. 53.

and the Improvement of Land Act, 1864 (*f*), passed to enable owners of limited interests in land to charge their land with the repayment of moneys advanced for the purpose of executing improvements of the kind specified in the act.

All these enactments were repealed by s. 51 of the Trustee Act, 1893, but were re-enacted in a consolidated form in s. 6 of that act, which provides that—

"A trustee having power to invest in the purchase of land or on mortgage of land may invest in the purchase or on mortgage of any land notwithstanding the same is charged with a rent under the powers of the Public Money Drainage Acts, 1846 to 1856, or the Landed Property Improvement (Ireland) Act, 1847, or by an absolute order made under the Improvement of Land Act, 1864, unless the terms of the trust expressly provide that the land to be purchased or taken in mortgage shall not be subject to any such prior charge."

(*f*) 27 & 28 Vict. c. 114, s. 61.

Section XXXV.—Trustees not to convert Inscribed Stock into Certificates to Bearer.

(1) A trustee, unless authorized by the terms of his trust, shall not apply for or hold any certificate to bearer issued under the authority of any of the following acts, that is to say:—

(a) The India Stock Certificate Act, 1863.
(b) The National Debt Act, 1870.
(c) The Local Loans Act, 1875.
(d) The Colonial Stock Act, 1877.

(2) Nothing in this section shall impose on the Bank of England or of Ireland, or on any person authorized to issue any such certificates, any obligation to inquire whether a person applying for such a certificate is or is not a trustee, or subject them to any liability in the event of their granting any such certificate to a trustee, nor invalidate any such certificate if granted (*a*).

It seems to be considered that generally trustees should not invest on securities payable to bearer, and where a settlement authorizes an investment "in the names of the trustees," the court has held that they are not entitled to invest in bearer securities. In order to give them this right they ought to be authorized to invest "in the names or under the legal control" of the trustees (*b*).

By the India Stock Certificate Act, 1863, provision was made for the registered holders of India stock obtaining certificates of title to their shares with coupons entitling the bearer to the dividends thereon, but a trustee was prohibited from doing so unless authorized by the terms of his trust (*c*).

(*a*) Trustee Act, 1893, s. 7.

(*b*) *In re Roth, Goldberger* v. *Roth* (1896), 74 L. T. 50.

(*c*) ss. 3 and 4.

Similar provisions were contained in the National Debt Conversion Act, 1870 (*d*), the Local Loans Act, 1875 (*e*), and the Colonial Stock Act, 1877 (*f*). But all the above acts contained provisions indemnifying the Banks of England and Ireland and other authorities under the acts in respect of a breach of their provisions by a trustee.

All the above enactments were repealed by s. 51 of the Trustee Act, 1893, s. 51, but s. 7 of the act provides that a trustee, unless authorized by the terms of his trust, shall not apply for or hold any certificate to bearer issued under the authority of any of the above acts, but continues the indemnity to the banks and persons authorized to issue such certificates.

Perhaps the feeling against bearer securities that exists in England is somewhat exaggerated. The holder of such securities can lodge them with a good bank, who will collect the dividends for him as they become due without making any charge, and if he does this the practical risk involved in this class of securities is very small, and even this may be insured against at a very trifling cost. On the continent of Europe and in the United States of America bearer securities seem to be regarded much more favourably by investors.

(*d*) ss. 26 and 29.

(*e*) s. 21.

(*f*) ss. 7 and 12.

Section XXXVI.—Loans and Investments by Trustees not chargeable as Breaches of Trust.

(1) A trustee lending money on the security of any property on which he can lawfully lend shall not be chargeable with breach of trust by reason only of the proportion borne by the amount of the loan to the value of the property at the time when the loan was made, provided that it appears to the court that in making the loan the trustee was acting upon a report as to the value of the property made by a person whom he reasonably believed to be an able practical surveyor or valuer instructed and employed independently of any owner of the property, whether such surveyor or valuer carried on business in the locality where the property is situate or elsewhere, and that the amount of the loan does not exceed two equal third parts of the value of the property as stated in the report, and that the loan was made under the advice of the surveyor or valuer expressed in the report.

(2) A trustee lending money on the security of any leasehold property shall not be chargeable with breach of trust only upon the ground that in making such loan he dispensed, either wholly or partly, with the production or investigation of the lessor's title.

(3) A trustee shall not be chargeable with breach of trust only upon the ground that in effecting the purchase of, or in lending money upon, the security of any property he has accepted a shorter title than the title which a purchaser is, in the absence of a special contract, entitled

to require if in the opinion of the court the title accepted be such as a person acting with prudence and caution would have accepted.

(4) This section applies to transfers of existing securities, and to investments made as well before as after the commencement of this act, except where an action or other proceeding was pending with reference thereto on the twenty-fourth day of December, one thousand eight hundred and eighty-eight (*a*).

Every trustee, unless he is expressly forbidden by the trust instrument, may now invest in "real or heritable securities in Great Britain or Ireland" (*b*), *i.e.*, on mortgage of real estate.

In exercising this power the attention of the trustee should be directed, Mr. Lewin says, to two leading topics—the value and sufficiency of the security and the title of the borrower (*c*).

With regard to the question of value a distinction was formerly drawn between land and houses, and it was considered that while a trustee might safely lend up to two-thirds of the value of the estate if it were freehold land he ought not to lend more than one-half if it consisted of houses (*d*).

With regard to the sufficiency of the security it was necessary for the trustee to get an independent valuation of it made on his own behalf by a competent valuer with local knowledge of it sufficient to enable him to arrive at a valuation, who had been instructed that the advance was to be made out of trust money and that it was desired to ascertain the actual value of the property (*e*).

These rules were materially modified in 1888 by s. 4 of the Trustee Act of that year, sub-s. (1) of which was as follows:—

"No trustee lending money upon the security of any property shall be chargeable with breach of trust by reason only of the proportion borne by the amount of the loan to the value of such property at the time when the loan was made, provided that it

(*a*) Trustee Act, 1893, s. 8.

(*b*) *Ante*, sect. XXIX.

(*c*) Lewin, Trusts, 11th ed. 368.

(*d*) Lewin, *ibid.*; *Fry* v. *Tapson* (1884), 28 Ch. D. 268; *Shaw* v. *Cates*, (1909) 1 Ch. at pp. 396 *et seq.*

(*e*) See Rudall & Greig, Trustee Acts, 3rd ed. 45, where the authorities are cited.

shall appear to the court that in making such loan the trustee was acting upon a report as to the value of the property made by a person whom the trustee reasonably believed to be an able practical surveyor or valuer instructed and employed independently of any owner of the property, *whether such surveyor or valuer carried on business in the locality where the property is situate or elsewhere*, and that the amount of the loan does not exceed two equal third parts of the value of the property as stated in such report, and that the loan was made under the advice of such surveyor or valuer expressed in such report. And this section shall apply to a loan upon any property of any tenure, *whether agricultural or house or other property*, on which the trustee can lawfully lend."

This was repealed by s. 51 of the Trustee Act, 1893, but re-enacted in the form set out above in s. 8 of that act, from which it will be seen that the last sentence in s. 4 of the act of 1888, to the effect that the section shall apply to a loan "upon any property of any tenure, whether agricultural or house or other property," &c., is omitted, and that the words "on which he can lawfully lend" are placed at the beginning of the section after the word "property." In s. 50 of the act of 1893, however, the word "property" is defined as including "real and personal property and any estate and interest in any property real or personal" unless the context otherwise requires, so that the meaning appears to be the same.

It is to be observed that the section only relieves the trustee in respect of "*the proportion borne by the amount of the loan to the value of the property at the time when the loan was made.*" The acts have therefore not enlarged the powers of a trustee with regard to the description of property on which he ought to invest, nor do they absolve him from exercising the care of a prudent man in selecting the security (*f*). In order for a trustee to be safe, he must consequently be able to show—

(1) That the property is of a kind on which he can lawfully lend. Unless expressly forbidden by the terms of the instrument creating the trust, he can lawfully lend on real securities. What the term "real securities" means has been discussed above.

(2) That in selecting the investment he exercised the same care as would have been exhibited by an ordinary prudent man of business in managing his own affairs. And in this connection,

(*f*) See *Shaw* v. *Cates*, (1909) 1 Ch. 389.

as Lord Justice Lindley has said, "care must be taken not to lose sight of the fact that the business of the trustee, and the business which the ordinary prudent man is supposed to be conducting for himself, is the business of investing money for the benefit of persons who are to enjoy it at some future time, not for the sole benefit of the person entitled to the present income. The duty of a trustee is not to take such care only as a prudent man would take if he had only himself to consider; the duty, rather, is to take such care as an ordinary prudent man would take if he were minded to make an investment for the benefit of other people for whom he felt morally bound to provide" (*g*). A trustee should therefore not invest on property unless it is (a) permanent in nature and value, (b) producing income, and (c) readily marketable. It follows that, in considering whether he shall lend money on mortgage of land on which a trade or business is carried on, the trustee must distinguish, and require the surveyor or valuer he employs to distinguish, between the value of the land and the value of the trade or business carried on upon it (*h*). It would seem also that all incorporeal hereditaments other than permanent rents—though they are "real securities"—must fail to comply with one or more of the above requirements. The result is that, although trustees are authorized to invest in any form of real security, in practice they can only properly lend on the security of land (regarded as a physical object), buildings, or permanent rents (*i*).

(3) That in making the loan he was acting upon a report as to the value of the property made by a person whom he reasonably believed to be an able practical surveyor or valuer. And he must himself reasonably believe this, that is to say, he must himself select the surveyor or valuer, not leave it to his solicitor—*delegatus non potest delegare*. If a solicitor is asked by a trustee to name a valuer, he should submit a name or names to the trustee, and tell him everything he knows to guide his choice, but leave the choice to him (*j*).

(*g*) *Whiteley* v. *Learoyd* (1886), 33 Ch. D. at p. 355. See, however, *Learoyd* v. *Whiteley* (1887), 12 App. Cas. at p. 732.

(*h*) See *Whiteley* v. *Learoyd* (1886), 33 Ch. D. 347; affirmed by H. L. as *Learoyd* v. *Whiteley* (1887), 12 App. Cas. 727; Birrell, Duties and Liabilities of Trustees, 48.

(*i*) Champernowne & Johnston, Trustee Acts, 20.

(*j*) *Fry* v. *Tapson* (1884), 28 Ch. D. 268.

(4) That the surveyor or valuer was instructed and employed independently of any owner of the property. And it seems that it is not sufficient that the trustee believed that he was so employed if in fact he was not. The words "reasonably believed to be" in the section do not govern the words "instructed and employed independently of any owner of the property" (*k*). The question has been raised whether the employment of a surveyor on the terms that he shall receive no fee or only a reduced fee if the business does not go through is proper, and a judicial opinion has been expressed that it is improper for a trustee to make such an arrangement. It is said that it is obvious in such a case that it is the interest of the surveyor to make such a report as will let the thing go on, whereas his duty is to advise the trustees independently and without reference to any question concerning his fees, and it has been suggested that a report obtained on these terms may not protect a trustee. Until there is a decision on the point, therefore, it will be dangerous for a trustee to make such an arrangement (*l*).

(5) That the amount of the loan does not exceed two equal third parts of the value of the property as stated in the report; and

(6) That the loan was made under the advice of the surveyor or valuer expressed in the report. The surveyor or valuer employed ought to be distinctly told in writing that the moneys in question are trust moneys, and that his report is to be made, having regard to the provisions of s. 8 of the Trustee Act, 1893, and he must be required at the end of his valuation formally to advise the trustees that they would be safe in advancing two-thirds of the amount of the valuation, though he ought not to advise an advance of so large a proportion, unless, having regard to the nature of the property and all the circumstances of the case, a prudent man would advance it. The report should be signed by the surveyor or valuer in his individual name, and not in that of any firm of which he may be a member. It is just as well not to tell the surveyor or valuer the amount of the proposed loan (*m*).

(*k*) Per Kekewich, J., *In re Walker* (1890), 59 L. J. Ch. at p. 391; and *In re Somerset, Somerset* v. *Poulett*, (1894) 1 Ch. at p. 253. This, however, does not seem clear. See per Parker, J., *Shaw* v. *Cates*, (1909) 1 Ch. at p. 403.

(*l*) See *Solicitors' Jour.* vol. liii. 236 and 260; *Law Jour.* vol. xliv. 124.

(*m*) Birrell, Duties and Liabilities of Trustees, 52. The duties of the valuer are discussed and explained in *Shaw* v. *Cates*, (1909) 1 Ch. 389.

With regard to the sufficiency of the title of the lessor, s. 8 (2) of the Trustee Act, 1893, which re-enacts s. 4 (2) of the Trustee Act, 1888, provides that " a trustee lending money on the security of any leasehold property shall not be chargeable with breach of trust only upon the ground that in making such loan he dispensed, either wholly or partly, with the production of the lessor's title."

This has reference to the provisions of s. 2 of the Vendor and Purchaser Act, 1874, which precludes an intended lessee or assign of a lease from calling for the title to the freehold, and of s. 13 of the Conveyancing Act, 1881, which precludes an intended lessee from an underlessee from calling for the title to the leasehold reversion. S. 3 of the former act, now re-enacted in s. 15 of the Trustee Act, 1893, and s. 66 of the Conveyancing Act protected trustees who were buying, but apparently did not apply to trustees who were merely lending on the security of leasehold property.

In pursuance of the same principle, s. 8 (3) of the Trustee Act, 1893, re-enacting s. 4 (3) of the Act of 1888, provides that " a trustee shall not be chargeable with breach of trust only upon the ground that in effecting the purchase of, or in lending money upon, the security of any property he has accepted a shorter title than the title which a purchaser is, in the absence of a special contract, entitled to require if, in the opinion of the court, the title accepted be such as a person acting with prudence and caution would have accepted."

Before the act, a trustee buying or lending money on the security of property had generally to see that the title to the property was marketable (*n*). The effect of the statute appears to be to put a trustee in exactly the same position as a person buying or lending his own money, so far as determining the length of title he shall accept goes.

(*n*) Rudall & Greig, Trustee Acts, 3rd ed. 48.

SECTION XXXVII.—LIABILITY FOR LOSS BY REASON OF IMPROPER INVESTMENTS.

(1) WHERE a trustee improperly advances trust money on a mortgage security which would at the time of the investment be a proper investment in all respects for a smaller sum than is actually advanced thereon, the security shall be deemed an authorized investment for the smaller sum, and the trustee shall only be liable to make good the sum advanced in excess thereof with interest.

(2) This section applies to investments made as well before as after the commencement of this act, except where an action or other proceeding was pending with reference thereto on the twenty-fourth day of December, one thousand eight hundred and eighty-eight (*a*).

As a general rule, a trustee who commits a breach of trust is liable for the whole of the loss sustained by the beneficiary as a consequence (*b*).

Formerly, therefore, if a trustee, on mortgage of a property valued at 3,000*l.*, lent 2,500*l.* out of the trust money, and on a subsequent realization of the security it only fetched 1,500*l.*, the trustee would have had to make good the 1,000*l.* lost. But it was provided by s. 5 of the Trustee Act, 1888, that "where a trustee shall have improperly advanced trust money on a mortgage security which would at the time of the investment have been a proper investment in all respects for a less sum than was actually advanced thereon, the security shall be deemed an authorized investment for such less sum, and the trustee shall only be liable to make good

(*a*) Trustee Act, 1893, s. 9. (*b*) See below, sect. LXI.

the sum advanced in excess thereof, with interest." This was repealed by s. 51 of the Trustee Act, 1893, but re-enacted in the form given in large type above by s. 9 of that act.

In the case put, the trustee would now only be liable for 500*l.*, that is, "the sum advanced in excess" of that for which the security is an authorized investment, namely, 2,000*l.*

But it is to be observed that the section only applies when the mortgage security is one "which would at the time of the investment be a proper investment in all respects" for the smaller sum (*c*).

(*c*) For an example of its application, see *Shaw* v. *Cates*, (1909) 1 Ch. 389.

SECTION XXXVIII.—LIABILITY OF TRUSTEE IN CASE OF CHANGE OF CHARACTER OF INVESTMENT.

A TRUSTEE shall not be liable for breach of trust by reason only of his continuing to hold an investment which has ceased to be an investment authorized by the instrument of trust or by the general law (*a*).

There appears to be no clear general rule defining the duty of a trustee with regard to the retention of investments of the trust property (*b*).

Where, on entering on his office, he finds the trust property invested in securities in which he is authorized by law or the instrument creating the trust to invest no question arises; but where he finds that it is not so invested, or where, though the investment was originally authorized, it has ceased to be so owing to a change in its character, the question arises whether he ought to retain it or not.

A trustee is bound to realize investments in three cases:—(1) Where the instrument creating the trust contains an express direction to convert; (2) where the rule in *Howe* v. *Earl Dartmouth* (*c*) applies; and (3) where it is necessary for the security of the trust fund. But, except in these cases, he appears to be under no general obligation to realize investments which are not of the kind he is authorized to make.

Where, for example, the trust property is invested on a mortgage of real estate, and owing to a fall in the value of the land the amount of the advance becomes in excess of two-thirds of the value of the land, the trustee was not bound by the rules of equity to call in the mortgage merely because the value of the security had fallen below the authorized limit. So long as he acted as a

(*a*) Trustee Act (1893) Amendment Act, 1894, s. 4.

(*b*) See Champernowne & Johnston, Trustee Acts, 176.

(*c*) (1802) 7 Vesey, 137, *supra*, sect. XXIII.

prudent man would have done he was under no liability, even though the retention of the security caused a loss to the beneficiaries (*d*).

On the other hand, where a change has taken place in the nature of the investment it has been decided that the trustee was bound to realize it. For instance, where trustees were authorized to invest a trust fund by lending it to a specified firm at interest, they were held bound to call it in on a change taking place in the membership of the firm (*e*).

In 1894 it was enacted by s. 4 of the Trustee Act Amendment Act that "a trustee shall not be liable for breach of trust *by reason only* of his continuing to hold an investment which has ceased to be an investment authorized by the instrument of trust or the general law."

It is not clear how far the section has altered the law, if it has done so at all.

(*d*) *In re Medland* (1889), 41 Ch. D. 476; *In re Chapman*, (1896) 2 Ch. 763.

(*e*) *In re Tucker*, (1894) 1 Ch. 724; C. A. (1894) 3 Ch. 429.

Part VI.—RIGHTS AND POWERS OF THE TRUSTEE.

SECTION XXXIX.—RIGHT TO POSSESSION OF TITLE DEEDS, &C.

A TRUSTEE is entitled to the possession of the instrument creating the trust, and, unless the court otherwise orders, to all the documents of title, if any, relating solely to the trust property.

The legal owner of property is entitled to the documents of title of the property. Therefore, as between trustee and *cestui que trust*, it is the trustee who is entitled to the documents of title of the trust property (*a*).

And even though the trustee has no estate in the trust property sufficient to carry the right to the title deeds, it seems that he may be entitled to them if he has active duties to perform—such as to receive rents—even against a legal owner for life (*b*).

Since the Settled Land Acts, however, the court will allow an equitable tenant for life to have the custody of the title deeds of the settled land to enable him to exercise the statutory powers conferred on him by those acts (*c*). But the court will not give

(*a*) *Barclay* v. *Collett* (1838), 4 Bing. N. C. 658. Compare *Harrington* v. *Price* (1832), 3 Barn. & Ad. 170; *Newton* v. *Beck* (1858), 3 H. & N. 220; and *Cooper* v. *Vesey* (1882), 20 Ch. D. 611, which were all successful actions by the legal owner of land to recover the title deeds from persons who claimed an equitable or other interest in the land. See also Lewin, Trusts, 11th ed. 853; and conf. the Indian Trusts Act, 1882, s. 31.

(*b*) *Garner* v. *Hannyngton* (1856), 22 Beav. at p. 630; *Stanford* v. *Roberts* (1871), L. R. 6 Ch. App. at p. 310.

(*c*) *In re Burnaby's Settled Estates* (1889), 42 Ch. D. 621; *In re Wythes*, (1893) 2 Ch. 369.

the title deeds to the tenant for life if he has mortgaged his interest. "The trustees are the proper custodians of the title deeds," said Mr. Justice Kekewich in a case in 1894, "the tenant for life is not. The mortgagee is entitled to say, 'If the tenant for life has the title deeds, I must have them. The tenant for life cannot hold the title deeds against me, her mortgagee, and I am entitled to that extent to stand in her shoes.' There is a great deal to be said in favour of that view. At any rate, I think there is sufficient to prevent the handing over of the title deeds by the trustees to the tenant for life for all purposes" (*d*).

Since the trustees of a settlement are the persons entitled to the possession of the settlement, it follows that the solicitors of a husband on whose instructions a marriage settlement has been prepared have no lien on it against the trustees for their costs of preparing it, but must hand it over on the request of the trustees (*e*).

(*d*) *In re Newen, Newen* v. *Barnes*, (1894) 2 Ch. at p. 307.

(*e*) *In re Lawrence, Bowker* v. *Austin*, (1894) 1 Ch. 556.

SECTION XL.—RIGHT TO RE-IMBURSEMENT AND INDEMNITY.

(1) A TRUSTEE may re-imburse himself or pay or discharge out of the trust property all expenses properly incurred in or about the execution of his trusts or powers (*a*).

(2) If he pays such expenses out of his own moneys, he has a charge therefor upon the trust property (both capital and income) in respect of which they were incurred.

(3) If the trust property is insufficient for the purpose, the trustee is entitled to recover such expenses from the beneficiary, provided that such beneficiary is under no disability, and is absolutely entitled to the trust property; and provided that the right to do so is not inconsistent with the expressed or implied terms of the trust.

A trustee is not entitled to any remuneration for his services, but he is entitled to be re-imbursed every expense he has properly incurred in the performance of his office. This is now a statutory rule, contained in s. 24 of the Trustee Act, 1893, which re-enacts s. 31 of the Law of Property Amendment Act, 1859 (*b*). This provides that "a trustee may re-imburse himself or pay or discharge out of the trust premises all expenses incurred in or about

(*a*) Trustee Act, 1893, s. 24. The word "properly" is not in the act, but the section is construed as if it were there. See *In re Beddoe*, *Downes* v. *Cottam*, (1893) 1 Ch. 547, per Lindley, L. J., at p. 558, and per Bowen, L. J., at p. 562; *Stott* v. *Milne* (1884), 25 Ch. D. 710, per Lord Selborne, at p. 715.

(*b*) Compare the Indian Trusts Act, 1882, s. 32. And see Lewin, Trusts, 11th ed. 770 *et seq.*; and Underhill, Trusts and Trustees, 6th ed. 347.

the execution of his trusts or powers." The word "properly" is not in the section, but it is construed as if it were there (*c*).

The rule, however, existed independently of statutory enactment. "It is in the nature of the office," said Lord Eldon, "whether expressed in the instrument or not, that the trust property shall re-imburse him all the charges and expenses incurred in the execution of the trust" (*d*). And the right extends to any person who has advanced money at the request of, or has given credit to the trustees for the purpose of the trust, or otherwise has a claim against them in their character of trustees; such a person is subrogated to the rights of the trustee (*e*).

The following are examples of expenses allowed:—

1. Expenses of employing a solicitor for the better conduct of the trust. *Macnamara* v. *Jones* (1784), Dick. 587.

2. Travelling expenses. *Ex parte Lovegrove* (1834), 3 D. & C. 763 (*f*).

3. Fees to counsel. *Poole* v. *Pass* (1839), 1 Beav. 600.

4. Damages for a tort committed by an agent employed by the trustee in the due performance of the trust. *Bennett* v. *Wyndham* (1862), 4 D. F. & J. 259 (*g*).

5. Calls on shares forming part of the trust property. *Jervis* v. *Wolferstan* (1874), L. R. 18 Eq. 18 (*h*).

6. Costs of reasonably defending an unsuccessful action against the trustee for the protection of the trust estate. *Walters* v. *Woodbridge* (1878), 7 Ch. D. 504.

7. Costs of properly bringing actions which are compromised. *Stott* v. *Milne* (1884), 25 Ch. D. 710.

(*c*) See *In re Beddoe*, *Downes* v. *Cottam*, (1893) 1 Ch. 547, per Lindley, L. J., at p. 558, and per Bowen, L. J., at p. 562.

(*d*) *Worrall* v. *Harford* (1802), 8 Vesey, 4.

(*e*) See *Todd* v. *Moorhouse* (1874), L. R. 19 Eq. 69; *Dowse* v. *Gorton*, (1891) A. C. 190; *In re Raybould*, *Raybould* v. *Turner*, (1900) 1 Ch. 199; *In re Frith*, *Newton* v. *Rolfe*, (1902) 1 Ch. 342.

(*f*) This was the case of an assignee in bankruptcy, but a trustee is on the same footing.

(*g*) *In re Raybould*, (1900) 1 Ch. 199, is similar.

(*h*) *Hardoon* v. *Belilios*, (1901) A. C. 118, is to the same effect.

8. Costs of defending a successful action for the rectification of the trust instrument. *James* v. *Couchman* (1885), 29 Ch. D. at p. 217.

9. Liabilities incurred in properly carrying on a testator's business in accordance with the terms of the will with the assent of the testator's creditors, in the interest of the creditors as well as of the beneficiaries. *Dowse* v. *Gorton*, (1891) A. C. 190 (*i*).

10. Costs of defending a successful action to declare the trust void. *Merry* v. *Pownall*, (1898) 1 Ch. 306.

The right of trustees to indemnity against all costs and expenses properly incurred by them in the execution of the trust is a first charge on all the trust property, both income and corpus. The trustees, therefore, have a right to retain the costs out of income until provision can be made for raising them out of the corpus (*j*).

As between tenant for life and remainderman, however, the trustee's costs seem generally to be payable out of capital (*k*).

If the trust estate is insufficient for the payment of the trustee's costs the trustee may sue the *cestui que trust* personally (*l*). "Where parties place others in the position of trustees for them they are in equity personally bound to indemnify them against the consequences resulting from that position," said Lord Justice Turner (*m*).

"I take it to be a general rule that where persons accept a trust at the request of another and that other is a *cestui que trust* he is personally liable to indemnify the trustees for any loss accruing in the due execution of the trust," said Sir George Jessel twenty years later (*n*).

But it is not necessary that the *cestui que trust* should request the trustee to accept the trust, as these passages seem to suggest. If the *cestui que trust* is *sui juris* and has accepted the beneficial

(*i*) The trustee's right of indemnity in this case has priority to the claims of the testator's creditors, and extends to the assets at the date of testator's death as well as those coming into existence afterwards. *In re Frith*, (1902) 1 Ch. 342, is a similar case which also shows that the right is not affected by one of the trustees being in default.

(*j*) *Stott* v. *Milne* (1884), 25 Ch. D. 710, per Lord Selborne, at p. 714.

(*k*) *In re Weall* (1889), 42 Ch. D. 674. And see Gover, Capital and Income, ch. vii.

(*l*) *Balsh* v. *Hyam* (1728), 2 P. W. 453; *Phené* v. *Gillan* (1845), 5 Hare, 1; *In re Southampton Imperial Hotel Co.* (1872), 22 L. T. 384; *Jervis* v. *Wolferstan* (1874), L. R. 18 Eq. 18.

(*m*) *Ex parte Chippendale* (1854), 4 D. M. & G. at p. 54.

(*n*) *Jervis* v. *Wolferstan* (1874), L. R. 18 Eq. at p. 24.

ownership of the trust property so as to be unable to disclaim, he is bound to indemnify his trustee whether the trust was created by him or some predecessor in title. "The plainest principles of justice require that the *cestui que trust* who gets all the benefit of the property should bear its burden unless he can show some good reason why his trustee should bear them himself" (*o*).

The right, however, appears to be limited to cases in which the beneficiary is absolutely entitled. All the reported cases in which a claim by the trustee has been successful have been of this character, and in *Hardoon* v. *Belilios* (*o*) Lord Lindley said: "It is quite unnecessary to consider in this case the difficulties which would arise if these shares were held by the plaintiff on trust for tenants for life, or for infants, or upon special trusts limiting the right to indemnity. In those cases there is no beneficiary who can be justly expected or required personally to indemnify the trustee against the whole of the burdens incident to his legal ownership; and the trustee accepts the trust knowing that under such circumstances and in the absence of special contract his right to indemnity cannot extend beyond the trust estate, *i.e.*, beyond the respective interests of his *cestuis que trustent*." Yet it is not confined to a bare trust merely, as appears from the case of *Jervis* v. *Wolferstan* (*p*). In that case the trustees held shares in a company on trust for the settlor's wife for life with remainders over. The remaindermen disclaimed, and there was consequently a resulting trust for the settlor's estate, the settlor himself being dead. A large liability was incurred by the trustees in respect of the shares. The wife, the tenant for life, was willing to pay her share, and it was held that the persons entitled to the residuary estate of the settlor must contribute to the balance in proportion to their interests.

Further, the principle cannot be applied to cases in which the nature of the transaction excludes it. So it has been held that the trustees of a club, which is formed upon the tacit understanding, judicially recognized, that no member as such becomes liable to pay to its funds or otherwise any money beyond the subscriptions required by its rules, are not entitled to be indemnified by the members personally (*q*).

(*o*) *Hardoon* v. *Belilios*, (1901) A. C. 118; see per Lord Lindley, at p. 127.

(*p*) (1874), L. R. 18 Eq. 18.

(*q*) *Wise* v. *Perpetual Trustee Co., Ltd.*, (1903) A. C. 139.

SECTION XLI.—POWER OF TRUSTEE FOR SALE TO SELL BY AUCTION, &c.

(1) WHERE a trust for sale or a power of sale of property is vested in a trustee, he may sell or concur with any other person in selling all or any part of the property either subject to prior charges or not, and either together or in lots by public auction or by private contract, subject to any such conditions respecting title or evidence of title or other matter as the trustee may think fit, with power to vary any contract for sale, and to buy in at any auction or to rescind any contract for sale and to re-sell, without being answerable for any loss.

(2) This section applies only if and as far as a contrary intention is not expressed in the instrument creating the trust or power, and shall have effect subject to the terms of that instrument and to the provisions therein contained.

(3) This section applies only to a trust or power created by an instrument coming into operation after the 31st of December, 1881 (*a*).

A trustee who held property upon a trust for sale or who had a power of sale might, apart from statutory enactment, concur with another person in selling, but it lay on him to show that to do so was beneficial to the *cestuis que trust*. He could also sell either together or in lots, and by public auction or by private

(*a*) Trustee Act, 1893, s. 13.

contract, and probably would be justified in selling subject to special conditions, if the conditions were such as a reasonably prudent man would employ in selling his own property in the like circumstances (*b*). But until the year 1860 it was the custom of conveyancers to insert an express authority to this effect in the trust instrument (*c*) so as to preclude any question, and in 1860, by s. 1 of Lord Cranworth's Act (*d*), a power to sell together or in lots, and either by auction or by private contract, was conferred on all trustees having a power to sell land; and by s. 2, where the trust instrument contained no declaration of a contrary intention they were entitled to insert in any conditions of sale or contract such special conditions as to title or evidence of title or otherwise as they might think fit. This enactment was superseded by the wider provision to the same effect contained in s. 35 of the Conveyancing Act, 1881, and was repealed, with a saving as to instruments executed before the act, by s. 64 of the Settled Land Act, 1882. The provision of the Conveyancing Act was itself repealed by s. 51 of the Trustee Act, 1893, but re-enacted in the form given above by s. 13 of that Act.

The authority conferred by this section extends to both real and personal property (*e*). But sub-ss. 2 and 3 appear to limit the operation of the enactment to trusts created by an instrument, so that it may be open to question whether an administrator selling personal property is within the section. But "instrument" includes act of parliament (*f*), so that an administrator selling real estate may be within it, since his power to deal with that is conferred by Part I. of the Land Transfer Act, 1897.

The words "any part of the property" seem not to authorize a sale of fixtures apart from the land to which they are annexed, nor to sell a house in flats. They mean that what is sold should be a separate part of the trust property in the state in which it was subjected to the trust (*g*). Nor do they authorize a sale of the surface apart from the minerals, or *vice versâ*, but the court may sanction a sale of this kind under s. 44 of the Trustee Act,

(*b*) See Rudall & Greig, Trusts and Trustees, 3rd ed. 76; Hood & Challis, Conv. Acts, 6th ed. 370; Lewin, Trusts, 11th ed. 507, 511.

(*c*) Vaizey, Settlements, 589.

(*d*) 23 & 24 Vict. c. 145.

(*e*) See definition of property in s. 50 of the Trustee Act, 1893.

(*f*) *Ibid.*

(*g*) See *In re Yates* (1888), 38 Ch. D. 112, a decision on similar words in s. 19 of the Conveyancing Act, 1881.

1893, below. The power to sell "subject to any conditions respecting title or evidence of title or other matter as the trustee thinks fit," authorize a trustee who is selling in lots a leasehold property held under one lease to carry out the sale by granting an underlease of the whole term less one day to the purchaser of each lot. This, though in form the grant of a lease, is in substance a sale, and in accordance with the ordinary conveyancing practice (*h*).

(*h*) *In re Judd and Poland and Skelcher's Contract*, (1906) 1 Ch. 684.

SECTION XLII.—POWER OF COURT TO SANCTION SALE OF LAND AND MINERALS SEPARATELY.

(1) WHERE a trustee or other person is for the time being authorized to dispose of land by way of sale, exchange, partition, or enfranchisement, the High Court may sanction his so disposing of the land with an exception or reservation of any minerals, and with or without rights and powers of or incidental to the working, getting, or carrying away of the minerals, or so disposing of the minerals with or without the said rights or powers, separately from the residue of the land.

(2) Any such trustee or other person with the said sanction previously obtained, may, unless forbidden by the instrument creating the trust or direction, from time to time, without any further application to the court, so dispose of any such land or minerals.

(3) Nothing in this section shall derogate from any power which a trustee may have under the Settled Land Acts, 1882 to 1890, or otherwise (*a*).

It was decided in the case of *Buckley* v. *Howell* (*b*), in 1861, that trustees who had a power of sale and exchange were not entitled to sell the land reserving the minerals.

It was therefore enacted by s. 2 of the Confirmation of Sales Act, 1862 (*c*), that "every trustee and other person now or hereafter to become authorized to dispose of land by way of sale, exchange, partition, or enfranchisement may, unless forbidden by the instru-

(*a*) Trustee Act, 1893, s. 44, as amended by the Trustee Act (1893) Amendment Act, 1894, s. 3.

(*b*) (1861), 29 Beav. 546.

(*c*) 25 & 26 Vict. c. 108.

ment creating the trust or power, so dispose of such land with an exception or reservation of any minerals, and with or without rights and powers of or incidental to the working, getting, or carrying away of such minerals, or may (unless forbidden as aforesaid) dispose of by way of sale, exchange, or partition the minerals with or without such rights or powers separately from the residue of the land, and in either case without prejudice to any future exercise of the authority with respect to the excepted minerals, or (as the case may be) the undisposed-of land; but this enactment shall not enable any such disposition as aforesaid, without the previous sanction of the court of chancery, to be obtained on petition in a summary way of the trustee or other person authorized as aforesaid, which sanction once obtained shall extend to the enabling from time to time of any disposition within this enactment of any part or parts of the lands comprised in any order to be made on such petition without the necessity of any further or other application to the court."

This act was repealed by the Trustee Act, 1893, s. 51, but substantially re-enacted in s. 44 of that act. As re-enacted in that section, however, the provision was limited to trustees, so that it did not include a mortgagee who was not also a trustee. The Trustee Act (1893) Amendment Act, 1894, s. 3, therefore enacted that "in section 44 of the Trustee Act, 1893, after the word 'trustee' in the first two places where it occurs shall be inserted the words 'or other person.'"

The application to the court for an order under this section should apparently be made by petition. Order LIVB. of the Rules of the Supreme Court provides that all applications under the Trustee Act, 1893, may be made by petition except as otherwise provided by Order LV.

SECTION XLIII.—POWER TO SELL SUBJECT TO DEPRECIATORY CONDITIONS.

(1) No sale made by a trustee shall be impeached by any beneficiary upon the ground that any of the conditions subject to which the sale was made may have been unnecessarily depreciatory unless it also appears that the consideration for the sale was thereby rendered inadequate.

(2) No sale made by a trustee shall, after the execution of the conveyance, be impeached as against the purchaser upon the ground that any of the conditions subject to which the sale was made may have been unnecessarily depreciatory, unless it appears that the purchaser was acting in collusion with the trustee at the time when the contract for sale was made.

(3) No purchaser, upon any sale made by a trustee, shall be at liberty to make any objection against the title upon the ground aforesaid.

(4) This section applies only to sales made after the 24th day of December, 1888 (*a*).

A trustee who holds property upon trust for or with a power of sale may sell "subject to any such conditions respecting title or evidence of title or other matter" as he may think fit (*b*), and has certainly had this power since 1860. But although he have such a power he must not, to quote Lord Justice James, "rashly or improvidently introduce a depreciatory condition for which there is no necessity" (*c*); the power must be exercised reasonably, and

(*a*) Trustee Act, 1893, s. 14.

(*b*) Trustee Act, 1893, s. 13. See above, Sect. XLI.

(*c*) *Dance* v. *Goldingham* (1873), L. R. 8 Ch. App. at p. 910.

formerly if a trustee used unduly depreciatory conditions the *cestuis que trust* could have the sale set aside, either before (*d*) or after completion (*e*). The purchaser also might take objection that the conditions were unduly depreciatory, and if he did so the trustee could not enforce the contract against him either by way of specific performance or damages (*d*). It was provided, however, by s. 3 of the Trustee Act, 1888, that (1) no sale made by a trustee should be impeached by any *cestui que trust* upon the ground that any of the conditions subject to which the sale was made may have been unduly depreciatory unless it also appeared that the consideration for the sale was thereby rendered inadequate; and (2) no sale made by a trustee should after the execution of the conveyance be impeached as against the purchaser on the ground that any of the conditions subject to which the sale was made may have been unnecessarily depreciatory unless it appeared that the purchaser was acting in collusion with the trustee at the time when the contract for such sale was made; and (3) no purchaser upon any sale made by a trustee should be at liberty to make any objection against the title upon the ground aforesaid.

This section was repealed by s. 51 of the Trustee Act, 1893, but re-enacted in the form given above by s. 14 of that act.

As a result a *cestui que trust* cannot now impeach the sale as against the trustee unless he can prove three things:—(1) that one or more of the conditions was unnecessarily depreciatory; (2) that the consideration for the sale was inadequate; and (3) that this was the consequence of the employment of the condition or conditions. Even then, if the purchase has been completed in order to get it set aside as against the purchaser, he must prove that the latter was acting in collusion with the trustee. But though as between the *cestui que trust* and the purchaser the transaction may be unimpeachable, there is nothing in the act to prevent the *cestui que trust* from requiring the trustee to make good the loss he has sustained if he can show that the consideration was inadequate.

(*d*) *Dunn* v. *Flood* (1885), 28 Ch. D. 586.

(*e*) *Rede* v. *Oakes* (1864), 4 De G. J. & S. at p. 513.

SECTION XLIV.—POWER TO SELL UNDER THE VENDOR AND PURCHASER ACT, 1874.

A TRUSTEE who is either a vendor or a purchaser may sell or buy without excluding the application of s. 2 of the Vendor and Purchaser Act, 1874 (*a*).

In the year 1874, with a view to facilitating the transfer of land, it was enacted by the Vendor and Purchaser Act, 1874, s. 2, that—

"In the completion of any contract [of sale of land] and subject to any stipulation to the contrary in the contract, the obligations and rights of vendor and purchaser shall be regulated by the following rules; that is to say,

"First.—Under a contract to grant or assign a term of years, whether derived or to be derived out of a freehold or leasehold estate, the intended lessee or assign shall not be entitled to call for the title to the freehold.

"Second.—Recitals, statements, and descriptions of facts, matters, and parties contained in deeds, instruments, acts of parliament, or statutory declarations twenty years old at the date of the contract, shall, unless and except so far as they shall be proved to be inaccurate, be taken to be sufficient evidence of the truth of such facts, matters, and descriptions.

"Third.—The inability of the vendor to furnish the purchaser with a legal covenant to produce and furnish copies of documents of title shall not be an objection to title in case the purchaser will on the completion of the contract have an equitable right to the production of such documents.

"Fourth.—Such covenants for production as the purchaser can and shall require shall be furnished at his expense, and the vendor shall bear the expense of perusal and execution on behalf of and

(*a*) Trustee Act, 1893, s. 15.

by himself, and on behalf of and by necessary parties other than the purchaser.

"Fifth.—Where the vendor retains any part of an estate to which any documents of title relate, he shall be entitled to retain such documents."

These rules materially curtailed the rights of a purchaser of land. But according to the general rule of equity trustees investing trust money in the purchase of land were bound to see that they obtained a good marketable title (*b*). In order to preclude any question where the parties were trustees the statute therefore provided that "trustees who are either vendors or purchasers may sell or buy without excluding the application of the second section of this act" (*c*). This was repealed by s. 51 of the Trustee Act, 1893, but re-enacted in the form given above in s. 15 of that act.

In pursuance of the same policy it was subsequently enacted by s. 4 (3) of the Trustee Act, 1888, that no trustee shall be chargeable with breach of trust upon the ground that in effecting the purchase of any property or in lending money upon the security of any property he shall have accepted a shorter title than the title which a purchaser is in the absence of a special contract entitled to require, if in the opinion of the court the title accepted be such as a person acting with prudence and caution would have accepted. This also was repealed by s. 51 of the Trustee Act, 1893, but re-enacted with a slight variation of language in s. 8 (3) of that act.

(*b*) Williams, Vendor and Purchaser, vol. i. 298.

(*c*) s. 3. Compare s. 66 (3) of the Conveyancing Act, 1881, which protects trustees who adopt the provisions of that act.

SECTION XLV.—POWER TO AUTHORIZE RECEIPT OF MONEY BY BANKER OR SOLICITOR.

(1) A TRUSTEE may appoint a solicitor to be his agent to receive and give a discharge for any money or valuable consideration or property receivable by the trustee under the trust by permitting the solicitor to have the custody of and to produce a deed containing any such receipt as is referred to in s. 56 of the Conveyancing and Law of Property Act, 1881; and a trustee shall not be chargeable with breach of trust by reason only of his having made or concurred in making any such appointment; and the producing of any such deed by the solicitor shall have the same validity and effect under the said section as if the person appointing the solicitor had not been a trustee.

(2) A trustee may appoint a banker or solicitor to be his agent to receive and give a discharge for any money payable to the trustee under or by virtue of a policy of assurance by permitting the banker or solicitor to have the custody of and to produce the policy of assurance with a receipt signed by the trustee, and a trustee shall not be chargeable with a breach of trust by reason only of his having made or concurred in making any such appointment.

(3) Nothing in this section shall exempt a trustee from any liability which he would have incurred if this act had not been passed in case he permits any such money, valuable consideration or property to remain in

the hands or under the control of the banker or solicitor for a period longer than is reasonably necessary to enable the banker or solicitor (as the case may be) to pay or transfer the same to the trustee.

(4) This section applies only where the money or valuable consideration or property is received after the 24th day of December, 1888.

(5) Nothing in this section shall authorize a trustee to do anything which he is in express terms forbidden to do, or to omit anything which he is in express terms directed to do by the instrument creating the trust (*a*).

It was enacted by s. 56 of the Conveyancing Act, 1881, that "where a solicitor produces a deed having in the body thereof, or indorsed thereon, a receipt for consideration money or other consideration, the deed being executed or the indorsed receipt being signed by the person entitled to give a receipt for that consideration, the deed shall be sufficient authority to the person liable to pay or give the same for his paying or giving the same to the solicitor without the solicitor producing any separate or other direction or authority in that behalf from the person who executed or signed the deed or receipt."

But previously to this act the rule of equity was that, under ordinary circumstances, trustees were not justified in authorizing their solicitors or other agents to receive purchase-money which ought to be paid personally by them (*b*); and in 1883, in the case of *In re Bellamy and the Metropolitan Board of Works* (*c*), it was decided by the majority of the Court of Appeal that the section had not enlarged the powers of trustees, and therefore generally a purchaser of property from trustees could not safely pay the purchase-money to the trustee's solicitor, even though he produced a deed containing such a receipt as is mentioned in the above section of the Conveyancing Act.

This led to some inconvenience, and it was therefore enacted by s. 2 of the Trustee Act, 1888, that "it shall be lawful for a trustee to appoint a solicitor to be his agent to receive and give a discharge

(*a*) Trustee Act, 1893, s. 17.

(*b*) Per Cotton, L. J., at 24 Ch. D. p. 400.

(*c*) (1883), 24 Ch. D. 387.

for any money or any valuable consideration or property receivable by such trustee under the trust by permitting the solicitor to have the custody of and to produce a deed containing any such receipt as is referred to in the 56th section of the Conveyancing and Law of Property Act, 1881; and no trustee shall be chargeable with breach of trust by reason only of his having made or concurred in making any such appointment; and the producing of any such deed by such solicitor shall have the same effect, by virtue of the said 56th section, as the same would have had if the person appointing such solicitor had not been a trustee . . . ."

At the same time, authority was given to a trustee to appoint a banker or a solicitor to be his agent to receive and give a discharge for money payable under a policy of assurance, by permitting him to have the custody of and to produce the policy, with a receipt signed by the trustee.

Both these enactments were repealed by s. 51 of the Trustee Act, 1893, but re-enacted in somewhat different language by s. 17 of that act.

SECTION XLVI.—POWER TO INSURE PROPERTY.

(1) A TRUSTEE may insure against loss or damage by fire any building or other insurable property to any amount (including the amount of any insurance already on foot) not exceeding three equal fourth parts of the full value of such building or property, and pay the premiums for such insurance out of the income thereof or out of the income of any other property subject to the same trusts without obtaining the consent of any person who may be entitled wholly or partly to such income.

(2) This section does not apply to any building or property which a trustee is bound forthwith to convey absolutely to any beneficiary upon being requested to do so.

(3) This section applies to trusts created either before or after the commencement of this act, but nothing in this section shall authorize any trustee to do anything which he is in express terms forbidden to do, or to omit to do anything which he is in express terms directed to do by the instrument creating the trust (*a*).

Before 1888 a trustee was in a difficult position with regard to insuring buildings or property against fire. If he omitted to continue or renew a policy, serious loss might be occasioned to the trust estate, while if he did insure, the beneficiaries interested might raise objections, for he could not safely insure without the assent of the person entitled to the income (*b*).

(*a*) Trustee Act, 1893, s. 18.

(*b*) Lewin, Trusts, 11th ed. 702; Rudall & Greig, Trustee Acts, 3rd ed. 88.

It was therefore enacted by s. 7 of the Trustee Act, 1888, that "it shall be lawful for, but not obligatory upon, a trustee to insure against loss or damage by fire any building or other insurable property to any amount (including the amount of any insurance already on foot) not exceeding three equal fourth parts of the full value of such building or property, and to pay the premium for such insurance out of the income thereof or out of the income of any other property, subject to the same trusts, without obtaining the consent of any person who may be entitled wholly or partly to such income."

The section, however, did not apply to any building or property which a trustee is bound forthwith to convey absolutely to any *cestui que trust* upon being requested so to do.

This enactment was repealed by s. 51 of the Trustee Act, 1893, but was re-enacted in the form given above in s. 18 of that act.

It has been held that the section justifies a trustee in insuring heirlooms, or rather chattels settled to devolve as such, and in paying the premiums for the insurance out of the income of capital money in their hands (*c*).

(*c*) *In re Earl of Egmont's Trusts*, (1908) 1 Ch. 821.

Section XLVII.—Power of Trustee of renewable Leaseholds to renew and raise Money for the Purpose.

(1) A trustee of any leaseholds for lives or years which are renewable from time to time, either under any covenant or contract, or by custom or usual practice, may, if he thinks fit, and shall if thereto required by any person having any beneficial interest, present or future or contingent, in the leaseholds, use his best endeavours to obtain from time to time a renewed lease of the same hereditaments on the accustomed and reasonable terms, and for that purpose may from time to time make, or concur in making, a surrender of the lease for the time being subsisting, and do all such other acts as are requisite: Provided that where by the terms of the settlement or will the person in possession for his life or other limited interest is entitled to enjoy the same without any obligation to renew or to contribute to the expense of renewal, this section shall not apply, unless the consent in writing of that person is obtained to the renewal on the part of the trustee.

(2) If money is required to pay for the renewal, the trustee effecting the renewal may pay the same out of any money then in his hands in trust for the persons beneficially interested in the lands to be comprised in the renewed lease, and if he has not in his hands sufficient money for the purpose, he may raise the money required by mortgage of the hereditaments to be com-

prised in the renewed lease, or of any other hereditaments for the time being subject to the uses or trusts to which those hereditaments are subject, and no person advancing money upon a mortgage purporting to be under this power shall be bound to see that the money is wanted, or that no more is raised than is wanted for the purpose.

(3) This section applies to trusts created either before or after the commencement of this act; but nothing in this section shall authorize any trustee to do anything which he is in express terms forbidden to do, or to omit to do anything which he is in express terms directed to do by the instrument creating the trust (*a*).

Before the 28th of August, 1860, in the absence of a direction expressed or implied in the trust instrument, a trustee of renewable leaseholds was not bound to renew them (*b*). But if he did renew, the renewed lease, although he might have taken it in his own name and for his own benefit, became subject to the trusts of the original term, the trustee having a lien on it for the expenses of the renewal with interest and a right to be indemnified by the beneficiaries against any covenants he might have entered into with the lessor (*c*).

By s. 8 of Lord Cranworth's Act (*d*), which came into force on that day, it was provided that "it shall be lawful for any trustees of any leaseholds for lives or years which are renewable from time to time either under any covenant or contract or by custom or usual practice, if they shall in their discretion think fit, and it shall be the duty of such trustees if thereunto required by any person having any beneficial interest, present or future or contingent, in such leaseholds to use their best endeavours to obtain from time to time a renewed lease of the same hereditaments on the accustomed and reasonable terms, and for that purpose it shall be lawful for any such trustees from time to time to make, or concur in making,

(*a*) Trustee Act, 1893, s. 19.

(*b*) Rudall & Greig, Trustee Acts, 3rd ed. 90.

(*c*) *Keech* v. *Sandford* (1726), Sel. Ch. Ca. 61, and other cases above, s. XVI.

(*d*) 22 & 23 Vict. c. 145.

such surrender of the lease for the time being subsisting, and to do all such other acts as shall be requisite in that behalf; but this section is not to apply to any case where, by the terms of the settlement or will, the person in possession for his life or other limited interest is entitled to enjoy the same without any obligation to renew the lease or to contribute to the expense of renewing the same." And by s. 9 provision was made for raising any money required for the purpose by mortgage of the hereditaments to be received in exchange or contained in the renewed lease or of any other hereditaments for the time being subject to the trusts.

These enactments were repealed by s. 64 of the Settled Land Act, 1882, with a saving for any rights accrued before the commencement of that act.

They were, however, re-enacted in somewhat different terms in ss. 10 and 11 of the Trustee Act, 1888, which were in their turn repealed by s. 51 of the Trustee Act, 1893, and replaced by s. 19 of that act in the above form.

SECTION XLVIII.—POWER OF TRUSTEE TO GIVE RECEIPTS.

(1) THE receipt in writing of any trustee for any money, securities, or other personal property or effects payable, transferable, or deliverable to him under any trust or power, shall be a sufficient discharge for the same, and shall effectually exonerate the person paying, transferring, or delivering the same from seeing to the application or being answerable for any loss or misapplication thereof.

(2) This section applies to trusts created either before or after the commencement of this act (*a*).

Formerly a person who paid money to a trustee in his capacity as such was bound to see that he applied it in accordance with the terms of his trust. There were exceptions to the rule, but they were of limited application (*b*).

This obligation was very onerous, and would seem to be indefensible on any principle (*c*). It therefore became the practice in well-drawn settlements and wills to insert a clause giving the trustees power to give receipts for money paid them, and exonerating purchasers and others dealing with them from seeing to the application of the money. At length the burden became intolerable and the legislature intervened (*d*), and after an abortive attempt to deal with the matter in 1844 (*e*), it was enacted by the Law of Property Amendment Act, 1859, s. 23, that "the *bonâ fide* payment to and the receipt of any person to whom any *purchase or mortgage money* shall be payable upon any express or implied trust

(*a*) Trustee Act, 1893, s. 20.

(*b*) See *Elliot* v. *Merryman* (1740), Barnardiston, Chy. R. 78, and notes in White & Tudor, L. C. Eq. 7th ed. 896 *et seq.*

(*c*) See Ames, Cases on the Law of Trusts, 271.

(*d*) See as to the law in the United States of America, Ames, *supra*.

(*e*) By the statute 7 & 8 Vict. c. 76, s. 10, repealed by 8 & 9 Vict. c. 106 (The Real Property Act, 1845), s. 1.

shall effectually discharge the person paying the same from seeing to the application or being answerable for the misapplication thereof, unless the contrary shall be expressly declared by the instrument creating the trust or security."

The act came into force on the 13th August, 1859, and this section is apparently still in force. However, it was practically superseded by the wider provisions of Lord Cranworth's Act, which came into force just a year later (*f*).

S. 29 of this act provided that "the receipts in writing of any trustees or trustee for any money payable to them or him by reason or in the exercise of any trusts or powers reposed or vested in them or him shall be sufficient discharges for the money therein expressed to be received, and shall effectually exonerate the persons paying such money from seeing to the application thereof, or from being answerable for any loss or misapplication thereof." This section was, however, repealed by s. 71 of the Conveyancing Act, 1881, but was re-enacted by s. 36 of that act in the following terms:—

"(1) The receipt in writing of any trustees or trustee for any money, securities, or other personal property or effects payable, transferable, or deliverable to them or him under any trust or power shall be a sufficient discharge for the same, and shall effectually exonerate the person paying or transferring or delivering the same from seeing to the application or being answerable for any loss or misapplication thereof.

"(2) This section applies to trusts created either before or after the commencement of this act."

This, in its turn, was repealed by s. 51 of the Trustee Act, 1893, and re-enacted in s. 20 of that act, which is as follows:—

"(1) The receipt in writing of any trustee for any money, securities, or other personal property or effects payable, transferable, or deliverable to him under any trust or power shall be a sufficient discharge for the same, and shall effectually exonerate the person paying, transferring, or delivering the same from seeing to the application, or being answerable for any loss or misapplication thereof.

"(2) This section applies to trusts created either before or after the commencement of this act."

(*f*) 22 & 23 Vict. c. 145, which came into force on the 28th August, 1860.

SECTION XLIX.—POWER TO COMPOUND AND SETTLE CLAIMS.

(1) AN executor or administrator may pay or allow any debt or claim on any evidence that he thinks sufficient.

(2) An executor or administrator, or two or more trustees, acting together, or a sole acting trustee where by the instrument (if any) creating the trust a sole trustee is authorized to execute the trusts and powers thereof, may, if and as he or they may think fit, accept any composition or any security, real or personal, for any debt or for any property, real or personal, claimed, and may allow any time for payment of any debt, and may compromise, compound, abandon, submit to arbitration or otherwise settle any debt, account, claim or thing whatever relating to the testator's or intestate's estate or to the trust, and for any of those purposes may enter into, give, execute and do such agreements, instruments of composition or arrangement, releases and other things as to him or them seem expedient without being responsible for any loss occasioned by any act or thing so done by him or them in good faith.

(3) This section applies only if and as far as a contrary intention is not expressed in the instrument (if any) creating the trust, and shall have effect subject to the terms of that instrument, and to the provisions therein contained.

(4) This section applies to executorships, adminis-

tratorships, and trusts constituted or created either before or after the commencement of this act (*a*).

Independently of statutory enactment trustees might release or compound a debt or allow a reasonable time for payment, but it was somewhat risky for them to do so, for it lay on them to prove that it was for the benefit of the estate to do it (*b*).

It therefore became usual in properly drawn settlements and wills to give them express power, and in 1860 it was enacted by s. 30 of Lord Cranworth's Act (*c*) that "it shall be lawful for any *executors* to pay any debts or claims upon any evidence that they may think sufficient and to accept any composition or any security, real or personal, for any debts due to the deceased, and to allow any time for payment of any such debts as they shall think fit, and also to compromise, compound or submit to arbitration all debts, accounts, claims and things whatsoever relating to the estate of the deceased" . . . .

This, it will be seen, only applied to executors and was repealed by s. 71 of the Conveyancing Act, 1881, but s. 37 of that act re-enacted it in a wider form, extending it to two or more trustees acting together or a sole acting trustee, where by the instrument (if any) creating the trust, a sole trustee is authorized to act, and applied to executorships and trusts constituted or created either before or after the commencement of the act.

This, again, was repealed by s. 51 of the Trustee Act, 1893, and re-enacted in s. 21 of that act, which extended the power to administrators in the form given above.

Apparently the result of the enactment is that, so long as the trustee or personal representative has acted in good faith, it is not necessary for him to show that any transaction coming within the terms of the section was a proper one but for the beneficiary impeaching it to show its impropriety (*d*).

(*a*) Trustee Act, 1893, s. 21.

(*b*) *Blue* v. *Marshall* (1735), 3 P. W. 381; *Forshaw* v. *Higginson* (1857), 8 De G. M. & G. 827.

(*c*) 22 & 23 Vict. c. 145.

(*d*) See Underhill, Trusts and Trustees, 6th ed. 210, 212; Rudall & Greig, Trustee Acts, 3rd ed. 97. See also per Sir G. Jessel, in *Re Owens* (1882), 47 L. T. 61, at p. 64.

Section L.—Power to apply Income of Property of Infant for Maintenance, &c.

(1) Where any property is held by trustees in trust for an infant, either for life or for any greater interest, and whether absolutely or contingently on his attaining the age of twenty-one years, or on the occurrence of any event before his attaining that age, the trustees may, at their sole discretion, pay to the infant's parent or guardian, if any, or otherwise apply for or towards the infant's maintenance, education, or benefit, the income of that property or any part thereof, whether there is any other fund applicable to the same purpose or any person bound by law to provide for the infant's maintenance or education or not.

(2) The trustees shall accumulate all the residue of that income in the way of compound interest by investing the same and the resulting income thereof from time to time on securities on which they are by the settlement (if any) or by law authorized to invest trust money, and shall hold those accumulations for the benefit of the person who ultimately becomes entitled to the property from which the same arise; but so that the trustees may at any time, if they think fit, apply those accumulations or any part thereof as if the same were income arising in the then current year.

(3) This section applies only if and as far as a contrary intention is not expressed in the instrument under which the interest of the infant arises, and shall have

effect subject to the terms of that instrument and to the provisions therein contained.

(4) This section applies whether that instrument comes into operation before or after the commencement of this act (*a*).

It often happens that when a beneficiary is under age it is necessary to make provision for his or her maintenance. Before 1860 this could only be done by the trustees without application to the court if there was an express power conferred on them by the trust instrument.

In that year it was, however, enacted by Lord Cranworth's Act (22 & 23 Vict. c. 145), s. 26, that where any property was held by trustees in trust for an infant, either absolutely or contingently on his attaining the age of twenty-one years, or on the occurrence of any event previously to his attaining that age, it should be lawful for such trustees at their sole discretion to pay to the guardians (if any) of such infant, or otherwise to apply for or towards the maintenance or education of such infant, the whole or any part of the income *to which such infant might be entitled in respect of such property.*

It was held by the courts that, having regard to the words italicized, the section did not apply in the case where an infant was contingently entitled, unless on the contingency happening the infant would be entitled to the interest which had accrued on the capital during his minority as well as to his share of the capital (*b*).

In 1881 this enactment was repealed by s. 71 of the Conveyancing Act, 1881, s. 43 of which provides that—

"(1) Where any property is held by trustees in trust for an infant, either for life or for any greater interest, and whether absolutely or contingently on his attaining the age of twenty-one years, or on the occurrence of any event before his attaining that age, the trustees may at their sole discretion pay to the infant's parent or guardian (if any), or otherwise apply for or towards the infant's maintenance, education or benefit the income of *that property*, or any part thereof, whether there is any other fund applicable to the same purpose, or any person bound by law to provide for the infant's maintenance or education or not."

(*a*) Conveyancing Act, 1881, s. 43.

(*b*) *In re George* (1877), 5 Ch. D. 837.

It will be seen that this is framed in wider terms than the act of 1860, and it was not unreasonably argued that the alteration in the language of the act conferred power on the trustees to apply income for the maintenance of an infant entitled to property from which it was derived contingently on his attaining the age of twenty-one, even if when he attained that age he would not be entitled to the past income. However, the Court of Appeal held that such an important alteration could only be effected by a much clearer expression of intention to that effect than the act contained, and that the same construction was to be given it (*c*).

The following cases illustrate this:—

Illustrations.

1. Testator gives to each of the children who shall be living at his death and attains twenty-one, of A., B. and C., the sum of 1,000*l.*, and gives his residuary estate to X. and Y. in equal shares. Testator is not *in loco parentis* to any of the children. The trustees of the will are not entitled to utilize the income accruing on the sums of 1,000*l.* for the maintenance of the children under age. *In re Dickson*, *Hill* v. *Grant* (1885), 29 Ch. D. 331.

2. Testator gives real estate to trustees upon trust to pay the rents and profits to A. for life, and after her death in trust for A.'s children who, being sons, attain twenty-one, or being daughters attain that age or marry. A. dies, leaving six children under age. The trustees are not entitled to apply the income of the real estate for the maintenance of the children, and when the eldest attains twenty-one he is entitled to the whole of the rents and profits until the next attains twenty-one or (if a daughter) marries. *In re Averill*, *Salsbury* v. *Buckle*, (1898) 1 Ch. 523.

In neither of the foregoing cases were the infants, when they attained the age of twenty-one, entitled to the income accruing due during their minority on the property then vesting in them.

But if, when the infant attains a vested interest, by attaining the required age or otherwise, he will become entitled not merely to the corpus but to the income accruing due thereon during his minority, the section applies, and the trustees can apply the income

(*c*) *In re Dickson*, *Hill* v. *Grant* (1885), 29 Ch. D. 331.

for his maintenance. And when there is a class of infants contingently entitled on attaining twenty-one, each one as he attains that age acquires a vested interest in his share of the capital, and a like share of the income only, so that the balance of the income is applicable for the maintenance of the remaining members of the class. Thus, if a testator gives the residue of his estate upon trust to pay and divide the same among the children of X., who shall be living at his decease and who shall attain the age of twenty-one years, in equal shares, and there are six children of X., when the eldest child attains twenty-one she is entitled to only one-sixth of the income of the residue, and the remaining five-sixths are applicable for the maintenance of the other children during their minority, and so on (*d*). In this case the gift being of residuary personalty, the gift, although contingent, carries with it the intermediate income (*e*), as does a contingent gift of blended residuary, realty and personalty (*f*).

The section of the Conveyancing Act, 1881, continues:—

"(2) The trustees shall accumulate all the residue of that income in the way of compound interest by investing the same, and the resulting income thereof from time to time, on securities on which they are by the settlement (if any) or by law authorized to invest trust money, and shall hold those accumulations for the benefit of the person who ultimately becomes entitled to the property from which the same arise; but so that the trustees may at any time if they think fit apply those accumulations, or any part thereof, as if the same were income arising in the then current year."

The words "the property from which the same arise" mean the property the income arising from which has been accumulated, so that if a contingent legacy is settled on trust for a legatee for life, and after his death on trust for his children or remoter issue, the tenant for life is, on the happening of the contingency, entitled only to the interest during his life of the amount of the surplus

(*d*) *In re Holford, Holford* v. *Holford*, (1894) 3 Ch. 30. Conf. *In re Averill*, *supra*, where the gift did not carry the intermediate income.

(*e*) *Green* v. *Ekins* (1742), 2 Atk. 473; *In re Adams*, (1893) 1 Ch. 329.

(*f*) *In re Burton's Will*, (1892) 2 Ch. 38.

income and the accumulations thereof—the surplus income and accumulations forming an accretion to the capital (*g*).

The section goes on—

"(3) This section applies only if and as far as a contrary intention is not expressed in the instrument under which the interest of the infant arises, and shall have effect subject to the terms of that instrument and to the provisions therein contained.

"(4) This section applies whether that instrument comes into operation before or after the commencement of this act."

These two sub-sections taken together mean, Lord Justice Fry has said, "that all that has gone before with regard to maintenance is made subject to the will or other instrument under which the infant claims, and that the construction of the will or other instrument is not in terms affected by this section." Consequently a gift either by express words or by implication of the intermediate income of a legacy to some other person than the infant legatee excludes the section (*h*).

(*g*) *In re Bowlby*, (1904) 2 Ch. 685.

(*h*) *In re Dickson, Hill* v. *Grant* (1885), 29 Ch. D. at p. 339.

SECTION LI.—POWERS EXERCISABLE BY SURVIVOR OF TWO OR MORE TRUSTEES.

(1) WHERE a power or trust is given to or vested in two or more trustees jointly, then, unless the contrary is expressed in the instrument, if any, creating the power or trust, the same may be exercised or performed by the survivor or survivors of them for the time being.

(2) This section applies only to trusts constituted after or created by instruments coming into operation after the 31st day of December, 1881 (*a*).

It appears to have always been the rule that a power given to two or more trustees as part of the trust is exercisable by the survivors or survivor, although if a mere power were given to several persons, and one or more of them died, the power could not be exercised (*b*).

"If," says Mr. Lewin, "a *mere* power be given to A., B. and C., and one of them die, it is perfectly clear that the power cannot be exercised by the survivors: but if trustees have an *equitable* power annexed to the trust and forming an integral part of it, as if an estate be vested in three trustees upon trust to sell, then as the power is coupled with an interest and the interest survives, the power also survives," and he continues: "it seems now to be decided that even where the trust is reposed in the trustees by name, the survivor who takes the estate with the duty annexed to it can execute the trust: and the rule of survivorship applies not only to trusts or powers imperative which are construed as trusts but also to such discretionary powers as are annexed to the office of trustee and are meant to form an integral part of it" (*c*).

(*a*) Trustee Act, 1893, s. 22.

(*b*) See Coke, Litt. 113 a.

(*c*) Lewin, Trusts, 11th ed. 746, 748, cited and applied by Swinfen Eady, J., in *In re Bacon, Toovey* v. *Turner*, (1907) 1 Ch. at p. 479.

The following cases illustrate this:—

> Testator devises freehold land to X. and Y. upon trust that the sum of 2,000*l.* shall be raised thereout by sale or otherwise, at the discretion of the trustees, and that the 2,000*l.* shall be invested and applied for the maintenance of his daughter. Y. dies. X. can sell the land for the purpose of raising the 2,000*l.* *Lane* v. *Debenham* (1853), 11 Hare, 188 (*d*).

"The main question is whether or not, there being a direct trust to raise 2,000*l.* by sale or otherwise—and thus a discretion to be exercised, and one of the trustees being dead—it is thereby rendered impossible for the surviving trustee to execute this trust without the direction of the court. The money, it is clear, must be raised; can the surviving trustee raise it by means of a sale, or is it necessary to come to the court in order that the court may exercise its discretion whether it is to be by sale, by mortgage, or by some other appropriation? Mr. Walker has argued that whether the case be one of a power or a trust, if it be confided to two persons, or if it be a mere trust for sale, if it is said that the sale is to be made by two persons, a survivor of the two can never execute it. The argument proceeds, as it appears to me, upon an entire disregard of the distinction between powers and trusts. No doubt where it is a naked power given to two persons, that will not survive to one of them unless there be express words or a necessary implication upon the whole will showing it to be the intention that it should do so. But the ground of that rule is, that where the testator has disposed of his property in one direction, subject to a power in two or more persons, enabling them to divert it in another direction, the property will go as the testator has first directed, unless the person to whom he has given the power of controlling the disposition exercise that power. He, therefore, to whom the testator has given the property, subject to having it taken from him by the exercise of the power, has a right to say that it must be exercised *modo et forma.* It is therefore a rule of law that in all cases of powers the previous estate is not to be defeated unless the power be exercised in the manner specifically directed. When, on the other hand, a testator gives his property,

(*d*) *In re Bacon, Toovey* v. *Turner*, (1907) 1 Ch. 475, is to the same effect.

not to one party subject to a power in others, but to trustees upon special trusts, with a direction to carry his purposes into effect, it is the duty of the trustees to execute the trust. Thus, if the direction be to raise a certain sum of money, the estate is thereby at once charged, and it becomes the duty of the trustee to raise the charge so created. If an estate be devised to A. and B. upon trust to sell, and thereby raise such a sum, it is, I think, a novel argument that after A.'s death B. cannot sell the estate and execute the trust. . . ." (*e*).

By an agreement for a marriage settlement the tenant for life is authorized to divert the trusts of the settled fund with the assent of the "undersigned trustees." Both trustees die. The power of assent may be exercised by new trustees appointed by the court. *Byam* v. *Byam* (1854), 19 Beav. 58.

"There is no question but that a power to consent given to named and specified persons cannot be exercised after the death of any of them; but it is also equally certain that when such a power is conferred on persons not in their individual character, but in their character of trustees, the power will belong to the trustees for the time being" (*f*).

Testator devises his real and personal estate to his wife for life, and from and after her decease to A. and B., their heirs, executors and administrators, upon trust to sell and dispose thereof "at such times and in such manner as they, my said trustees, shall deem expedient." A. and B. both die before the tenant for life, B., the survivor, having devised his trust estates to X. and Y. The latter can exercise the power of sale. *Osborne* to *Rowlett* (1880), 13 Ch. D. 774.

"The true view appears to me to be this: that the person to execute the trust for sale is the person who takes the estate, not by accident, so to speak, but in accordance with the provisions of the will. There is a trust annexed to the estate, and when we

(*e*) Per Page Wood, V.-C., *Lane* v. *Debenham*, *supra*, at p. 191.

(*f*) Per Sir J. Romilly, M. R., *Byam* v. *Byam*, *supra*, at p. 66. See also *In re Smith*, *Eastick* v. *Smith*, (1904) 1 Ch. 139.

find who is the person who takes the estate under the will, we find who is the person to execute the trust" (*g*).

> Testator devises his freehold and copyhold estates to A. and B. and their heirs "upon trust that they, my said trustees, or the trustees or trustee for the time being of this my will" shall sell. A. dies, and afterwards B. dies intestate. B.'s customary heir can sell the copyholds. *In re Morton and Hallett* (1880), 15 Ch. D. 143.

"If an estate is given to A. and B. and their heirs on trust to sell, the heir of the survivor of A. and B. is a trustee under the will, takes the estate on trust for sale and can sell it" (*h*).

Before 1882, in view of the questions which had been raised, conveyancers were in the habit, in conferring powers on two or more executors or trustees, of adding the words "and the survivors and survivor of them." It was, however, enacted by s. 38 of the Conveyancing Act, 1881, that—(1) "Where a power or trust is given to or vested in two or more executors or trustees jointly, then, unless the contrary is expressed in the instrument (if any) creating the power or trust, the same may be exercised or performed by the survivor or survivors of them for the time being." But this section applied only to executorships and trusts constituted after or created by instruments coming into operation after the commencement of the act—the 1st of January, 1882.

The section was repealed by s. 51 of the Trustee Act, 1893, but re-enacted in s. 22 of that act, with the omission of the words "executors or."

The result of the enactments seems to be merely to declare the law so far as regards powers annexed to trusts, and possibly to extend the same rule to a mere power, thus abolishing the distinction which formerly existed between them (*i*). This, however, is

(*g*) Per Sir G. Jessel, M. R., *Osborne to Rowlett*, *supra*, at p. 783, treating *Cooke* v. *Crawford* (1842), 13 Sim. 91, *contra*, as overruled. *In re Waidanis*, (1908) 1 Ch. 123, appears to support this. See, however, per James and Baggallay, L. JJ., in *In re Morton and Hallett*, *supra*.

(*h*) Per James, L. J., in *In re Morton and Hallett*, *supra*, at p. 149. It would seem that the same applies to personal representatives where the estate devolves on them under the Conveyancing Act, 1881, s. 30. See *In re Waidanis*, (1908) 1 Ch. 123.

(*i*) See Clerke & Brett, Conv. Acts, 3rd ed. 159.

not clear, since the section only applies where a power is vested in two or more *trustees* (*j*).

"The result of the authorities, and of ss. 22 and 37 of the Trustee Act," Lord Justice Farwell has said, "is, in my opinion, this: every power given to trustees which enables them to deal with or affect the trust property is *primâ facie* given them *ex-officio* as an incident of their office, and passes with the office to the holders or holder thereof for the time being" (*k*).

(*j*) Lewin, Trusts, 11th ed. 748; Rudall & Greig, Trustee Acts, 3rd ed. 98; Champernowne & Johnston, Trustee Acts, 85 *et seq.*

(*k*) *In re Smith*, *Eastick* v. *Smith*, (1904) 1 Ch. at p. 144.

SECTION LII.—POWER OF TRUSTEE TO ACT UNDER POWERS OF ATTORNEY.

A TRUSTEE acting or paying money in good faith under or in pursuance of any power of attorney shall not be liable for any such act or payment by reason of the fact that at the time of the payment or act the person who gave the power of attorney was dead, or had done some act to avoid the power, if this fact was not known to the trustee at the time of his so acting or paying:

Provided that nothing in this section shall affect the right of any person entitled to the money against the person to whom the payment is made, and that the person so entitled shall have the same remedy against the person to whom the payment is made as he would have had against the trustee (*a*).

It not infrequently happens that a trustee has to pay the income of the trust property to an agent of the beneficiary, the agent being appointed to receive it by a power of attorney from the beneficiary. A power of attorney can be revoked either expressly or impliedly, as by the death, lunacy, or unsoundness of mind or bankruptcy of the principal. Probably the revocation is only effective as regards persons dealing with the attorney in good faith when it is made known to them (*b*), but in the case of a trustee this was expressly enacted by s. 26 of the Law of Property Amendment Act, 1859 (*c*), which was as follows:—

"No trustee, executor, or administrator making any payment, or doing any act *bonâ fide* under or in pursuance of any power of

(*a*) Trustee Act, 1893, s. 23.

(*b*) See Story, Agency, 470.

(*c*) 22 & 23 Vict. c. 35 (Lord St. Leonards' Act).

attorney, shall be liable for the moneys so paid or the act so done by reason that the person who gave the power of attorney was dead at the time of such payment or act, or had done some act to avoid the power, provided that the fact of the death, or of the doing of such act as last aforesaid, at the time of such payment or act *bonâ fide* done as aforesaid by such trustee, executor, or administrator, was not known to him:

"Provided always that nothing herein contained shall in any manner affect or prejudice the right of any person entitled to the money against the person to whom such payment shall have been made, but that such person so entitled shall have the same remedy against such person to whom such payment shall be made as he would have had against the trustee, executor, or administrator, if the money had not been paid away under such power of attorney."

A further provision on the same point is made by the Conveyancing Act, 1881, s. 47 of which is as follows:—

"(1) Any person making or doing any payment or act in good faith in pursuance of a power of attorney shall not be liable in respect of the payment or act by reason that before the payment or act the donor of the power had died, or become lunatic, of unsound mind, or bankrupt, or had revoked the power if the fact of death, lunacy, unsoundness of mind, bankruptcy, or revocation was not, at the time of the payment or act, known to the person making or doing the same.

"(2) But this section shall not affect any right against the payee of any person interested in any money so paid; and that person shall have the like remedy against the payee as he would have had against the payor if the payment had not been made by him.

"(3) This section applies only to payments and acts made and done after the commencement of this act."

The provision of the Conveyancing Act is much more extensive than that of the act of 1859 in that it applies to any person, and not only to revocation by the death or some act of the donor of the power, but to revocation by lunacy, unsoundness of mind, and bankruptcy as well.

The provision of the Conveyancing Act is still in force, but s. 26 of the Law of Property Amendment Act, 1859, was repealed by s. 51 of the Trustee Act, 1893, though it was substantially re-enacted in s. 23 of that act. The re-enacted section only expressly refers to a trustee; but by s. 50 of the act the word "trustee" includes "the duties incident to the office of personal representative," so that the effect is the same. It is not clear why, having regard to s. 47 of the Conveyancing Act, the provision of the act of 1859 should have been re-enacted. If it was intended to make it plain that a trustee was to have the same protection as other people, it is curious that the narrower language of the earlier section was adopted.

SECTION LIII.—POWERS OF TRUSTEE NOT SUBJECT TO ANY CONTROL WHEN EXERCISED IN GOOD FAITH.

WHERE a discretion as to the mode of performing the trust is conferred on a trustee by the settlor, the trustee is not subject to any control in exercising such discretion, provided that he exercises it in good faith.

"Where a testator has given a pure discretion to trustees as to the exercise of a power," said Sir George Jessel, "the court does not enforce the exercise of the power against the wish of the trustees, but it does prevent them from exercising it improperly. The court says that the power, if exercised at all, is to be properly exercised. But in all cases where there is a trust or duty coupled with the power the court will then compel the trustee to carry it out in a proper manner and within a reasonable time" (*a*). Putting the matter in another form, it comes to this: although the court will always compel a trustee to perform his duty, where anything is left to his discretion it will not interfere with him so long as he *is* exercising his discretion, and exercising it in good faith. But if he does not exercise any discretion at all the court will interfere (*b*).

Vice-Chancellor Malins seems to have drawn a distinction between a discretion which is expressed to be absolute and uncontrollable and a discretion without those adjectives. He admitted that the court could not interfere with the former, but held that it could control the latter. "The view I have always acted upon," he says, "which I think is the proper view, and which I shall continue to act upon, is this: That where the trustee acts in the exercise of his discretion it is incumbent on the court to pay every

(*a*) *Tempest* v. *Lord Camoys* (1882), 21 Ch. D. at p. 578. See generally Lewin, Trusts, 11th ed. 748; Underhill, Trusts and Trustees, 6th ed. 277. Compare Indian Trusts Act, 1882, s. 49.

(*b*) See, for example, *Wilson* v. *Turner* (1883), 22 Ch. D. 521.

respect to that exercise, but it must consider whether it is properly done" (*c*). But it seems somewhat doubtful whether the addition of the adjectives "free," "absolute," or "uncontrollable," can make any difference. Cases in which there was no adjective have been treated on the same footing as those in which they appeared (*d*).

The following cases illustrate the rule:—

Illustrations.

1. Testator gives property to trustees upon trust (*inter alia*) that they "in their discretion and of their uncontrollable authority pay and apply the whole *or such portion only* of the annual income as they shall think expedient" for the maintenance of his wife. The wife has property of her own and is a lunatic. The trustees *bonâ fide* refuse to apply any more of the income for her maintenance than is necessary to supply the deficiency of the income of her own property. The court will not interfere. *Gisborne* v. *Gisborne* (1877), 2 App. Cas. 300.

2. Trustees of a marriage settlement have power to apply the income of the settled fund for the benefit of the husband and wife and their children as they shall "in their uncontrolled and irresponsible discretion think proper." The husband is a hopeless drunkard, and in consequence of his intemperance and violence the wife cannot live with him. The wife has no means of support, but, notwithstanding this, the trustees pay the whole of the income of about 360*l.* to the husband, with the exception of 60*l.* a year, which they pay for the school expenses of the only child of the marriage. There being no *mala fides*, the court will not interfere. *Tabor* v. *Brooks* (1878), 10 Ch. D. 273.

3. Testator gives his residuary estate upon trust to sell and hold the proceeds on specified trusts, and gives the trustees power to postpone the sale "for such period as they in their free discretion shall think fit." The trustees do not sell any part of the

(*c*) See *In re Hodges*, *Davey* v. *Ward* (1878), 7 Ch. D. at pp. 761, 762, and *Tabor* v. *Brooks* (1878), 10 Ch. D. at p. 278.

(*d*) See *Wilson* v. *Turner* (1883), 22 Ch. D. 521; *In re Bryant*, (1894) 1 Ch. 324. See also Brett, L. C. Eq. 4th ed. 164.

residuary estate, which includes Egyptian bonds and shares in an unlimited bank. Several years afterwards the bonds are sold at a heavy loss and the bank fails. The trustees are not liable. *In re Norrington* (1879), 13 Ch. D. 654.

4. Testator gives trustees power to sell the trust property, and at their absolute discretion to lay out the money to be received from such sale in the purchase of other hereditaments. One of the trustees wishes to purchase an old family mansion formerly belonging to the testator's family; the other *bonâ fide* objects. The court will not order the purchase to be made. *Tempest* v. *Lord Camoys* (1882), 21 Ch. D. 571.

5. Testator directs his trustees to invest moneys coming to their hands in such investments "as they in their uncontrolled discretion shall think proper." The trustees in good faith invest in bonds of a foreign government, bonds of a colonial railway and shares in a bank on which there is a liability. In an administration action the court must allow the investments. *In re Brown* (1885), 29 Ch. D. 889.

6. Testator declares that the trustees of his will shall apply "the whole or such part as they shall think fit" of the income of the expectant share of any child of his for or towards the maintenance, education and benefit of such child. The testator's children reside with their mother, who maintains and educates them out of her separate estate, but who applies to the trustees (of whom she is one) to make her an allowance of 300*l.* a year for the purpose. The co-trustees, *bonâ fide* in the exercise of their discretion, refuse. The court will not interfere. *In re Bryant*, (1894) 1 Ch. 324.

SECTION LIV.—SUSPENSION OF TRUSTEE'S POWERS BY JUDGMENT.

WHERE judgment has been given in an action for the execution of the trust, a trustee must not exercise any power conferred by the terms of the trust without the sanction of the court.

"The powers assigned in the preceding pages to trustees," says Mr. Lewin, "must be taken subject to the qualification that if a suit has been instituted and a decree made for the execution of the trust, the powers of the trustees are thenceforth so far paralysed that the authority of the court must sanction every subsequent proceeding" (*a*).

So in the case of *Walker* v. *Smalwood* (*b*), Lord Chancellor Camden set aside a sale by a trustee which had been made after the commencement of a suit by creditors of the deceased settlor for a sale of deceased's estate for payment of their debts.

So also in the case of *Bethell* v. *Abraham* (*c*) Sir George Jessel refused to permit trustees of a will to invest trust money in their hands in the purchase of specified securities under a power contained in the will after a suit had been commenced for the administration of the trust estate. "As long," he said, "as an estate remains to be administered in this court, the court does not allow a purchase to be made, or a mortgage or any other investment to be made, unless the court is satisfied of its safety. There is a reason for that. The court has to protect the property for all claimants, and even where the trustees have an undisputed power to make a purchase or to make a mortgage a reference is made, generally to chambers, to ascertain the propriety of the investment which is intended to be made, that is to say, its propriety in all respects."

(*a*) Lewin, Trusts, 11th ed. 730; Underhill, Trusts and Trustees, 6th ed. 293. Compare Indian Trusts Act, 1882, s. 45.

(*b*) (1768), Amb. 676.

(*c*) (1873), L. R. 17 Eq. 24.

And so in the case of *Minors* v. *Battison* (*d*), where a testator had left his residuary property to trustees upon trust after his widow's death "at the sole discretion of my trustees" to sell the same, and a decree for administration of the estate had been made, Lord Chelmsford said that "even assuming . . . . that the trustees had an absolute discretion (which the House of Lords decided they had not) . . . . the trustees had retired from the trust and placed themselves in the hands of the court by the bill filed by the trustees for administration of the trusts and the order founded thereon, after which the trustees could not exercise any discretion with which they were invested without the sanction of the court."

A decree for administration does not, however, deprive the trustees of their powers; they may still exercise them, but the court will see that they do so in a proper manner. For instance, a power of appointing new trustees may be exercised, but it can only be exercised subject to the supervision of the court. If a fit and proper person is nominated he must be appointed, but if the person nominated is not fit, the court can only require that someone else shall be nominated. If the person having the power repeatedly nominated improper persons, it would amount to a refusal to exercise the power, and then the court can itself appoint (*e*).

(*d*) (1876), 1 App. Cas. 428.

(*e*) *Tempest* v. *Lord Camoys* (1882), 21 Ch. D. at p. 578; *In re Gadd* (1883), 23 Ch. D. 134; *In re Norris* (1884), 27 Ch. D. 333.

Part VII.—DISABILITIES OF THE TRUSTEE.

SECTION LV.—TRUSTEE MAY NOT RENOUNCE.

SUBJECT to the provisions of this Digest, a trustee may not renounce the trust after having accepted it, unless—

(a) the court authorizes him to do so; or

(b) the beneficiary, or if more than one, all the beneficiaries, have legal capacity to contract and consent to his doing so; or

(c) he is authorized to do so by the terms of the trust.

The first of the disabilities under which a trustee labours is that he cannot renounce his office once he has undertaken it. "A trustee who has accepted the trust cannot afterwards renounce," says Mr. Lewin. "It is a rule without any exception, that a person who has once undertaken the office, either by actual or constructive acceptance, cannot discharge himself from liability by a subsequent renunciation. The only mode by which he can obtain a release is either under the sanction of a court of equity, or by virtue of a special power in the instrument creating the trust or of a statutory power, or with the consent of all the parties interested in the estate and being *sui juris*" (*a*).

Before 1882, however, it was usual in settlements to give a trustee the power of retiring from the trust by making provision for the appointment of a new trustee in place of one who desired to be discharged. And by s. 31 of the Conveyancing Act, 1881, this power was conferred on every trustee unless a contrary intention was expressed in the instrument creating the trust. This section was repealed by s. 51 of the Trustee Act, 1893, but re-enacted in s. 10 of that act, which will be discussed hereafter.

(*a*) Lewin, Trusts, 11th ed. 276. Conf. Indian Trusts Act, 1882, s. 46.

SECTION LVI.—TRUSTEE MAY MAKE NO PROFIT OUT OF HIS TRUST.

(1) SUBJECT to the provisions of this Digest, and of any statute in that behalf, a trustee is not entitled to any remuneration for performing the trust, except as follows:—

(a) a trustee is entitled to remuneration where the terms of the trust so provide:

(b) where a trustee who is a solicitor acts as such on behalf of himself and a co-trustee or a beneficiary in any action or other proceeding in court [brought against the trustees (?)], he is entitled to his profit costs of so doing if the costs which would have been incurred by the trustees or beneficiary have not been increased by his so acting:

(c) the court may make such allowance to a trustee for his trouble and loss of time as it may think fit.

(2) Nothing herein contained is to affect the provisions of any contract.

Subject to a few exceptions, it is the established rule that a trustee or executor or administrator can make no charge against his *cestui que trust* for his services.

This rule was definitely established by the case of *Robinson* v. *Pett*, decided in 1734 (*a*), in which Lord Chancellor Talbot stated the reason to be that, "if allowed, the trust estate might be loaded and rendered of little value"; a reason of which Lord Cottenham

(*a*) (1734), 3 P. W. 132. Conf. the Indian Trusts Act, 1882, s. 50.

expressed his approval a hundred years later (*b*). It is now, however, more generally put upon the ground that a trustee ought not to put himself in a position in which his interest and his duty are in conflict (*c*). It has been put on this ground by Lord Lyndhurst (*d*), by Baron Alderson (*e*), by Lord Langdale (*f*), by Lord Cranworth (*g*), and by Mr. Justice Chitty (*h*).

In *New* v. *Jones* (*d*), where the rule was applied to prevent a solicitor-trustee charging for professional services, Lord Lyndhurst said: "A trustee placed in the situation of a solicitor might, if he were allowed to perform the duties of a solicitor and to be paid for them, be so placed that he might find it very often proper to institute and carry on legal proceedings which he would not do were he to derive no emolument from them."

In fact, this and all the other rules which impose disabilities on trustees are derived from the same principle that a person standing in a fiduciary relation towards another ought not to place himself in a position in which his duty and his interest will be in conflict. Human nature is weak; it is best not to subject it to temptation. The law of Scotland is the same in this respect (*i*).

Illustrations.

1. Testator directs certain businesses to be carried on by his trustees and executors, and directs several other onerous trusts to be performed by his trustees. A trustee devotes considerable time and travels many hundred miles in performing the trusts. He is not entitled to compensation for personal trouble and loss of time. *Brocksopp* v. *Barnes* (1820), 5 Madd. 90.

2. A trustee, being a solicitor, acts professionally in the execution of the trust. Neither he nor his firm is entitled to charge for his services. *New* v. *Jones* (1833), 1 Hall & Tw. 632 (*j*).

(*b*) In *Moore* v. *Frowd* (1837), 3 My. & Cr. 50.

(*c*) See White & Tudor, L. C. Eq. 7th ed. vol. ii. 608.

(*d*) In *New* v. *Jones* (1833), 1 Hall & Tw. at p. 634.

(*e*) In *Fraser* v. *Palmer* (1841), 4 Y. & C. Exch. Ca. at p. 517.

(*f*) In *Bainbrigge* v. *Blair* (1845), 8 Beav. at p. 595.

(*g*) In *Broughton* v. *Broughton* (1855), 5 De G. M. & G. at p. 164.

(*h*) In *In re Barber* (1886), 34 Ch. D. at p. 81.

(*i*) *Hamilton* v. *Wright* (1842), 9 Cl. & F. 111.

(*j*) *Moore* v. *Frowd* (1837), 3 My. & Cr. 45; *Collins* v. *Cary* (1839), 2 Beav. 129; *Fraser* v. *Palmer* (1841), 4 Y. & C. Exch. Ca. 517; *Burge* v. *Brutton* (1843), 2

3. An auctioneer, being executor and trustee of a will, acts as such on the sale of portions of the testator's property. He is not entitled to charge commission. *Kirkman* v. *Booth* (1848), 11 Beav. 273.

4. A solicitor who is an executor of a will brings an action to recover part of the testator's assets. He acts as his own solicitor. He cannot charge profit costs. *Pollard* v. *Doyle* (1860), 1 Dr. & Sm. 319.

5. Three trustees, two of whom are bankers, are empowered to carry on a business and to borrow money "from any bankers or other persons" for that purpose. The banker trustees make advances of money to the trust at compound interest. They are only entitled to simple interest at 5 per cent. *Crosskill* v. *Bower* (1863), 32 Beav. 86.

Exceptions.

Like most rules, however, it is subject to exceptions.

I.—The case of *Robinson* v. *Pett* itself shows that the trustee is entitled to any remuneration which the settlor has expressly conferred on him, and in practice it is common for a settlor to authorize a trustee who is a professional man to make professional charges, even for business not of a strictly professional character (*k*). But if an authority of this kind is conferred on an executor or trustee of a will who attests the will he will not be entitled to make use of it owing to s. 15 of the Wills Act, 1837 (*l*). Further, if the estate turns out to be insolvent, the trustee will get

Hare, 373; *Bainbrigge* v. *Blair* (1845), 8 Beav. 588 (now overruled; see per Chitty, J., *In re Barber* (1886), 34 Ch. D. at p. 83); *Todd* v. *Wilson* (1846), 9 Beav. 486; *Lincoln* v. *Windsor* (1851), 9 Hare, 158; *Lyon* v. *Baker* (1852), 5 De G. & Sm. 622; *Broughton* v. *Broughton*, (1855), 5 De G. M. & G. 160, are to the same effect.

(*k*) See *In re Sherwood* (1840), 3 Beav. 338 (solicitor); *Douglas* v. *Archbutt* (1858), 2 De G. & J. 148 (auctioneer); *In re Ames* (1883), 25 Ch. D. 72 (solicitor); *In re Chapple* (1884), 27 Ch. D. 584 (solicitor); *In re Barber* (1886), 31 Ch. D. 665 (solicitor); *In re Bedingfield* (1887), 57 L. T. 332 (solicitor); *In re Pooley* (1888), 40 Ch. D. 1 (solicitor); *Shepherd* v. *Harris*, (1905) 2 Ch. 310 (stockbroker).

(*l*) *In re Barber*, *supra*; *In re Pooley*, *supra*.

nothing under it, for the effect of the clause is to confer on him a legacy, and a legatee has no claim to anything until the creditors of the testator are satisfied (*m*). Lastly, being a legacy, it is liable to legacy duty (*n*).

II.—Another important exception to the rule was established by Lord Cottenham in the case of *Cradock* v. *Piper* (*o*), in which a solicitor-trustee who defended actions brought against himself and his co-trustees was held entitled to the ordinary costs, the costs not being increased by him so doing. Referring to the case of *Fraser* v. *Palmer*, cited above, Lord Cottenham said: "This is clear from the decision of the learned judge, that in a case in which a solicitor, being a trustee of the fund in question, acts for the *cestui que trust*, not acting for himself purely, but for the *cestui que trust*, the fact of his being a trustee of the fund in question does not prevent him obtaining costs as solicitor of the *cestui que trust*. This is established by the first suit and clearly pointed out by the judgment. It also points out—and that is not a matter in dispute or a matter of doubt with me—that where he acts for himself, he himself being a party, he cannot be allowed his costs. That falls within all the former cases. There is no case that I can find in which the principle has been extended beyond the dealing of a trustee for himself and acting for himself as solicitor in the execution of those trusts. It is not extended to a case where the mere circumstance of being a trustee and solicitor, but not performing the duty as a trustee, he is within the rule that he is not entitled to his costs, though acting as trustee for other parties."

This decision has been adversely commented on, but has been acted on too long to be overruled now (*p*). In *In re Corsellis*, in which the Court of Appeal followed *Cradock* v. *Piper*, Lord Justice Cotton states the rule thus: "Where there is work done in a suit not on behalf of the trustee, who is a solicitor, alone, but on behalf of himself and a co-trustee, the rule will not prevent the solicitor or his firm from receiving the usual costs, if the costs of appearing for and acting for the two have not increased the expense; that is to say, if the trustee himself has not added to the expense which

(*m*) *In re White, Pennell* v. *Franklin*, (1898) 2 Ch. 217.

(*n*) *In re Thorley*, (1891) 2 Ch. 613.

(*o*) (1850), 1 Hall & Tw. 617; 1 Mac. & G. 664.

(*p*) See *In re Barber* (1886), 34 Ch. D. at p. 83; and *In re Corsellis* (1887), 34 Ch. D. at pp. 682, 688. In both these cases it was followed.

would have been incurred if he or his firm had appeared only for his co-trustee."

But, as Lord Justice Cotton went on to point out, the exception in *Cradock* v. *Piper* is limited expressly to the costs incurred in respect of business done in an action or a suit, although, as was decided in *In re Corsellis*, it is not confined to costs in a hostile action, but extends to proceedings on an originating summons. "It is an anomalous rule," said Lord Justice Lindley, "applicable to the case to which it applies, and which ought not to be extended. But although we ought not to extend the rule, it will not do to fritter it away."

It has been said that the rule in *Cradock* v. *Piper* is "fiercely restricted to proceedings in Chancery in cases where the solicitor-trustee is co-defendant with trustees who are not solicitors" (*q*). But in Ireland it has been held to apply where the solicitor-trustee was co-petitioner (*r*). The solicitor-trustee had presented a petition on behalf of himself and his co-trustee for a sale of part of the trust property, and in deciding that he was entitled to his costs, Mr. Justice Monroe said, "Mr. Todd sought to narrow the exception made in *Cradock* v. *Piper* to the cases in which a trustee-solicitor and his co-trustee were made co-defendants in a suit, and where the solicitor represented both, and he contended that it did not include those cases where a trustee-solicitor instituted proceedings on behalf of himself and his co-trustees as plaintiff. For this he relied on some observations of Lord Justice Turner in *Lincoln* v. *Windsor* (*s*), and of Lord Cranworth in *Broughton* v. *Broughton* (*t*). There is, however, no decision to this effect, and the distinction is not taken by the Court of Appeal in *In re Corsellis*. Indeed, I find that part of the costs given to the solicitor in *Cradock* v. *Piper* were profit costs, which he claimed as solicitor for himself and his co-trustee in instituting proceedings for the administration of the estate" (*r*).

III.—The court also has power to make an allowance to trustees for trouble and loss of time, and occasionally does so (*u*).

(*q*) Birrell, Duties and Liabilities of Trustees, 74.

(*r*) *In re Smith's Estate* (1894), 1 Ir. 60. It is to be observed that in the report of *Cradock* v. *Piper* in 1 Mac. & G. it is stated (p. 666) that "bills of costs were left in the office of the Taxing Master on behalf of the several *defendants* represented by J. Watson" (the trustee), and it was as to these bills that the question came before the court.

(*s*) (1851), 9 Hare, 158.

(*t*) (1855), 5 De G. M. & G. 160.

(*u*) It did so in *Forster* v. *Ridley*

IV.—Lastly, a trustee is sometimes entitled to remuneration by the express provisions of a statute. For example, a trustee in bankruptcy is so entitled by ss. 72 and 73 of the Bankruptcy Act, 1883, a judicial trustee by s. 1 (5) of the Judicial Trustees Act, 1896, and the Public Trustee by ss. 8 and 9 of the Public Trustee Act, 1906.

Besides the above exceptions to the rule, the trustee may make a contract that he is to receive remuneration, and there is nothing in his position of trustee merely to prevent the enforcement of such a contract. "Whether upon general grounds," said Lord Hardwicke in 1740, "a trustee may make an agreement with a *cestui que trust* for an extraordinary allowance, over and above what he is allowed by the terms of the trust, I think there may be cases where this court would establish such agreements, but at the same time would be extremely cautious and wary in doing of it" (*v*). For often in cases in which such an agreement is alleged the beneficiary is not a free agent. He is in the hands of the trustee, and has no choice but to assent to his proposals. "In order to render a contract, or an agreement of any kind, binding," as Vice-Chancellor Stuart pointed out in a case of this kind, "there must be the assent of both parties to the agreement under such circumstances as to show that there was no pressure—no influence existing of a kind to make the assent an imperfect assent which under other circumstances would have been refused. If the assent to the agreement is not an assent given under such circumstances as that both parties are on an equal footing, and the agreement one perfectly free from any influence or pressure in the eye of this court, it is not an assent sufficient to constitute an agreement" (*w*).

(1864), 4 De G. J. & S. 452, and in *In re Freeman's Settlement Trusts* (1887), 37 Ch. D. 148.

(*v*) *Ayliffe* v. *Murray* (1740), 2 Atkyns, 58.

(*w*) *Barrett* v. *Hartley* (1866), L. R. 2 Eq. 789.

SECTION LVII.—TRUSTEE MAY NOT TAKE GIFT FROM BENEFICIARY.

(1) A TRUSTEE may not retain a gift made to him by the beneficiary unless he can prove that in making it the beneficiary was acting upon competent independent advice, and that the influence arising from the relationship of trustee and beneficiary had wholly ceased at the time it was made.

(2) [This section does not apply if it appears that the gift was not made under any influence exercised by the trustee over the beneficiary (?).]

It is a corollary to the rule that a trustee must work without reward, that he has no right to a gift made to him by his beneficiary while the relation of trustee and *cestui que trust* subsists between them, or even after it has been determined, if the influence arising from the relation continues. Such gifts are treated on the same footing as gifts to a solicitor from his client, or to a guardian from his ward (*a*).

In the case of *Hatch* v. *Hatch* (*b*), in 1804, Lord Eldon said: "This case proves the wisdom of the court in saying it is almost impossible in the course of the connection of guardian and ward, attorney and client, trustee and *cestui que trust*, that a transaction shall stand purporting to be bounty for the execution of antecedent duty. There may not be a more moral act, one that would do more credit to a young man beginning the world, or afford a better omen for the future, than if a trustee having done his duty, the *cestui que trust* taking it into his fair, serious and well-informed consideration, were to do an act of bounty like this. But the court

(*a*) Williams, Vendor and Purchaser, vol. ii. 887.
(*b*) (1804), 9 Ves. at p. 296.

cannot permit it; except [it be] quite satisfied that the act is of that nature . . ." (*c*).

Lord Eldon's judgment in *Hatch* v. *Hatch* was cited and discussed at length by the Court of Appeal in the case of *Wright* v. *Carter* (*d*)—a case of solicitor and client. The effect of the decision in this case is that the presumption that the gift is the result of undue influence in such cases is not irrebuttable, but before the gift can stand the court must be satisfied that the *cestui que trust* had competent independent advice, and that the influence arising from the relation had ceased to exist.

The employment of an independent adviser is not sufficient by itself; there must be not only a cessation of the confidential relation, but a cessation of the influence arising from that relation.

"In other words," as Lord Justice Stirling said, "the court in dealing with such a transaction starts with the presumption that undue influence exists on the part of the donee, and throws upon him the burden of satisfying the court that the gift was uninfluenced by the position of the [trustee]. Secondly, this presumption is not a presumption which is entirely irrebuttable, though it is one which is extremely difficult to be rebutted. Lord Eldon puts it that it was 'almost impossible' to uphold such a gift in the case of the relationships which he specified. . . . Now it has been laid down in recent cases, and particularly in two cases in this court—*Mitchell* v. *Homfray* (*e*) and *Liles* v. *Terry* (*f*)—that in order to uphold a gift of this kind the donor must have competent independent advice in conferring the gift. That is to say, the transaction cannot be upheld unless that condition is satisfied; but if the old rule still remains—that the court must look to all the circumstances of the case—the introduction of a new solicitor, although a highly important element, does not conclude the matter, and the court still has to be satisfied that the influence arising from the relationship can no longer be supposed to exist" (*g*).

It has been objected by several very distinguished equity lawyers that the statement of the rule in sub-s. 1 above is too wide, and that unless it is qualified, absurd and unreasonable results

(*c*) Sir John Romilly also, in the case of *Vaughton* v. *Noble* (1861), 30 Beav. at p. 39, said that "a *cestui que trust* cannot give a benefit to a trustee."

(*d*) (1903) 1 Ch. at p. 49 *et seq.*

(*e*) (1881), 8 Q. B. D. 587, a case of medical adviser and patient.

(*f*) (1895) 2 Q. B. 679, a case of solicitor and client.

(*g*) *Wright* v. *Carter*, (1902) 1 Ch. at p. 57.

follow. For example, suppose a son is trustee for his mother, tenant for life under his father's will. The evidence shows that she is a masterful woman and has always exercised a commanding influence over her son. Without taking independent advice she makes him gifts of money, say to pay debts, or to educate his children. For the court to be compelled to make him account to her or her estate would be a manifest injustice.

Again, suppose a father appoints his son, on the latter attaining his majority, to be a trustee of the father's marriage settlement, and subsequently gives his son 5,000*l.* and dies leaving all his property to his daughter. If the rule is as stated the daughter could recover the 5,000*l.* from the son unless it were shown that the father had acted upon competent independent advice, and that some influence the existence of which on the case supposed is really negatived by the circumstances, had ceased.

Again, if one brother is trustee of another brother's settlement the rule as stated would preclude the latter from making the former a birthday present of a horse or a pair of guns without at least calling in the assistance of a lawyer (*h*).

Probably, therefore, the rule is subject to the qualification, that if the circumstances show that the gift was in fact not due to any influence exercised by the trustee over the *cestui que trust* the trustee can retain the gift, and Lord Eldon seems to have had some such qualification in his mind when he said in *Hatch* v. *Hatch*, *supra*, that "the court cannot permit it, *except* [it be] *quite satisfied that the act is of that nature.*" Beyond this phrase there does not seem to be any reported case in which the qualification has been recognized.

(*h*) Report of Select Committee on Trusts Bill (1908), Appendices 2 and 4.

SECTION LVIII.—TRUSTEE MAY NOT PURCHASE THE TRUST PROPERTY.

(1) SUBJECT as hereinafter mentioned, a trustee who is selling property under a trust or power of sale must not, either directly or indirectly, buy the trust property or any interest in it, or take a mortgage or lease thereof either from himself or a co-trustee, unless—

(a) he is expressly authorized to do so by the terms of the trust; or

(b) he obtains the leave of the court.

But a trustee may buy or otherwise acquire for value the interest of the beneficiary in the trust property, provided that he complies with the following conditions, namely—

(a) he gives a fair price therefor:

(b) he makes a full disclosure to the beneficiary of all facts within his knowledge relating to the trust property and the circumstances of the transaction: and

(c) the beneficiary has competent and independent advice in respect of the transaction.

(2) This disability does not apply to a bare trustee.

The rule that a trustee must not purchase the trust property is yet another application of the principle that a trustee must not place himself in a position in which his interest and his duty may conflict (*a*).

(*a*) See per Lord Cottenham in *In re Bloye's Trust* (1849), 1 Macn. & G. at p. 495.

This rule is generally regarded as having been established by the leading case of *Fox* v. *Mackreth* (*b*). In this case Fox, on the 16th January, 1778, executed a conveyance of real estate to Mackreth in trust to sell and pay the debts of Fox. Immediately after the execution of the deed Mackreth offered to buy the estate from Fox for 39,500*l*., and Fox accepted his offer. On the 28th January a formal agreement for sale was prepared, and on the 24th April Fox executed a conveyance to Mackreth. In the meantime Mackreth had entered into a contract to sell the estate to Page for 50,500*l*. Fox discovered this fact three years later, and brought his action. The court (Lord Thurlow affirming the M. R.) decreed an account of the moneys received from Page, with interest. This decree was subsequently affirmed by the House of Lords (*c*).

It is not necessary in these cases to show that the trustee has, in fact, made any advantage out of the transaction. The law prohibits the transaction altogether on grounds of public policy. "The principle is that, as the trustee is bound by his duty to acquire all the knowledge possible to enable him to sell to the utmost advantage for the *cestui que trust*, the question what knowledge he has obtained, and whether he has fairly given the benefit of that knowledge to the *cestui que trust* (which he always acquires at the expense of the *cestui que trust*), no court can discuss with competent sufficiency or safety to the parties" (*d*).

The rule applies with as much force to a sale by public auction as to one by private treaty; for the knowledge that the trustee was a bidder might keep other people away—they might consider that he would bid to the utmost value of the property, and then if anyone else bid more would leave it (*e*). It also applies whether the purchase be direct or indirect, and it extends to a mortgage and lease as well as to a sale in the strict sense, and whether the trustee acquires the property from himself alone or his co-trustees.

It follows that if any beneficiary impeaches a sale of this kind it will always be set aside unless it appears to be for the benefit of

(*b*) (1788—1791), 2 Bro. Ch. 400; 2 Cox, 320.

(*c*) 4 B. P. C. 258.

(*d*) Lord Eldon, *Ex parte James* (1803), 8 Ves. at p. 348.

(*e*) Lord Hatherley, *Tennant* v. *Trenchard* (1869), L. R. 4 Ch. App. at p. 547.

the beneficiary that it should stand. In order to determine this the court orders the property to be put up for sale again, and if anyone bids more than the trustee gave will set aside the sale to him; otherwise it will hold him to his bargain (*f*).

The following are illustrations: —

Illustrations.

1. A. being trustee for sale of property buys it himself, and subsequently re-sells at an enhanced price. He must account to the beneficiary for the profit made. Per Lord Thurlow in *Fox* v. *Mackreth* (1788), 2 Cox, 320.

2. A. conveys real estate to B., C., D. and E. in trust to sell for the benefit of creditors. The real estate is put up for sale by auction in lots, and B. purchases some of the lots. The conveyances to him are executed by his co-trustees. B. re-sells at a profit. A.'s creditors are entitled to an account of the profits. *Whichcote* v. *Lawrence* (1798), 3 Ves. 739.

3. A. devises the "Link Farm" and "Quarry Brewhouse" to B. and C. in trust to sell. The trustees put up the Link Farm for sale by auction, and it is bought by X. on behalf of B. They then put up the Quarry Brewhouse, which is bought by X. on behalf of B. and C. Both sales are perfectly fair and open, but they must be set aside at the instance of the beneficiaries. *Campbell* v. *Walker* (1800), 5 Ves. 678; 13 Ves. 601 (*g*).

4. An assignee (trustee) in bankruptcy sells the bankrupt's leaseholds by auction, and they are bought on his behalf by an agent. The court will order them to be put up again, and if any one bids more the sale will be set aside. *Ex parte Lacey* (1802), 6 Ves. 625.

5. Trustees put up the trust property for sale by auction and bid themselves, and the property is sold to them. The court will

(*f*) See *Lister* v. *Lister* (1802), 6 Ves. 631 a; *Ex parte Hughes* (1802), 6 Ves. 616; *Hickley* v. *Hickley* (1876), 2 Ch. D. at p. 193.

(*g*) Compare *Ingle* v. *Richards* (No. 1) (1860), 28 Beav. 361; *Dyson* v. *Lunn* (1866), 14 L. T. 588.

order it to be put up again, and if any one bids more the sale will be set aside, otherwise it will stand good. *Lister* v. *Lister* (1802), 6 Ves. 631 a.

6. An assignee (trustee) in bankruptcy leases a mill forming part of the bankrupt's estate to himself. He must account for any profit he may have made out of the lease. *Ex parte Hughes* (1802), 6 Ves. 616.

7. A. assigns real and leasehold property and shares in lead mines to B. and C. in trust to sell and pay A.'s debts, and subject thereto in trust for A. At the auction X. buys part of the real estate on behalf of B. and C., and the shares on behalf of C. After A.'s death his next of kin can have the sales set aside. *Randall* v. *Errington* (1805), 10 Ves. 423.

8. A., holding real estate in trust to sell, executes a conveyance purporting to be made with the concurrence of the beneficiaries to himself in consideration of 200*l.* paid to himself by his agent X. The deed must be set aside. *Franks* v. *Bollans* (1867), 17 L. T. 309.

9. In the bankruptcy of a medical man his house and practice are put up for sale by auction by the trustee. They are bought by an agent for the trustee's brother, with whom the trustee is in partnership. The sale must be set aside. *In re Moore, Ex parte Moore* (1881), 51 L. J. Ch. 72.

10. A. devises property to B. and C. in trust to sell. B. and C. sell and convey the property to B. B. subsequently contracts to sell the property to X. The title is too doubtful to be forced upon X. *Williams* v. *Scott*, (1900) A. C. 499 (*h*).

The settlor may, however, authorize the trustee to purchase the trust property by the express terms of the trust instrument (*i*), and

(*h*) In the following cases a purchase by a trustee was held good: *Clarke* v. *Swaile* (1762), 2 Eden, 134 (special circumstances and acquiescence); *Coles* v. *Trecothick* (1804), 9 Ves. 234 (special circumstances); *Naylor* v. *Wynch* (1824), 1 Sim. & Stu. 555 (no possibility of advantage to trustee). And see *Hickley* v. *Hickley* (1876), 2 Ch. D. 190, which was not strictly a purchase by a trustee though he was indirectly interested.

(*i*) For an example, see the case of *Allen* v. *Taylor* (1880), 16 Ch. D. 355.

the court may give him leave to bid at an auction or even to buy the property by private treaty (*j*).

Purchase by Trustee from Beneficiary.

A distinction, moreover, is always drawn between a trustee buying from himself or his co-trustee or co-trustees and a trustee buying from the beneficiary.

For example, Mr. Lewin says, "A trustee for sale, that is, a trustee who is selling, is absolutely and entirely disabled from purchasing the trust property." But he goes on to say that "the meaning must be understood to be that the trustee may not purchase from himself, that is, that he cannot perform the two functions of seller and buyer; for there is no rule that a trustee, whether for sale or otherwise, may not purchase from his *cestui que trust*" (*k*).

This distinction is derived from Lord Eldon, who had been one of the counsel for Fox in the leading case, and who explained the matter in the case of *Ex parte Lacey* (*l*), some fourteen years later, thus: "The rule I take to be this; not that a trustee cannot buy from his *cestui que trust*, but that he shall not buy from himself. If a trustee so deal with his *cestui que trust* that the amount of the transaction shakes off the obligation that attaches upon him as trustee, then he may buy. . . The rule is this. A trustee who is entrusted to sell and manage for others undertakes in the same moment in which he becomes a trustee not to manage for the benefit and advantage of himself. It does not preclude him from bargaining that he will no longer act as trustee."

This seems rather to suggest that the relation of trustee and *cestui que trust* must have been dissolved altogether before the trustee can buy the latter's interest, but apparently Lord Eldon did not mean that, for he said later, in the case of *Coles* v. *Trecothick* (*m*), that "a trustee may buy from the *cestui que trust* provided

(*j*) *Campbell* v. *Walker* (1800), 5 Ves. at p. 682, per Sir R. P. Arden, M. R.; *Tennant* v. *Trenchard* (1869), L. R. 4 Ch. App. 537; *Boswell* v. *Coaks* (1883), 23 Ch. D. 302; affirmed by H. L. s. n. *Coaks* v. *Boswell* (1886), 11 App. Cas. 232.

(*k*) Lewin, Trusts, 11th ed. 562, 565. See also Underhill, Trusts and Trustees, 6th ed. 263 *et seq.*; White & Tudor, L. C. Eq. 7th ed. vol. ii. 730; Williams, Vendor and Purchaser, vol. ii. 878, 885; Ashburner, Equity, 428, 432. And compare Indian Trusts Act, 1882, ss. 52 and 53.

(*l*) (1802), 6 Ves. 625.

(*m*) (1804), 9 Ves. at p. 246. See

there is a distinct and clear contract, ascertained to be such after a jealous and scrupulous examination of all the circumstances, proving that the *cestui que trust* intended the trustee should buy; and there is no fraud, no concealment, no advantage taken by the trustee of information acquired by him in the character of trustee."

What then was the meaning of the decision in *Fox* v. *Mackreth*, which, it will be seen, was not a purchase by the trustee from himself, but from his *cestui que trust?* Lord Eldon always explained it on the ground that the trustee, Mackreth, had not divested himself of the character of trustee with the consent of the *cestui que trust* freely given after full information; for he had not made a full disclosure of all he knew about the value of the property he was buying (*n*).

But for practical purposes there is not very much in the distinction, for, as Lord Eldon said, a purchase by a trustee from his *cestui que trust* "is a transaction of great delicacy, and [one] which the court will watch with the utmost diligence; so much that it is very hazardous for a trustee to engage in such a transaction" (*o*); and Lord Erskine thought that the distinction between a purchase by a trustee from himself and a purchase from his *cestui que trust* was so fine that they might both have been equally forbidden as against the policy of the law (*p*).

The only point seems to be that if the trustee sells to himself, whether the sale be direct or indirect, the transaction is always liable to be set aside at the instance of the beneficiary on the ground of public policy; there is an irrebuttable presumption that the sale was made under undue influence (*q*). Whereas if the *cestui que trust* sells to the trustee, although there is a presumption that the *cestui que trust* was acting under undue influence, and therefore the transaction is invalid, the presumption is rebuttable; and if the trustee rebuts it by showing that he gave a fair price for

Lord Erskine's remarks on these statements of Lord Eldon in *Morse* v. *Royal* (1806), 12 Ves. at p. 372.

(*n*) See *Gibson* v. *Jeyes* (1801), 6 Ves. at p. 277; *Ex parte Lacey* (1802), *ibid.* at p. 627; *Ex parte James* (1803), 8 Ves. at pp. 352, 353; *Coles* v. *Trecothick* (1804), 9 Ves. at p. 247.

(*o*) See *Coles* v. *Trecothick*, *supra*, at p. 244.

(*p*) *Morse* v. *Royal* (1806), 12 Ves. at p. 372.

(*q*) Sir J. Romilly, M. R., said, in *Denton* v. *Donner* (1856), 23 Beav. at p. 290, "the transaction is absolutely and *ipso facto* void," but this does not appear to be correct. It is binding unless the *cestui que trust* desires it to be set aside. See judgment of Sir R. P. Arden in *Campbell* v. *Walker* (1800), 5 Ves. 678. And see *Lister* v. *Lister* (1802), 6 Ves. 631 a.

the property, that he fully disclosed all he knew respecting the property and the transaction to the beneficiary, and that the latter had adequate and independent advice, the purchase is valid; but unless he can show all these things—and the onus is on him—the sale will be set aside (*r*). In this respect the law of Scotland is the same as that of England (*s*).

It seems, however, to have been the opinion of Vice-Chancellor Kindersley that there would not even be any presumption against the trustee if he were only a bare trustee. "Take the case," he says, "of a trustee to preserve contingent remainders; he may clearly purchase. So, if an estate is vested in A. in fee in trust for B. in fee, it is quite obvious that B. may sell to A." (*t*). However, as he was only using this illustration to combat the untenable argument that in no circumstances can a trustee purchase from his beneficiary, it is not clear that he intended to put a bare trustee in a different category from an active trustee buying the interest of his beneficiary. It may well be, however, that the distinction should be drawn. The foundation of the presumption against the validity of a purchase by a trustee from his beneficiary is that the trustee's position in regard to the property gives him opportunities of acquiring knowledge which there is a danger he may make use of to the disadvantage of his beneficiary, and this is hardly applicable to a bare trustee.

(*r*) See *Denton* v. *Donner* (1856), 23 Beav. 285; per Lord Cairns, *Thomson* v. *Eastwood* (1877), 2 App. Cas. at p. 236; *Wright* v. *Carter*, (1903) 1 Ch. 27; *Dougan* v. *Macpherson*, (1902) A. C. 197.

(*s*) *Dougan* v. *Macpherson*, *supra*.

(*t*) See *Pooley* v. *Quilter* (1858), 4 Drew. at p. 189.

Section LIX.—Trustee may not use the Trust Property for his own benefit.

Subject to the terms of the trust, a trustee must not use or deal with the trust property for his own benefit or for any purpose unconnected with the trust.

It is a still further corollary from the rule that a trustee must make no profit out of his trust, that he must not use or deal with the trust property for his own benefit in any way whatever (*a*).

Suppose, for example, the trust property consists of a landed estate which comprises a shooting. The trustee has no right to shoot over the property, even though the beneficiary, by reason of infancy or otherwise, cannot enjoy the shooting himself. The trustee ought to let the shooting if he can, and if he cannot, the heir-at-law is entitled to it rather than the trustee (*b*).

So a trustee of an advowson has no right to present to the living if it becomes vacant; if the right of presentation has not been disposed of by the settlor, his heir-at-law is entitled to it (*c*).

(*a*) Lewin, Trusts, 11th ed. 303; Underhill, Trusts and Trustees, 6th ed. 263. Compare the Indian Trusts Act, 1882, s. 51.

(*b*) *Webb* v. *Earl of Shaftesbury* (1802), 7 Ves. 480.

(*c*) *Sherrard* v. *Lord Harborough* (1753), Amb. 165.

SECTION LX.—CO-TRUSTEES MAY NOT LEND TO ONE OF THEMSELVES.

A TRUSTEE who holds money in trust to invest, or who has power to invest it on mortgage or personal security, must not invest it on a mortgage by or on the personal security of himself or any of his co-trustees.

Where trustees have trust moneys in their hands for investment, they must all exercise an impartial judgment with reference to the investment. It follows that they must not lend the money to one of themselves, even upon mortgage, for they cannot *all* have exercised an impartial judgment in the matter (*a*).

Mr. Coote, however, says (*b*): "No reported case seems to go so far as to decide that a loan by trustees to one of themselves, if otherwise proper at the time of taking the security, as regards the nature and value of the mortgaged property, and in all other respects, and in the absence of subsequent misconduct or want of care on the part of the trustees constitutes such a breach of trust as will of itself render the other trustees liable for loss to the trust fund through failure of the security and insolvency of the debtor. But it is obvious that a loan to a co-trustee is objectionable and improper, inasmuch as the beneficiaries are entitled to have the unbiassed judgment of all the trustees as to the expediency of the proposed security; and such a loan places the borrowing trustee in a position in which his interest is liable to conflict with his duty, and tends to put difficulties in the way of the proper exercise by the other trustees of their rights and remedies as mortgagees; moreover, it may happen that by the death or the retirement of the other trustees the borrowing trustee may be left in the inconsistent character of mortgagor and sole mortgagee. The court would certainly regard such a loan with the utmost jealousy."

(*a*) —— v. *Walker* (1828), 5 Russ. 7. See Lewin, Trusts, 11th ed. 343, 374; and compare Indian Trusts Act, 1882, s. 54. A loan on mortgage by trustees to one of themselves was also treated as a breach of trust by the C. A. in *Francis* v. *Francis* (1854), 5 De G. M. & G. 108; and it appears to have been treated as one of the grounds for holding the trustees liable in *Stickney* v. *Sewell* (1835), 1 My. & Cr., see at pp. 14, 15.

(*b*) Coote, Law of Mortgages, 7th ed. vol. i. 542.

Part VIII.—LIABILITIES OF THE TRUSTEE FOR A BREACH OF TRUST.

Section LXI.—Trustee failing to Perform his Obligation liable to make good Loss.

(1) A trustee who fails to perform the obligation imposed on him without lawful excuse is liable to make good to the beneficiary the loss sustained by him as a consequence.

(2) Provided that a beneficiary who has fraudulently induced a trustee to commit the breach of trust, or who, having legal capacity to contract, has instigated the breach of trust or knowingly concurred therein, or with full knowledge of the circumstances and of his rights against the trustee has subsequently acquiesced therein or released the trustee therefrom, cannot claim to have the loss resulting to him from such breach of trust made good to him by the trustee.

A trustee who fails to perform the obligation imposed on him is said to be guilty of a breach of trust.

A trustee who has committed a breach of trust is liable to make good to the beneficiary any loss which he has sustained as a consequence (*a*).

(*a*) Lewin, Trusts, 11th ed. 1134. Compare the Indian Trusts Act, 1882, s. 23.

This liability can be enforced by an action brought by the beneficiary, or if there be more than one, by any of the beneficiaries against the trustee (*b*).

It is unnecessary to discuss this elementary liability further, for the whole law of trusts has grown out of it. Formerly, it is needless to say, the liability could only be enforced by a suit in a court of equity, but in England this is now rendered a matter of historical importance merely by the Judicature Acts. It is, however, expressly provided by s. 34 of the Judicature Act, 1873, that all actions for the execution of trusts shall be assigned to the Chancery Division.

Although, however, a trustee may have incurred liability for a breach of trust the beneficiary may be precluded from enforcing the liability against him, if he himself instigated the commission of the breach or concurred in it, or has subsequently acquiesced in it or has released or confirmed it (*c*).

It is a general rule that he who comes into equity must come with clean hands. If, therefore, the beneficiary has induced the trustee to commit a breach of trust by his own fraud, he cannot hold the trustee liable; and this applies even though the beneficiary is not *sui juris* (*d*).

Similarly, if the beneficiary has acquiesced in a breach of the trust, he has no right to complain afterwards. "It is established by all the cases," said Lord Eldon in the case of *Walker* v. *Symonds* (*e*), "that if the *cestui que trust* joins with the trustee in that which is a breach of trust knowing the circumstances, such a *cestui que trust* can never complain of such a breach of trust. I go further, and agree that either concurrence in the act or acquiescence without original concurrence will release the trustees" (*f*).

A fortiori the beneficiary is precluded from complaining of a breach of trust if he has executed a formal release or confirmation to the trustee (*g*).

There can be no acquiescence, however, without full knowledge

(*b*) See Lewin, Trusts, 11th ed. 864.

(*c*) Lewin, Trusts, 11th ed. 1167 *et seq.*

(*d*) See per Wigram, V.-C., in *Overton* v. *Banister* (1844), 3 Hare, 503.

(*e*) (1818), 3 Swanst. at p. 64.

(*f*) See for examples *Brice* v. *Stokes* (1805), 11 Ves. 319; *Nail* v. *Punter* (1832), 5 Sim. 555; *Fletcher* v. *Collis*, (1905) 2 Ch. 24.

(*g*) Lewin, Trusts, 10th ed. 1133; 11th ed. 1171. See *French* v. *Hobson* (1803), 9 Ves. 103; *Wilkinson* v. *Parry* (1828), 4 Russ. 272; *Blackwood* v. *Borrowes* (1843), 2 Conn. & Laws. 459.

by the beneficiary of the circumstances and of his rights against the trustee. "Acquiescence, as I conceive, imports knowledge, for I do not see how a man can be said to have acquiesced in what he did not know, and in cases of this sort I think that acquiescence imports full knowledge, for I take the rule to be quite settled that a *cestui que trust* cannot be bound by acquiescence unless he has been fully informed of his rights and of all the material facts and circumstances of the case" (*h*). And the same applies to a release or confirmation (*i*).

Further, in order for his acquiescence, release, or confirmation to bind a beneficiary, he must be *sui juris* (*j*), and in the case of a release the release must have been obtained fairly and without any duress or undue influence.

Since 1857, breach of trust has been a criminal offence. The law is now contained in s. 80 of the Larceny Act, 1861, which provides that—

"Whosoever being a trustee of any property for the use or benefit either wholly or partially of some other person, or for any public or charitable purpose, shall with intent to defraud, convert, or appropriate the same or any part thereof to or for his own use or benefit, or the use or benefit of any person other than such person as aforesaid, or for any purpose other than such public or charitable purpose as aforesaid, or otherwise dispose of or destroy such property or any part thereof, shall be guilty of a misdemeanour". . . .

But no prosecution can take place without the consent of the Attorney-General, or in case that office be vacant, of the Solicitor-General; nor if civil proceedings are pending, without the sanction of the court before which they are pending.

The term "trustee" in this enactment means a trustee on some express trust created by some deed, will, or instrument in writing, and includes the heir or personal representative of any such trustee and any other person upon or to whom the duty of such trust shall have devolved or come, and also an executor or administrator.

(*h*) Per Turner, L. J., in *Life Association of Scotland* v. *Siddal* (1861), 3 De G. F. & J. at p. 74.

(*i*) *In re Garnett* (1885), 31 Ch. D. 1.

(*j*) Lewin, Trusts, 11th ed. 1172; *Wilkinson* v. *Parry* (1828), 4 Russ. 272.

SECTION LXII.—TRUSTEES' LIABILITY JOINT AND SEVERAL.

WHERE there is more than one trustee, each one is liable for the whole loss although all have been guilty of the breach of trust, and a judgment against all is enforceable against any one or more.

Where several co-trustees are implicated in a breach of trust, all are equally liable, and the *cestui que trust* may proceed against any one, or some, or all of them. And though he obtains a decree against the trustees jointly, he may have process of execution against any one of them separately; for as regards the remedy of the *cestui que trust* there is no primary liability, but each trustee is responsible for the entirety of the loss incurred (*a*).

"When three trustees are involved in one common breach of trust," said Lord Eldon in 1818, "a *cestui que trust* suffering from that breach, and proving that the transaction was neither authorized nor adopted by him, may proceed against either or all the trustees" (*b*).

And so in an action against three trustees for investing the trust fund on an insufficient security, Sir John Romilly said, "It is clear that the three trustees are jointly and severally liable, and that the plaintiffs are entitled to a decree against them all to make good the amount. . . . . If any one of the trustees should pay the whole he may come against the others for contribution, and I shall then determine the question between the co-defendants. At present I cannot decide whether there is any priority of liability. All are equally liable, and the plaintiff is entitled to levy the whole against any one of them. If one should pay the whole, I shall be able to determine to what extent the others are liable to contribute" (*c*).

(*a*) Lewin, Trusts, 11th ed. 1149; *Ex parte Shakshaft* (1791), 3 Bro. C. C. 197; and *Wilson* v. *Moore* (1832), 1 My. & K. 126; *Att.-Gen.* v. *Wilson* (1840), Cr. & Ph. 28 (both cases of constructive trustees). See also *Taylor* v. *Tabrum* (1833), 6 Sim. 281; *Ex parte Norris, In re Biddulph* (1869), L. R. 4 Ch. App. 280. Compare the Indian Trusts Act, 1882, s. 27.

(*b*) *Walker* v. *Symonds* (1818), 3 Swanst. at p. 75.

(*c*) *Fletcher* v. *Green* (1864), 33 Beav. at p. 429.

SECTION LXIII.—MEASURE OF TRUSTEE'S LIABILITY.

(1) SUBJECT as herein otherwise stated, the extent of the liability of a trustee who has committed a breach of trust is the amount by which the trust property has been diminished as a consequence, together with the interest which he has received on that amount, or which it may be reasonably inferred that he ought to have received, or which he is estopped from denying that he has received.

(2) Provided that where the breach of trust consists in or involves the use of the trust money or property for the purposes of trade or speculation he is chargeable at the option of the beneficiary either (i) with such interest as aforesaid, or (ii) with the profits made by him by such use.

As a general rule, the measure of a trustee's liability for a breach of trust is the amount by which the trust property has been diminished by the breach, together with the interest which he has received on that amount, or which it may be reasonably inferred that he ought to have received, or which he is estopped from saying that he did not receive (a).

The leading authority on this point is the judgment of Lord Cranworth in the case of *Att.-Gen.* v. *Alford* (a), in which he said, "What the court ought to do, I think, is to charge him only with the interest which he has received, or which it is justly entitled to say he ought to have received, or which it is so fairly to be

(a) See per Lord Cranworth, *Att.-Gen.* v. *Alford* (1855), 4 D. M. & G. at p. 851; *Stafford* v. *Fiddon* (1857), 23 Beav. 386; *Burdick* v. *Garrick* (1870), L. R. 5 Ch. App. 233.

presumed that he did receive that he is estopped from saying that he did not receive it."

As a rule, the court does not hold a trustee liable for anything more than this. It is not a court of penal jurisdiction. The principle on which it proceeds is that it compels restitution of property unconscientiously withheld; it gives full compensation for any loss or damage through failure of some equitable duty ; but it has no power of punishing anyone (*b*).

The interest chargeable against the trustee under this general rule is simple interest, and the rate is now 3 per cent. (*c*).

There are cases, however, in which the trustee may be liable for more than this. First, he may be liable for a higher rate of interest than 3 per cent., and secondly, he may be liable for compound interest. These cases appear to be governed by the same rule as that applied in charging the trustee with simple interest (*d*). That is to say, he will be charged with a higher rate of interest when (1) he has received a higher rate, or (2) when the court is justly entitled to say he ought to have received a higher rate, or (3) when it is so fairly to be presumed that he did receive it that he is estopped from saying that he did not.

The case in which the trustee has actually received a higher rate of interest, and is charged with it accordingly, needs no further discussion (*e*).

The principal cases in which he ought to have received a higher rate, though there may be others, are :—

(a) *When the trustee has appropriated the trust fund to his own use.* "In such a case," says Lord Cranworth in the judgment quoted, "I think the court would be justified in dealing in point of interest very hardly with an executor; because it might fairly infer that he used the money in speculation, by which he either did make 5 per cent. or ought to be estopped from saying that he did not. The court would not enquire what had been the actual proceeds, but in application of the principle, *in odium spoliatoris*

(*b*) See per James, L. J., in *Vyse* v. *Foster* (1872), L. R. 8 Ch. App. at p. 333; affirmed by H. L. (1874), L. R. 7 H. L. 318.

(*c*) *In re Barclay, Barclay* v. *Andrew*, (1899) 1 Ch. 674.

(*d*) See per Fry, J., in *Gilroy* v. *Stephen* (1882), 30 W. R. 745, followed by Stirling, J., in *In re Barclay*, *supra*. See also *Burdick* v. *Garrick* (1870), L. R. 5 Ch. App. 233.

(*e*) See for an example, *In re Emmet's Estate* (1881), 17 Ch. D. 142.

omnia præsumuntur, would assume that he did make the higher rate, that is, if that were a reasonable presumption" (*f*).

(b) *When the trustee uses the trust fund for the purposes of trade or speculation.* "If," said Sir J. Romilly, after stating the general rule with regard to a trustee's liability, "in addition to such retention, he has committed a direct breach of trust, or if the fund has been taken by him from a proper state of investment in which it was producing 5 per cent., he will be charged with interest after the rate of 5 per cent. per annum; if, in addition to this, he has employed the money so obtained by him in trade or speculation for his own benefit and advantage, he will be charged either with the profits actually so obtained by him from the use of the money, or with interest at 5 per cent. per annum, and also with yearly rests, that is, with compound interest" (*g*).

It is still presumed that 5 per cent. interest has been made in these cases (*h*).

Similarly, the cases in which the trustee ought to have received compound interest, or in which it is so fairly to be presumed that he did receive it that he is estopped from saying that he did not, are:—

(a) *When the trustee neglects to comply with an express trust for accumulation, or in any other case neglects to accumulate the income when he ought to do so.* In such a case, if the trustee had done his duty, compound interest would have been obtained (*i*). Even though there is no express trust for accumulation, the trustee may be liable for compound interest if it was his duty to accumulate the fund and he has omitted to do so. For example, in *Gilroy* v. *Stephen* (*j*), an executrix and trustee set aside certain securities as representing the share of the trust estate belonging to an infant. She allowed her solicitor to receive the dividends on these securities, and he used them in his business. The dividends were paid half-

(*f*) See also per Sir J. Romilly in *Jones* v. *Foxall* (1852), 15 Beav. at p. 392; and in *Knott* v. *Cottee* (1852), 16 Beav. at p. 80; and per Lord Cranworth in *Mayor of Berwick* v. *Murray* (1857), 7 D. M. & G. at p. 519; and per Giffard, L. J., in *Burdick* v. *Garrick* (1870), L. R. 5 Ch. App. at p. 243. Compare *Price* v. *Price* (1880), 42 L. T. 626, where after retaining the trust fund for some time the trustee re-invested it, but on an improper security, and was held liable for 5 per cent.

(*g*) *Jones* v. *Foxall*, *supra*. See also *In re Davis*, *Davis* v. *Davis*, (1902) 2 Ch. 314.

(*h*) *In re Davis*, *supra*.

(*i*) *Knott* v. *Cottee* (1852), 16 Beav. 77; *In re Emmet's Estate* (1881), 17 Ch. D. 142; *In re Barclay*, *Barclay* v. *Andrew*, (1899) 1 Ch. 674.

(*j*) (1882), 30 W. R. 745.

yearly, and the trustee ought to have directed payment of them to a banker, and to have instructed him to invest them in consols as they were received, as also the income from such investments as it came in, in which case she would have received 3 per cent. compound interest. Mr. Justice Fry ordered her to pay compound interest at 3 per cent. with half-yearly rests.

(b) *When the trustee uses the trust funds for the purposes of trade or speculation.* "If the court finds," said Lord Hatherley in 1870, "that the money received (by the trustee) has been invested in ordinary trade, the whole course of decision has tended to this, that the court presumes that the party against whom relief is sought has made that amount of profit which persons ordinarily do make in trade, and in those cases the court directs rests to be made" (*k*).

When the trustee uses the trust fund for the purposes of trade or speculation, the beneficiaries have an option whether they will make the trustee liable for interest or for all the profits made by him from the use of the trust funds (*l*).

There is one case in which the measure of a trustee's liability for breach of trust has been defined by statute, for it is provided by s. 9 of the Trustee Act, 1893, that "where a trustee improperly advances trust money on a mortgage security, which would at the time of the investment be a proper investment in all respects for a smaller sum than is actually advanced thereon, the security shall be deemed an authorized investment for the smaller sum, and the trustee shall only be liable to make good the sum advanced in excess thereof with interest."

(*k*) *Burdick* v. *Garrick* (1870), L. R. 5 Ch. App. at p. 241.

(*l*) See *Robinson* v. *Robinson* (1851), 1 D. M. & G. at p. 256; *Jones* v. *Foxall* (1852), 15 Beav. at p. 392; *Vyse* v. *Foster* (1872), L. R. 8 Ch. App. at p. 329; affirmed (1874), L. R. 7 H. L. 318; *In re Davis*, *Davis* v. *Davis*, (1902) 2 Ch. at p. 317.

SECTION LXIV.—NO SET-OFF OF GAIN ON ONE BREACH AGAINST LOSS ON ANOTHER ALLOWED.

A TRUSTEE who is liable for a loss occasioned by a breach of trust in respect of one portion of the trust property is not entitled to set off against his liability a gain which has accrued to another portion of the trust property through another and distinct breach of trust.

It seems now well established that, in an action against a trustee to make good a breach of trust, the trustee is not entitled to set off against the loss incurred by that breach a gain which he has made by another and distinct breach of trust (*a*). As Vice-Chancellor Kindersley put it: "When there are two separate funds subject to trusts, and the trustees commit a breach of trust as to one by which it is lost, I think it impossible to permit the trustees to say—'We have improved the other fund, and that fund is bound to make up the loss on the other.' That I cannot hold. If the trustees have lost one part of the settled fund they must answer for it, whatever may be the improvement of the other part" (*b*).

Accordingly, in a case in which an executor and trustee had lent money of the deceased on personal security at high rates of interest whereby the estate had benefited to the extent of between 4,000*l.* and 5,000*l.*, but on another loan of 1,000*l.* the borrower failed, so that the money was lost, he was held liable to account for the profits, and at the same time to bear the loss, although he had acted quite honourably and not unnaturally in the circumstances (*c*).

(*a*) See Lewin, Trusts, 11th ed. 1147; Underhill, Trusts and Trustees, 6th ed. 379. And compare the Indian Trusts Act, 1882, s. 24, which adopts the rule as stated in Lewin almost verbatim.

(*b*) *Wiles* v. *Gresham* (1854), 2 Drew at p. 271.

(*c*) *Adye* v. *Feuilletau* (1783), 3 Swanst. 84, n.

So where it was the duty of a trustee to convert wasting securities under the rule in *Howe* v. *Earl Dartmouth*, and he did not sell within a year from the testator's death, but went on paying the income produced by the securities to the tenant for life for eleven years, when the securities were sold at a much higher price than they would have fetched a year after the testator's death. In an action against the trustee by the remainderman to make good the amount overpaid to the tenant for life, the trustee was held liable for the whole loss without allowing for the gain which had resulted from the postponement of the sale (*d*).

In another case in which trustees of a marriage settlement were bound to get in a bond debt of 2,000*l.* from the husband within six months of the marriage, but omitted to do so, and as a consequence the money was lost, they were held not entitled to set off the gain to the trust estate accruing from the fact that they had invested another part of the trust fund in the purchase of land (itself a breach of trust, as they had no power to buy land), on which the husband had erected buildings, which increased its value far beyond the 2,000*l.* (*e*).

It is not easy, however, to reconcile all the cases with this rule. For example, in a case in which trustees had committed a breach of trust by lending 4,000*l.* trust moneys on mortgage, they had subsequently instituted an action to realize the security in which the property was sold, and the proceeds paid into court and invested in consols. At a later stage of the proceedings the stock was ordered to be sold, and the price of consols having risen a net gain of 251*l.* was made on the investment. In an action afterwards brought against the trustees by the beneficiaries to make good the loss, it was held by Sir J. Romilly that they were only liable to make good the difference between the amount in their hands, including the 251*l.*, and the 4,000*l.* (*f*).

There were not two breaches of trust in this case, but only one, whereas in the cases above cited there were two separate breaches of trust, and perhaps the decisions can be distinguished, and the

(*d*) *Dimes* v. *Scott* (1828), 4 Russ. 195; *Barker* v. *Barker* (1898), 77 L. T. 712, is similar.

(*e*) *Wiles* v. *Gresham* (1854), 2 Drew. 258; *Ex parte Lewis* (1819), 1 G. & J. 69, is a case of a somewhat similar character.

(*f*) *Fletcher* v. *Green* (1864), 33 Beav. 426.

difference between them justified on this ground. The judgments, as reported, throw no light on the matter.

Perhaps it ought to be added to the rule above stated, that a trustee who is liable for a breach of trust consisting in retaining an unauthorized investment, or in any other act, in consequence whereof a beneficiary has received more income than would have been received by that beneficiary if there had been no breach of trust, cannot set off against his liability for diminution of the capital value of the trust property the excess of income received by that beneficiary.

SECTION LXV.—TRUSTEE ANSWERABLE FOR HIS OWN DEFAULTS ONLY.

A TRUSTEE shall, without prejudice to the provisions of the instrument, if any, creating the trust, be chargeable only for money and securities actually received by him, notwithstanding his signing any receipt for the sake of conformity, and shall be answerable and accountable only for his own acts, receipts, neglects or defaults and not for those of any other trustee, nor for any banker, broker or other person with whom any trust moneys or securities may be deposited, nor for the insufficiency or deficiency of any securities, nor for any other loss, unless the same happens through his own wilful default (*a*).

Where there is more than one trustee, we have seen that all must concur in performing the trust (*b*). It follows that when money is paid to co-trustees on account of the trust the receipt, in order to protect the person paying it, must be authenticated by the signature of all the trustees. Consequently, since it is not always convenient for all the trustees to be present when money is paid, it frequently happens that though a receipt is signed by all the trustees the money acknowledged was in fact received by only one.

It seems that at one time the courts held that the signature of the receipt rendered the trustee signing it responsible for the money acknowledged although he did not actually receive it and only joined in it "for conformity," as it was called. But it was obviously tyrannical to punish the unfortunate trustee for an act which the very nature of his office gave him no option to decline, and by the time of Lord Eldon it was established that a trustee

(*a*) Trustee Act, 1893, s. 24. (*b*) *Ante*, Sect. XXVIII.

who only joined in a receipt for conformity without actually receiving the money acknowledged was not answerable for a misapplication of it by the trustee who did receive it (*c*).

Perhaps it was the memory of the older state of the law that caused conveyancers to insert in trust deeds and wills an express provision that one of several trustees should not be answerable for the receipts, acts, or defaults of his co-trustee (*d*). For although it was superfluous, it was usual to find such a clause in well-drawn documents until at length it was enacted by the Law of Property Amendment Act, 1859, s. 31, that every deed, will, or other instrument creating a trust either expressly or by implication, should be deemed to contain the usual indemnity and re-imbursement clauses.

This was repealed by s. 51 of the Trustee Act, 1893, its place being taken by s. 24 of that act, which provides that "a trustee shall, without prejudice to the provisions of the instrument, if any, creating the trust, be chargeable only for money and securities actually received by him, notwithstanding his signing a receipt for the sake of conformity, and shall be answerable and accountable only for his own acts, receipts, neglects or defaults, and not for those of any other trustee, nor for any banker, broker, or other person with whom any trust moneys or securities may be deposited, nor for the insufficiency or deficiency of any securities, nor for any other loss unless the same happens through his own wilful default; and may re-imburse himself, or pay or discharge out of the trust premises, all expenses incurred in or about the execution of his trusts or powers."

This is somewhat wider in its terms than the earlier act, which only applied to trustees under an instrument, whilst the present section applies to every trustee. But although it makes a trustee "answerable for his own acts or defaults, and not for those of any other trustee," it gives no protection to him if by any neglect or default of his own he has enabled his co-trustee to commit a breach of trust. For instance, suppose an estate is vested in A. and B. in trust to sell and to invest the proceeds in government or real

(*c*) Lewin, Trusts, 11th ed. 291. See *Brice* v. *Stokes* (1805), 11 Ves. at p. 324.

(*d*) The practice may, however, have arisen only from its being satisfactory to trustees to see what they were told was the rule of equity made an express part of the contract instead of being left to implication. See Davidson, Precedents, 2nd ed. vol. iii. 183, 184.

securities, and A. and B. sell and convey to C., acknowledging receipt of the purchase-money, which, however, is in fact received by A. alone. If A. does not invest it, but retains it in his own hands and subsequently dies insolvent, B. will be liable, not for signing the receipt or for A.'s default, but for his own in not seeing that the money was properly invested (*e*).

But it is, of course, open to any settlor to define what shall be the duties of a trustee, so long as he keeps within the bounds of the law—the section is "without prejudice to the provisions of the instrument, if any, creating the trust," so that by an express indemnity clause in the settlement the trustee may be exonerated from liability even in such a case as the last, and a wide indemnity clause of this kind is sometimes used and will be given effect to by the courts (*f*).

By s. 50 of the Trustee Act, 1893, "unless the context otherwise requires," "the expression . . . . . trustee" includes "the duties incident to the office of personal representative of a deceased person." This definition seems to extend the right of indemnity given by the act to executors and administrators, though the section of the Law of Property Amendment Act, 1859, which it replaces, was confined to trustees (*g*).

(*e*) *Brice* v. *Stokes* (1805), 11 Ves. 319; 8 R. R. 164; and other cases cited in the notes to this case in Wh. & Tud. L. C. Eq. 7th ed. 673 *et seq.*

(*f*) *Wilkins* v. *Hogg* (1861), 8 Jur. N. S. 25; *Pass* v. *Dundas* (1880), 43 L. T. 665. The form of clause is given in Hayes & Jarman, Concise Forms of Wills, 12th ed. 365.

(*g*) Champernowne & Johnston, Trustee Acts, 92.

SECTION LXVI.—RIGHT TO BE INDEMNIFIED BY BENEFICIARY INSTIGATING BREACH OF TRUST.

(1) WHERE a trustee commits a breach of trust at the instigation or request or with the consent in writing of a beneficiary, the High Court may, if it thinks fit, and notwithstanding that the beneficiary may be a married woman, entitled for her separate use and restrained from anticipation, make such order as to the court seems just for impounding all or any part of the interest of the beneficiary in the trust estate by way of indemnity to the trustee or person claiming through him.

(2) This section shall apply to breaches of trust committed as well before as after the passing of this act, but shall not apply so as to prejudice any question in an action or other proceeding which was pending on the twenty-fourth day of December, one thousand eight hundred and eighty-eight, and is pending at the commencement of this act (*a*).

By the rules of the old courts of equity, if a trustee committed a breach of trust at the instigation or request of a beneficiary, the trustee, on making good the breach, was entitled to be indemnified out of the interest of the beneficiary in the trust property, though the court would not order the beneficiary personally to recoup the trustee (*b*). But if the beneficiary was a married woman whose interest was subject to restraint against anticipation, her interest could not be made liable for this purpose (*c*). This right of the trustee constituted an equitable lien on the interest of the

(*a*) Trustee Act, 1893, s. 45.

(*b*) *Raby* v. *Ridehalgh* (1855), 7 De G. M. & G. 104. See, as to the extent of the liability, *Chillingworth* v. *Chambers*, (1896) 1 Ch. 685.

(*c*) Lewin, Trusts, 11th ed. 1153.

beneficiary, and bound that interest, even though it had been assigned before an order of the court impounding it had been obtained by the trustee (*d*).

The Trustee Act, 1888 (which came into operation on the 24th of December, 1888), s. 6, provided that where a trustee committed a breach of trust at the instigation or request or with the consent in writing of a beneficiary, the court might, notwithstanding that the beneficiary was a married woman restrained from anticipation, impound the interest of the beneficiary by way of indemnity to the trustee. This section was repealed by s. 51 of the Trustee Act, 1893, but re-enacted in the words given above by s. 45 of that act.

These sections were only intended to enlarge the powers of the court, not to curtail the previously-existing rights and remedies of trustees, so that if, before the passing of the act, the court would in a proper case have enforced the equity of a trustee and impounded the interest of the beneficiary in the hands of an assignee, the court is bound to do the same in a similar case after the act. The trustee's equity still arises, as it did before the act, at the time of the breach of trust, not from the date of the order of the court made under the section (*e*).

It will be observed that the section only refers to the case "where a trustee commits a *breach of trust* at the instigation or request or with the consent in writing of a beneficiary," so that it does not apply, although the act which involved the breach of trust was done at the instigation of the beneficiary, unless the latter intended the trustees to commit a breach of trust in doing it. "In order to bring a case within this section, the *cestui que trust* must instigate or request or consent in writing to some act or omission which is itself a breach of trust, and not to some act or omission which only becomes a breach of trust by reason of want of care on the part of the trustees" (*f*). It is not sufficient that the beneficiary has instigated a particular investment; he must instigate such an investment as, upon the facts, he knows amounts to a breach of trust.

It has been argued that the "instigation or request" of the beneficiary must be in writing, but it has been decided, as indeed

(*d*) See *Bolton* v. *Curre*, (1895) 1 Ch. 544.

(*e*) Per Romer, J., *Bolton* v. *Curre*, (1895) 1 Ch. 544.

(*f*) Per Lindley, L. J., *In re Somerset*, (1894) 1 Ch. at p. 265.

seems fairly obvious, that the words "in writing" only apply to the consent of the beneficiary (*g*).

When the beneficiary is a married woman restrained from anticipation, it is the duty of the trustee to protect her against herself when she asks him to commit a breach of trust, and the court will not readily exercise the discretion vested in it by the section in his favour where he has not resisted her importunity (*h*).

The section authorizes the court to make an order impounding "all or any part of the interest of the beneficiary." It may, therefore, order the whole to be impounded, even though the beneficiary has not derived any benefit at all from the breach of trust (*i*).

Illustrations.

1. A. and B., trustees of X.'s marriage settlement, hold securities in trust for X. for life, remainder as she shall appoint. X. appoints to her son Y. subject to her life interest. Y., on his marriage with Z., covenants with the trustees of his settlement to pay them 10,000*l.* within six months after the death of X., to be held in trust for himself and Z. and their issue, and assigns the securities in the hands of A. and B. as security for payment of the 10,000*l.* Notice of the assignment is given to A. and B., who, however, are subsequently induced by Y., X. and Z. to apply a large portion of the funds in their hands in discharge of Y.'s debts. A. and B. being held liable to make good the breach of trust are not entitled to be indemnified out of the interest of either Y. or Z. under Y.'s settlement, such interest not being an interest of a "beneficiary in the trust estate" of which A. and B. are trustees. *Ricketts* v. *Ricketts* (1891), 64 L. T. 263.

2. A. holds property in trust for B. for her life without power of anticipation and after her death for her children. B. verbally requests A. to advance her 80*l.* out of the trust estate to save her home from being sold up, as she and her husband were being pressed for payment of debts amounting to that sum. A. complies, not understanding the meaning of the words "without power of anticipation." A. on making good the 80*l.* is entitled to be

(*g*) *In re Somerset*, *supra.*

(*h*) *Bolton* v. *Curre*, *supra.*

(*i*) *Chillingworth* v. *Chambers*, (1896) 1 Ch. 685, explaining *Raby* v. *Ridehalgh*, *supra.*

indemnified out of the income payable to B. *Griffith* v. *Hughes*, (1892) 3 Ch. 105.

3. A tenant for life under a settlement instigates the trustees to invest the trust funds on a mortgage of a particular estate. The trustees obtain a valuation of the property and advance more than the valuation shows that they ought, and on a subsequent realization there is a loss. The valuation is not disclosed to the tenant for life, and he is not informed of its effect, and does not instigate the advance of any specified sum. The trustees are not entitled to be indemnified out of his life interest. *In re Somerset, Somerset* v. *Earl Poulett*, (1894) 1 Ch. 231.

4. Trustees of a marriage settlement hold a sum of 4,000*l.* railway stock on trust for the wife for life without power of anticipation, with remainder to her husband and issue. The husband being in pecuniary difficulties requests the trustees to sell the stock and invest the proceeds on an equitable mortgage of his estates. The wife consents, in writing, to the investment, but she does not know that it is a breach of trust. On making good the 4,000*l.* the trustees are entitled to have the life interest of the husband impounded, but not that of the wife. *Bolton* v. *Curre*, (1895) 1 Ch. 544.

SECTION LXVII.—RIGHT TO CONTRIBUTION FROM CO-TRUSTEE AND TO BE INDEMNIFIED BY CO-TRUSTEE IN CERTAIN CASES.

(1) IF one of several trustees, all of whom are liable for a breach of trust, has made good the loss, he is entitled to contribution from his co-trustee or trustees. Provided that—

[(2) There is no right to contribution if the breach of trust is fraudulent (?).]

(3) The court may, if in the circumstances it appears just to do so, order any one trustee to indemnify the other or others.

(4) Where any one of the trustees is a beneficiary, he cannot claim contribution in respect of so much of the loss as represents his own loss as a beneficiary from the breach of trust.

At common law, if one of two or more wrong-doers has been sued alone and compelled to pay the whole damages, he has generally no right to indemnity or contribution from the other or others (*a*).

But this rule is not applicable to liability for breach of trust (*b*). "When trustees are equally to blame for a breach of trust, and are made jointly and severally liable to the *cestui que trust*, if one of them pays the whole, his right to enforce contribution from his co-trustee is clear" (*c*).

(*a*) *Merryweather* v. *Nixan* (1799), 8 T. R. 186; 8 R. R. 810. See Pollock, Torts, 7th ed. 195.

(*b*) *Lingard* v. *Bromley* (1812), 1 Ves. & Bea. 114.

(*c*) Per Kay, L. J., *Chillingworth* v. *Chambers*, (1896) 1 Ch. at p. 701.

This right of contribution is enforceable against the trustee himself during his life or his estate after his death (*d*).

Exceptions.

I. It would appear, however, that if the breach of trust is fraudulent the common law rule would apply, and there would be no right of contribution among the trustees. There seems to be no judicial decision directly in point; but in the case of *Att.-Gen.* v. *Wilson* (*e*), which was an information by the Attorney-General against a number of persons who had been members of the old unreformed corporation of the borough of Leeds for misapplying the borough funds, Lord Cottenham said: "In cases of this kind, where the liability arises from the wrongful act of the parties, each is liable for all the consequences, and there is no contribution between them, and each case is distinct, depending upon the evidence of each party. It is therefore not necessary to make all parties who may more or less have joined in the act complained of, nor would anyone derive any advantage from their being all made defendants, because, as the decree would be general against all found to be guilty of the charge, it might be executed against any of them" (*f*). The text-book writers treat this as deciding that a fraudulent breach of trust is outside the equitable right (*g*).

II. In some cases also, although all the trustees are equally liable to the beneficiary, as between themselves one may be liable to bear the whole loss, the other or others being entitled to be indemnified by him. The cases in which this obligation will arise appear at present to be undefined. Lord Justice Cotton said, in 1886: "I think it wrong to lay down any limitation of the circumstances under which one trustee would be held liable to the other for indemnity, both having been held liable to the *cestui que trust*; but so far as cases have gone at present, relief has only been

(*d*) The right was enforced in *Lingard* v. *Bromley*, *supra*; *Birks* v. *Micklethwait* (1864), 33 Beav. 409; *Bahin* v. *Hughes* (1886), 31 Ch. D. 390; and *Jackson* v. *Dickinson*, (1903) 1 Ch. 947. Other cases are cited in 20 Beav. 585, n.

(*e*) (1840), Cr. & Ph. 1, see at p. 28.

(*f*) Compare the judgments in *Lingard* v. *Bromley*, *supra*; and *Tarleton* v. *Hornby* (1835), 1 Y. & C. Exch. at p. 336.

(*g*) See Lewin, Trusts, 11th ed. 1150; Underhill, Trusts and Trustees, 6th ed. 404.

granted against a trustee who has himself got the benefit of the breach of trust, or between whom and his co-trustees there has existed a relation which will justify the court in treating him as solely liable for the breach of trust" (*h*).

In the case of *Baynard* v. *Woolley* (*i*), a trustee who had received 500*l.* trust money on loan to himself was held liable for the whole amount at the suit of the other trustee—the two having been sued by the beneficiaries for the breach of trust.

In the case of *Lockhart* v. *Reilly* (*j*), where there were two trustees, one of whom was a solicitor, and intrusted by the other with the management of the trust property, loss having been incurred by a breach of trust which was attributable to the negligence of the solicitor-trustee, it was held that the solicitor-trustee must reimburse his co-trustee all expenses properly incurred by him as such. And the cases of *Thompson* v. *Finch* (*k*), *In re Turner* (*l*), and *In re Linsley* (*m*) are similar.

III. There is a further exception when the trustee seeking contribution is also a beneficiary. The situation is then complicated by a conflict of rights. On the one hand is the clear rule that if two trustees are jointly and severally liable to make good a breach of trust, and are as between themselves *in pari delicto*, they are as between themselves entitled to contribution so as to equalize the loss to which both are equally liable. On the other hand, it is an equally clear rule that a beneficiary who concurs or acquiesces in a breach of trust cannot obtain any relief against his trustee. What is the result of these rules when the two conflict? This problem was presented to the court in the case of *Chillingworth* v. *Chambers* (*n*). In this case a fund was held by two trustees in trust for five persons in equal shares. The trustees advanced a sum of 8,650*l.* on mortgages, which were a breach of trust. On being realized the mortgages produced only 7,070*l.*, leaving a deficiency of 1,580*l.* In the meantime, one of the trustees had become entitled to one of the five shares. The four beneficiaries other than the trustee beneficiary were each entitled out of the 7,070*l.* to be paid their

(*h*) *Bahin* v. *Hughes* (1886), 31 Ch. D. at p. 395.

(*i*) (1855), 20 Beav. 583.

(*j*) (1856), 25 L. J. Ch. 697.

(*k*) (1856), 22 Beav. 316.

(*l*) (1897) 1 Ch. 536.

(*m*) (1904) 2 Ch. 785.

(*n*) (1896) 1 Ch. 685.

one-fifth share, namely, 1,730*l.* This accounted for 6,920*l.*, leaving only 150*l.* for the trustee beneficiary, and it was held by the Court of Appeal, affirming the decision of Mr. Justice North, that the trustee beneficiary could not recover any part of his loss from his co-trustee. If the trustee beneficiary, in recouping the loss to the other beneficiaries, had paid more than the amount of his share in the trust fund, he would have been entitled, in his character of trustee, to claim contribution in respect of the excess from his co-trustee; but not having done so, in his character of beneficiary, he was, by his concurrence in the breach of trust, precluded from recovering anything.

SECTION LXVIII.—STATUTE OF LIMITATIONS MAY BE PLEADED BY TRUSTEE.

(1) IN any action or other proceeding against a trustee or any person claiming through him, except where the claim is founded upon any fraud or fraudulent breach of trust to which the trustee was party or privy, or is to recover trust property, or the proceeds thereof still retained by the trustee, or previously received by the trustee and converted to his use, the following provisions shall apply:—

(a) All rights and privileges conferred by any statute of limitations shall be enjoyed in the like manner and to the like extent as they would have been enjoyed in such action or other proceeding if the trustee or person claiming through him had not been a trustee or person claiming through him:

(b) If the action or other proceeding is brought to recover money or other property, and is one to which no existing statute of limitations applies, the trustee or person claiming through him shall be entitled to the benefit of and be at liberty to plead the lapse of time as a bar to such action or other proceeding in the like manner and to the like extent as if the claim had been against him in an action of debt for money had and received, but so nevertheless that the statute shall run against a married woman entitled in possession for her separate use, whether with or without a restraint upon anticipation, but shall not begin to run against any beneficiary unless and until the interest of such beneficiary shall be an interest in possession.

(2) No beneficiary, as against whom there would be a good defence by virtue of this section, shall derive any greater or other benefit from a judgment or order obtained by another beneficiary than he could have obtained if he had brought such action or other proceeding and this section had been pleaded.

(3) This section shall apply only to actions or other proceedings commenced after the first day of January one thousand eight hundred and ninety, and shall not deprive any executor or administrator of any right or defence to which he is entitled under any existing statute of limitations.

(4) For the purposes of this section the expression "trustee" shall be deemed to include an executor or administrator and a trustee whose trust arises by construction or implication of law as well as an express trustee, but not the official trustee of charitable funds.

(5) The provisions of this section relating to a trustee shall apply as well to several joint trustees as to a sole trustee (*a*).

It was a well-established rule of the Court of Chancery that, as between trustee and *cestui que trust*, in the case of an express trust no length of time was a bar to the enforcement of the

(*a*) Trustee Act, 1888, ss. 1 and 8.

trust (*b*), and this was made a statutory rule by the Judicature Act, 1873, which provides that:—

"25 (2). No claim of a *cestui que trust* as against his trustee for any property held on an express trust, or in respect of any breach of such trust, shall be held to be barred by any statute of limitations."

In the case of trusts arising by implication of law, whether resulting or constructive, the law was not quite so clear. Generally they were within the statutes of limitations. Lord Commissioner Ashurst said, in a case in 1783, "as to trusts being an exception to the statute of limitations, the rule holds only as between trustees and *cestui que trusts*. It is true that a trustee cannot set it up against his *cestui que trust;* but this is merely the case of a trustee by implication, and as such affected by an equity; but that equity must be pursued within some reasonable time" (*c*). So, again, Sir William Grant said: "It is certainly true that no time bars a direct trust as between *cestui que trust* and trustee; but if it is meant to be asserted that a court of equity allows a man to make out a case of constructive trust at any distance of time after the facts and circumstances happened out of which it arises, I am not aware that there is any ground for a doctrine so fatal to the security of property as that would be" (*d*).

But there are some kinds of constructive trusts in which the statutes of limitation are no defence. "The result [of the authorities] seems to be that there are certain cases of what are strictly speaking constructive trusts in which the statute of limitations cannot be set up as a defence. Amongst these are the case where a stranger to the trust has assumed to act and has acted as a trustee, and the case where a stranger has concurred with the trustee in committing a breach of trust and has taken possession of the trust property knowing that it was trust property, and has not duly discharged himself of it by handing it over to the proper trustees or to the persons absolutely entitled to it" (*e*).

It would appear, then, that all constructive trusts coming within Section XVII., above, are on the same footing as express

(*b*) Lewin, Trusts, 11th ed. 1082.

(*c*) *Townshend* v. *Townshend* (1783), 1 Bro. Ch. Ca. at p. 554.

(*d*) *Beckford* v. *Wade* (1805), 17 Ves. at p. 97.

(*e*) Per Kay, L. J., in *Soar* v. *Ashwell*, (1893) 2 Q. B. at p. 405. The decisions will be found collected and discussed in this judgment.

trusts in this respect. And so, it seems, are some others; for example, in the case of *Wassell* v. *Leggatt* (*f*) it was held by Mr. Justice Romer that a husband who had forcibly possessed himself of his wife's separate property was a constructive trustee for her, and that the statute of limitations could not be pleaded in bar of her claim. But in the case of most constructive trusts and resulting trusts the statute of limitations could be pleaded.

In this state of the law the Trustee Act, 1888, was passed, s. 8 of which provides that:—

"(1) In an action or other proceeding against a trustee, or any person claiming through him, except where the claim is founded upon any fraud or fraudulent breach of trust to which the trustee was party or privy, or is to recover trust property or the proceeds thereof still retained by the trustee, or previously received by the trustee and converted to his use, the following provisions shall apply—

"(a) All rights and privileges conferred by any statute of limitations shall be enjoyed in the like manner and to the like extent as they would have been enjoyed in such action or other proceeding if the trustee or person claiming through him had not been a trustee or person claiming through him:

"(b) If the action or other proceeding is brought to recover money or other property, and is one to which no existing statute of limitations applies, the trustee or person claiming through him shall be entitled to the benefit of, and be at liberty to plead the lapse of time as a bar to such action or other proceeding, in the like manner and to the like extent as if the claim had been against him in an action of debt for money had and received, but so, nevertheless, that the statute shall run against a married woman entitled in possession for her separate use, whether with or without a restraint upon anticipation, but shall not begin to run against any beneficiary unless and until the interest of such beneficiary shall be an interest in possession.

"(2) No beneficiary, as against whom there would be a good defence by virtue of this section, shall derive any greater or other

(*f*) (1896) 1 Ch. 554.

benefit from a judgment or order obtained by another beneficiary than he could have obtained if he had brought such action or other proceeding and this section had been pleaded.

"(3) This section shall apply only to actions or other proceedings commenced after the first day of January, one thousand eight hundred and ninety, and shall not deprive any executor or administrator of any right or defence to which he is entitled under any existing statute of limitations."

The statute is not very happily framed, and it is not easy to determine its precise application. The chief difficulty is presented by para. (a) of sub-s. 1. In an action by a new trustee against an old one to compel him to make good trust funds which had been misapplied, it was contended that it protected the defendant, but Lord Justice Fry held that it could not apply. "In the first place," he said, "it is obvious that if a person had not been a trustee, he could not be sued for a breach of trust; and further, that there is no right or privilege, that I am aware of, conferred by any statute of limitations in respect of a breach of trust" (*g*).

But, as was subsequently pointed out by Lord Justice Lindley, to exclude the operation of the paragraph on this ground would be to deprive it of all meaning whatever (*h*). And in the same case, Lord Justice Rigby expressed the view that this clause had to do with remedies only and not with causes of action, and did not intend to suppose a case in which the cause of action or the corresponding obligation had gone. "That was supposed to continue, and if in such a case there had been any statute of limitations applicable as against a person who was not a trustee, I understand clause (a) provides that that particular right or privilege is to be given to him as though he had not been a trustee: not as though he had not committed any breach of duty or had been guilty of any negligence—not that at all—but as though the breach of duty being the same as it was he had not been a trustee. . . . . You must suppose the right of action to exist, and generally one may say that a trustee who undertakes a trust agrees to perform that trust. Throw away the idea of a breach of trust and the equitable position in which he is placed by that reason, he is still guilty of a breach of duty. . . . . Of course it may happen that a duty is

(*g*) *In re Bowden* (1890), 45 Ch. D. at p. 450.

(*h*) *How* v. *Earl Winterton*, (1896) 2 Ch. at pp. 638, 639.

thrown on him by virtue of his simple contract to undertake the trust, or it may be by reason of a covenant to undertake it as where the duty is thrown on him by a deed. Then you must look to the appropriate act of limitations, that which would have been applicable if the duty had not been performed" (*i*).

If this is the correct view of paragraph (a), it would appear that when the form of the trust instrument is a covenant by the trustee to hold the trust property on specified trusts for specified persons, the period of limitation will be twenty years from the breach of trust (*j*).

Whatever may be the effect of paragraph (a) it will generally be under paragraph (b) that the trustee is entitled to relief if at all. It will be seen that this enables him to plead lapse of time as a bar, "*as if the claim had been against him in an action of debt for money had and received*"; the result is that the period of limitation is six years from the time when the right of recovery accrued (*k*); unless in the meantime there has been an acknowledgment in writing or payment sufficient to take the case out of the statute.

The statute is *not to* "*begin to run against any beneficiary unless and until the interest of such beneficiary shall be an interest in possession*" (*l*); but as against a beneficiary whose interest is in possession it begins to run from the commission of the breach, not from the time of its discovery, unless its commission was concealed by fraud to which the trustee was party or privy, when of course it does not run at all (*m*).

In the excepted cases, namely—

(1) where the claim is founded upon any fraud or fraudulent breach of trust to which the trustee was party or privy, or—

(2) is to recover trust property or the proceeds thereof still retained by the trustee, or—

(3) is to recover trust property or the proceeds thereof previously received by the trustee and converted to his use—

(*i*) *How* v. *Earl Winterton*, (1896) 2 Ch. at p. 641.

(*j*) See Champernowne & Johnston, Trustee Acts, 8.

(*k*) 21 Jac. I. c. 16, s. 3; *In re Somerset, Somerset* v. *Earl Poulett*, (1894) 1 Ch. 231.

(*l*) The meaning of these words was discussed by North, J., in *Mara* v. *Browne*, (1895) 2 Ch. at p. 95.

(*m*) *Thorne* v. *Heard*, (1894) 1 Ch. 599; affirmed by H. L. (1895) A. C. 495.

the position remains as it was before the act. But if fraud is to be relied on to take the case out of the statute, it must be the fraud of, or in some way imputable to, the person who invokes the aid of the statute. It is only when a person has in some way participated in a fraud that he can be said to be party or privy to it (*n*). If the fraud is that of an agent it must have been committed while he was acting within the scope of his employment by the trustee. Similarly trust property is not "still retained by the trustee" unless it is actually in the trustee's hands or under his control when the action is brought.

Both these points arose for consideration in the case of *Thorne* v. *Heard* (*o*). The facts were, that property had been mortgaged to Heard as first mortgagee and to Thorne by way of second mortgage, one Searle acting as solicitor for both mortgagor and mortgagee in each case. In 1878 Heard sold the property under his power of sale, employing Searle to conduct the sale. Out of the proceeds of sale the latter paid Heard the amount due and kept the balance for himself, not telling Thorne of the sale and continuing to pay the interest on the second mortgage to him as if it were still subsisting. In 1892 Thorne discovered the fraud and brought an action against Heard for the balance of the proceeds of sale. It was held that he could not recover. The action did not come within the excepted cases because the fraud of Searle was not imputable to Heard, he was not acting as the latter's agent in paying the interest, nor was the trust property still retained by the trustee, and the action was therefore barred by the statute (*p*).

(*n*) See per Lindley, L. J., in *Thorne* v. *Heard*, (1894) 1 Ch. at p. 606.

(*o*) (1893) 3 Ch. 530; (1894) 1 Ch. 599; (1895) A. C. 495.

(*p*) Other cases on the section are: *In re Bowden* (1890), 45 Ch. D. 444; *Moore* v. *Knight*, (1891) 1 Ch. 547; *In re Swain*, (1891) 3 Ch. 233; *In re Page*, (1893) 1 Ch. 304; *In re Gurney*, (1893) 1 Ch. 590; *In re Somerset, Somerset* v. *Earl Poulett*, (1894) 1 Ch. 231; *In re Lands Allotment Co.*, (1894) 1 Ch. 616; *Wassell* v. *Leggatt*, (1896) 1 Ch. 554; *How* v. *Earl Winterton*, (1896) 2 Ch. 626; *In re Timmis*, (1902) 1 Ch. 176.

SECTION LXIX.—POWER OF COURT TO GRANT RELIEF FOR BREACH OF TRUST.

IF it appears to the court that a trustee (whether appointed under this act or not) is or may be personally liable for any breach of trust, whether the transaction alleged to be a breach of trust occurred before or after the passing of this act, but has acted honestly and reasonably, and ought fairly to be excused for the breach of trust and for omitting to obtain the directions of the court in the matter in which he committed such breach, then the court may relieve the trustee either wholly or partly from personal liability for the same.

Under the law, as settled by the decisions of the courts, if a trustee was proved to have committed a breach of trust it was impossible for him to avoid liability, however honest and reasonable his conduct had been, unless he could show that the beneficiary had concurred in the breach of trust or had subsequently acquiesced in it, or released the trustee from it in manner already discussed. This rule was felt to operate very harshly at times and to deter many people from undertaking the office of trustee, and a Select Committee of the House of Commons, which sat in 1895 to inquire into the administration of trusts, by their report recommended, "that the court be empowered to relieve any trustee from personal liability when satisfied that he has acted honestly and reasonably with the intention of carrying out the terms of the trust, and ought fairly to be excused for having acted without the direction of the court" (*a*).

Pursuant to this recommendation it was enacted by s. 3 of the Judicial Trustees Act, 1896, that "if it appears to the court that a trustee, whether appointed under this act or not, is or may be

(*a*) See Rudall & Greig, Trustee Acts, 3rd ed. 200.

personally liable for any breach of trust, whether the transaction alleged to be a breach of trust occurred before or after the passing of this act, but has acted honestly and reasonably and ought fairly to be excused for the breach of trust, and for omitting to obtain the directions of the court in the matter in which he committed such breach, then the court may relieve the trustee either wholly or partly from personal liability for the same."

The section, it will be seen, is framed very nearly in the words of the Committee's report.

"It would be impossible to lay down any general rules or principles to be acted on in carrying out the provisions of the section," said Mr. Justice Byrne shortly after it came into force (*b*), "and I think that each case must depend upon its own circumstances." A view expressed also by Mr. Justice Romer (*c*).

"The power is meant to be acted on freely and fairly in the exercise of judicial discretion," said the former judge in the case cited, "but the court must, before exercising the power, be satisfied by sufficient evidence that the trustee acted reasonably as well as honestly."

The onus of proving that he has acted "reasonably" lies upon the trustee (*d*), and "reasonably" means reasonably as a trustee (*e*). If, although the trustee has acted honestly and reasonably, it does not appear that he ought fairly to be excused for his breach of trust, he will not be entitled to relief (*f*).

The following cases illustrate the application of the section :—

Illustrations.

1. A. by her will appoints B., a solicitor, and C., a linendraper, executors and trustees. B. and C. invest the trust funds upon a mortgage which is an improper investment both as to nature and value. C. acts honestly in so doing, but although he relied on B.'s advice he cannot obtain relief, for he must show that he also acted reasonably. *In re Turner, Barker* v. *Ivimey*, (1897) 1 Ch. 536.

(*b*) In *In re Turner*, (1897) 1 Ch. at p. 542.

(*c*) In *In re Kay*, (1897) 2 Ch. at p. 524.

(*d*) *In re Stuart*, (1897) 2 Ch. at p. 583.

(*e*) Per Chitty, L. J., in *In re Grindley*, (1897) 2 Ch. at p. 601.

(*f*) *Waite* v. *Parkinson* (1901), 85 L. T. 456 : *National Trustees Co. of Australasia, Ltd.* v. *General Finance Co. of Australasia, Ltd.*, (1905) A. C. 373; *Davis* v. *Hutchings*, (1907) 1 Ch. 356.

2. A. dies in June, 1894, leaving assets amounting to 22,000*l*., and debts as then ascertained of about 100*l*. By his will he gives to his widow an immediate legacy of 300*l*. and the income of his estate for her life. B., the executor, pays the legacy and allows the widow to receive the income. In December, 1894, an action claiming an account against A. on the footing of wilful default is commenced. B., without going to the court for directions, defends the action, and continues to allow the widow to receive the income. In April, 1896, judgment for 26,000*l*. is given against A.'s estate. B. acts reasonably in paying the 300*l*. legacy and income up to the date of the writ, but not after, and having acted honestly is entitled to relief to this extent. *In re Kay, Mosley* v. *Kay*, (1897) 2 Ch. 518.

3. A., the executor of B., a deceased solicitor, omits to take any steps to obtain payment from a client of B. of costs due to B. A. believes in good faith and on reasonable grounds that he cannot maintain an action against the client personally. Supposing this omission to amount to a breach of trust, A., having acted honestly and reasonably, is entitled to be relieved. *In re Roberts, Knight* v. *Roberts* (1897), 76 L. T. 479.

4. A. invests trust funds upon mortgage partly in reliance upon the advice of the solicitor to the trust, and partly upon valuations made by a surveyor employed by the latter, but A. does not in several respects comply with the requirements of s. 8 of the Trustee Act, 1893, and does not reasonably believe the surveyor to be employed independently of the mortgagor. A. has not acted reasonably, and is not entitled to relief. *In re Stuart, Smith* v. *Stuart*, (1897) 2 Ch. 583.

5. A. and B., trustees, honestly and reasonably believing that they have power to do so, sell part of the trust property. They have no power of sale, but if they had the sale would be a proper one. A. and B. are entitled to relief. *Perrins* v. *Bellamy*, (1898) 2 Ch. 521; (1899) 1 Ch. 797.

6. A., by his will, gives his real and personal estate to his executors and trustees X. and Y., upon trust to maintain the same in the like mode of investment as at his death, until his son B. should attain the age of twenty-four years. The estate comprises

a debt of 166*l.* due upon a promissory note payable on demand; X. and Y. believing the debtor to be a man of good credit, neither call it in nor apply to the court for directions. The debtor dies insolvent before B. attained twenty-four. X. and Y. have acted honestly and reasonably, and are entitled to be relieved. *In re Grindley, Clews* v. *Grindley*, (1898) 2 Ch. 593.

7. In the course of the administration of the estate of a testator, which continues for upwards of five years, the executors knowing that large sums are required for the payment of debts, disbursements, and other purposes, pay various sums from time to time to their solicitors in reliance on their statements that these sums are in each case required for those purposes to which they are in fact in great part applied. Shortly before the completion of the administration the solicitors become bankrupt, and it is then found that the total amount paid to the solicitors is in excess of the amount properly applied by them by over 500*l.* The executors are entitled to relief. *In re Lord de Clifford's Estate*, (1900) 2 Ch. 707.

8. The trustees of a marriage settlement have power to invest in real securities in England, Wales, or Ireland, and to vary with the consent of the husband and wife during their joint lives. The trustees without the consent of the wife sell out stock forming part of the trust funds and invest the proceeds, 5,000*l.*, on a transfer of a sub-mortgage of a second mortgage of land in Ireland. They take no legal advice as to the propriety of the investment before making it, and on a realization the security only produces 75*l.* 1*s.* The investment is a breach of trust and the trustees are not entitled to relief. *Chapman* v. *Browne*, (1902) 1 Ch. 785.

9. A beneficiary mortgages his interest in the trust property to secure an advance and the mortgagee subsequently transfers the mortgage. Afterwards the beneficiary assigns his interest absolutely to the solicitor of the trustees by a deed which recites the mortgage and assigns the interest subject thereto. No notice of the mortgage or transfer is given to the trustees. Upon the trust fund becoming distributable the trustees pay the share of the beneficiary to the solicitor in reliance on his statement that he is the assignee of the share and without calling on him to prove his title. In an action by the transferee of the mortgage the trustees

are not entitled to relief, since, although they may have acted honestly and reasonably, they ought not fairly to be excused for the breach of trust. *Davis* v. *Hutchings*, (1907) 1 Ch. 356.

10. A trustee holds a fund in trust to invest it "in his name or under his legal control" in (*inter alia*) freehold, copyhold, leasehold, or chattel real securities. He invests 2,000*l.* on a contributory mortgage of leaseholds, which security is introduced by a surveyor to the trustees' solicitor; the latter recommends the investment to the trustee and acts throughout as his solicitor, and on his suggestion the trustee appoints the surveyor to value the property on his behalf; the surveyor (whose fee depends on whether the mortgage goes through or not) makes a report in which he values the property at 6,045*l.*, and advises that it is a good security for 4,000*l.*, and on this the solicitor advises the trustee to make the advance. Some years later the mortgagor becomes insolvent, and on realization the security produces only 500*l.* In an action against the trustee for breach of trust, he is not entitled to relief since he has not acted reasonably. *In re Dive, Dive* v. *Roebuck*, (1909) 1 Ch. 328 (*g*).

(*g*) See also *Shaw* v. *Cates*, (1909) 1 Ch. 389.

Part IX.—RIGHTS OF THE BENEFICIARY.

SECTION LXX.—RIGHT TO PERFORMANCE OF TRUST.

(1) EVERY beneficiary has the right to enforce performance by the trustee of his obligations by an action for the execution of the trust.

(2) If there is more than one beneficiary, any one of them may maintain the action.

Right and duty or obligation are correlative terms. Except within the sphere of the criminal law, whenever one person is under an obligation some other person is invested with a corresponding right (*a*). The extent of the obligations of the trustee is therefore the measure of the rights of the beneficiary. The beneficiary has the right to enforce performance of all or any of the obligations of the trustee by bringing an action for the execution of the trust (*b*).

If there be more than one beneficiary, any one or more of them may bring the action. Ord. XVI. r. 36 of the Rules of the Supreme Court provides that "any one of several *cestuis que trust* under any deed or instrument entitled to a judgment or order for the execution of the trusts of the deed or instrument may have the same without serving any other *cestui que trust.*"

However, a beneficiary is not now entitled to a judgment for execution of a trust as of right, for Ord. LV. r. 10 provides that "it shall not be obligatory on the court or a judge to pronounce or

(*a*) See Austin, Lectures on Jurisprudence, Lect. XVII. 5th ed. 400 *et seq.*
(*b*) Lewin, Trusts, 11th ed. 1069.

make a judgment or order, whether on summons or otherwise, for the administration of any trust or of the estate of any deceased person if the questions between the parties can be properly determined without such judgment or order."

This is a natural corollary to the provisions of Ord. LV. r. 3, which enable an application to be made for directions on any specific question arising in the course of the administration of the trust.

Section LXXI.—Right to transfer Beneficial Interest.

(1) A beneficiary who has legal capacity to dispose of property has the right to assign his beneficial interest (subject to all equities affecting it) so as to confer on the assignee the right of enforcing the obligations of the trustee and the beneficiary's remedies therefor, and the power to give a good discharge for the same.

(2) Every such assignment must be in writing, signed by the assignor (*a*).

(3) Where there are several assignments of the same beneficial interest, the assignees are entitled as against the trustee in the order in which the trustee has notice of their assignments, subject as follows:—

(a) notice to one of two or more co-trustees is deemed to be notice to them all;

(b) if notice has been given, the priority obtained thereby is not lost by reason that the trustee or trustees to whom it has been given have ceased to act in the trust, but if all the trustees to whom notice has been given cease to act, and the new trustee or trustees dispose of the beneficial interest in ignorance of the assignment, they are not liable to the assignee;

(c) if two or more assignees give simultaneous notice of their assignments, they are entitled in the order in which the assignments are made;

(*a*) Statute of Frauds, s. 9.

(d) an assignee claiming under a voluntary disposition made without valuable consideration or by a testamentary disposition, cannot claim priority over assignments prior in point of date, whether notice has been given of such prior assignments or not; and

(e) assignments of the beneficial interest in land rank in the order in which they are made

(4) Where the beneficiary is a married woman whose interest is subject to restraint against anticipation, she has no right to assign her beneficial interest during the continuance of the marriage.

"It may be laid down," says Mr. Lewin, "as a general rule that an equitable interest may be assigned though it be a mere possibility, and that either with or without the intervention of the trustee. And the assignee of the *cestui que trust* may call upon the trustee to clothe the equitable interest with the legal estate, and on his refusal may by suit compel a conveyance without making the assignor a party" (*a*).

But the assignment must be in writing, for s. 9 of the Statute of Frauds provides that—

"All grants and assignments of any trust or confidence shall likewise be in writing signed by the party granting or assigning the same, or by such last will or devise, or else shall likewise be utterly void and of none effect."

The section refers to the assignment of the beneficiary's interest (*b*), but though its scope is not so clear as it might be, there appear to be no reported decisions upon it.

The assignment of the equitable interest is subject to all equities which could be set up against the assignor, or as it is commonly

(*a*) Lewin, Trusts, 11th ed. 868. An assignment of a mere possibility is not, however, enforceable unless it be for valuable consideration. See *In re Ellenborough, Towry-Law* v. *Burne*, (1903) 1 Ch. 697. Compare Indian Trusts Act, 1882, ss. 58 and 69.

(*b*) Per Page Wood, V.-C., *Jerdein* v. *Bright* (1861), 2 J. & H. at p. 330.

expressed, "the assignee of an equity is bound by all equities affecting it."

"If there is one rule more perfectly established in a court of equity than another," Lord St. Leonards once said, "it is this, that whoever takes an assignment of a chose in action . . . . takes it subject to all the equities of the person who made the assignment" (c).

Lord Justice James has also asserted: "It is a rule and principle of this court, and of every court I believe, that where there is a chose in action, whether it is a debt or an obligation or a trust fund, and it is assigned, the person who holds the debt or obligation or has undertaken to hold the trust fund has as against the assignee exactly the same equities that he would have as against the assignor" (d).

Moreover, although the assignee's title is complete from the date of the assignment as between himself and the assignor or his representatives (e), yet his title is not complete as between himself and the trustee until he has given notice to the latter, and a trustee who performs his obligation to the original beneficiary without notice of any assignment by the latter is thereby discharged.

This rule was established in 1828 in the cases of *Dearle* v. *Hall* and *Loveridge* v. *Cooper* (f), where it seems to have been based on the necessity of protecting third persons who might otherwise be deceived into dealing with the assignor as still the owner; "any other decision would facilitate fraud by the *cestui que trust*, and cause loss to those who might have used every precaution that was possible to ascertain, before parting with their money, that the title they were taking was a valid one, and who might have done everything they could to render that title secure" (g). It has also been said by a learned writer that the true reason is the protection of the trustee, who has a right to look to the person for whom he undertook his obligation to give him a discharge unless and until he is distinctly informed that he is to

(c) *Mangles* v. *Dixon* (1852), 3 H. L. C. at p. 731.

(d) *Phipps* v. *Lovegrove* (1873), L. R. 16 Eq. at p. 88.

(e) See *Fortescue* v. *Barnett* (1834), 3 M. & K. 36; *Pearson* v. *Amicable Assurance Office* (1859), 27 Beav. 229; *Justice* v. *Wynne* (1860), 12 Ir. Ch. 289. And see *ante*, under sect. VIII.

(f) (1828), 3 Russ. 48. The rule was affirmed, or supposed to have been affirmed, by the House of Lords in *Foster* v. *Cockerell* (1835), 3 Cl. & Fin. 456.

(g) See per Lord Herschell in *Ward* v. *Duncombe*, (1893) A. C. at p. 378.

look to some other person (*h*). It seems difficult, however, to reduce the decisions of the courts to any consistent theory, and it may be questioned whether it rests upon any satisfactory principle (*i*). The rule is independent of any consideration of the conduct of the competing assignees. The earlier assignee is not postponed to the later on the ground that he has been guilty of negligence. Priority depends solely on priority of notice (*j*).

A similar rule has been adopted in Scotland, France, and some of the United States of America, but the opposite rule prevails in Germany and many of the states of America (*k*).

Where the trust property is under the control of several trustees, it is desirable to give notice to all of them, for though notice to one is sufficient so long as he remains a trustee at the time a later assignment is made (*l*), if at that time a trustee to whom notice has been given is dead and the second assignee gives notice to all the then existing trustees who are ignorant of the title of the first, it seems that the second gets priority (*m*). When, however, an assignee has given notice to all the trustees in existence at the time of his assignment, it is unnecessary, for the purpose of preserving his priority, that he should give any further notice when all the trustees to whom he gave notice have ceased to act and new trustees have taken their place (*n*).

At the same time, where there are several trustees, though notice be given to them all, if they all die or retire, and the new trustees appointed in their place, having no notice of the assignment, dispose of the trust property to some one other than the assignee, they are not liable to the latter. They are not bound to make inquiry of the retiring trustee or trustees (*o*).

It is clear that express notice need not be given by the assignee; it is sufficient if he can show that the trustee had notice

(*h*) See Pollock, Contracts, 7th ed. 220.

(*i*) See remarks of Lord Macnaghten in *Ward* v. *Duncombe*, *supra*, at p. 391.

(*j*) *In re Dallas*, (1904) 2 Ch. 385. See also per Lord Macnaghten in *Ward* v. *Duncombe*, *supra*, at p. 390.

(*k*) Ames, Cases on Trusts, 2nd ed. 327.

(*l*) *Ward* v. *Duncombe*, (1893) A. C. 369.

(*m*) *Timson* v. *Ramsbotham* (1837), 2 Keen, 35. The authority of this case was, however, questioned by Lord Macnaghten in *Ward* v. *Duncombe*, *supra*, at p. 394.

(*n*) *In re Wasdale*, *Brittin* v. *Partridge*, (1899) 1 Ch. 163.

(*o*) *Phipps* v. *Lovegrove* (1873), L. R. 16 Eq. 80.

of the assignment (*p*). But notice to a trustee who is himself the beneficiary making the assignment is not sufficient (*q*).

It is also clear that if two assignees give simultaneous notice to the trustee they rank in the order of the date of the assignments to them. In the case of *Johnstone* v. *Cox* (*r*) an army captain charged the fund payable to Cox & Co., army agents, on his behalf under the statute 34 & 35 Vict. c. 86, s. 3, first, to A. on the 5th October, 1875, second, to B. on the 14th December, 1877, and the 5th February, 1878, and third, to C. on the 14th May, 1878. Cox & Co. received the fund on behalf of the captain on the 16th May, 1878. B. and C. both gave notice of their charges as soon as Cox & Co.'s office was opened at 10 o'clock on the 17th May, 1878, and A. gave notice on the 21st May, 1878. In an action by C. against Cox & Co., A. and B., to establish his charge, it was held that B. was entitled first, then C., and then A.

It is settled that the rule in *Dearle* v. *Hall* does not apply to equitable estates or interests in land, whether freehold or leasehold, and if these be assigned the assignee's title is for all purposes complete from the date of the assignment, so that if there be several assignees they rank according to the respective dates of their assignments (*s*).

The above rules are applicable as between the assignees themselves as well as between the assignees and the trustees if the assignments are for valuable consideration (*t*). But it would appear that, at any rate as between the assignees themselves, the rules are only applicable where all the assignments are for valuable consideration. If there are several voluntary assignments of the same fund they rank as between themselves in the order of their date, and a later assignee cannot obtain priority by giving notice. This was one of the grounds on which the Court of Appeal in Ireland decided the case of *Justice* v. *Wynne* (*u*). In that case A.,

(*p*) *Lloyd* v. *Banks* (1868), L. R. 3 Ch. App. 488; *Ward* v. *Duncombe*, (1893) A. C. 369.

(*q*) *Browne* v. *Savage* (1859), 4 Drew. 635; *In re Dallas*, (1904) 2 Ch. 385.

(*r*) *Johnstone* v. *Cox* (1880), 16 Ch. D. 571; *In re Dallas*, (1904) 2 Ch. 385, is to the same effect.

(*s*) See *Wiltshire* v. *Rabbits* (1844), 14 Sim. 76; *Lee* v. *Howlett* (1856), 2 Kay & J. 531; *Humber* v. *Richards* (1890), 45 Ch. D. 589; *Ward* v. *Duncombe*, (1893) A. C. 369.

(*t*) Most, if not all, the cases will be found to be contests of one sort or another between the assignees.

(*u*) (1860), 12 Ir. Ch. 289.

by a voluntary deed executed in 1830, assigned a policy of assurance on his own life to trustees for his children. No notice of the assignment was given to the assurance company. The entire interest in the policy having become vested in B. and C. as trustees of and beneficiaries under this deed, C. married D., and in 1854 A. assigned the moiety of the policy not belonging to C. to D., who gave notice to the assurance company. The Irish Court of Appeal held that, as between B. and D., the former was entitled to the moiety of the policy moneys. In giving judgment Lord Justice Blackburne said (*v*), "it would be a total perversion of the doctrine of this court to allow want of notice of a prior title to be a ground of defence of a puisne title or incumbrance acquired without consideration. That doctrine is founded on and limited to the purpose of protecting purchasers, and never can be called in aid of the right of a party claiming under a voluntary instrument, which is the claim of the respondent here." Lord Chancellor Brady likewise said, "taking as a volunteer a mere chose in action, he is bound by all the equities which affected [the assignor] and cannot rely on the notice given to the company as conferring upon him any better title" (*w*).

The same case shows that as between the several assignees the later cannot obtain priority over the earlier by giving notice if at the time of doing so he has notice, actual or constructive, of the earlier assignment.

"The principle is well established," said Mr. Justice Ball, "that if a person having notice of a previous assignment of a trust fund, take an assignment of the same fund to himself, he cannot rely on being first to give notice to the trustee of the fund in order to obtain priority."

But these latter rules cannot be applicable as between the assignees and the trustees. If there are two voluntary assignees of a trust fund, and the later in time gives notice to the trustee before the earlier, and the trustee pays the fund to him in ignorance of the assignment to the earlier, he could be under no liability to the earlier (*x*).

The general rule that the owner of an equitable interest may

(*v*) See p. 299 of the report.

(*w*) See p. 304 of the report.

(*x*) See per Lord Macnaghten in *Ward* v. *Duncombe*, (1893) A. C. at p. 392.

assign it, is subject to the qualification that if the owner is a married woman whose interest has been subjected to a restraint against anticipation she has no power to dispose of her beneficial interest so long as the marriage continues. "In no case, and by no device whatever, can the restraint upon anticipation be evaded" (*y*).

(*y*) *Stanley* v. *Stanley* (1878), 7 Ch. D. 589, per Malins, V.-C. at p. 591. See also *Robinson* v. *Wheelwright* (1855), 21 Beav. 214; Underhill, Trusts and Trustees, 6th ed. 301.

SECTION LXXII.—RIGHT TO HAVE BREACH OF TRUST MADE GOOD.

EVERY beneficiary has the right to have the loss occasioned by a breach of trust made good by the trustee liable therefor.

It follows from the fact that a trustee is under an obligation to make good a breach of trust, that the beneficiary has a right to bring an action against the trustee to compel him personally to make compensation for the loss which the trust property has sustained (*a*).

There are two forms of account in an action by a beneficiary against a trustee, namely:—

A.—*An account of all such of the moneys or funds comprised in the trust instrument or from time to time subject to the trusts thereof as have been possessed or received by the trustee, or by any person by his order or for his use.* This is called the common account, and—

B.—*An account, in addition to the foregoing, of the moneys or funds comprised in the instrument of trust or from time to time subject to the trusts thereof which might without the wilful neglect or default of the trustee have been so possessed or received.* This is called the account on the footing of wilful default (*b*).

Judgment for the former is given as a matter of course in every action for the execution of the trust. In taking it the beneficiary is not permitted to charge the trustee with anything beyond his actual receipts. He is not permitted to show that there is some part of the trust property which the trustee ought to have got in, but has not (*c*).

If the beneficiary wants relief on the footing of wilful default, he must allege some specific act of wilful default in his pleadings, and claim consequential relief, and prove at least one act of wilful default at the hearing, or at any rate establish a case for inquiry (*d*).

(*a*) Lewin, Trusts, 11th ed. 1134; Ashburner, Equity, 192.

(*b*) See Seton, Decrees, 6th ed. 1125, 1157, 1162.

(*c*) See per Lord Macnaghten in *Dowse* v. *Gorton*, (1891) A. C. at p. 202.

(*d*) Lewin, Trusts, 11th ed. 1141.

SECTION LXXIII.—RIGHT TO FOLLOW TRUST PROPERTY.

(1) WHEN a trustee disposes of the trust property in a way not authorized by the terms of the trust, if the beneficiary can identify the property bought with, or the property or money received in exchange for, the trust property, or any subsequent product of either, he may—

(a) waive the breach of trust, and require that property, money, or product to be dealt with as if it were the trust property; or

(b) require the trustee to make good the breach of trust, and enforce a charge therefor on that property, money, or product.

(2) If the trust property or its product has been converted into or is money, and is mixed with the money of the trustee or of some other person, then, whether it remains a money fund, or whether the mixed fund has been invested in the purchase of any property, the beneficiary is entitled (subject to the rights of such other person) to a charge on the fund or property purchased therewith for the amount of the trust property.

(3) If there is more than one beneficiary, all must concur in exercising the option conferred by sub-s. 1 (a) of this section, and for this purpose all must have legal capacity to dispose of property.

When a trustee disposes of the trust property in a way not authorized by the terms of the trust instrument, the rights of the beneficiary depend upon the circumstances.

First.—If he can identify the property bought with, or property or money received in exchange for, the trust property or any subsequent product of either, he may—

(a) waive the breach of trust and take that property, money, or product; or,

(b) require the trustee to make good the breach of trust and enforce a lien therefor on that property, money, or product (*a*).

"The modern doctrine of equity," said Sir George Jessel in the case of *In re Hallett's Estate* (*a*), "as regards property disposed of by persons in a fiduciary position, is a very clear and well-established doctrine. You can, if the sale was rightful, take the proceeds of the sale if you can identify them. If the sale was wrongful, you can still take the proceeds of the sale, in a sense adopting the sale for the purpose of taking the proceeds, if you can identify them. There is no distinction therefore between a rightful and a wrongful disposition of the property so far as regards the right of the beneficial owner to follow the proceeds . when the purchase is clearly made with . . . the trust money . . the beneficial owner has a right to elect either to take the property purchased or to hold it as a security for the amount of the trust money laid out in the purchase; or as we generally express it, he is entitled at his election either to take the property or to have a charge on the property for the amount of the trust money" (*b*).

Illustrations.

1. A client hands to his stockbroker 22,200*l.* which he directs him to lay out in the purchase of exchequer bills. The stockbroker buys 6,500*l.* worth of exchequer bills, but with the balance pays for fifty shares in an American bank, funded stock of the United States, and certain bullion which he had previously bought for himself, but had not any money of his own to pay with. The stockbroker then absconds, but is followed by the client, to whom he surrenders the American securities mentioned. The client is

(*a*) *Taylor* v. *Plumer* (1815), 3 M. & S. 562; *Frith* v. *Cartland* (1865), 34 L. J. Ch. 301; *In re Hallett's Estate* (1879), 13 Ch. D. 696; *In re Champion*, (1893) 1 Ch. 101. See also *In re Oatway*, (1903) 2 Ch. 356; Harvard Law Review, vol. xix. 511; Lewin, Trusts, 11th ed. 1124 *et seq.* Compare Indian Trusts Act, 1882, s. 63.

(*b*) The beneficiary has an equitable charge or lien of the same description as that created by an equitable mortgage. See per Fry, J., *Cave* v. *Cave* (1880), 15 Ch. D. at p. 649.

entitled to retain these as against the trustee in bankruptcy of the stockbroker. *Taylor* v. *Plumer* (1815), 3 M. & S. 562.

2. The trustee of a settlement has power to invest the trust funds "on real securities." He invests part of the funds on the debenture of an English railway company which in the circumstances is not an authorized investment, and is therefore a breach of trust. In an action by the beneficiary for the restoration of the trust fund the beneficiary is entitled to a charge on the debenture until the breach of trust is made good. *Mant* v. *Leith* (1852), 15 Beav. 524.

Secondly.—If the beneficiary cannot identify the trust property or its product because it has been converted into or is money, and is mixed with the money of the trustee or of some third person, then, whether it remains money or whether the mixed fund has been invested in the purchase of any property, he is entitled (subject to the rights of such other person) to a lien on the fund or property purchased therewith for the amount of the trust property (*c*).

When the trustee has mixed the trust money with his own [or some third party's] "there is this distinction, that the *cestui que trust* or beneficial owner can no longer elect to take the property, because it is no longer bought with the trust money simply and purely but with a mixed fund. He is, however, still entitled to a charge on the property purchased for the amount of the trust money laid out in the purchase; and that charge is quite independent of the fact of the amount laid out by the trustee" (*d*).

This applies equally where the product of the trust property is money. "Supposing," as Sir George Jessel said, "instead of being invested in the purchase of land or goods, the moneys were simply mixed with other moneys of the trustee, does it make any difference according to the modern doctrine of equity? I say none. It would be very remarkable if it were so. Supposing the trust money was 1,000 sovereigns, and the trustee put them into a bag and, by mistake or accident or otherwise, dropped a sovereign of his own into the bag. Could anybody suppose that a judge in equity would

(*c*) *In re Hallett's Estate* (1879), 13 Ch. D. at p. 709; *Gibert* v. *Gonard* (1884), 54 L. J. Ch. 439; *Hancock* v. *Smith* (1889), 41 Ch. D. 456. Compare the Indian Trusts Act, 1882, s. 66.

(*d*) *In re Hallett's Estate* (1879), 13 Ch. D. at p. 709.

find any difficulty in saying that the *cestui que trust* has a right to take 1,000 sovereigns out of that bag? I do not like to call it a charge of 1,000 sovereigns on the 1,001 sovereigns, but that is the effect of it. I have no doubt of it. It would make no difference if, instead of one sovereign, it was another 1,000 sovereigns; but if instead of putting it into his bag, or after putting it into his bag, he carries the bag to his bankers, what then? According to law, the bankers are his debtors for the total amount. But if you lend the trust money to a third person, you can follow it. If in the case supposed the trustee had lent the 1,000*l.* to a man without security, you could follow the debt and take it from the debtor. If he lent it on a promissory note, you could take the promissory note; or a bond, if it were a bond. If instead of lending the whole amount in one sum simply he had added a sovereign, or had added 500*l.* of his own to the 1,000*l.*, the only difference is this, that instead of taking the bond or the promissory note, the *cestui que trust* would have a charge for the amount of the trust money on the bond or promissory note. So it would be on a simple contract debt; that is, if the debt were of such a nature as that between the creditor and the debtor you could not sever the debt in two so as to show what part was trust money, then the *cestui que trust* would have a right to a charge upon the whole."

Illustrations.

1. A. accepts bills of exchange, and entrusts them to B. for B. to get them discounted and pay the amount to A. B. gets them discounted with other bills of his own, mixes the money thus obtained together, makes certain payments out of the mixed fund, and invests the balance in letters of credit and foreign bills. B. becomes a bankrupt, and the letters of credit and foreign bills are realized and the moneys paid into the Bank of England. A. is entitled to be paid the amount of the bills accepted by him, less discount, before B.'s general creditors can have anything. *Frith* v. *Cartland* (1865), 34 L. J. Ch. 301.

2. A trustee holds bonds for 2,892*l.* in trust for a beneficiary. He improperly sells them and pays the proceeds (2,145*l.*) into his account at the bank. He draws cheques on the account for his own purposes, and subsequently pays in money of his own, but

the balance at the bank is never less than 2,145*l.* (*e*), and at his death is 3,029*l.* The beneficiary is entitled to a charge on the money for the amount of the proceeds of the bond. *In re Hallett's Estate* (1879), 13 Ch. D. 696 (*f*).

3. On the 30th October a stockbroker has in his bank, along with other moneys, 60*l.* belonging to a client, A. Subsequently he pays into the account moneys belonging to other clients and draws out sums exceeding those paid in by more than 60*l.*, but on the 5th November he has 301*l.* to the credit of his account, all of which belongs to his clients. There being enough to pay all the clients exclusive of A., and leave a balance of 60*l.*, A. is entitled to that balance in preference to a judgment creditor of the stockbroker, who obtains a garnishee order on the 5th November. *Hancock* v. *Smith* (1889), 41 Ch. D. 456.

If there is more than one beneficiary, and they propose to elect to take the unauthorized investment, all must concur in so doing. This rule is important when the trustee wants to realize the unauthorized investment in determining whether he can make a title to a purchaser. Suppose, for example, a trustee has improperly bought land with the trust money, and on the breach of trust being pointed out to him he wishes to sell the land. It is his duty to do this, because he is accountable for the money. If the purchaser has notice of the breach of trust, he will be bound to see that the beneficiaries have not elected to keep the land. If all of them are *sui juris*, the only safe course is to get one of them to join in the conveyance. But if any of them is not *sui juris*, since they cannot all concur in electing to keep the land, the trustee can make a good title without the concurrence of any of them (*g*).

(*e*) It would appear that in the opinion of Baggallay, L. J., if the balance had fallen below 2,145*l.*, the right of the *cestui que trust* to a charge would have been reduced *pro tanto* (see p. 731 of the report), and this appears to have been decided to be the law in America. See Harvard Law Review, vol. xix. 519.

(*f*) *Gibert* v. *Gonard* (1884), 54 L. J. Ch. 439, is similar.

(*g*) *In re Jenkins and Randall's Contract*, (1903) 2 Ch. 362.

SECTION LXXIV.—RIGHT TO CHARGE ON TRUSTEE'S BENEFICIAL INTEREST.

(1) A TRUSTEE who is himself a beneficiary, and who has committed a breach of trust, is not entitled to receive any part of the trust property until he has made good the breach of trust, and, if necessary, the other beneficiaries are entitled to a charge on his beneficial interest for the amount due from him.

(2) This section does not apply to prevent a trustee who is a married woman from receiving income from the trust property which is subject to restraint against anticipation, or to give other beneficiaries a charge on that income so long as the restraint continues.

It is well settled that a defaulting trustee cannot claim as against his *cestui que trust* any beneficial interest in the trust property so long as he remains in default (*a*).

This is sometimes expressed by saying that the other beneficiaries can impound the trustee beneficiary's beneficial interest. But the theory on which the rule is based is that the court treats the trustee as having received his share of the trust property by anticipation, and the answer to any claim made by him is, "You have already received your share; you have it in your hands" (*b*). Generally, therefore, it is hardly correct to say that the other beneficiaries can impound the defaulting trustee's share. There is nothing to impound; the trustee has had his share (*c*). It is rather a right to prevent him from taking any part of the trust property until he has made good his breach of trust. But there may conceivably be cases in which the other beneficiaries would be

(*a*) *Irby* v. *Irby* (1858), 25 Beav. 632; *Jacubs* v. *Rylance* (1874), L. R. 17 Eq. 341; *In re Brown* (1886), 32 Ch. D. 597; *Doering* v. *Doering* (1889), 42 Ch. D. 203.

(*b*) Per Stirling, J., *Doering* v. *Doering*, *supra*, at p. 207.

(*c*) Per Jessel, M. R., *Jacubs* v. *Rylance*, *supra*, at p. 342.

entitled to a charge on the trustee's share of the trust property. For example, suppose a testator gives property to a trustee upon trusts for his wife and children, directing that each child shall take a life interest, with remainder to his or her children, and he has eight children, one of whom is the sole trustee. Suppose an action for administration is commenced by the beneficiaries against the trustee, and in this action it is ordered that the estate shall be realized, and that eight separate accounts shall be opened in the names of the eight beneficiaries. Suppose it is then ascertained that the trustee is liable for a breach of trust. The other seven beneficiaries would be entitled to a charge on the amount standing to his account for the amount due from him in respect of the breach of trust (*d*).

The rule applies not only to an interest in the trust property conferred on the trustee by the instrument creating the trust, but even to one to which the trustee has become entitled derivatively, for example, as being the next of kin of a *cestui que trust* who has died intestate (*e*), or the assignee or mortgagee of a *cestui que trust* (*f*).

The right of the *cestui que trust* is exerciseable against an assignee of the trustee's beneficial interest, even though the breach of trust was committed after the assignment, for the assignee cannot be in any better position than his assignor; he takes subject to all equities (*g*). But the right is not enforceable against a *bonâ fide* purchaser without notice who has the legal title (*h*).

It seems pretty clear that the right is also not enforceable where the trustee is a married woman whose beneficial interest is subject to a restraint against anticipation (*i*).

(*d*) See *Edgar* v. *Plomley*, (1900) A. C. 431, where such an order was made, though the decree was subsequently reversed on appeal by reason of the trustee having assigned his share to a purchaser without notice.

(*e*) *Jacubs* v. *Rylance*, *supra*.

(*f*) *Doering* v. *Doering*, *supra*.

(*g*) *Morris* v. *Livie* (1842), 1 Y. & C. Ch. 380; *Doering* v. *Doering*, *supra*.

(*h*) See *Edgar* v. *Plomley*, (1900) A. C. 431.

(*i*) See *Stanley* v. *Stanley* (1878), 7 Ch. D. 589. See, however, Underhill, Trusts and Trustees, 6th ed. 418.

SECTION LXXV.—RIGHT TO AN INJUNCTION TO RESTRAIN A THREATENED BREACH OF TRUST.

IF it appears to the court that a trustee is about to commit a breach of trust, an injunction may be granted to restrain the same at the instance of any beneficiary.

"As the *cestui que trust* may compel the trustee to the observance of his duty, so on the other hand, if the *cestui que trust* have reason to suppose and can satisfy the court that the trustee is about to proceed to an act not authorized by the true scope of the trust, he may obtain an injunction from the court to restrain the trustee from such a wanton exercise of his legal power" (*a*).

(*a*) Lewin, Trusts, 11th ed. 1071; citing *Balls* v. *Strutt* (1841), 1 Hare, 146.

Part X.—RETIREMENT OF TRUSTEE AND APPOINTMENT OF NEW TRUSTEES.

SECTION LXXVI.—POWER OF APPOINTING NEW TRUSTEE WHEN TRUSTEE DEAD, ETC.

(1) WHERE a trustee, either original or substituted, and whether appointed by a court or otherwise, is dead, or remains out of the United Kingdom for more than twelve months, or desires to be discharged from all or any of the trusts or powers reposed in or conferred on him, or refuses or is unfit to act therein, or is incapable of acting therein, then the person or persons nominated for the purpose of appointing new trustees by the instrument, if any, creating the trust, or if there is no such person, or no such person able and willing to act, then the surviving or continuing trustees or trustee for the time being, or the personal representatives of the last surviving or continuing trustee, may, by writing, appoint another person or other persons to be a trustee or trustees in the place of the trustee dead, remaining out of the United Kingdom, desiring to be discharged, refusing, or being unfit or being incapable, as aforesaid.

(2) On the appointment of a new trustee for the whole or any part of trust property—

(a) the number of trustees may be increased; and

(b) a separate set of trustees may be appointed for any part of the trust property held on trusts distinct from those relating to any other part or parts of the trust property, notwithstanding that no new trustees or trustee are or is to be appointed for other. parts of the trust property, and any existing trustee may be appointed or remain one of such separate set of trustees; or, if only one trustee was originally appointed, then one separate trustee may be so appointed for the first-mentioned part; and

(c) it shall not be obligatory to appoint more than one new trustee where only one trustee was originally appointed, or to fill up the original number of trustees where more than two trustees were originally appointed; but, except where only one trustee was originally appointed, a trustee shall not be discharged under this section from his trust unless there will be at least two trustees to perform the trust; and

(d) any assurance or thing requisite for vesting the trust property, or any part thereof, jointly in the persons who are the trustees, shall be executed or done.

(3) Every new trustee so appointed, as well before as after all the trust property becomes by law, or by assurance, or otherwise, vested in him, shall have the same powers, authorities, and discretions, and may in all respects act, as if he had been originally appointed a trustee by the instrument, if any, creating the trust.

(4) The provisions of this section relative to a trustee who is dead include the case of a person nominated trustee in a will but dying before the testator, and those

relative to a continuing trustee include a refusing or retiring trustee, if willing to act in the execution of the provisions of this section.

(5) This section applies only if and as far as a contrary intention is not expressed in the instrument, if any, creating the trust, and shall have effect subject to the terms of that instrument and to any provisions therein contained.

(6) This section applies to trusts created either before or after the commencement of this act (*a*).

Originally, if the trustee or trustees appointed by the settlor died or became incapable of acting in the trust, there was no one who could continue its administration, and it was necessary to commence a suit for the execution of the trust in order to get a new trustee appointed, unless the settlor had provided for the contingency.

But even those who were familiar with the law might overlook the necessity for making this provision. For example, it is recorded that Lord Thurlow himself omitted to insert any power to appoint new trustees in his will though he had appointed Lord Eldon one of his trustees, and it became necessary as a consequence for the latter to obtain a private act of parliament (49 Geo. 3, cap. clxxv) to supply the defect (*b*).

Further, as has already been shown, a trustee who had once accepted office had no power of relinquishing it unless the court allowed it, or the beneficiaries were *sui juris* and consented, or there was a power in the instrument of trust enabling him to do so.

In well-drawn settlements and wills, however, it became usual to insert a provision that in case the trustees or any of them should die or be abroad for twelve calendar months, or should be desirous of being discharged from or refuse, decline or become incapable to act in the trusts, it should be lawful for some person named, or for the surviving or continuing trustee, or the executors or administrators of the survivor, by deed or writing to nominate some other person to be a trustee; and to declare that the trust estate should

(*a*) Trustee Act, 1893, s. 10.

(*b*) Lewin, Trusts, 11th ed. 786.

forthwith be vested jointly in the persons appointed, and that they should be capable of exercising all the same powers as if originally named in the settlement (*c*).

In 1860 Lord Cranworth's Act (22 & 23 Vict. c. 145) by s. 27 conferred a power somewhat in this form on the person or persons nominated for the purpose by the instrument creating the trust, or, if there were no such person, the surviving or continuing trustee or trustees, or the acting executor or administrator of the last surviving or continuing trustee, or the last retiring trustee. The provisions of the act were, however, less complete than the forms of powers then commonly in use, and it was consequently often not relied on in practice (*d*).

It was in consequence repealed in 1881 by s. 71 of the Conveyancing Act, 1881, and replaced by the much wider provisions of s. 31 of that act. Even these, however, were found not wide enough, and were supplemented by s. 5 of the Conveyancing Act, 1882, which authorized the appointment of a separate set of trustees for any part of the trust property held on trusts distinct from those relating to any other part or parts of the trust property; and by s. 6 of the Conveyancing Act, 1892, which enabled such an appointment to be made notwithstanding that no new trustees or trustee were to be appointed of other parts of the trust property. These enactments were all in their turn repealed by s. 51 of the Trustee Act, 1893, and replaced in slightly different language by s. 10 of that act, which provides:—

"(1) Where a trustee, either original or substituted, and whether appointed by a court or otherwise, is dead, or remains out of the United Kingdom for more than twelve months, or desires to be discharged from all or any of the trusts or powers reposed in or conferred on him, or refuses or is unfit to act therein, or is incapable of acting therein, then the person or persons nominated for the purpose of appointing new trustees by the instrument (if any) creating the trust, or if there is no such person, or no such person able and willing to act, then the surviving or continuing trustees or trustee for the time being, or the personal representatives of the last surviving or continuing trustee, may by writing appoint another person or other persons to be a trustee or trustees in the place of the trustee dead, remaining out of the United Kingdom,

(*c*) Lewin, Trusts, 786, 787.

(*d*) See Bythewood & Jarman, Conveyancing, 4th ed. vol. ii. 4.

desiring to be discharged, refusing or being unfit, or being incapable as aforesaid."

By s. 50 of the Trustee Act, 1893, the term "trustee" includes the duties incident to the office of personal representative of a deceased person unless the context otherwise requires. But the better opinion seems to be that the section does not authorize the appointment of a new executor or trustee to perform the duties of an executor (*e*).

The power to appoint "where a trustee is dead" includes the case of a person nominated trustee in a will, but dying before the testator, by the express provisions of sub-s. (4) of s. 10 of the Trustee Act, 1893. But where the sole trustee or trustees die before the testator, unless a person has been nominated for the purpose there will be no one capable of exercising the power.

Illustration.

A. by his will appoints B. and C. his trustees and executors, both of whom pre-decease A. The personal representatives of the survivor of B. and C. cannot appoint new trustees. *Nicholson* v. *Field*, (1893) 2 Ch. 511.

The words "remains out of the United Kingdom for more than twelve months," mean an uninterrupted absence for twelve consecutive months. The section does not apply if during the twelve months the trustee pays even a very short visit to the United Kingdom.

Illustration.

X., one of the trustees of a settlement, leaves the United Kingdom on the 1st April, 1899. In November 1899, he returns and remains one week, during which he visits the office of the solicitors to the trust and transacts trust business. On the 1st June, 1900, a new trustee is appointed in his place. The appointment is void. *In re Walker*, *Summers* v. *Barrow*, (1901) 1 Ch. 259.

(*e*) See *In re Moore* (1882), 21 Ch. D. 778; *In re Willey* (1890), W. N. 1; *Eaton* v. *Daines* (1894), W. N. 32; Rudall & Greig, Trustee Acts, 3rd ed. 54; Champerowne & Johnston, Trustee Acts, 50; Easton, Appointment of New Trustees, 11.

The power to appoint where a trustee "desires to be discharged," has the effect of giving a trustee a power to retire whenever he pleases, though of course only upon the appointment of a new trustee; and as the new trustee can only be appointed by the person or persons nominated for the purpose, or if there be none by the surviving or continuing trustees or trustee, he can only retire if the latter give their consent. The desire of the trustee to be discharged should be stated in express terms in the instrument appointing the new trustee, so as to preserve evidence of the fact.

A doubt has been suggested whether the expression "refuses to act" covers the case of a person appointed trustee who disclaims (*f*). It is argued (1), that such a person is not a "trustee" at all, and (2) that he cannot be said to "refuse," though he may be said to "decline" to act, and that the expression only covers the case of a trustee who has undertaken the office but afterwards declines to take any further part in the execution of the trust. But this appears a quite unnecessary subtlety, and the great majority of text-writers seem to be of opinion that both classes of cases are included (*g*).

It has been held that payment into court of the trust fund by the trustee under the Trustee Relief Act (now s. 42 of the Trustee Act, 1893) amounts to a refusal to act (*h*).

There have been but few decisions to explain when a trustee is "unfit to act" within the meaning of this section. The court has inherent jurisdiction in an action for that purpose to remove a trustee and appoint a new one in his place on the ground of unfitness, and probably in any case in which the court would exercise its jurisdiction it will be safe for the person having the statutory power to exercise it (*i*). It is clear that the court will remove a bankrupt trustee. "It is the duty of the court," said Sir George Jessel, "to remove a bankrupt trustee who has trust money to receive or deal with, so that he can misappropriate it. There may be exceptions under special circumstances to that general rule; and it may also be that where a trustee has no money to receive he

(*f*) Lewin, Trusts, 11th ed. 788. But see also 798.

(*g*) Rudall & Greig, Trustee Acts, 3rd ed. 57; Champernowne & Johnston, Trustee Acts, 52; Easton, Appointment of New Trustees, 19.

(*h*) *In re Williams' Settlement* (1858), 4 K. & J. 87.

(*i*) See Rudall & Greig, Trustee Acts, 3rd ed. 58.

ought not to be removed merely because he has become bankrupt; but I consider the general rule to be as I have stated. The reason is obvious. A necessitous man is more likely to be tempted to misappropriate trust funds than one who is wealthy; and, besides, a man who has not shown prudence in managing his own affairs is not likely to be successful in managing those of other people" (*j*). The person or persons who have power to appoint new trustees under this section can therefore appoint a new trustee in place of one who has become bankrupt, at any rate as a general rule (*k*).

A trustee is "incapable of acting" if he is of unsound mind (*l*), but the expression does not refer to mere legal incapacity, such as that of infancy or coverture.

The words "the person or persons nominated for the purpose of appointing new trustees," mean the person or persons nominated for the purpose of appointing new trustees in the particular event which has happened.

Illustration.

A settlement nominates persons to have the power of appointing new trustees in specified events, including the event of a trustee becoming incapable, but not including the event of a trustee becoming unfit. One of the trustees becomes a bankrupt and absconds. This makes him "unfit" but not "incapable" of acting, and the appointment of new trustees must be made, not by the persons nominated, but by the continuing trustees under the provisions of this section. *In re Wheeler and De Rochow*, (1896) 1 Ch. 315.

The words "the instrument, if any, creating the trust" show that the section is applicable to all trusts, whether created in writing or not, and this is emphasized by the definition clause of the act, where "trust" is defined as including implied and constructive trusts.

The provision that "if there is no such person or no such

(*j*) *In re Barker's Trusts* (1875), 1 Ch. D. 43; *In re Adam's Trust* (1879), 12 Ch. D. 634; *Bowen* v. *Phillips*, (1897) 1 Ch. 174; Trustee Act, 1893, s. 25 (1).

(*k*) Certainly they can if he has absconded as well: *In re Wheeler and De Rochow*, (1896) 1 Ch. at p. 322.

(*l*) *In re Blake* (1887), W. N. 173.

person able and willing to act" covers the case of the persons nominated being unable to agree on their appointee.

Illustration.

By a settlement the power of appointing new trustees is vested in a husband and his wife during their joint lives. They are living apart, and are unable to agree in the selection of new trustees. The legal personal representatives of the last surviving trustee are entitled to exercise the statutory power. *In re Sheppard's Settlement Trusts* (1888), W. N. 234.

By the words "the surviving or continuing trustee or trustees for the time being" is meant one who is to continue to act after the completion of the appointment (*m*).

Illustrations.

A. and B. are trustees of a will. B. desires to retire. A. appoints X. in his place without the concurrence of B. The appointment is properly made. *In re Norris* (1884), 27 Ch. D. 333.

2. A., B. and C. are trustees of a settlement. C. remains out of the United Kingdom for more than twelve months. A. and B., without the concurrence of C., appoint X. a trustee in his place. The appointment is valid. *In re Coates to Parsons* (1886), 34 Ch. D. 370.

By sub-s. (4), however, the provisions of this section relative to a continuing trustee include a refusing or retiring trustee if willing to act in the execution of the provisions of the section. So that if a trustee who wishes to retire cares to join in the appointment of a new trustee in his place, he is entitled to do so; but if he does not care to do so, the appointment can be made by the continuing trustee without him.

"The personal representatives of the last surviving or continuing trustee" means, it would seem, the persons who are for the

(*m*) *In re Norris, Allen* v. *Norris* (1884), 27 Ch. D. 333; *In re Coates to Parsons* (1886), 34 Ch. D. 370.

time being entitled to administer the estate of the last surviving or continuing trustee under a grant of probate or administration. For example, a sole surviving trustee of a will by his will appointed A. and B. "general executors" thereof, and C. and D. executors "for the purpose of executing in continuation to" himself the trusts in question. A. and B. obtained a grant of probate to themselves as "general executors," and proceeded by deed to appoint two persons to be trustees of the will of the original testator. Subsequently D. obtained a grant of administration "for the purpose only of executing in continuation to the said testator" the trusts of the original will. Mr. Justice Kekewich held, though not without some hesitation, that the appointment by A. and B. was valid, they being at the time in possession of the only grant of probate then in existence, and therefore the "personal representatives" within the meaning of the section (*n*).

A sole trustee may be a "last surviving or continuing trustee" within the meaning of the section, so that if a sole trustee dies having by his will appointed an executor, the latter can appoint new trustees (*o*).

It is to be observed that the section says the person having the power "may" by writing appoint. He is not bound, therefore, to appoint, and if he does not choose to exercise the power he cannot be compelled to do so. In that event the court will appoint, and if the person having the power has acted vexatiously, he will not be allowed costs (*p*).

The appointment is to be "by writing," so that a deed is not necessary, although it is often used. But the language of the section seems inapplicable to an appointment by will, even if made by a last surviving trustee, and such an appointment has been held void (*q*).

The power is to appoint "another person or other persons," and the question arises whether this means some person or persons other than the trustee who is dead, remaining out of the United King-

(*n*) *In re Parker's Trusts*, (1894) 1 Ch. 707.

(*o*) *In re Shafto's Trusts* (1885), 26 Ch. D. 247.

(*p*) *In re Sarah Knight's Will* (1883), 26 Ch. D. 82.

(*q*) *In re Parker's Trusts*, (1894) 1 Ch. 707.

dom, or as the case may be, or whether it means some person or persons other than the person exercising the power of appointment. Mr. Justice Kekewich has held that, since it must mean the latter where the person appointing is a surviving or continuing trustee, or retiring or refusing trustee, it must mean the same where the person appointing is a person nominated for the purpose, and that therefore he cannot appoint himself either alone or with any other person (*r*). Apart from this, however, it has been said that in any case a power to appoint new trustees is a fiduciary power, and that as a consequence the person having it cannot appoint himself (*s*). On the other hand, it has been said that there is no rule that a donee of a power to appoint new trustees is unable to appoint himself where the language of the power permits, and that the court will sanction such an appointment in special circumstances (*t*).

S. 10 of the Trustee Act, 1893, proceeds as follows :—

"(2) On the appointment of a new trustee for the whole or any part of trust property—

"(a) The number of trustees may be increased; and

"(b) A separate set of trustees may be appointed for any part of the trust property held on trusts distinct from those relating to any other part or parts of the trust property, notwithstanding that no new trustees or trustee are or is to be appointed for other parts of the trust property, and any existing trustee may be appointed or remain one of such separate set of trustees: or, if only one trustee was originally appointed, then one separate trustee may be so appointed for the first-mentioned part; and

"(c) It shall not be obligatory to appoint more than one new trustee where only one trustee was originally appointed, or to fill up the original number of trustees where more than two trustees were originally appointed; but except where only one trustee was originally appointed, a trustee shall not be discharged under this section

(*r*) *In re Sampson*, (1906) 1 Ch. 435.

(*s*) *In re Skeat's Settlement* (1889), 42 Ch. D. 522, Kay, J.; *In re Newen*, *Newen* v. *Barnes*, (1894) 2 Ch. 297, Kekewich. J.

(*t*) *Montefiore* v. *Guedalla*, (1903) 1 Ch. 723, Buckley, J. In this case the power was to "appoint a new trustee or trustees."

from his trust unless there will be at least two trustees to perform the trust; and

"(d) Any assurance or thing requisite for vesting the trust property or any part thereof jointly in the persons who are the trustees shall be executed or done."

Paragraphs (a), (c) and (d) of this sub-section are re-enactments of sub-ss. (2), (3) and (4) respectively of s. 31 of the Conveyancing Act, 1881, and paragraph (b) is substantially a re-enactment of s. 5 of the Conveyancing Act, 1881, and s. 6 of the Conveyancing Act, 1892.

S. 10 of the Trustee Act, 1893, continues as follows :—

"(3) Every new trustee so appointed as well before as after all the trust property becomes by law or by assurance or otherwise vested in him, shall have the same powers, authorities and discretions, and may in all respects act as if he had been originally appointed a trustee by the instrument (if any) creating the trust.

"(4) The provisions of this section relative to a trustee who is dead include the case of a person nominated trustee in a will but dying before the testator, and those relative to a continuing trustee include a refusing or retiring trustee if willing to act in the execution of the provisions of this section.

"(5) This section applies only if and as far as a contrary intention is not expressed in the instrument (if any) creating the trust, and shall have effect subject to the terms of that instrument and to any provisions therein contained.

"(6) This section applies to trusts created either before or after the commencement of this act."

These sub-sections are a re-enactment of sub-ss. (5), (6), (7) and (8) respectively of the Conveyancing Act, 1881.

SECTION LXXVII.—POWER FOR TRUSTEE TO RETIRE UNDER CERTAIN CONDITIONS.

(1) WHERE there are more than two trustees, if one of them by deed declares that he is desirous of being discharged from the trust, and if his co-trustees and such other person, if any, as is empowered to appoint trustees, by deed consent to the discharge of the trustee, and to the vesting in the co-trustees alone of the trust property, then the trustee desirous of being discharged shall be deemed to have retired from the trust, and shall, by the deed, be discharged therefrom under this act, without any new trustee being appointed in his place.

(2) Any assurance or thing requisite for vesting the trust property in the continuing trustees alone shall be executed or done.

(3) This section applies only if and as far as a contrary intention is not expressed in the instrument, if any, creating the trust, and shall have effect subject to the terms of that instrument and to any provisions therein contained.

(4) This section applies to trusts created either before or after the commencement of this act (*a*).

Previously to the coming into operation of the Conveyancing Act, 1881, a trustee could not retire from the trust unless some person was appointed in his place, or unless the instrument creating the trust authorized him to do so, which, however, it very rarely did.

(*a*) Trustee Act, 1893, s. 11.

By s. 32 of that act, however, it was provided that, where there were more than two trustees, if one of them by deed declared that he was desirous of being discharged from the trust, and if his co-trustees and such other person, if any, as was empowered to appoint trustees by deed consented to the discharge of the trustee and to the vesting in the co-trustees alone of the trust property, then the trustee desirous of being discharged should be deemed to have retired from the trust, and should by the deed be discharged therefrom . . . without any new trustee being appointed in his place. This section was repealed by s. 51 of the Trustee Act, 1893, and replaced by s. 11 of that act, which is in the words above given.

It is to be observed that a deed is essential when a trustee is retiring under this provision.

SECTION LXXVIII.—VESTING OF TRUST PROPERTY IN NEW OR CONTINUING TRUSTEES.

(1) WHERE a deed by which a new trustee is appointed to perform any trust contains a declaration by the appointor to the effect that any estate or interest in any land subject to the trust, or in any chattel so subject, or the right to recover and receive any debt or other thing in action so subject, shall vest in the persons who by virtue of the deed become and are the trustees for performing the trust, that declaration shall, without any conveyance or assignment, operate to vest in those persons, as joint tenants, and for the purposes of the trust, that estate, interest, or right.

(2) Where a deed by which a retiring trustee is discharged under this act contains such a declaration as is in this section mentioned by the retiring and continuing trustees, and by the other person, if any, empowered to appoint trustees, that declaration shall, without any conveyance or assignment, operate to vest in the continuing trustees alone, as joint tenants, and for the purposes of the trust, the estate, interest, or right to which the declaration relates.

(3) This section does not extend to any legal estate or interest in copyhold or customary land, or to land conveyed by way of mortgage for securing money subject to the trust, or to any such share, stock, annuity, or property as is only transferable in books kept by a company or other body, or in manner directed by or under act of parliament.

(4) For purposes of registration of the deed in any registry, the person or persons making the declaration shall be deemed the conveying party or parties, and the conveyance shall be deemed to be made by him or them under a power conferred by this act.

(5) This section applies only to deeds executed after the thirty-first of December one thousand eight hundred and eighty-one (*a*).

When a new trustee is appointed or a trustee retires, it of course becomes necessary for the trust property to be transferred from the old to the new or continuing trustee or trustees, as the case may be.

This sometimes caused difficulty when a new trustee was being appointed in the place of one who was out of the jurisdiction or incapable of acting; the latter could not transfer the trust property, and it was necessary to apply to the court for a vesting order under the Trustee Acts. With a view to saving parties the expense of such an application, it was provided by s. 34 of the Conveyancing Act, 1881, that—

"(1) Where a deed by which a new trustee is appointed to perform any trust contains a declaration by the appointor to the effect that any estate or interest in any land subject to the trust or in any chattel so subject, or the right to recover and receive any debt or other thing in action so subject, shall vest in the persons who, by virtue of the deed, become and are the trustees for performing the trust, that declaration shall, without any conveyance or assignment, operate to vest in those persons, as joint tenants and for the purposes of the trust, that estate, interest, or right.

"(2) Where a deed by which a retiring trustee is discharged under this act contains such a declaration as in this section mentioned by the retiring and continuing trustees, and by the other person, if any, empowered to appoint trustees, that declaration shall, without any conveyance or assignment, operate to vest in the continuing trustees alone, as joint tenants and for the purposes of the trust, the estate, interest, or right to which the declaration relates."

(*a*) Trustee Act, 1893, s. 12.

It will be observed that on the appointment of a new trustee the declaration may be made by "the appointor," thus dispensing with the concurrence of the old trustee and saving the expense of an application for a vesting order by giving the appointor practically the same power as the court. The declaration must, however, be in the same document as the appointment of the new trustee, and the document must be a deed.

On the other hand, on the retirement of a trustee where no new trustee is being appointed in his place, the declaration must be made by both the retiring and the continuing trustees, and in addition the person empowered to appoint new trustees if any, so that no saving of expense or saving in the length of the document of any importance is effected.

However, with a view to protecting the rights of the lord of the manor in which any copyhold property belonging to the trust is situate, and to preventing the trusts getting on to the title of property in mortgage to the trust, and to preserving the statutory methods of transferring stocks and shares, it was provided by the third sub-section of s. 34 of the Conveyancing Act that—

"(3) This section does not extend to any legal estate or interest in copyhold or customary land, or to land conveyed by way of mortgage for securing money subject to the trust, or to any such share, stock, annuity or property as is only transferable in books kept by a company or other body or in manner prescribed by or under act of parliament."

In these cases, therefore, a surrender and admission or transfer, as the case may be, is necessary, or else an application to the court for a vesting order must be made.

Where the trust property includes land in the county of Middlesex or Yorkshire, registration of a memorial of the transaction becomes necessary, and the section therefore provided that—

"(4) For the purposes of registration of the deed in any registry, the person or persons making the declaration shall be deemed the conveying party or parties, and the conveyance shall be deemed to be made by him or them under a power conferred by this act."

These provisions of the Conveyancing Act were repealed by s. 51 of the Trustee Act, 1893, but re-enacted word for word in s. 12 of that act.

SECTION LXXIX.—POWER OF THE COURT TO APPOINT NEW TRUSTEES.

(1) THE High Court may, whenever it is expedient to appoint a new trustee or new trustees, and it is found inexpedient, difficult, or impracticable so to do without the assistance of the court, make an order for the appointment of a new trustee or new trustees either in substitution for or in addition to any existing trustee or trustees, or although there is no existing trustee. In particular and without prejudice to the generality of the foregoing provision, the court may make an order for the appointment of a new trustee in substitution for a trustee who is convicted of felony, or is a bankrupt.

(2) An order under this section, and any consequential vesting order or conveyance, shall not operate further or otherwise as a discharge to any former or continuing trustee than an appointment of new trustees under any power for that purpose contained in any instrument would have operated.

(3) Nothing in this section shall give power to appoint an executor or administrator (*a*).

The Court of Chancery always had inherent jurisdiction to appoint new trustees of trust property in an action; it had, however, no inherent jurisdiction to divest a person of an estate legally vested in him and vest it in another. The statute 11 Geo. IV. & 1 Will. IV. c. 60, was, with some others, passed with the view of providing a remedy in certain cases where it was difficult or

(*a*) Trustee Act, 1893, s. 25.

impossible to obtain a conveyance or assignment of property held on trust, and at the same time the opportunity was taken to empower the court in those cases to appoint new trustees in a more summary manner than had previously been possible, namely, upon petition instead of by suit (*b*).

These statutes were all repealed and, with some modifications, re-enacted by the Trustee Act, 1850, of which ss. 32 and 33 related to the appointment of new trustees, and authorized the court to make an order appointing new trustees upon petition, whenever it should be expedient to appoint them and it should be found inexpedient, difficult, or impracticable so to do without the assistance of the court. These provisions were amended by the Trustee Amendment Act, 1852, ss. 8 and 9, and the Bankruptcy Act, 1883, s. 147, and all these enactments were repealed by s. 51 of the Trustee Act, 1893, and re-enacted in a consolidated form by s. 25 of that act in the words given above. The section, however, does not deal exhaustively or generally with the powers of the court to appoint new trustees. It, like the sections it replaces, merely provides a simple and expeditious method of appointing new trustees in comparatively simple cases, substituting proceedings by petition or summons in place of a suit or action. The general jurisdiction to remove and replace trustees in an action remains unaffected by the statutory provision (*c*).

It was decided, very soon after the act of 1850 came into operation, that though s. 32 enabled the court to appoint new trustees whenever it was expedient to do so, and it should be found inexpedient, difficult, or impracticable to make the appointment without the assistance of the court, the court had no power to appoint under the act if there were a person who had a power of appointing and who was capable of exercising and willing to exercise the power, although he might have disclosed an intention to exercise it corruptly; and further that the court had no power under the act to remove a trustee against his wishes (*d*). The court therefore can only appoint under the act when there is no person who will, or no person who can, exercise the power (*e*).

(*b*) Easton, Appointment of New Trustees, 1.

(*c*) Champernowne & Johnston, Trustee Acts, 96.

(*d*) *In re Hodson's Settlement* (1851), 9 Hare, 118; followed on the former point in *In re Higginbottom*, (1892) 3 Ch. 132; and on the latter point by the C. A. in *Re Combs* (1884), 51 L. T. 45.

(*e*) The cases in which the court has held it expedient to appoint a new trustee will be found collected in Rudall

The power is to appoint "a new trustee or new trustees," and therefore the court has no power in ordinary circumstances to re-appoint the existing trustees for the purpose of making a consequential vesting order. This device, though formerly resorted to, has been disapproved except in cases in which there is a reasonable question whether the existing trustees have been validly appointed. The proper course is to obtain a vesting order under some other sub-section of the act, and if there is none applicable, one of the trustees should retire so as to enable the court to appoint a new trustee in his place (*f*).

An application for the appointment of a new trustee under this section is made by summons (*g*). If there is a pending action or proceeding in which the summons can be issued it will be by summons in that action or proceeding, otherwise it will be by originating summons (*h*).

& Greig, Trustee Acts, 3rd ed. 111; and Champernowne & Johnston, Trustee Acts, 97.

(*f*) Champernowne & Johnston, Trustee Acts, 101.

(*g*) Rules of the Supreme Court, Ord. LV. r. 13a.

(*h*) For forms, see Rudall & Greig, Trustee Acts, 3rd ed. App. V. Forms 8, 9, 10 and 11, pp. 336 *et seq.*

SECTION LXXX.—VESTING ORDERS AS TO LAND.

IN any of the following cases, namely:—

(i) Where the High Court appoints or has appointed a new trustee; and

(ii) Where a trustee entitled to or possessed of any land, or entitled to a contingent right therein, either solely or jointly with any other person,—

(a) is an infant, or

(b) is out of the jurisdiction of the High Court, or

(c) cannot be found; and

(iii) Where it is uncertain who was the survivor of two or more trustees jointly entitled to or possessed of any land; and

(iv) Where, as to the last trustee known to have been entitled to or possessed of any land, it is uncertain whether he is living or dead; and

(v) Where there is no heir or personal representative to a trustee who was entitled to or possessed of land and has died intestate as to that land, or where it is uncertain who is the heir or personal representative or devisee of a trustee who was entitled to or possessed of land and is dead; and

(vi) Where a trustee jointly or solely entitled to or possessed of any land, or entitled to a contingent right therein, has been required, by or on behalf of a person entitled to require a conveyance of the land or a release of the right, to convey the land or to release the right, and has wilfully refused or neglected to convey the land or release the right for twenty-eight days after the date of the requirement;

the High Court may make an order (in this act called a vesting order) vesting the land in any such person in any such manner and for any such estate as the court may direct, or releasing or disposing of the contingent right to such person as the court may direct.

Provided that—

(a) Where the order is consequential on the appointment of a new trustee the land shall be vested for such estate as the court may direct in the persons who on the appointment are the trustees; and

(b) Where the order relates to a trustee entitled jointly with another person, and such trustee is out of the jurisdiction of the High Court or cannot be found, the land or right shall be vested in such other person, either alone or with some other person (*a*).

When a new trustee is appointed it is necessary to get the trust property transferred from the old to the new trustees. This, as has been already pointed out, is often a matter of difficulty, as for example where a sole trustee is of unsound mind, or where all the trustees have died and the trust property is vested in an infant as heir to the last survivor of them, and the like.

To provide for difficulties of this kind power was conferred on

(*a*) Trustee Act, 1893, s. 26.

the court by several statutes and especially by Lord St. Leonards' Trustee Act—11 Geo. IV. & 1 Will. IV. c. 60—either to direct a trustee under disability to convey or to appoint some person to convey for him.

In 1850 a new procedure was invented. By ss. 3, 4, 5 and 6 of the Trustee Act of that year power was conferred on the Lord Chancellor, as exercising jurisdiction over lunatics, to make an order vesting land, or the right to transfer stock or choses in action held on trust or by way of mortgage by a lunatic in such person, in such manner and for such estate as he should direct; and by other sections as amended by the Trustee Extension Act, 1852, and the Merchant Shipping Act, 1855, power was conferred on the Court of Chancery to make a similar order vesting land, or the right to transfer stock or choses in action, or ships held on trust or by way of mortgage when the trustee was an infant or out of the jurisdiction, or could not be found, or when it was uncertain which of two trustees was the survivor, or whether a trustee were living or dead, and other specified eventualities, and particularly upon the appointment of a new trustee under s. 32 of the act.

Such an order has come to be called a vesting order.

The provisions of these acts were terribly involved, and exhibit all the prolixity which characterizes legal draftsmanship of the time. Each section provided only for one specified event, and a repetition of the consequences to arise thereupon was rendered necessary in each. Such of them as relate to lunacy were repealed by s. 342 of the Lunacy Act, 1890, and replaced by ss. 133 to 143 of that act, and the others by s. 51 of the Trustee Act, 1893, being for the most part replaced by ss. 26 to 41 of that act.

The powers of the court to make vesting orders in the case of land were re-enacted in a consolidated form in s. 26 of the last mentioned act, which is in the words given above.

The history of the various enactments above mentioned has led to a conflict of jurisdiction between the court in lunacy and the Chancery Division of the High Court which has produced a somewhat absurd result. It has already been stated that s. 32 of the Trustee Act, 1850, conferred power on the court to appoint a new trustee whenever it was expedient, and ss. 34 and 35 gave it power to make a vesting order on the appointment of a new trustee. The language of these sections was wide enough to give the court power to appoint a new trustee in the case of a trustee becoming a lunatic, and to make a vesting order thereupon, and would probably have been held to be so had it not been that ss. 3, 4, 5 and 6 made special provision for the making of vesting orders in the case of a lunatic trustee, not by the Court of Chancery, but by the Lord Chancellor sitting in lunacy. It was accordingly held that although a trustee could be appointed in place of a lunatic trustee by the Court of Chancery, no order divesting the trust property from him and vesting it in the new trustee could be made in lunacy. By s. 10 of the Trustee Extension Act, 1852, power was given to the Lord Chancellor in Lunacy to make an order for the appointment of a new trustee in every case in which, under the Trustee Act, 1850, he had jurisdiction to make a vesting order. Consequently, in the case of a lunatic trustee, there was jurisdiction in lunacy to appoint a new trustee and to make a vesting order consequential thereon, and there was jurisdiction in Chancery to appoint a new trustee but not to make a vesting order. The repeal and re-enactment of these various provisions in the Lunacy Act, 1890, and the Trustee Act, 1893, respectively, which are only consolidating acts, has made no difference in this respect. It follows that although the Chancery Division of the High Court has jurisdiction under the Trustee Act, 1893, to appoint a new trustee in the place of a lunatic, it has still no jurisdiction to make a vesting order consequential thereon. If a vesting order is required, resort must be had to the court in lunacy (*b*).

The above did not apply where a trustee was both a lunatic and an infant (*c*), or both a lunatic and out of the jurisdiction (*d*), for in these cases power to make vesting orders was conferred on the Court of Chancery, apart from any appointment of new trustees by ss. 7 to 12 of the Trustee Act, 1850, and presumably this also has not been altered by the repeal and re-enactment of the sections (*b*). But owing to the provisions of s. 30 of the Conveyancing Act, 1881, and Part I. of the Land Transfer Act, 1897, it is not likely that trust property will be vested in an infant except in rare cases.

In certain cases vesting orders must be made and intituled both in Chancery and in lunacy. This necessity occurs whenever a new trustee is appointed in place of a lunatic who is one of

(*b*) *In re M.*, (1899) 1 Ch. 79, where the history of the matter is traced and the authorities cited. See also Champernowne & Johnston, Trustee Acts, 104.

(*c*) *Re Arrowsmith's Trusts* (1858), 6 W. R. 642.

(*d*) *In re Gardner's Trusts* (1878), 10 Ch. D. 29.

two or more trustees, for, in such a case, it is necessary for the whole property to be divested from the old trustees and vested in the new trustees, otherwise the joint tenancy will be severed (*e*). In these cases the application is made in lunacy, and the order is made by the Lords Justices exercising jurisdiction as commissioners in lunacy under the Lunacy Act, and as additional judges of the Chancery Division under the Judicature Acts (*f*). The court must be asked to appoint a new trustee as well as to make a vesting order.

A similar situation arises when the trust property consists of or includes land or stock in Ireland, and the trustee becomes a lunatic, for the Lunacy Act, 1890, does not extend to Ireland, and the Lords Justices in Lunacy have no jurisdiction under it to vest property in Ireland, so that it becomes necessary to resort to the Chancery jurisdiction to appoint a new trustee (*g*).

It would be an improvement if the Trustee Act were amended so as to give complete jurisdiction in all these cases to the Chancery Division, if not to the court in lunacy also.

It will be seen that s. 26 of the Trustee Act authorizes the making of a vesting order of land when a trustee is (a) an infant; or (b) is out of the jurisdiction; or (c) cannot be found; but it makes no provision for doing so where the trustee is a bankrupt, or is convicted of felony, or is otherwise unfit or unwilling to act.

A curious controversy has been raised upon sub-s. (ii) (c), which gives the court power to make a vesting order where a trustee "cannot be found." Suppose a company registered under the Companies Acts goes into liquidation and its property is sold, but before a formal conveyance or assignment of it has been executed to the buyer, the company becomes finally dissolved under s. 143 of the Companies Act, 1862, can it be said to be a trustee who "cannot be found," so as to entitle the court to make an order vesting the property in the buyer?

Mr. Justice Farwell thought the case fell within the section, and made the order in *In re General Accident Assurance Corporation, Limited* (*h*).

Mr. Justice Buckley, however, expressed himself unable to

(*e*) *In re Pearson* (1877), 5 Ch. D. 982; *In re Chell* (1883), 49 L. T. 196; Champernowne & Johnston, Trustee Acts, 105.

(*f*) See Judicature Act, 1873, s. 51; and *In re Platt* (1887), 36 Ch. D. 410.

(*g*) Champernowne & Johnston, Trustee Acts, 105.

(*h*) (1904) 1 Ch. 147.

accept this view in *In re Taylor's Agreement Trusts* (i), in which he said: "To my mind, the words 'cannot be found' in that context mean that the trustee is, or presumably is, somewhere, but that you do not know where he is; that the difficulty arises not because he is nowhere, but because you do not know where to find him"; and he held accordingly that a vesting order could not be made. He also held that even if a new trustee were appointed under s. 25, on the ground that there was no existing trustee, a vesting order could not be made, because if there be no existing trustee the legal estate must be in the crown, and could not be divested from the crown since it is not bound by the act.

But in a more recent case, Mr. Justice Warrington held that it was clearly "expedient to appoint a new trustee" in such a case under s. 25, and that on such appointment a vesting order could be made under s. 26 (j).

(i) (1904) 2 Ch. 737.

(j) *In re No. 9, Bomore Road*, (1906) 1 Ch. 359.

SECTION LXXXI.—ORDERS AS TO CONTINGENT RIGHTS OF UNBORN PERSONS.

WHERE any land is subject to a contingent right in an unborn person or class of unborn persons who, on coming into existence would, in respect thereof, become entitled to or possessed of the land on any trust, the High Court may make an order releasing the land from the contingent right, or may make an order vesting in any person the estate to or of which the unborn person or class of unborn persons would, on coming into existence, be entitled or possessed in the land (*a*).

With a view to facilitate sales of land subject to trusts for the benefit of unborn children, it was provided by s. 16 of the Trustee Act, 1850, that when lands were subject to a contingent right in unborn persons who, upon coming into existence would in respect thereof become seised or possessed of such lands upon any trust, the court might make an order which should wholly release and discharge the lands from such contingent right, or to make an order which should vest in any person the estates which such unborn persons would, upon coming into existence, be seised or possessed of in the lands.

Suppose, for example, by a deed disentailing and re-settling a family estate land is limited to such uses as A., a father, and B., his son, shall jointly appoint and subject thereto to the use of A. for life, remainder to B. for life, remainder to the first and other sons of B. successively in tail, remainders over; and under their power A. and B. contract to sell, and B. dies before conveyance; upon the classes of remaindermen coming into existence they will hold the land subject to a constructive trust for the purchaser. This section will then apply, and enable the court to release their contingent right, or vest it in the purchaser (*b*).

S. 16 of the Trustee Act, 1850, was repealed by s. 51 of the Trustee Act, 1893, and re-enacted in the words printed above by s. 27 of that act.

(*a*) Trustee Act, 1893, s. 27.

(*b*) *Hargreaves* v. *Wright* (1852), 1 W. R. 408. See also *Wake* v. *Wake* (1853), 17 Jurist, 545.

SECTION LXXXII.—VESTING ORDER IN PLACE OF CONVEYANCE BY INFANT MORTGAGEE.

WHERE any person entitled to or possessed of land, or entitled to a contingent right in land, by way of security for money, is an infant, the High Court may make an order vesting or releasing or disposing of the land or right in like manner as in the case of an infant trustee (*a*).

Formerly, when a mortgagee of real estate died intestate and his heir was an infant, there was no one capable of reconveying the mortgaged property to the mortgagor when the latter desired to redeem. This difficulty was provided for by ss. 7 and 8 of the Trustee Act, 1850, which enabled the Court of Chancery to make a vesting order in the same way as it could do in the case of an infant trustee.

These sections were repealed by s. 51 of the Trustee Act, 1893, and re-enacted in a consolidated form by s. 28 of the Trustee Act, 1893, in the words given above. The matter is, however, of little practical importance, owing to s. 30 of the Conveyancing Act, 1881, which provides that, on the death of a sole trustee or mortgagee of real estate, the real estate shall, notwithstanding any testamentary disposition, devolve to and become vested in his personal representatives as if it were a chattel real. Copyhold property is, however, excepted from the operation of this section if it is vested in the deceased as tenant on the court rolls by s. 88 of the Copyhold Act, 1894, and the provision may therefore occasionally be useful where a sole or sole surviving mortgagee of copyhold land who has been admitted dies intestate and his customary heir is an infant.

(*a*) Trustee Act, 1893, s. 28.

SECTION LXXXIII.—VESTING ORDER IN PLACE OF CONVEYANCE BY HEIR OR DEVISEE OR PERSONAL REPRESENTATIVE OF MORTGAGEE.

WHERE a mortgagee of land has died without having entered into the possession or into the receipt of the rents and profits thereof, and the money due in respect of the mortgage has been paid to a person entitled to receive the same, or that last-mentioned person consents to any order for the reconveyance of the land, then the High Court may make an order vesting the land in such person or persons in such manner and for such estate as the court may direct in any of the following cases, namely,—

(a) Where an heir or personal representative or devisee of the mortgagee is out of the jurisdiction of the High Court or cannot be found; and

(b) Where an heir or personal representative or devisee of the mortgagee on demand made by or on behalf of a person entitled to require a conveyance of the land has stated in writing that he will not convey the same or does not convey the same for the space of twenty-eight days next after a proper deed for conveying the land has been tendered to him by or on behalf of the person so entitled; and

(c) Where it is uncertain which of several devisees of the mortgagee was the survivor; and

(d) Where it is uncertain as to the survivor of several devisees of the mortgagee or as to the heir or personal representative of the mortgagee whether he is living or dead; and

(e) Where there is no heir or personal representative to a mortgagee who has died intestate as to the land, or where the mortgagee has died and it is uncertain who is his heir or personal representative or devisee (*a*).

The above enactment is to be found in s. 29 of the Trustee Act, 1893, which re-enacted s. 19 of the Trustee Act, 1850, with some verbal alterations, the latter being repealed by s. 51 of the act of 1893. It, like the preceding section, was intended to provide for cases of difficulty in obtaining the reconveyance or transfer of a mortgage. It seems, however, very doubtful whether it is needed at all; for it was decided by Vice-Chancellor Page Wood, in a case in 1856, that even though the mortgagee had been in possession, so that the 19th section of the Trustee Act, 1850, did not enable the court to make a vesting order, there was power to make it under the 9th section—now s. 26 of the Trustee Act, 1893—since the heir of the deceased (who in that case was out of the jurisdiction) was a trustee for the executors who had received the mortgage money (*b*). And on similar grounds it could be held in every case to which this section applies, namely, where the money due in respect of the mortgage has been paid to a person entitled to receive it, that the deceased mortgagee or his heir, personal representative or devisee was a trustee.

Since the passing of s. 30 of the Conveyancing Act, 1881, it can only be in the case of copyhold land, and then only rarely, that mortgaged property can be vested in the heir or devisee of a deceased mortgagee; and where it is vested in a personal representative the section seems to be of very little practical value, since if he were absent abroad, or could not be found, there would, as a rule, be no one entitled to receive the money due in respect of the mortgage, so that the section could not apply.

(*a*) Trustee Act, 1893, s. 29.

(*b*) *In re Skitter's Mortgage Trust* (1856), 4 W. R. 791. See also *In re Lea's Trust* (1858), 6 W. R. 482.

The section was applied in a case in 1895, in which the mortgagor had repaid the mortgage money, but the mortgagee had died before any reconveyance had been executed. He had made a will appointing executors, but the validity of the will was disputed and an action to establish it had been commenced but had not been set down for trial. Mr. Justice North held that par. (e) of the section applied, and made an order vesting the mortgaged property in the mortgagor (*c*). But the deceased mortgagee was here clearly a constructive trustee for the mortgagor, so that the order might just as well have been made under s. 26 (v) of the Trustee Act, 1893 (*d*).

(*c*) *In re Cook's Mortgage*, (1895) 1 Ch. 700.

(*d*) See Champernowne & Johnston, Trustee Acts, 116.

SECTION LXXXIV.—VESTING ORDER CONSEQUENTIAL ON JUDGMENT FOR SALE OR MORTGAGE OF LAND.

WHERE any court gives a judgment or makes an order directing the sale or mortgage of any land, every person who is entitled to or possessed of the land, or entitled to a contingent right therein, and is a party to the action or proceeding in which the judgment or order is given or made or is otherwise bound by the judgment or order, shall be deemed to be so entitled or possessed, as the case may be, as a trustee within the meaning of this act; and the High Court may, if it thinks expedient, make an order vesting the land or any part thereof for such estate as that court thinks fit in the purchaser or mortgagee or in any other person (*a*).

With a view to enabling the court to make a vesting order, it was enacted by s. 29 of the Trustee Act, 1850, that "when a decree shall have been made by any court of equity directing the sale of any lands *for the payment of the debts of a deceased person*, every person seised or possessed of such lands or entitled to a contingent right therein as heir, or under the will of such deceased debtor, shall be deemed to be so seised or possessed or entitled, as the case may be, upon a trust within the meaning of this act; and the Court of Chancery is hereby empowered to make an order wholly discharging the contingent right under the will of such deceased debtor of any unborn person."

This being confined to sales for payment of debts was found to be too narrow in its operation, and it was therefore enacted by

(*a*) Trustee Act, 1893, s. 30, as amended by s. 1 of the Trustee Act (1893) Amendment Act, 1894.

s. 1 of the Trustee Extension Act, 1852, that "when any decree or order shall have been made by any court of equity directing the sale of any lands *for any purpose whatever*, every person seised or possessed of such land, or entitled to a contingent right therein, being a party to the suit or proceeding in which such decree or order shall have been made, and bound thereby, or being otherwise bound by such decree or order, shall be deemed to be so seised or possessed or entitled (as the case may be) upon a trust within the meaning of the Trustee Act, 1850; and in every such case it shall be lawful for the Court of Chancery, if the said court shall think it expedient for the purpose of carrying such sale into effect, to make an order vesting such lands, or any part thereof, for such estate as the court shall think fit, either in any purchaser or in such other person as the court shall direct; and every such order shall have the same effect as if such person so seised or possessed or entitled had been free from all disability, and had duly executed all proper conveyances and assignments of such lands for such estate."

It will be seen that these sections are confined to the case of the sale of land and after a decree or order of the court, but it was held in the case of *In re Angelo* (*b*) in 1852 that, since the act of 1850 applied to constructive trusts, even on a sale of stock standing in the name of A., if properly made by B., the court could treat A. as a trustee for the purchaser and make a vesting order under the provisions of ss. 22 to 25 of the act. In view of this decision, it was not unreasonable to suppose that a vendor of land was no less a trustee and that the above sections were really unnecessary, and it was in fact so argued in the case of *In re Carpenter* (*c*) shortly afterwards; but Vice-Chancellor Page-Wood held that in the case of land, the constructive trust must first have been declared by a decree of the court, on the ground that there might always be a question in the case of land whether the contract could be enforced by a suit for specific performance, and it would be extremely inconvenient to declare the vendor to be a trustee upon a petition on which that point could not be decided. And this has been approved and followed by the Court of Appeal (*d*). There is one case, however, in which a vendor of land is a trustee for

(*b*) (1852), 5 De G. & Sm. 278.

(*c*) (1854), Kay, 418.

(*d*) *In re Colling* (1886), 32 Ch. D. 333.

this purpose without a decree, and that is where the contract for sale has been executed by the purchaser by payment of the purchase-money (*e*).

It has been held that s. 1 of the Trustee Extension Act, 1852, applies to a decree for sale in a partition suit, notwithstanding s. 7 of the Partition Act, 1868, referred to in the next section below (*f*).

The above sections of the Trustee Act, 1850, and the Trustee Extension Act, 1852, were repealed by s. 51 of the Trustee Act, 1893, and replaced by s. 30 of that act. This was amended by s. 1 of the Trustee Act (1893) Amendment Act, 1894, and in its amended form is in the words given above.

(*e*) *In re Cuming* (1869), L. R. 5 Ch. App. 72.

(*f*) *Beckett* v. *Sutton* (1882), 19 Ch. D. 646.

SECTION LXXXV.—VESTING ORDER CONSEQUENTIAL ON JUDGMENT FOR SPECIFIC PERFORMANCE, ETC.

WHERE a judgment is given for the specific performance of a contract concerning any land, or for the partition, or sale in lieu of partition, or exchange, of any land, or generally where any judgment is given for the conveyance of any land either in cases arising out of the doctrine of election or otherwise, the High Court may declare that any of the parties to the action are trustees of the land or any part thereof within the meaning of this act, or may declare that the interests of unborn persons who might claim under any party to the action, or under the will or voluntary settlement of any person deceased who was during his lifetime a party to the contract or transactions concerning which the judgment is given, are the interests of persons who, on coming into existence, would be trustees within the meaning of this act, and thereupon the High Court may make a vesting order relating to the rights of those persons, born and unborn, as if they had been trustees (*a*).

It was provided by s. 30 of the Trustee Act, 1850, that "when any decree shall be made by any court of equity for the specific performance of a contract concerning any lands or for the partition or exchange of any lands, or generally when any decree shall be made for the conveyance or assignment of any lands either in cases arising out of the doctrine of election or otherwise, it shall be lawful for the said court to declare that any of the parties to the

(*a*) Trustee Act, 1893, s. 31.

said suit wherein such decree is made are trustees of such lands or any part thereof within the meaning of this act, or to declare concerning the interests of unborn persons who might claim under any party to the said suit or under the will or voluntary settlement of any person deceased who was during his lifetime a party to the contract or transactions concerning which such decree is made that such interests of unborn persons are the interests of persons who upon coming into existence would be trustees within the meaning of this act," and the court was thereupon given power to make the same orders as in the case of trustees.

This section was extended to cases where, in suits for partition, the court directs a sale instead of a division of the property by s. 7 of the Partition Act, 1868.

Both sections were repealed by sect. 51 of the Trustee Act, 1893, and re-enacted by s. 31 of that Act in the words given above.

The following cases illustrate the application of the sections :—

Illustrations.

1. A. and B. purchase real estate as tenants in common. A. settles his share by his will, under which unborn issue might become entitled to legal estates. A. and B. die, and the interests in the real estate being very numerous, a partition suit is commenced, and a decree for sale made. The court can declare that the parties to the suit are trustees, and that the interests of the unborn issue are those of trustees. *Lees* v. *Coulton* (1875), L. R. 29 Eq. 20 (*b*).

2. In an action for specific performance of a contract to grant a lease the defendant is ordered to execute a lease to the plaintiff. On defendant refusing the court can declare him a trustee, and appoint a person to execute the lease on his behalf. *Hall* v. *Hale* (1884), 51 L. T. 226 (*c*).

(*b*) But a separate application ought to be made to appoint new trustees, and for a vesting order. *Ibid.*

(*c*) Conf. *Cowper* v. *Harmer* (1887), 57 L. J. Ch. 460.

3. In a partition suit the property is ordered to be sold. One-third of it belongs to a lunatic resident out of the jurisdiction, whose committee refuses to convey. The court can declare the lunatic a trustee, and appoint a person to convey his share. *Caswell* v. *Sheen* (1894), 69 L. T. 854.

4. In an application to the court for the purpose, it is declared to be for the benefit of an infant to elect to take under a will disposing of his property. The infant being tenant in tail in possession of that property, the court can declare him a trustee, and appoint a person to convey the property for such estate as the infant could if of full age convey. *In re Montagu, Faber* v. *Montagu*, (1896) 1 Ch. 549.

SECTION LXXXVI.—EFFECT OF VESTING ORDER.

A VESTING order under any of the foregoing provisions shall, in the case of a vesting order consequential on the appointment of a new trustee, have the same effect as if the persons who before the appointment were the trustees (if any) had duly executed all proper conveyances of the land for such estate as the High Court directs, or if there is no such person, or no such person of full capacity, then as if such person had existed and been of full capacity and had duly executed all proper conveyances of the land for such estate as the court directs, and shall in every other case have the same effect as if the trustee or other person or description or class of persons to whose rights or supposed rights the said provisions respectively relate had been an ascertained and existing person of full capacity, and had executed a conveyance or release to the effect intended by the order (*a*).

Provision was contained in ss. 7 to 15, 19 and 34 of the Trustee Act, 1850, and in ss. 1, 2 and 8 of the Trustee Extension Act, 1852, stating the effect of the vesting orders made in the various eventualities specified in those sections. These provisions being repealed by s. 51 of the Trustee Act, 1893, were re-enacted in a consolidated form by s. 32 of that act in the words given above.

The "foregoing provisions" all relate to "land," which by virtue of the Interpretation Act, 1889, includes copyhold and customary land, and it is probably in respect of such land that vesting orders will in future most often be required. The effect is then as if the trustee or person whose rights are dealt with had made a surrender, so that admittance is still necessary except in the case provided for below, where the order is made with the consent of the lord or lady of the manor (*b*).

(*a*) Trustee Act, 1893, s. 32.

(*b*) See Champernowne & Johnston, Trustee Acts, 126: Lewin, Trusts, 11th ed. 830.

SECTION LXXXVII.—POWER OF COURT TO APPOINT PERSON TO CONVEY.

IN all cases where a vesting order can be made under any of the foregoing provisions, the High Court may, if it is more convenient, appoint a person to convey the land or release the contingent right, and a conveyance or release by that person in conformity with the order shall have the same effect as an order under the appropriate provision (*a*).

S. 20 of the Trustee Act, 1850, provided that, instead of making a vesting order under the foregoing provisions the court might, if it was more convenient, appoint a person to convey the land or release the contingent right. This was repealed by s. 51 of the Trustee Act, 1893, and re-enacted in the words given above by s. 33 of that act.

Whether a vesting order shall be made, or some person appointed to convey, is chiefly a matter of expense (*b*).

The conveyance should contain a recital showing that it is made in obedience to the order of the court, and should be executed by the person appointed to convey in his own name (*c*).

(*a*) Trustee Act, 1893, s. 33.

(*b*) See *Hancox* v. *Spittle* (1857), 3 Sm. & G. 478; *Shepherd* v. *Churchill* (1857), 25 Beav. 21.

(*c*) Lewin, Trusts, 11th ed. 832.

SECTION LXXXVIII.—EFFECT OF VESTING ORDER AS TO COPYHOLD LAND.

(1) WHERE an order vesting copyhold land in any person is made under this act with the consent of the lord or lady of the manor, the land shall vest accordingly without surrender or admittance.

(2) Where an order is made under this act appointing any person to convey any copyhold land, that person shall execute and do all assurances and things for completing the assurance of the land; and the lord and lady of the manor and every other person shall, subject to the customs of the manor and the usual payments, be bound to make admittance to the land and to do all other acts for completing the assurance thereof, as if the persons in whose place an appointment is made were free from disability and had executed and done those assurances and things (*a*).

In the case of copyhold land, the Trustee Act, 1850, gave the court power to vest the land in any person for all the estate vested in the person in respect of whom the inconvenience to be remedied arose, without any consent on the part of the lord of the manor. On the order being made the person in whom the land is vested by it applies for admission as if the land had been surrendered. Or, instead of making a vesting order, the court might—again without the consent of the lord of the manor—appoint a person to convey the land, in which case the person appointed must surrender and the person in whose favour the order is made be admitted (*b*).

(*a*) Trustee Act, 1893, s. 34.

(*b*) See Lewin, Trusts, 11th ed. 833.

In order to simplify matters, however, it was provided by s. 28 of the Trustee Act, 1850, that if the lord of the manor consented to the vesting order being made the estate should vest, without the necessity for any surrender or admittance. This was repealed by s. 51 of the Trustee Act, 1893, and re-enacted by s. 34 of that act in the words given above.

The consent of the lord of the manor should be proved by a verified certificate. He should not be made a party to the application (*c*).

(*c*) *Ayles* v. *Cox* (1853), 17 Beav. 584.

SECTION LXXXIX.—VESTING ORDERS AS TO STOCK AND CHOSES IN ACTION.

(1) IN any of the following cases, namely :—

(i) Where the High Court appoints or has appointed a new trustee ; and

(ii) Where a trustee entitled alone or jointly with another person to stock or to a chose in action—

(a) is an infant, or

(b) is out of the jurisdiction of the High Court, or

(c) cannot be found, or

(d) neglects or refuses to transfer stock or receive the dividends or income thereof, or to sue for or recover a chose in action, according to the direction of the person absolutely entitled thereto for twenty-eight days next after a request in writing has been made to him by the person so entitled, or

(e) neglects or refuses to transfer stock or receive the dividends or income thereof, or to sue for or recover a chose in action for twenty-eight days next after an order of the High Court for that purpose has been served on him ; or

(iii) Where it is uncertain whether a trustee entitled alone or jointly with another person to stock or to a chose in action is alive or dead,

the High Court may make an order vesting the right to

transfer or call for a transfer of stock, or to receive the dividends or income thereof, or to sue for or recover a chose in action, in any such person as the court may appoint:

Provided that—

(a) Where the order is consequential on the appointment by the court of a new trustee, the right shall be vested in the persons who, on the appointment, are the trustees; and

(b) Where the person whose right is dealt with by the order was entitled jointly with another person, the right shall be vested in that last-mentioned person either alone or jointly with any other person whom the court may appoint.

(2) In all cases where a vesting order can be made under this section, the court may, if it is more convenient, appoint some proper person to make or join in making the transfer.

(3) The person in whom the right to transfer or call for the transfer of any stock is vested by an order of the court under this act, may transfer the stock to himself or any other person, according to the order, and the Banks of England and Ireland and all other companies shall obey every order under this section according to its tenor.

(4) After notice in writing of an order under this section it shall not be lawful for the Bank of England or of Ireland or any other company to transfer any stock to which the order relates or to pay any dividends thereon except in accordance with the order.

(5) The High Court may make declarations and give directions concerning the manner in which the right to any stock or chose in action vested under the provisions of this act is to be exercised.

(6) The provisions of this act as to vesting orders shall apply to shares in ships registered under the acts relating to merchant shipping as if they were stock (*a*).

It has already been stated that power was conferred on the Court of Chancery by various sections of the Trustee Act, 1850, as amended by the Trustee Extension Act, 1852, and the Merchant Shipping Act, 1855, to make an order vesting in such persons as it should think fit, the right to transfer stock, or choses in action, or ships held on trust, or by way of mortgage when the trustee was an infant, or out of the jurisdiction, or could not be found, or other specified eventualities, and particularly upon the appointment of new trustees.

The numerous sections in which these provisions were to be found were all repealed by s. 51 of the Trustee Act, 1893, and replaced by s. 35 of that act in a consolidated and condensed form, just as those relating to vesting orders in the case of land were replaced by s. 26. These two sections are of similar character, but not identical. For example, under s. 26 there is power to make a vesting order "where it is uncertain who was the survivor of two or more trustees"; there is no such power in s. 35. On the other hand, there is power under the latter section to make a vesting order as to stock when a trustee "neglects or refuses to transfer stock . . . . or to sue for or recover a chose in action for twenty-eight days next after an order of the High Court for that purpose has been served on him"; there is no such power in s. 26. The reason for these distinctions is not apparent. It would be an improvement if the powers conferred on the court were made the same in both classes of cases and consolidated into one section. It has more than once been suggested by text writers, that instead of enumerating a number of particular cases in which the powers may be exercised, which has been the plan adopted in all the statutes hitherto, it would be better to frame a general enactment wide enough to cover all cases (*b*).

The conflict of jurisdiction referred to in connection with vesting orders as to land (*c*), arises also in connection with this section.

(*a*) Trustee Act, 1893, s. 35.

(*b*) See Easton, Appointment of New Trustees, 2; Champernowne & Johnston, Trustee Acts, 106.

(*c*) See above under sect. LXXX., p. 360.

Section XC.—Persons entitled to apply for Orders.

(1) An order under this act for the appointment of a new trustee or concerning any land, stock, or chose in action subject to a trust, may be made on the application of any person beneficially interested in the land, stock, or chose in action, whether under disability or not, or on the application of any person duly appointed trustee thereof.

(2) An order under this act concerning any land, stock, or chose in action subject to a mortgage may be made on the application of any person beneficially interested in the equity of redemption, whether under disability or not, or of any person interested in the money secured by the mortgage (*a*).

S. 37 of the Trustee Act, 1850, provided that an order under the act for the appointment of a new trustee, or concerning any lands, stock, or chose in action subject to a trust, might be made upon the application of any person beneficially interested, whether under disability or not, or of any person duly appointed as a trustee thereof, and that an order concerning any lands, stock, or chose in action subject to a mortgage might be made on the application of any person beneficially interested in the equity of redemption, whether under disability or not, or of any person interested in the moneys secured by the mortgage.

It has been held that a person having a contingent interest in a trust fund, as distinguished from a mere possibility of an interest, is a person "beneficially interested" for this purpose (*b*).

Where an order for the sale of property has been made, the purchaser, if he has paid his purchase-money, is a proper person to apply (*c*).

The above section of the act of 1850 was repealed by s. 51 of the Trustee Act, 1893, and re-enacted by s. 36 of that act.

(*a*) Trustee Act, 1893, s. 36.

(*b*) *In re Sheppard's Trusts* (1862), 4 De G. F. & J. 423.

(*c*) *Rowley* v. *Adams* (1851), 14 Beav. 130; *Ayles* v. *Cox* (1853), 17 Beav. 584.

SECTION XCI.—POWERS OF NEW TRUSTEE APPOINTED BY THE COURT.

EVERY trustee appointed by a court of competent jurisdiction shall, as well before as after the trust property becomes by law, or by assurance, or otherwise, vested in him, have the same powers, authorities, and discretions, and may in all respects act as if he had been originally appointed a trustee by the instrument, if any, creating the trust (*a*).

It was provided by s. 33 of the Conveyancing Act, 1881—which re-enacted in an amplified form s. 27 of Lord Cranworth's Act—that every trustee appointed by the Court of Chancery or by the Chancery Division of the court, or by any other court of competent jurisdiction, shall, as well before the trust property becomes by law or by assurance, or otherwise, vested in him, have the same powers, authorities and discretions, and may in all respects act as if he had been originally appointed a trustee by the instrument, if any, creating the trust.

This was repealed by s. 51 of the Trustee Act, 1893, but re-enacted, in the words given above, by s. 37 of the Trustee Act, 1893.

(*a*) Trustee Act, 1893, s. 37.

SECTION XCII.—POWER TO CHARGE COSTS OF ORDER APPOINTING NEW TRUSTEE, ETC. ON TRUST ESTATE.

THE High Court may order the costs and expenses of and incident to any application for an order appointing a new trustee, or for a vesting order, or of and incident to any such order, or any conveyance or transfer in pursuance thereof, to be paid or raised out of the land or personal estate in respect whereof the same is made, or out of the income thereof, or to be borne and paid in such manner and by such persons as to the court may seem just (*a*).

When the court was exercising the powers conferred on it by the Trustee Act, 1850, it was exercising a special statutory jurisdiction, which was limited entirely by the act. In order, therefore, to give it power to deal with costs of the proceedings taken under the act, s. 51 provided that the court might order the costs and expenses of and relating to the petitions, orders, directions, conveyances, assignments and transfers to be made in pursuance of the act, or any of them, to be paid and raised out of or from the lands or personal estate, or the rents or produce thereof, in respect of which the same respectively should be made or in such manner as the court should think proper.

The court, however, was strictly limited by the words of the section, and it was consequently held that it could make no order for the costs of an application under the act to be paid by the respondent whose conduct rendered the application necessary (*b*), since the section only authorized it to order the costs to be paid and raised out of the property.

The section was therefore repealed by s. 51 of the Trustee Act, 1893, and re-enacted in a wider form by s. 38 of that act in the words given above, from which it will be seen that the court may now order the costs to be borne and paid in such manner *and by such persons* as to the court may seem just.

(*a*) Trustee Act, 1893, s. 38.

(*b*) *In re Primrose* (1857), 23 Beav. 590; *In re Sparks* (1877), 6 Ch. D. 361; *In re Sarah Knight's Will* (1883), 26 Ch. D. 82; *In re Mills' Estate* (1886), 33 Ch. D. 24.

SECTION XCIII.—TRUSTEES OF CHARITIES.

THE powers conferred by this act as to vesting orders may be exercised for vesting any land, stock, or chose in action in any trustee of a charity or society over which the High Court would have jurisdiction upon action duly instituted, whether the appointment of the trustee was made by instrument under a power or by the High Court under its general or statutory jurisdiction (*a*).

s. 45 of the Trustee Act, 1850, authorized the court to exercise the power of making vesting orders conferred by it in the case of a trustee of any charity or society over which the court "would have jurisdiction upon suit duly instituted."

This was repealed by s. 51 of the Trustee Act, 1893, and re-enacted in the words given above by s. 39 of that act.

(*a*) Trustee Act, 1893, s. 39.

Section XCIV.—Orders made on certain Allegations to be conclusive Evidence.

Where a vesting order is made as to any land under this act or under the Lunacy Act, 1890, or under any act relating to lunacy in Ireland, founded on an allegation of the personal incapacity of a trustee or mortgagee, or on an allegation that a trustee or the heir or personal representative or devisee of a mortgagee is out of the jurisdiction of the High Court or cannot be found, or that it is uncertain which of several trustees or which of several devisees of a mortgagee was the survivor, or whether the last trustee or the heir or personal representative or last surviving devisee of a mortgagee is living or dead, or on an allegation that any trustee or mortgagee has died intestate without an heir, or has died and it is not known who is his heir or personal representative or devisee, the fact that the order has been so made shall be conclusive evidence of the matter so alleged in any court upon any question as to the validity of the order; but this section shall not prevent the High Court from directing a reconveyance or the payment of costs occasioned by any such order if improperly obtained (*a*).

The making of a vesting order of land on an allegation of the personal incapacity of a trustee or mortgagee, or of any other fact founding the jurisdiction to make the order, was made conclusive evidence of the matter alleged in any court upon any question as to the legal validity of the order by s. 44 of the Trustee Act, 1850.

This was repealed and re-enacted in the words given above by s. 40 of the Trustee Act, 1893.

(*a*) Trustee Act, 1893, s. 40.

SECTION XCV.—APPLICATION OF VESTING ORDER TO PROPERTY OUT OF ENGLAND.

THE powers of the High Court in England and Ireland to make vesting orders under this act shall extend to all land and personal estate in Her Majesty's dominions, except Scotland (*a*).

The Trustee Act, 1850, s. 54, provided that—
"the powers and authorities given by this act to the Court of Chancery in England shall extend to all lands and personal estate within the dominions, plantations, and colonies belonging to Her Majesty (except Scotland)."

and s. 55 provided that—
"the powers and authorities given by this act to the Court of Chancery in England shall and may be exercised in like manner, and are hereby given and extended to the Court of Chancery in Ireland with respect to all lands and personal estate in Ireland."

These two sections were repealed by s. 51 of the Trustee Act, 1893, and re-enacted in a consolidated form by s. 41 of that act, which was as follows:—

"The powers of the High Court in England to make vesting orders under this act shall extend to all land and personal estate in Her Majesty's dominions, except Scotland."

The result was that the English court could make vesting orders of land in any part of the Empire, except Scotland, and the Irish court could make such orders of land in Ireland, but nowhere else. This, however, was regarded by Irishmen as a grievance (*b*), and it was accordingly provided by s. 2 of the Trustee Act (1893) Amendment Act, 1894, that "the powers conferred on the High Court in England by s. 41 of the Trustee Act, 1893, to make vesting orders as to all land and personal estate in Her Majesty's dominions, except Scotland, are hereby also given to and may be exercised by the High Court in Ireland."

(*a*) Trustee Act, 1893, s. 41, as amended by the Trustee Act (1893) Amendment Act, 1894, s. 2.

(*b*) Lord Ashbourne called it "a real Irish grievance." Hansard, Parl. Debates, 4th series, vol. 23 (1894), 448. It seems odd that it should not have been discovered for forty-four years.

Part XI.—JUDICIAL TRUSTEES.

Section XCVI.—Power of Court on Application to appoint Judicial Trustee.

(1) Where application is made to the court by or on behalf of the person creating or intending to create a trust, or by or on behalf of a trustee or beneficiary, the court may, in its discretion, appoint a person (in this act called a judicial trustee) to be a trustee of that trust, either jointly with any other person or as sole trustee, and, if sufficient cause is shown, in place of all or any existing trustees.

(2) The administration of the property of a deceased person, whether a testator or intestate, shall be a trust, and the executor or administrator a trustee, within the meaning of this act.

(3) Any fit and proper person nominated for the purpose in the application may be appointed a judicial trustee, and, in the absence of such nomination, or if the court is not satisfied of the fitness of a person so nominated, an official of the court may be appointed, and in any case a judicial trustee shall be subject to the control and supervision of the court as an officer thereof.

(4) The court may, either on request or without request, give to a judicial trustee any general or special directions in regard to the trust or the administration thereof.

(5) There may be paid to a judicial trustee out of the trust property such remuneration, not exceeding the prescribed limits, as the court may assign in each case, subject to any rules under this act respecting the application of such remuneration where the judicial trustee is an official of the court, and the remuneration so assigned to any judicial trustee shall, save as the court may for special reasons otherwise order, cover all his work and personal outlay.

(6) Once in every year the accounts of every trust of which a judicial trustee has been appointed shall be audited, and a report thereon made to the court by the prescribed persons, and, in any case where the court shall so direct, an inquiry into the administration by a judicial trustee of any trust, or into any dealing or transaction of a judicial trustee, shall be made in the prescribed manner (*a*).

On the 14th June, 1894, a question was asked in the House of Commons by Sir Howard Vincent whether, having regard to the heavy losses sustained by the public by the laches of trustees, the increasing difficulty of finding competent persons to undertake such onerous duties, and the failure of the public companies formed to discharge the task, the Chancellor of the Exchequer would appoint a select committee to consider the subject. And shortly afterwards a committee was appointed to inquire into the liabilities to which persons are exposed under the present law, as to the administration of trusts, and whether any further legislative provision might be made for securing adequate administration of trusts without the necessity of subjecting private trustees and executors to the risks which they now run (*b*).

In due course the committee reported. They found that, although the difficulty of finding competent persons to act as trustees had been exaggerated, it was real and increasing, and that

(*a*) Judicial Trustees Act, 1896, s. 1.

(*b*) Hansard, Parl. Debates, 4th series, vol. 25, 1095; vol. 26, 515; vol. 30, 1059.

though misappropriations by trustees bore but a small proportion to the vast sums held on trust, it was a serious matter. They therefore reported in favour of the establishment of a system under which private trusts could be administered, if so desired, by or under the control of some official or judicial authority, which should also have the custody of the funds; and after considering the various methods by which such a system could be worked—including the establishment of a Public Trustee—they recommended a system by which trusts might be administered under judicial supervision, on the same lines as they are administered by a "judicial factor" in Scotland (*c*).

In accordance with the recommendations of the committee a bill for the appointment of judicial trustees was introduced in the House of Commons in the next session (*d*), and this, in due course, passed into law as the Judicial Trustees Act, 1896. The first section of the act provides that, "Where application is made to the court by or on behalf of the person creating or intending to create a trust, or by or on behalf of a trustee or beneficiary, the court may in its discretion appoint a person (in this act called a judicial trustee) to be a trustee of that trust, either jointly with any other person, or as sole trustee, and if sufficient cause is shown in place of all or any existing trustees."

By the rules made under the act the application must be made to the Chancery Division, and if not made in a pending cause or matter must be made by originating summons; if made in a pending cause or matter it must be made as part of the relief claimed, or by summons in the cause or matter (*e*).

The jurisdiction conferred on the court is purely discretionary; no one is entitled as of right to the appointment (*f*), and, in fact, very few judicial trustees have been appointed.

The administration of the property of a deceased person, whether a testator or intestate, is a trust, and the executor or administrator a trustee within the meaning of the act (*g*).

Any "fit and proper person" nominated for the purpose in the application may be appointed a judicial trustee, and in the absence

(*c*) Sessional Papers, 1895, vol. 9. The report is dated 6th May, 1895.

(*d*) Hansard, 4th series, vol. 37, 570; vol. 41, 1297; vol. 42, 1047; vol. 43, 117, 588, 1439; vol. 44, 93, 823.

(*e*) Judicial Trustee Rules, 1897, r. 2.

(*f*) *In re Ratcliff*, (1898) 2 Ch. 352.

(*g*) s. 1 (2).

of such nomination, or if the court is not satisfied of the fitness of a person so nominated, an official of the court may be appointed.

In any case a judicial trustee is subject to the control and supervision of the court as an officer of the court (*h*). The word "person" in an act of parliament includes a corporation, and in a few cases guarantee societies have been appointed under the act. The administration of trusts by such societies is quite common in several of the British colonies.

Where an "official of the court" is appointed judicial trustee, the official solicitor of the court must be appointed, unless, for special reasons, the court directs that some other official of the court should be so appointed (*i*).

But the court is not bound to appoint the official solicitor merely because the person nominated by the applicant is not a fit person, so long as some fit person is suggested by one of the parties before the court (*j*).

The committee had expressed the opinion in their report that whoever was appointed to administer a trust, whether an official or non-official person, ought to be required to act precisely as private trustees now act; using his own discretion, and proceeding not as a judge but as a man of business. But in all respects he should be in the situation of an officer of the court able to ask for directions and bound to obey them whether asked for or not. In any case of difficulty he should be at liberty without either formality or expense to consult the judge who might, if he thought it necessary, give other parties an opportunity of presenting their views, or informing his mind before giving his directions (*k*). In accordance with this recommendation the act provides that the court may either, on request or without request, give to a judicial trustee any general or special directions in regard to the trust or its administration (*l*). And the rules authorize a judicial trustee to communicate with the court as to the administration of the trust by letter addressed to the Chancery Master without any further formality, and provide that the court may give any direction to a judicial trustee with regard to the administration of his trust by letter signed by the

(*h*) s. 1 (3).

(*i*) Judicial Trustee Rules, 1897, r. 7. See, however, rr. 29, 30 and 31.

(*j*) *Douglas* v. *Bolam*, (1900) 2 Ch. 749.

(*k*) Sessional Papers, 1895, vol. 9, p. viii. of the report.

(*l*) s. 1 (4).

Chancery Master without drawing up any order or formal document (*m*).

The committee recommended the payment of a judicial trustee by commission upon a scale to be fixed by the Lord Chancellor and the Treasury, and the act provides that there shall be paid to a judicial trustee out of the trust property such remuneration not exceeding the prescribed limits as the court may assign in each case, subject to any rules under the act respecting the application of such remuneration where the judicial trustee is an official of the court, and the remuneration so assigned shall, save as the court may for special reasons otherwise order, cover all his work and personal outlay (*n*).

The committee also recommended that accounts should be rendered at fixed periods by all persons appointed to administer trusts, and audited officially, and that the official auditor should be enabled to make representation to the court as to any trust being administered under the control of the court at any time, and might be required by the court to investigate and report upon its management. Accordingly the act provides that once in every year the accounts of every trust of which a judicial trustee has been appointed shall be audited, and a report thereon made to the court by prescribed persons, and in any case where the court shall so direct, an inquiry into the administration by a judicial trustee of any trust, or into any dealing or transaction of a judicial trustee, shall be made in the prescribed manner (*o*).

(*m*) Judicial Trustee Rules, 1897, r. 28.

(*n*) s. 1 (5). See, further, Judicial Trustee Rules, 1897, rr. 17, 18 and 19.

(*o*) s. 1 (6). See Judicial Trustee Rules, 1897, rr. 14, 15 and 16.

SECTION XCVII.—COURT BY WHICH JURISDICTION TO BE EXERCISED.

THE jurisdiction of the court under this act may be exercised by the High Court, and as respects trusts within its jurisdiction by a palatine court, and (subject to the prescribed definition of the jurisdiction) by any county court judge to whom such jurisdiction may be assigned under this act (*a*).

A judicial trustee may be appointed either by the High Court, or as regards trusts within its jurisdiction by a palatine court, or subject to the rules made under the act by a county court to which the jurisdiction is assigned (*a*).

By rule 31 of the Judicial Trustee Rules, 1897, it is provided that—

"(1) For the purpose of the act and these rules the jurisdiction of the county court judge shall extend to any trust in which the trust property does not exceed in value 500*l*. as if that jurisdiction had been given under s. 67 of the County Courts Act, 1888, but that jurisdiction shall be exercised only in a metropolitan county court, or in a county court for the time being having bankruptcy jurisdiction. . . . .

"(5) For the purposes of this rule the expression 'Metropolitan County Court' means any of the county courts mentioned in the third schedule of the Bankruptcy Act, 1883."

(*a*) Judicial Trustees Act, 1896, s. 2.

SECTION XCVIII.—POWER TO MAKE RULES.

(1) RULES may be made for carrying into effect this act, and especially—

(1) for requiring judicial trustees, who are not officials of the court, to give security for the due application of any trust property under their control:

(2) respecting the safety of the trust property, and the custody thereof:

(3) respecting the remuneration of judicial trustees and for fixing and regulating the fees to be taken under this act so as to cover the expenses of the administration of this act, and respecting the payment of such remuneration and fees out of the trust property, and, where the judicial trustee is an official of the court, respecting the application of the remuneration and fees payable to him:

(4) for dispensing with formal proof of facts in proper cases:

(5) for facilitating the discharge by the court of administrative duties under this act without judicial proceedings, and otherwise regulating procedure under this act and making it simple and inexpensive:

(6) for assigning jurisdiction under this act to county court judges and defining such jurisdiction:

(7) respecting the suspension or removal of any judicial trustee, and the succession of another person to the office of any judicial trustee who may cease to hold office, and the vesting in such person of any trust property:

(8) respecting the classes of trusts in which officials of the court are not to be judicial trustees, or are to be so temporarily or conditionally:

(9) respecting the procedure to be followed where the judicial trustee is executor or administrator:

(10) for preventing the employment by judicial trustees of other persons at the expense of the trust, except in cases of strict necessity:

(11) for the filing and auditing of the accounts of any trust of which a judicial trustee has been appointed.

(2) The rules under this act may be made by the Lord Chancellor, subject to the consent of the Treasury in matters relating to fees and to salaries and numbers of officers, and to the consent of the authority for making orders under the Solicitors Remuneration Act, 1881, in matters relating to the remuneration of solicitors. The rules shall be laid before parliament and have the same force as if enacted in this act, provided that if, within thirty days after such rules have been laid before either house of parliament during which that house has sat, the house presents to her majesty an address against such rules or any of them, such rules or the rule specified in the address shall thenceforward be of no effect (*a*).

(*a*) Judicial Trustees Act, 1896, s. 4.

Section XCIX.—Definitions.

In this act—

The expression "official of the court" means the holder of such paid office in or connected with the court as may be prescribed.

The expression "prescribed" means prescribed by rules under this act (*a*).

(*a*) Judicial Trustees Act, 1896, s. 5.

Section C.—Extent of this Part.

(1) This act may be cited as the Judicial Trustees Act, 1896.

(2) This act shall not extend to any charity, whether subject to or exempted from the Charitable Trusts Acts, 1853 to 1894.

(3) This act shall not extend to Scotland or Ireland.

(4) This act, except as by this act otherwise provided, shall come into operation on the first day of May, one thousand eight hundred and ninety-seven (*a*).

The select committee above referred to reported that in Ireland there did not seem to be any widespread desire for change or complaint of the existing law, and accordingly the Judicial Trustees Act, 1896, was confined in its operation to England. Being based on the system already in force in Scotland, there was, of course, no necessity to make it apply to that country.

(*a*) Judicial Trustees Act, 1896, s. 6.

Part XII.—DETERMINATION OF THE TRUST.

SECTION CI.—DETERMINATION OF TRUST BY PERFORMANCE, &C.

A TRUST is determined—

(a) When the trustee completely performs the obligation imposed on him,

(b) When the trust becomes impossible in consequence of the destruction of the trust property or otherwise without the fault of the trustee, or

(c) When the whole legal and beneficial interests in the trust property become vested in the same person or persons.

A trust may be determined in any of the following ways:—

1. By the performance by the trustee of the obligation imposed on him.

2. By the trust becoming impossible in consequence of the destruction of the subject-matter or otherwise.

3. By the union of the whole legal and equitable estates in the same person.

4. If the trust is revocable, by the settlor revoking it.

5. If the beneficiary is *sui juris* and solely entitled, by his determining it.

The first three of these modes of determination may be grouped together.

1. *Performance by the Trustee of the Obligation imposed on him.*

It is obvious that if the trustee performs the obligation imposed on him by the trust, the trust is at an end. It would probably be impossible to find any decision of the court to this effect, for the very reason that it is obvious; but the Indian Trusts Act, 1882, may be cited. Section 77 expressly enacts that "a trust is extinguished (a) when its purpose is completely fulfilled." The language of this enactment seems to limit its application, as was no doubt intended, to express trusts only; and for the purpose of the English law it seems better to say that "a trust is determined when the trustee completely performs the obligation imposed on him."

2. *Trust becoming impossible.*

It is as difficult to find any direct decision of the courts that a trust is determined by becoming impossible, as it is to find one that it is determined by performance by the trustee of his obligation. It seems equally obvious, for "lex non cogit ad impossibilia" (*a*).

Where the impossibility arises from the destruction of the trust property, it is indirectly involved in the decisions that a trustee is not bound to insure property against loss by fire (*b*), and that the trustee is not liable for the theft of the trust property without any fault on his part. Lord Hardwicke said in 1750, "it is proved (and I think reasonably) that if a trustee is robbed (of the trust fund), that robbery properly proved shall be a discharge, provided he keeps them so as he would keep his own" (*c*).

3. *Union of the whole Legal and Equitable Titles in the same person.*

It is easier to find authority for the proposition that a trust is determined by the union of the whole legal and equitable titles. "The moment both meet in the same person there is an end of the trust. A man cannot be trustee for himself," said Lord Mansfield (*d*). "It is universally true," said Lord Thurlow, "that where the

(*a*) See also Indian Trusts Act, 1882, s. 77.

(*b*) See *Bailey* v. *Gould* (1840), 4 Y. & C. Exch. 221; *Fry* v. *Fry* (1859), 27 Beav. 146.

(*c*) *Jones* v. *Lewis* (1750), 2 Ves. 240.

(*d*) *Goodright* v. *Wells* (1781), Doug. at p. 778.

estates unite, the equitable must merge in the legal" (*e*). Chancellor Kent called it "a settled principle" (*f*).

Such a union may come about by act of the parties or by operation of law. The following cases illustrate it.

Illustrations.

1. A. holds property in trust for B. A. and B. convey to C. The trust is determined.

2. A. contracts to buy real estate and pays for it, but dies before conveyance, having devised all his real estate to his widow in trust for his eldest son in fee. After testator's death the real estate is conveyed to his widow, who dies intestate without having conveyed it to the son. The latter thus succeeding to both legal and equitable estates, the trust is determined. *Goodright* v. *Wells* (1781), Doug. 771 (*g*).

3. A lease of a colliery is granted to A. who takes three-eighths of the colliery as to one moiety for himself, and as to the other moiety in trust for B. B., being indebted to A., assigns his moiety of the three-eighths to A. The trust is determined. *Newman* v. *Newman* (1885), 28 Ch. D. 674.

4. A. holds a leasehold house in trust for B. and C. *as tenants in common.* At the request of B. and C., A. assigns the house to them to hold *as joint tenants* for the residue of the lease. The trust is determined. *In re Selous*, (1901) 1 Ch. 921.

(*e*) *Wade* v. *Paget* (1784), 1 Bro. C. C. at p. 368. See also *Selby* v. *Alston* (1797), 3 Ves. 339.

(*f*) *Nicholson* v. *Halsey* (1815), 1 Johns. N. Y. at p. 422.

(*g*) *Selby* v. *Alston*, *supra*, is to the same effect.

Section CII.—Determination of a Revocable Trust by the Settlor.

When the settlor has expressly reserved a power of revocation at the time of creating the trust, he may determine the trust in accordance with the terms of the power.

Although when a trust has once been perfectly created, the settlor, as a rule, has no power of determining it (*a*) or modifying it (*b*), yet he may expressly reserve such a power at the time of creating the trust, and it is very common to reserve the power when the trust is voluntary (*c*).

When such a power is reserved, the effect of exercising it is to determine the trust (*d*).

(*a*) See authorities cited under Sect. VIII., *ante*.

(*b*) See *Perrins* v. *Bellamy*, (1898) 2 Ch. 521; (1899) 1 Ch. 797.

(*c*) See Vaizey, Settlements, ch. xvii.

(*d*) Ames, Cases on Trusts, 2nd ed. 448.

SECTION CIII.—DETERMINATION OF TRUST BY THE BENEFICIARY.

WHERE the beneficiary or, if there is more than one, all the beneficiaries is or are absolutely entitled to the whole beneficial interest in the trust property and have legal capacity to dispose of property, he or they may determine the trust.

It is now well established that if the sole beneficiary, or all the beneficiaries if more than one, is or are *sui juris* he or they may put an end to the trust at any time (*a*).

"For whatever modifications of the estate the settlor may have contemplated, through whatever channel he may have originally intended his bounty to flow, the *cestuis que trust* as the persons to be eventually benefited are in equity from the creation of the trust and before the trustees have acted in the execution of it, the absolute beneficial proprietors" (*b*).

Illustrations.

1. Testator gives securities to his trustees upon trust to accumulate the interest and dividends thereon until B. shall attain the age of 25 years, and then to pay or transfer the same together with the accumulated interest and dividends to B. absolutely. As soon as B. attains the age of 21 he may demand an immediate transfer of the fund. *Saunders* v. *Vautier* (1841), 4 Beav. 115 (*c*).

(*a*) See per Fry, J., *In re Cotton's Trustees and the School Board for London* (1882), 19 Ch. D. at p. 629.

(*b*) Lewin, Trusts, 11th ed. 864.

(*c*) The principle of this decision is equally applicable where the donee of a vested interest, payment of which is postponed with a trust to accumulate meanwhile, is a charity corporate or unincorporate. *Wharton* v. *Masterman*, (1895) A. C. 186.

2. Testator gives real estate upon specified uses, adding, "it is my particular desire that no one shall be put in possession of my estate or shall enjoy the rent, dividends and profits of any part thereof or of any property left by my will or codicil until he shall attain the age of 25 years; and in the meantime the rent, dividends and profits to accumulate." This provision is inoperative. *Gosling* v. *Gosling* (1859), Johns. 265.

3. Testator by his will gives certain shares of his property to each of his two daughters "to be settled on themselves at their marriage." At his death the two daughters are infants. On their attaining 21 and being unmarried, they are entitled to have their shares transferred to them absolutely. *Magrath* v. *Morehead* (1871), L. R. 12 Eq. 491.

SECTION CIV.—DISCHARGE OF THE TRUSTEE.

(1) UPON the determination of the trust the trustee is entitled to have the accounts of his administration of the trust property examined and settled by the beneficiary, and to an acknowledgment in writing by the beneficiary to that effect, and discharging him from any further liability in respect of the trust property.

(2) If the beneficiary refuses to discharge the trustee in manner in sub-s. (1) mentioned, the trustee is entitled to have his accounts taken by the court.

"On the final adjustment of the trust accounts," Mr. Lewin says, "it is usual for the trustee on handing over the balance to the parties entitled to require from them an acknowledgment that all claims and demands have been settled" (*a*).

The trustee is entitled to have his accounts examined and settled in order, as Vice-Chancellor Knight Bruce said, "that he and his family should be delivered from the anxiety and misery attending unsettled accounts,—the possible ruin which they who are acquainted with the affairs daily litigated in the Court of Chancery well know to be a frequent result of neglect in such a matter"—but generally he seems not to be entitled to a formal release by deed (*b*). However, Vice-Chancellor Page Wood once qualified this by saying, "unless the trust was created by an instrument under seal" (*c*); and Sir John Romilly on another occasion said, "I think where money is due to *cestuis que trust* who have settled it, the trustee is entitled to a release from the *cestuis que trust*, but to a receipt only from the persons to whom they

(*a*) Lewin, Trusts, 11th ed. 411.

(*b*) *Chadwick* v. *Heatley* (1845), 2 Coll. 137; *In re Wright's Trusts* (1857), 3 K. & J. 419; and see *Warter* v. *Anderson* (1853), 3 Hare, at p. 303. Compare Indian Trusts Act, 1882, s. 35.

(*c*) *In re Wright's Trusts*, *supra*, at p. 422.

desire it to be paid" (*d*). And Vice-Chancellor Kindersley actually decided that when the trust was verbal only, and the trustee was asked to deal with the trust property in a manner not in accordance with the tenor of the trusts, he was entitled to demand a release by deed (*e*). Mr. Lewin, however, who was one of the counsel engaged in the case, says his reasons are not satisfactory. The first, namely, that the trust was by parol and therefore obscure, might, he says, have been an excuse for not paying at all or ground for demanding an indemnity, but seems to afford no reason for requiring a release under seal as distinguished from a simple receipt or acquittance in writing, and moreover, Vice-Chancellor Page Wood's dictum, quoted above, appears to be in direct conflict with it. And the second, the anticipation of the time of payment, is also not material, for all the beneficiaries were ready to join in giving a receipt to the trustee (*f*).

Since all the authorities are agreed as to the general rule, presumably it may be taken to be now established, but whether there are any exceptions, and if so, what they are, must be taken to be doubtful. The Indian Trusts Act has adopted the general rule without qualification, s. 35 providing that—

> "When the duties of a trustee, as such, are completed he is entitled to have the accounts of his administration of the trust property examined and settled; and where nothing is due to the beneficiary under the trust to an acknowledgment in writing to that effect."

And this was adopted with a verbal alteration in s. 57 of the abortive Trusts Bill of 1892.

It has been decided that if the *cestui que trust* has assigned his share in the trust fund, on the distribution of the fund the trustee is not entitled to have the assignments handed over to him. He is no doubt entitled to see them, and probably to an acknowledgment of the right to their production, and an undertaking for their safe custody, but nothing more (*g*).

(*d*) *In re Cater's Trusts* (1858), 25 Beav. at p. 367.

(*e*) *King* v. *Mullins* (1852), 1 Drew. 308.

(*f*) Lewin, Trusts, 11th ed. 411.

(*g*) *In re Palmer*, (1907) 1 Ch. 486.

Section CV.—Payment into Court by Trustee.

(1) Trustees, or the majority of trustees, having in their hands or under their control money or securities belonging to a trust, may pay the same into the High Court; and the same shall, subject to rules of court, be dealt with according to the orders of the High Court.

(2) The receipt or certificate of the proper officer shall be a sufficient discharge to trustees for the money or securities so paid into court.

(3) Where any moneys or securities are vested in any persons as trustees, and the majority are desirous of paying the same into court, but the concurrence of the other or others cannot be obtained, the High Court may order the payment into court to be made by the majority without the concurrence of the other or others; and where any such moneys or securities are deposited with any banker, broker, or other depositary, the court may order payment or delivery of the moneys or securities to the majority of the trustees for the purpose of payment into court, and every transfer payment and delivery made in pursuance of any such order shall be valid and take effect as if the same had been made on the authority or by the act of all the persons entitled to the moneys and securities so transferred, paid, or delivered (*a*).

Any sole trustee may now rid himself of liability for trust money or securities by paying them into court, and, if there is more than one trustee, all, or a majority of them, may do so.

(*a*) Trustee Act, 1893, s. 42.

This right was first conferred by the Legacy Duty Act, 1796 (*b*), s. 32 of which authorized executors and administrators to pay into court any legacy or share of residuary personalty where they were unable to pay it to the person entitled by reason of his infancy or absence beyond the seas.

It was extended to trustees by the act 10 & 11 Vict. c. 96, commonly called the Trustee Relief Act, 1847, s. 1 of which provided that "all trustees, executors, administrators, or other persons having in their hands any moneys belonging to any trust whatever, or the major part of them," might pay the same or transfer stocks and securities into court. This act was extended to Ireland by the 11 & 12 Vict. c. 68, and by the 12 & 13 Vict. c. 74, commonly called the Trustee Relief Act, 1849. The court was authorized to direct transfer or payment into court where the majority of such persons so desired, but the concurrence of the other or others of them could not be had.

All these enactments were repealed by s. 51 of the Trustee Act, 1893, s. 42 of which provides that—

"(1) Trustees or the majority of trustees having in their hands or under their control money or securities belonging to a trust may pay the same into the High Court; and the same shall, subject to the rules of court, be dealt with according to the orders of the High Court.

"(2) The receipt or certificate of the proper officer shall be a sufficient discharge to trustees for the moneys or securities so paid into court.

"(3) Where any moneys or securities are vested in any persons as trustees, and the majority are desirous of paying the same into court, but the concurrence of the other or others cannot be obtained, the High Court may order the payment into court to be made by the majority without the concurrence of the other or others; and where any such moneys or securities are deposited with any banker, broker or other depository, the court may order payment or delivery of the moneys or securities to the majority of the trustees for the purpose of payment into court, and every transfer, payment and delivery made in pursuance of any such order shall be valid and take effect as if the same had been made on the authority or by the act of all the persons entitled to the moneys and securities so transferred, paid or delivered."

(*b*) 56 Geo. III. c. 52.

This repeal and re-enactment may in one respect give rise to some difficulty, for the payment into court of a fund belonging to an infant under the Trustee Relief Acts made the infant a ward of court, while a payment into court under the Legacy Duty Act, 1796, did not have that effect (*c*). Under s. 42 of the Trustee Act, 1893, the distinction as to the provision under which the payment in is made is abolished, and it is not easy to see now what the effect is. It has been suggested that the solution of the difficulty is that the court will consider the circumstances in each case (*d*).

The procedure to be followed by a trustee or personal representative on paying into court under this section is to be found in Order LIVB. of the Rules of the Supreme Court and in rule 41 of the Supreme Court Funds Rules. If it is a trustee who is making the payment, he must make and file an affidavit entitled in the matter of the trust (described so as to be distinguishable) and of the act, and setting forth:—

(a) a short description of the trust and of the instrument creating it;

(b) the names of the persons interested in and entitled to the money or securities and their places of residence, to the best of his knowledge and belief;

(c) his submission to answer all such inquiries relating to the application of the money or securities paid into court as the court or judge may make or direct;

(d) the place where he is to be served with any petition, summons or order or notice of any proceeding relating to the money or securities (*e*).

A form of affidavit will be found in Daniell's Chancery Forms. There must be annexed to the affidavit a schedule in the same printed form as the lodgment schedule to an order, setting forth:—

(a) the trustee's own name and address:

(b) the amount and description of the funds proposed to be lodged in court:

(c) the ledger credit in the matter of the particular trust to which the funds are to be placed:

(*c*) *In re Hodges* (1857), 3 K. & J. 213.

(*d*) Rudall & Greig, Trustee Acts, 3rd ed. 153.

(*e*) Ord. LIVB. r. 4 (1).

(d) a statement whether duty (if chargeable) or any part thereof has or has not been paid:

(e) a statement whether the money or the dividends on the securities so to be lodged in court, and all accumulations of dividends thereon, are desired to be invested in any and what description of Government securities, or whether it is deemed unnecessary so to invest the same.

And an office copy of the schedule must be left with the paymaster (*f*).

The affidavit may be written or printed; the lodgment schedule must be printed.

If the fund consists of money or securities being or being part of or representing a legacy or residue to which an infant or person beyond seas is absolutely entitled, and on which the trustee has paid the legacy duty, or on which no duty is chargeable, the trustee may make the lodgment without an affidavit (*g*). In this case he must leave with the paymaster a "request," signed by him or his solicitor, with a certificate of the Commissioners of Inland Revenue that the duty has been paid, or that no duty is payable, as the case may be (*h*).

The usual practice is for the trustee to deduct his costs of payment in from the fund before bringing it into court, and he is entitled to deduct any other costs that may be due to him so long as they are such as ought properly to be allowed him. But where a trustee knows that the amount of the costs he proposes to deduct are disputed, he ought to pay in the whole amount, leaving the court to decide the amount to which he is entitled when application is made for payment out (*i*). But if the trustee does improperly deduct costs, the only way to obtain redress is to bring an action against him to recover the amount. The court has no jurisdiction to order him to repay them on an application for payment out of the fund (*j*).

(*f*) Supreme Court Funds Rules, r. 41 (b).

(*g*) Ord. LIVB. r. 4.

(*h*) Supreme Court Funds Rules, r. 41 (a). The forms of request and certificate are No. 16 in the Appendix to the Rules.

(*i*) *Beaty* v. *Curson* (1868), L. R. 7 Eq. 194.

(*j*) *In re Parker's Will* (1888), 39 Ch. D. 303.

Part XIII.—MISCELLANEOUS AND SUPPLEMENTAL.

SECTION CVI.—POWER OF COURT TO GIVE JUDGMENT IN ABSENCE OF A TRUSTEE.

WHERE in any action the High Court is satisfied that diligent search has been made for any person who, in the character of trustee, is made a defendant in any action, to serve him with a process of the court, and that he cannot be found, the court may hear and determine the action and give judgment therein against that person in his character of a trustee, as if he had been duly served, or had entered an appearance in the action, and had also appeared by his counsel and solicitor at the hearing, but without prejudice to any interest he may have in the matters in question in the action in any other character (*a*).

SECTION CVII.—JURISDICTION OF PALATINE AND COUNTY COURTS.

THE provisions of this act with respect to the High Court shall, in their application to cases within the jurisdiction of a palatine court or county court, include that court, and the procedure under this act in palatine courts and county courts shall be in accordance with the acts and rules regulating the procedure of those courts (*b*).

(*a*) s. 43 of the Trustee Act, 1893.

(*b*) s. 46 of the Trustee Act, 1893.

Section CVIII. — Application to Trustees under Settled Land Acts of Provisions as to Appointment of Trustees.

(1) All the powers and provisions contained in this act with reference to the appointment of new trustees, and the discharge and retirement of trustees, are to apply to and include trustees for the purposes of the Settled Land Acts, 1882 to 1890, whether appointed by the court or by the settlement, or under provisions contained in the settlement.

(2) This section applies and is to have effect with respect to an appointment or a discharge and retirement of trustees taking place before as well as after the commencement of this act.

(3) This section is not to render invalid or prejudice any appointment or any discharge and retirement of trustees effected before the passing of this act, otherwise than under the provisions of the Conveyancing and Law of Property Act, 1881 (*a*).

Section CIX.—Indemnity.

This act, and every order purporting to be made under this act, shall be a complete indemnity to the Banks of England and Ireland, and to all persons for any acts done pursuant thereto; and it shall not be necessary for the Bank or for any person to inquire concerning the propriety of the order, or whether the court by which it was made had jurisdiction to make the same (*b*).

(*a*) s. 47 of the Trustee Act, 1893.

(*b*) s. 49 of the Trustee Act, 1893.

Section CX.—Interpretation of Terms.

In this act, unless the context otherwise requires,—

The expression "bankrupt" includes, in Ireland, insolvent:

The expression "contingent right," as applied to land, includes a contingent or executory interest, a possibility coupled with an interest, whether the object of the gift or limitation of the interest, or possibility is or is not ascertained, also a right of entry, whether immediate or future, and whether vested or contingent:

The expressions "convey" and "conveyance" applied to any person include the execution by that person of every necessary or suitable assurance for conveying, assigning, appointing, surrendering, or otherwise transferring or disposing of land whereof he is seised or possessed, or wherein he is entitled to a contingent right, either for his whole estate or for any less estate, together with the performance of all formalities required by law to the validity of the conveyance, including the acts to be performed by married women and tenants in tail in accordance with the provisions of the acts for abolition of fines and recoveries in England and Ireland respectively, and also including surrenders and other acts which a tenant of customary or copyhold lands can himself perform preparatory to or in aid of a complete assurance of the customary or copyhold land:

The expression "devisee" includes the heir of a devisee and the devisee of an heir, and any person who may claim right by devolution of title of a similar description:

The expression "instrument" includes act of parliament:

The expression "land" includes manors and lordships, and reputed manors and lordships, and incorporeal as well as corporeal hereditaments, and any interest therein, and also an undivided share of land:

The expressions "mortgage" and "mortgagee" include and relate to every estate and interest regarded in equity as merely a security for money, and every person deriving title under the original mortgagee:

The expressions "pay" and "payment" as applied in relation to stocks and securities, and in connection with the expression "into court" include the deposit or transfer of the same in or into court:

The expression "possessed" applies to receipt of income of, and to any vested estate less than a life estate, legal or equitable, in possession or in expectancy, in, any land:

The expression "property" includes real and personal property, and any estate and interest in any property, real or personal, and any debt, and any thing in action, and any other right or interest, whether in possession or not:

The expression "rights" includes estates and interests:

The expression "securities" includes stocks, funds, and shares; and so far as relates to payments into court has the same meaning as in the Court of Chancery (Funds) Act, 1872:

The expression "stock" includes fully paid up shares; and, so far as relates to vesting orders made by the court under this act, includes any fund, annuity, or security transferable in books kept by any company or society, or by instrument of transfer either alone or accompanied by other formalities, and any share or interest therein:

The expression "transfer," in relation to stock, includes the performance and execution of every deed, power of attorney, act, and thing on the part of the transferor to effect and complete the title in the transferee:

The expression "trust" does not include the duties incident to an estate conveyed by way of mortgage; but with this exception the expressions "trust" and "trustee" include implied and constructive trusts, and cases where the trustee has a beneficial interest in the trust property, and the duties incident to the office of personal representative of a deceased person (*a*).

(*a*) s. 50 of the Trustee Act, 1893.

APPENDIX.

PUBLIC TRUSTEE ACT, 1906.
(6 Edw. 7, c. 55.)

ARRANGEMENT OF SECTIONS.

PUBLIC TRUSTEE ACT, 1906.

(6 Edw. 7, c. 55.)

An Act to provide for the appointment of a Public Trustee and to amend the Law relating to the administration of Trusts.

[21st December, 1906.]

Be it enacted by the King's most Excellent Majesty, by and with the advice and consent of the Lords Spiritual and Temporal, and Commons, in this present Parliament assembled, and by the authority of the same, as follows:—

Establishment of Public Trustee.

Office of public trustee.

1.—(1) There shall be established the office of public trustee.

(2) The public trustee shall be a corporation sole under that name, with perpetual succession and an official seal, and may sue and be sued under the above name like any other corporation sole, but any instruments sealed by him shall not, by reason of his using a seal, be rendered liable to a higher stamp duty than if he were an individual.

Powers and Duties of Public Trustee.

General powers and duties of public trustee.

2.—(1) Subject to and in accordance with the provisions of this act and rules made thereunder, the public trustee may, if he thinks fit—

(a) act in the administration of estates of small value;

(b) act as custodian trustee;

(c) act as an ordinary trustee;

(d) be appointed to be a judicial trustee;

(e) be appointed to be the administrator of the property of a convict under the Forfeiture Act, 1870.

33 & 34 Vict. c. 23.

(2) Subject to the provisions of this act, and to the rules made thereunder, the public trustee may act either alone or jointly with any person or body of persons in any capacity to which he may be appointed in pursuance of this act, and shall have all the same powers, duties, and liabilities, and be entitled to the same rights and immunities and be subject to the control and orders of the court, as a private trustee acting in the same capacity.

(3) The public trustee may decline, either absolutely or except on the prescribed conditions, to accept any trust, but he shall not decline to accept any trust on the ground only of the small value of the trust property.

(4) The public trustee shall not accept any trust which involves the management or carrying on of any business, except in the cases in which he may be authorised to do so by rules made under this act, nor any trust under a deed of arrangement for the benefit of creditors, nor the administration of any estate known or believed by him to be insolvent.

(5) The public trustee shall not accept any trust exclusively for religious or charitable purposes, and nothing in this act contained, or in the rules to be made under the powers in this act contained, shall abridge or affect the powers or duties of the official trustee of charity lands or official trustees of charitable funds.

(1) *In the administration of small Estates.*

Administration of small estates.

3.—(1) Any person who in the opinion of the public trustee would be entitled to apply to the court for an order for the administration by the court of an estate, the gross capital value whereof is proved to the satisfaction of the public trustee to be less than one thousand pounds, may apply to the public trustee to administer the estate, and, where any such application is made and it appears to the public trustee that the persons beneficially entitled are persons of small means, the public trustee shall administer the estate, unless he sees good reason for refusing to do so.

(2) On the public trustee undertaking, by declaration in writing signed and sealed by him, to administer the estate the trust property other than stock shall, by virtue of this act, vest in him, and the right to transfer or call for the transfer of any stock forming part of the estate shall also vest in him, in like manner as if vesting orders had been made for the purpose by the High Court under the Trustee Act, 1893, and that act shall apply accordingly. As from such vesting any trustee entitled under the trust to administer the estate shall be discharged from all liability attaching to the administration, except in respect of past acts:

56 & 57 Vict. c. 53.

Provided that—

(a) the public trustee shall not exercise the right of himself transferring the stock without the leave of the court; and

(b) this subsection shall not apply to any copyhold land forming part of the estate, but the public trustee shall, as respects such land, have the like powers as if he had been appointed by the court under section thirty-three of the Trustee Act, 1893, to convey the land, and section thirty-four of that act shall apply accordingly.

(3) For the purposes of the administration the public trustee may exercise such of the administrative powers and authorities of the High Court as may be conferred on him by rules under this act, subject to such conditions as may be imposed by the rules.

(4) Rules shall be made under this act for enabling the public trustee to take the opinion of the High Court on any question arising in the course of any administration without judicial proceedings, and otherwise for making the procedure under this section simple and inexpensive.

(5) Where proceedings have been instituted in any court for the administration of an estate, and by reason of the small value of the estate it appears to the court that the estate can be more economically administered by the public trustee than by the court, or that for any other reason it is expedient that the estate should be administered by the public trustee instead of the court, the court may order that the estate shall be administered by the public trustee, and thereupon (subject to any directions by the court) this section shall apply as if the administration of the estate had been undertaken by the public trustee in pursuance of this section.

(2) *As Custodian Trustee.*

4.—(1) Subject to rules under this act the public trustee may, if he consents to act as such, and whether or not the number of trustees has been reduced below the original number, be appointed to be custodian trustee of any trust—

(a) by order of the court made on the application of any person on whose application the court may order the appointment of a new trustee; or

(b) by the testator, settlor, or other creator of any trust; or

(c) by the person having power to appoint new trustees.

(2) Where the public trustee is appointed to be custodian trustee of any trust—

(a) The trust property shall be transferred to the custodian trustee as if he were sole trustee, and for that purpose vesting orders may, where necessary, be made under the Trustee Act, 1893:

(b) The management of the trust property and the exercise of any power or discretion exerciseable by the trustees under the trust shall remain vested in the trustees other than the custodian trustee (which trustees are herein-after referred to as the managing trustees):

(c) As between the custodian trustee and the managing trustees, and subject and without prejudice to the rights of any other persons, the custodian trustee shall have the custody of all securities and documents of title relating to the trust property, but the managing trustees shall have free access thereto and be entitled to take copies thereof or extracts therefrom :

(d) The custodian trustee shall concur in and perform all acts necessary to enable the managing trustees to exercise their powers of management or any other power or discretion vested in them (including the power to pay money or securities into court), unless the matter in which he is requested to concur is a breach of trust, or involves a personal liability upon him in respect of calls or otherwise, but, unless he so concurs, the custodian trustee shall not be liable for any act or default on the part of the managing trustees or any of them :

(e) All sums payable to or out of the income or capital of the trust property shall be paid to or by the custodian trustee : Provided that the custodian trustee may allow the dividends and other income derived from the trust property to be paid to the managing trustees or to such person as they direct, or into such bank to the credit of such person as they may direct, and in such case shall be exonerated from seeing to the application thereof and shall not be answerable for any loss or misapplication thereof :

(f) The power of appointing new trustees, when exerciseable by the trustees, shall be exerciseable by the managing trustees alone, but the custodian trustee shall have the same power of applying to the court for the appointment of a new trustee as any other trustee :

(g) In determining the number of trustees for the purposes of the Trustee Act, 1893, the custodian trustee shall not be reckoned as a trustee :

(h) The custodian trustee, if he acts in good faith, shall not be liable for accepting as correct and acting upon the faith of any written statement by the managing trustees as to any birth, death, marriage, or other matter of pedigree or relationship, or other matter of fact, upon which the title to the trust property or any part thereof may depend, nor for acting upon any legal advice obtained by the managing trustees independently of the custodian trustee :

(i) The court may, on the application of either the custodian trustee, or any of the managing trustees, or of any beneficiary, and on proof to their satisfaction that it is the general wish of the beneficiaries, or that on other grounds it is expedient, to terminate the custodian trusteeship, make an order for that purpose, and the court may thereupon make such vesting orders and give such directions as under the circumstances may seem to the court to be necessary or expedient.

(3) The provisions of this section shall apply in like manner as to the public trustee to any banking or insurance company or other body corporate entitled by rules made under this act to act as custodian trustee, with power for such company or body corporate to charge and retain or pay out of the trust property fees not exceeding the fees chargeable by the public trustee as custodian trustee.

(3) *As an ordinary Trustee.*

Appointment of public trustee to be trustee, executor, &c.

5.—(1) The public trustee may by that name, or any other sufficient description, be appointed to be trustee of any will or settlement or other instrument creating a trust or to perform any trust or duty belonging to a class which he is authorised by the rules made under this act to accept, and may be so appointed whether the will or settlement or instrument creating the trust or duty was made or came into operation before or after the passing of this act, and either as an original or as a new trustee, or as an additional trustee, in the same cases, and in the same manner, and by the same persons or court, as if he were a private trustee, with this addition, that, though the trustees originally appointed were two or more, the public trustee may be appointed sole trustee.

(2) Where the public trustee has been appointed a trustee of any trust, a co-trustee may retire from the trust under and in accordance with section eleven of the Trustee Act, 1893, notwithstanding that there are not more than two trustees, and without such consents as are required by that section.

(3) The public trustee shall not be so appointed either as a new or additional trustee where the will, settlement, or other instrument creating the trust or duty contains a direction to the contrary, unless the court otherwise order.

(4) Notice of any proposed appointment of the public trustee either as a new or additional trustee shall where practicable be given in the prescribed manner to all persons beneficially interested who are resident in the United Kingdom and whose addresses are known to the persons proposing to make the appointment, or, if such beneficiaries

are infants, to their guardians, and if any person to whom such notice has been given within twenty-one days from the receipt of the notice applies to the court, the court may, if having regard to the interests of all the beneficiaries it considers it expedient to do so, make an order prohibiting the appointment being made, provided that a failure to give any such notice shall not invalidate any appointment made under this section.

Power as to granting probate.

6.—(1) If in pursuance of any rule under this act, the public trustee is authorised to accept by that name probates of wills or letters of administration, the court having jurisdiction to grant probate of a will or letters of administration may grant such probate or letters to the public trustee by that name, and for that purpose the court shall consider the public trustee as in law entitled equally with any other person or class of persons to obtain the grant of letters of administration, save that the consent or citation of the public trustee shall not be required for the grant of letters of administration to any other person, and that, as between the public trustee and the widower widow or next-of-kin of the deceased, the widower widow or next-of-kin shall be preferred, unless for good cause shown to the contrary.

(2) Any executor who has obtained probate or any administrator who has obtained letters of administration, and notwithstanding he has acted in the administration of the deceased's estate, may, with the sanction of the court, and after such notice to the persons beneficially interested as the court may direct, transfer such estate to the public trustee for administration either solely or jointly with the continuing executors or administrator, if any. And the order of the court sanctioning such transfer shall, subject to the provisions of this act, give to the public trustee all the powers of such executor and administrator, and such executor and administrator shall not be in any way liable in respect of any act or default in reference to such estate subsequent to the date of such order, other than the act or default of himself or of persons other than himself for whose conduct he is in law responsible.

LIABILITY : OFFICERS AND OFFICES : FEES.

Liability of Consolidated Fund.

7.—(1) The Consolidated Fund of the United Kingdom shall be liable to make good all sums required to discharge any liability which the public trustee, if he were a private trustee, would be personally liable to discharge, except where the liability is one to which neither the public trustee nor any of his officers has in any way contributed, and which neither he nor any of his officers could by the exercise of reasonable diligence have averted, and in that case the public trustee shall not, nor shall the Consolidated Fund, be subject to any liability.

(2) All sums payable in pursuance of this section out of the Consolidated Fund shall be charged on and issued out of that fund or the growing produce thereof.

8.—(1) The Lord Chancellor shall appoint a fit person to the office of public trustee, who shall hold office during pleasure, and receive such salary or fees, and be appointed on such terms, as the Treasury may determine.

(2) The Lord Chancellor shall appoint such persons to be officers of the public trustee as, subject to the sanction of the Treasury, he may consider necessary for the purposes of this act, and those officers shall hold office upon such terms, and be remunerated at such rates and in such manner, as the Treasury may sanction.

(3) Any person appointed to be public trustee or an officer of the public trustee may, and shall, if the Treasury so require, be a person already in the public service.

(4) The public trustee shall, if so directed by the Lord Chancellor with the concurrence of the Treasury, maintain offices in London and elsewhere, and, so far as practicable, buildings already used for public purposes shall be used for such offices.

(5) The salary or remuneration of the public trustee and his officers and such other expenses of executing his office or otherwise carrying this act into effect as may be sanctioned by the Treasury shall be paid out of moneys provided by Parliament.

9.—(1) There shall be charged in respect of the duties of the public trustee such fees, whether by way of percentage or otherwise, as the Treasury with the sanction of the Lord Chancellor may fix, and such fees shall be collected and accounted for by such persons, and in such manner, and shall be paid to such account, as the Treasury direct.

(2) Any expenses which might be retained or paid out of the trust property if the public trustee were a private trustee shall be so retained or paid, and the fees shall be retained or paid in the like manner as and in addition to such expenses.

(3) Such fees shall, under the regulations of the Treasury, be applied as an appropriation in aid of moneys provided by Parliament for expenses under this act, and so far as not so applied shall be paid into the Exchequer.

(4) The fees under this section shall be arranged from time to time so as to produce an annual amount sufficient to discharge the salaries and other expenses incidental to the working of this act (including such sums as the Treasury may from time to time determine to be required to insure the Consolidated Fund against loss under this act) and no more.

(5) The incidence of the fees and expenses under this section as between capital and income shall be determined by the public trustee.

SUPPLEMENTAL PROVISIONS AS TO PUBLIC TRUSTEE.

10.—(1) A person aggrieved by any act or omission or decision of the public trustee in relation to any trust may apply to the court, and the court may make such order in the matter as the court thinks just. **Appeal to the court.**

(2) Subject to rules of court, an application under this section to the High Court shall be made to a judge of the Chancery Division of the High Court in Chambers.

11.—(1) The public trustee shall not, nor shall any of his officers, act under this act for reward, except as provided by this act. **Mode of action of public trustee.**

(2) The public trustee may, subject to the rules made under this act, employ for the purposes of any trust such solicitors, bankers, accountants, and brokers, or other persons as he may consider necessary, and in determining the persons to be so employed in relation to any trust the public trustee shall have regard to the interests of the trust, but subject to this shall, whenever practicable, take into consideration the wishes of the creator of the trust and of the other trustees (if any), and of the beneficiaries, either expressed or as implied by the practice of the creator of the trust, or in the previous management of the trust.

(3) On behalf of the public trustee such person as may be prescribed may take any oath, make any declaration, verify any account, give personal attendance at any court or place, and do any act or thing whatsoever which the public trustee is required or authorised to take, make, verify, give, or do: Provided that nothing in this act or in any rule made under this act shall confer upon any person not otherwise entitled thereto any right to appear, or act, or be heard in or before any court or tribunal, on behalf or instead of the public trustee, or to do any act whatsoever on behalf or on the instructions of the public trustee, which could otherwise only be lawfully done by a barrister or a duly certificated solicitor.

(4) Where any bond or security would be required from a private person upon the grant to him of administration, or upon his appointment to act in any capacity, the public trustee, if administration is granted to him or if he is appointed to act in such capacity as aforesaid, shall not be required to give such bond or security, but shall be subject to the same liabilities and duties as if he had given such bond or security.

(5) The entry of the public trustee by that name in the books of a company shall not constitute notice of a trust, and a company shall not be entitled to object to enter the name of the public trustee on its books by reason only that the public trustee is a corporation, and, in dealings with property, the fact that the person or one of the persons dealt with is the public trustee, shall not of itself constitute notice of a trust.

Application of act to palatine courts.

12. The provisions of this act with respect to the High Court shall, in their application to cases within the jurisdiction of a palatine court, include that court, and the public trustee shall provide an address within the county palatine where service upon him of any proceedings under this act in such palatine court may be effected; the rules of court relating to the exercise of the jurisdiction of a palatine court under this act shall be made by the authority having power to make general rules and orders of that court.

INVESTIGATION AND AUDIT OF TRUST ACCOUNTS.

Investigation and audit of trust accounts.

13.—(1) Subject to rules under this act and unless the court otherwise orders, the condition and accounts of any trust shall, on an application being made and notice thereof given in the prescribed manner by any trustee or beneficiary, be investigated and audited by such solicitor or public accountant as may be agreed on by the applicant and the trustees or, in default of agreement, by the public trustee or some person appointed by him:

Provided that (except with the leave of the court) such an investigation or audit shall not be required within twelve months after any such previous investigation or audit, and that a trustee or beneficiary shall not be appointed under this section to make an investigation or audit.

(2) The person making the investigation or audit (herein-after called the auditor) shall have a right of access to the books, accounts, and vouchers of the trustees, and to any securities and documents of title held by them on account of the trust, and may require from them such information and explanation as may be necessary for the performance of his duties, and upon the completion of the investigation and audit shall forward to the applicant and to every trustee a copy of the accounts, together with a report thereon, and a certificate signed by him to the effect that the accounts exhibit a true view of the state of the affairs of the trust and that he has had the securities of the trust fund investments produced to and verified by him or (as the case may be) that such accounts are deficient in such respects as may be specified in such certificate.

(3) Every beneficiary under the trust shall, subject to rules under this act, be entitled at all reasonable times to inspect and take copies of the accounts, report, and certificate, and, at his own expense, to be furnished with copies thereof or extracts therefrom.

(4) The auditor may be removed by order of the court, and, if any auditor is removed, or resigns, or dies, or becomes bankrupt or incapable of acting before the investigation and audit is completed,

a new auditor may be appointed in his place in like manner as the original auditor.

(5) The remuneration of the auditor and the other expenses of the investigation and audit shall be such as may be prescribed by rules under this act, and shall, unless the public trustee otherwise directs, be borne by the estate; and, in the event of the public trustee so directing, he may order that such expenses be borne by the applicant or by the trustees personally or partly by them and partly by the applicant.

(6) If any person having the custody of any documents to which the auditor has a right of access under this section fails or refuses to allow him to have access thereto or in anywise obstructs the investigation or audit, the auditor may apply to the court, and thereupon the court shall make such order as it thinks just.

(7) Subject to rules of court, applications under or for the purposes of this section to the High Court shall be made to a judge of the Chancery Division in Chambers.

(8) If any person in any statement of accounts, report, or certificate required for the purposes of this section wilfully makes a statement false in any material particular, he shall be liable on conviction on indictment to imprisonment for a term not exceeding two years, and on summary conviction to imprisonment for a term not exceeding six months, with or without hard labour, and in either case to a fine in lieu of or in addition to such imprisonment.

Rules: Definitions: Short Title and Extent.

14.—(1) The Lord Chancellor shall, with the concurrence of the Treasury, make rules for carrying into effect the objects of this act, and in particular for all or any of the following purposes (that is to say):— **Rules.**

(a) establishing the office of public trustee and prescribing the trusts or duties he is authorised to accept or undertake, and the security, if any, to be given by the public trustee and his officers:

(b) the transfer to and from the public trustee of any property:

(c) the accounts to be kept and an audit thereof:

(d) the establishment and regulation of any branch office:

(e) excluding any trusts from the operation of this act or any part thereof:

(f) the classes of corporate bodies entitled to act as custodian trustees:

(g) the form and manner in which notices under this act shall be given.

(2) Every rule under this act shall be laid before each House of Parliament forthwith, and, if an address is presented to His Majesty by either House of Parliament, within the next subsequent thirty days on which the House has sat next after any such rule is laid before it, praying that the rule may be annulled, His Majesty in Council may annul the rule, and it shall thenceforth be void, but without prejudice to the validity of anything previously done thereunder.

(3) If the rules require a declaration to be made for any purpose, a person who makes such declaration, knowing the same to be untrue in any material particular, shall be guilty of a misdemeanour.

15. In this act, unless the context otherwise requires,—

the expression "court" means the High Court and, as respects trusts within its jurisdiction, the county court:

the expression "letters of administration" means letters of administration of the estate and effects of a deceased person, whether general or with a will annexed, or limited either in time or otherwise:

the expression "trust" includes an executorship or administratorship; and the expression "trustee" shall be construed accordingly; and the expression "trust property" shall include all property in the possession or under the control wholly or partly of the public trustee by virtue of any trust:

the expression "private trustee" means a trustee other than the public trustee:

the expression "expenses" includes costs and charges:

the expression "prescribed" means prescribed for the time being by rules under this act:

other expressions have the same meaning as in the Trustee Act, 1893.

16. This act shall come into operation on the first day of January one thousand nine hundred and eight.

17.—(1) This act may be cited as the Public Trustee Act, 1906.

(2) This act shall not extend to Ireland or Scotland.

THE PUBLIC TRUSTEE RULES, 1907.

Dated November 29, 1907.

I, the Right Honourable Robert Threshie, Baron Loreburn, Lord High Chancellor of Great Britain, with the concurrence of the Treasury, by virtue and in pursuance of the Public Trustee Act, 1906, and of all other powers and authorities enabling me in this behalf, do make the following rules for carrying into effect the objects of that act.

Interpretation.

1. In these rules the expression "the act" means the Public Trustee Act, 1906; and unless there is anything in the context or in the act inconsistent therewith—

The expression "trust instrument" includes any instrument by which a trust is created;

The expression "trust property" includes all property subject to a trust, or comprised in an estate, which is proposed to be administered by the public trustee;

The expression "deputy" means a deputy public trustee.

2. The Interpretation Act, 1889, applies for the purpose of the interpretation of these rules as it applies for the purpose of the interpretation of an act of parliament.

Establishment of Office.

3. The office of public trustee is hereby established.

Offices.

4.—(1) The central office of the public trustee shall be situate in London.

(2) Branch offices may from time to time be established as may be prescribed by the Lord Chancellor by notice in the London Gazette.

Deputy Public Trustees.

5. There shall be deputy public trustees at any branch offices so established who shall be officers of the public trustee, and shall have the powers and perform the duties assigned to them by or under these rules. Their number shall be such as the Lord Chancellor, with th sanction of the Treasury, may from time to time prescribe, and every such appointment shall be notified in the London Gazette.

Security.

6. Security shall be given by such persons employed under the act as the Treasury may direct for the due performance of their duties, and for the due accounting for and payment of all moneys received by them in pursuance of the act and these rules. The security shall be for such sum and shall be given in such manner and form as the Treasury shall order in the case of each such person, and the Treasury may at any time require that the amount or nature of any such security be varied.

Trusteeships.

7.—(1) Subject to the act and these rules the public trustee is authorised—

(a) to accept as ordinary trustee and to act as custodian trustee of any trust created by any trust instrument or arising upon an intestacy; and

(b) to accept by the name of the public trustee probates or letters of administration of any kind.

Provided that he shall not accept the trusts of any instrument made solely by way of security for money.

8. The public trustee may if he thinks fit—

(1) act as custodian trustee of a trust which involves the management or carrying on of any business but upon the conditions that (a) he shall not act in the management or carrying on of such business, and (b) he shall not hold any property of such a nature as will expose the holder thereof to any liability except under exceptional circumstances and when he is satisfied that he is fully indemnified or secured against loss; and

(2) accept as ordinary trustee under exceptional circumstances a trust which involves the management or carrying on of any business, but upon the conditions that except with the consent of the Treasury he shall only carry on the same (a) for a short time not exceeding eighteen months, and (b) with a view to sale disposition or winding-up, and (c) if satisfied that the same can be carried on without risk of loss.

9.—(1) A testator may appoint the public trustee to be trustee or custodian trustee under any testamentary instrument without previously applying to him for his consent to act as such.

(2) No such appointment by a testator shall have effect, and no appointment of the public trustee to be trustee or custodian trustee shall be made except by a testator, unless and until (in either case) the consent of the public trustee to act as such trustee shall have been applied for and obtained in accordance with these rules. Provided that in the case of any such appointment by a testator the public trustee shall at any time after the fact of his appointment shall have come to his knowledge be at liberty to act as if such application had been received by him.

10.—(1) An application to the public trustee to act as trustee or custodian trustee may be made

(a) where the appointment has been made by a testator—by any trustee or beneficiary under the testamentary instrument; and

(b) in the case of the estate of an intestate—by any person appearing to be beneficially interested in the estate; and

(c) in any case—by the persons or any one of the persons having power under the act to make the appointment.

(2) It shall be the duty of any person appointed by a testator to be co-trustee with the public trustee, and not renouncing or disclaiming the trust, to give to the public trustee notice in writing of such appointment as soon as practicable after the same has come to his knowledge.

11.—(1) Any application under the last preceding rule shall be made in writing addressed to the public trustee at his office in London, or any branch office for the time being in existence, and may be left at or sent by post to any such office as aforesaid.

(2) Upon receiving any such application the public trustee may require to be produced to him the trust instrument (if any), and may require to be supplied to him a copy of that instrument, and of any other document affecting the trust, and such particulars as to the nature and value of the trust property, and the liabilities (if any) attaching to such property, or the holder thereof, and the names and places of abode of any beneficiaries and trustees under the trust, and such other information relating to the trust as he may consider it desirable to obtain in any particular case.

12. As soon as may be after receiving any such application the public trustee shall take into consideration upon such evidence as may appear to him sufficient—

(a) the gross capital value of the trust property;

(b) the mode of investment and the condition of the trust property;

(c) the situation, tenure, and character of any land comprised in the trust property;

(d) any liabilities attaching to the trust property or the holder thereof;

(e) the places of abode and circumstances of the beneficiaries; and

(f) all the circumstances of the case.

13.—(1) Upon any application the public trustee shall decide whether the same ought to be accepted or refused, and shall forthwith give notice to the applicant of such acceptance or refusal, and in case of acceptance shall execute an instrument expressing his consent to act in the trust.

(2) Upon the acceptance of any application the public trustee shall consider and determine whether the trust shall be administered from his central office or from a branch office, and shall give directions accordingly, and any such direction may at any time be rescinded or varied by the public trustee at his discretion.

Administration of Small Estates.

14.—(1) An application under section 3 (1) of the act shall be made in the manner provided by rule 11 hereinbefore contained.

(2) Upon receiving any such application the public trustee shall require to be supplied to him such evidence as to the value of the estate, and the circumstances of the persons beneficially entitled, and such other information relating thereto as he may consider it desirable to obtain in any particular case.

15.—(1) If it is not proved to the satisfaction of the public trustee that the gross capital value of the estate is less than 1,000*l.*, or if it does not appear to him that the persons beneficially entitled are persons of small means, or if he sees any other good reason for refusing the application, he shall refuse the same, and shall forthwith give notice to the applicant of such refusal.

(2) In any other case the public trustee shall make in respect of the estate the declaration mentioned in section 3 (2) of the act, and shall give notice to the applicant that the application is accepted, and shall take such other steps as may be necessary or proper to enable him to administer the estate; and any person having the custody of the probate or letters of administration or other document relating to the estate shall, upon the request in writing of the public trustee, deliver the same to him or as he shall direct.

(3) A refusal under this rule shall not prevent the public trustee from exercising with respect to the estate any powers (other than powers under section 3 of the act) exerciseable by him with respect thereto under the act and these rules, if duly appointed to exercise the same.

(4) Upon the acceptance of any application the public trustee

shall consider and determine whether the estate shall be administered from his central office or from a branch office, and shall give directions accordingly, and any such direction may at any time be rescinded or varied by the public trustee at his discretion.

16. For the purposes of the administration the public trustee shall (subject as hereinafter provided) have all the administrative powers and authorities exerciseable by a master of the Supreme Court acting in the administration of an estate.

17.—(1) The public trustee may in manner hereinafter provided and without judicial proceedings take the opinion of the High Court upon any question arising in the course of an administration.

(2) The duty of advising upon any such question shall be assigned by the Lord Chancellor to a particular judge of the Chancery Division. Provided that in the absence or upon the request of such judge any other judge of that division, and during vacation any judge of the High Court, may act for such judge for the purposes of this rule.

(3) Any such question shall be submitted to the judge in such manner and at such time as he may direct, and shall be accompanied by such statement of facts, documents, and other information as he may require, and the public trustee shall, if the judge so desires, attend upon him at such time and place as the judge may appoint.

(4) The judge may before giving his opinion require the attendance of, or communicate with, any person interested in the estate as trustee or beneficiary, but no such person shall have a right to be heard by the judge unless he otherwise directs.

(5) The judge shall give his opinion to the public trustee, and the public trustee shall act in accordance with such opinion, and shall upon the request in writing of any such interested person communicate to him the effect of such opinion.

Administration of Trusts and Estates.

18. Subject to the provisions of the act and of these rules, and to the terms of any particular trust, the public trustee may, in the administration of any trust or estate, take and use professional advice and assistance in regard to legal and other matters, and may act on credible information (though less than legal evidence) as to matters of fact.

19.—(1) There shall be kept at the central office in London of the public trustee a register (hereinafter referred to as "the principal register") of all trusts in which the public trustee is acting as trustee or custodian trustee, and of all estates in course of administration under section 3 of the act, and whether the same are being administered from his central office or from any branch office.

(2) There shall be entered in the principal register in respect of each trust or estate—

(a) a distinctive letter and number;
(b) the date of the acceptance of the trust or of the declaration made under section 3 (2) of the act;
(c) particulars of the trust property from time to time;
(d) the names and place of abode of the person in receipt of the income of the trust property;
(e) a reference to any notice received of any dealing with any beneficial interest in the trust property and of any exercise or release of any power relating to the trust or estate;
(f) a record of any decision or opinion of the High Court in respect of the trust or estate;
(g) such records of his decisions and such other particulars as the public trustee may think fit.

20. The public trustee may invest or retain invested money belonging to any trust or estate and coming to his hands in any investment authorized by the trust instrument or (save as otherwise provided by that instrument) authorized by law for the investment of trust funds, and may (save as so provided) retain any investment existing at the date of the commencement of the trust, or (where the trust arises on an intestacy) at the date of the death of the intestate. Provided that he shall not invest in or hold any instrument in such manner as to expose him to liability as the holder thereof, unless he is satisfied that he is fully indemnified or secured against loss.

21. The securities and documents belonging or relating to a trust or estate of which the public trustee is a trustee, or which he is administering shall if under his control be kept at the bank to the trust or at some other safe place of deposit allowed generally or specially by the Treasury, so far as the convenience of business will admit.

22.—(1) A separate account shall be kept for every trust or estate.

(2) A separate account shall be kept of the capital of the trust property and of the mode in which it is from time to time invested, and all dealings with such capital shall be entered in such account.

(3) A separate account shall be kept of the income of the trust property and of the mode in which it is from time to time dealt with by the public trustee.

23. The accounts of the public trustee shall be audited and the securities held by him verified from time to time to the satisfaction of the controller and auditor-general, in accordance with such regulations as the Treasury may make.

24. All payments of money to or from the capital of the trust property shall be made through the bank to the trust or estate.

25.—(1) No transfer by the public trustee of any securities or assurance by him of any land forming part of the trust property shall be made except under the hand and official seal of the public trustee, or under the hand and seal of an officer of the public trustee authorized in writing by him to act in that behalf either generally or in any particular case.

(2) Any such transfer or assurance by an officer so authorized shall have the same effect as if the same were made by the public trustee under his hand and official seal.

26. All sums payable out of the income or capital of the trust property shall be made by a cheque on a bank signed by the public trustee or an officer of the public trustee authorized in writing by him to act in that behalf either generally or in any particular case. Provided that in any particular case the public trustee may authorize the payment of income by the person liable to pay the same direct to the person entitled to receive the same, or to his bank.

27.—(1) The income of the trust property may be paid to the person for the time being entitled to receive the same either through a bank or direct, and where such person is a married woman may be so paid notwithstanding any restraint on anticipation.

(2) Where authority is given to any corporation or bank to pay any income to any person the books of that corporation or bank showing the payment of that income in accordance with the authority shall be a sufficient discharge to the public trustee.

(3) Where authority is given to any person to pay any income to the bank of the person entitled, the certificate of that bank stating the receipt of that income shall be a sufficient discharge to the public trustee.

(4) Where any person is solely entitled to receive any income, without any restraint on anticipation, the public trustee may, on the request in writing of that person, authorise him for such period as the public trustee may think fit to collect or arrange for the collection of such income. During the continuance of any such authority such request in writing shall be a sufficient discharge to the public trustee in respect of such income.

28. The public trustee may, if the special circumstances of the case appear to him to render it desirable, pay to his co-trustee, or allow him to receive, the income of the trust property or any part thereof, on such co-trustee undertaking to apply it in manner directed by the trust.

29. The public trustee may make advances for the purposes of any trust or estate in course of administration, or about to be adminis-

tered, by him, out of any moneys which may be placed at his disposal by the Treasury for that purpose, and upon such terms as he may think proper.

30. The public trustee may at any time require a statutory declaration or other sufficient evidence that a person is alive and is the person to whom any money or property is payable or transferable, and may refuse payment or transfer until such declaration or evidence is produced.

31. Where a person appearing to be beneficially entitled to any sum of money under a trust or to be interested in the trust property cannot be found, or it is not known whether he is living or dead, the public trustee may apply to the court for directions as to the course to be taken with reference to such person, and until an order of the court is made shall keep any sum payable to such person, and if it is kept for more than six months shall invest the same or deposit the same at interest and shall accumulate the dividends or interest thereof.

32.—(1) Upon an application in writing by or with the authority of any person interested in the trust property the public trustee—

(a) shall permit the applicant or his solicitor or other authorized agent to inspect and take copies of any entry in any register relating to the trust or estate and (so far as the interest of the applicant in the trust property is or may be affected thereby) of any account notice or other document in the custody of the public trustee;

(b) shall at the expense of the applicant supply him or his solicitor or other authorized agent with a copy of any such entry, account, or document as aforesaid, or of any extract therefrom;

(c) shall give to such applicant or his solicitor or other authorized agent such information respecting the trust or estate and the trust property as shall be reasonably requested in the application and shall be within the power of the public trustee.

(2) Subject as aforesaid the public trustee shall observe strict secrecy in respect of every trust or estate in course of administration by him.

33.—(1) The public trustee may in writing authorize any deputy to exercise and perform (either generally or in relation to any particular case and subject to such conditions and restrictions (if any) as the public trustee may impose) all or any of the powers and duties of the public trustee under any of the foregoing rules except—

(a) the power or duty of determining whether a trust or estate shall be administered from his central office or from a branch office; and

(b) the powers of authorizing officers of the public trustee to transfer securities or assure land or to sign cheques;

(c) the power of making advances for the purpose of any trust or estate.

(2) Any such authority conditions or restrictions may at any time in like manner be withdrawn or varied by the public trustee at his discretion.

34. No deputy and no firm or member of a firm of solicitors of which such deputy is a member shall except with the consent in writing of the public trustee and subject to such conditions as he may impose act as solicitor or solicitors to a trust or estate which is in course of administration by such deputy.

35. Any officer of the public trustee who shall be authorized by him in writing in that behalf may take any oath, make any declaration, verify any account, and give personal attendance at any court or place.

Corporate Bodies as Custodian Trustees.

36.—(1) The bodies corporate entitled to act as custodian trustee shall be any such incorporated banking or insurance or guarantee or trust company or friendly society and any such body corporate established for charitable or philanthropic purposes as may be approved by the public trustee and the Treasury.

(2) The public trustee may require payment by any applicant for such approval of a fee not exceeding ten guineas.

(3) Such approval may be granted subject to such conditions as to the rendering by the body corporate, and verification, of periodical returns of business transacted, and fees and other emoluments received, and otherwise, as the Treasury may require either generally or in any particular case.

(4) Any such approval may at any time be withdrawn without reason assigned.

Investigation and Audit of Trust Accounts.

37. Any application under section 13 (1) of the act shall be made to the public trustee, and notice thereof shall be given (a) if the applicant is a beneficiary, to every trustee, and (b) if the applicant is a trustee, to each co-trustee and also to the person entitled to the receipt of the income of the trust property.

38. If within three months from the date of the receipt of the notice no solicitor or public accountant shall have been appointed by the applicant and the trustees to conduct the investigation and audit, there shall be deemed to be a default of agreement within the meaning of section 13 (1) of the act, and the applicant may apply to the public trustee accordingly.

39. The remuneration of the auditor and the other expenses of the investigation and audit shall be such as may be agreed on by the trustees and the person entitled to the receipt of the income of the trust property and the auditor, or (in default of such agreement) determined by the public trustee, who shall, in determining the same, have regard to the estimated value of the trust property, the time occupied or likely to be occupied by the investigation and audit, and the other circumstances of the case.

Miscellaneous.

40.—(1) Any notice or application required to be given or made for the purposes of the act or these rules to the public trustee may be addressed to the public trustee at his office in London, or if the same relates to a trust or estate in course of administration or proposed to be administered from a branch office then at that branch office.

(2) Any notice or application required to be given or made for the purposes of the act or these rules to any person other than the public trustee may be addressed to that person at his last known place of abode or place of business.

(3) Any such notice or application may be delivered at the place to which it is addressed or may be served by post.

41. Where any person who (if not under disability) might have made any application, given any consent, done any act, or been party to any proceeding in pursuance of these rules is an infant, idiot or lunatic, the guardian or (as the case may require) the committee or receiver of the estate of such person may make such application, give such consent, do such act, and be party to such proceedings as such person if free from disability might have made, given, done, or been party to, and shall otherwise represent such person for the purposes of these rules. Where there is no guardian or committee or receiver of the estate of any such infant, idiot or lunatic, or where any person is of unsound mind or incapable of managing his affairs but has not been found lunatic under any inquisition, it shall be lawful for the court to appoint a guardian of such person for the purpose of any proceedings under these rules and from time to time to change such guardian.

42. The public trustee may frame and cause to be printed and circulated or otherwise promulgated such forms and directions as he may deem requisite or expedient for facilitating proceedings under the act and these rules.

43. These rules may be cited as "The Public Trustee Rules, 1907."

LOREBURN, C.

November 29th, 1907.

We, being two of the Lords Commissioners of His Majesty's Treasury, hereby concur in the foregoing rules.

H. H. Asquith.
Joseph A. Pease.

INDEX.

PRINTED BY C. F. ROWORTH, 88, FETTER LANE, E.C.

Spotted something that isn't quite right?

Let us know and we'll fix it for future reprints. And as a thank you for your diligence, we'll send you a free Sothis book of your choice.

publisher@sothis.press

This page intentionally left blank

Made in United States
North Haven, CT
04 November 2026

21759933R00286